Cryptography and Information Security

Cryptography and Information Security

Editors

Lip Yee Por
Abdullah Ayub Khan

Basel • Beijing • Wuhan • Barcelona • Belgrade • Novi Sad • Cluj • Manchester

Editors
Lip Yee Por
Department of Computer
System and Technology,
University Malaya
Kuala Lumpur
Malaysia

Abdullah Ayub Khan
Department of Computer
Science and Information
Technology, Benazir Bhutto
Shaheed University Lyari
Karachi
Pakistan

Editorial Office
MDPI
St. Alban-Anlage 66
4052 Basel, Switzerland

This is a reprint of articles from the Special Issue published online in the open access journal *Applied Sciences* (ISSN 2076-3417) (available at: https://www.mdpi.com/journal/applsci/special_issues/NHRXO8RQUF).

For citation purposes, cite each article independently as indicated on the article page online and as indicated below:

Lastname, A.A.; Lastname, B.B. Article Title. *Journal Name* **Year**, *Volume Number*, Page Range.

ISBN 978-3-7258-0897-7 (Hbk)
ISBN 978-3-7258-0898-4 (PDF)
doi.org/10.3390/books978-3-7258-0898-4

© 2024 by the authors. Articles in this book are Open Access and distributed under the Creative Commons Attribution (CC BY) license. The book as a whole is distributed by MDPI under the terms and conditions of the Creative Commons Attribution-NonCommercial-NoDerivs (CC BY-NC-ND) license.

Contents

About the Editors vii

Lip Yee Por, Jing Yang, Chin Soon Ku and Abdullah Ayub Khan
Special Issue on Cryptography and Information Security
Reprinted from: *Applied Sciences* 2023, 13, 6042, doi:10.3390/app13106042 1

Abdullah Ayub Khan and Lip Yee Por
Special Issue on Information Security and Cryptography: The Role of Advanced Digital Technology
Reprinted from: *Applied Sciences* 2024, 14, 2045, doi:10.3390/app14052045 3

Raed Ahmed Alhamarneh and Manmeet Mahinderjit Singh
Strengthening Internet of Things Security: Surveying Physical Unclonable Functions for Authentication, Communication Protocols, Challenges, and Applications
Reprinted from: *Applied Sciences* 2024, 14, 1700, doi:10.3390/app14051700 6

Diego Antonio López-García, Juan Pérez Torreglosa, David Vera and Manuel Sánchez-Raya
Binary-Tree-Fed Mixnet: An Efficient Symmetric Encryption Solution
Reprinted from: *Applied Sciences* 2024, 14, 966, doi:10.3390/app14030966 35

Mira Lee and Minhye Seo
Secure and Efficient Deduplication for Cloud Storage with Dynamic Ownership Management
Reprinted from: *Applied Sciences* 2023, 13, 13270, doi:10.3390/app132413270 48

Hang Li, Junhao Li, Yulong Wang, Chunru Zhou and Mingyong Yin
Leaving the Business Security Burden to LiSEA: A Low-Intervention Security Embedding Architecture for Business APIs
Reprinted from: *Applied Sciences* 2023, 13, 11784, doi:10.3390/app132111784 70

Yuan Cao, Haotian Li, Lijuan Han, Xiaojin Zhao, Xiaofang Pan and Enyi Yao
AccFlow: Defending against the Low-Rate TCP DoS Attack in Drones
Reprinted from: *Applied Sciences* 2023, 13, 11749, doi:10.3390/app132111749 88

**Mohammed Al-Shatari, Fawnizu Azmadi Hussin, Azrina Abd Aziz,
Taiseer Abdalla Elfadil Eisa, Xuan-Tu Tran and Mhassen Elnour Elneel Dalam**
IoT Edge Device Security: An Efficient Lightweight Authenticated Encryption Scheme Based on LED and PHOTON
Reprinted from: *Applied Sciences* 2023, 13, 10345, doi:10.3390/app131810345 108

Ana Gavrovska
Effects on Long-Range Dependence and Multifractality in Temporal Resolution Recovery of High Frame Rate HEVC Compressed Content
Reprinted from: *Applied Sciences* 2023, 13, 9851, doi:10.3390/app13179851 129

Yang Li, Fei Kang, Hui Shu, Xiaobing Xiong, Yuntian Zhao and Rongbo Sun
APIASO: A Novel API Call Obfuscation Technique Based on Address Space Obscurity
Reprinted from: *Applied Sciences* 2023, 13, 9056, doi:10.3390/app13169056 155

Jiming Yin, Jie Cui
Secure Application of MIoT: Privacy-Preserving Solution for Online English Education Platforms
Reprinted from: *Applied Sciences* 2023, 13, 8293, doi:10.3390/app13148293 176

Ghanima Sabr Shyaa and Mishall Al-Zubaidie
Utilizing Trusted Lightweight Ciphers To Support Electronic-Commerce Transaction Cryptography
Reprinted from: *Applied Sciences* **2023**, *13*, 7085, doi:10.3390/app13127085 . . . . **194**

Jing Yang, Yen-Lin Chen, Lip Yee Por and Chin Soon Ku
A Systematic Literature Review of Information Security in Chatbots
Reprinted from: *Applied Sciences* **2023**, *13*, 6355, doi:10.3390/app13116355 . . . . **220**

About the Editors

Lip Yee Por

Lip Yee Por received their B.Sc., M.Sc., and Ph.D. degrees from Universiti Malaya, Malaysia. He has published more than 90 research articles in reputable journals. His research interests encompass various aspects of information security and quality assurance (NEC 2020: 0611), including authentication, graphic passwords, PIN-entry, cryptography, data hiding, steganography, and watermarking. Additionally, he specializes in machine learning (NEC 2020: 0613), with expertise in extreme learning machines, support vector machines, deep learning, long-short-term memory, computer vision, and AIoT.

Abdullah Ayub Khan

Abdullah Ayub Khan (Member, ACM) earned his Ph.D. degree from the Department of Computer Science at Sindh Madressatul Islam University in Karachi (Batch 2019). He has published more than 50 research articles in well-reputed journals and publishers (such as IEEE Access, IEEE Transactions, MDPI, Elsevier, Spring, Wiley, Hindawi, etc.) in the domains of digital forensics, cybersecurity, blockchain, Hyperledger technology, information security, Internet of Things federated learning, artificial intelligence, and deep learning.

Editorial

Special Issue on Cryptography and Information Security

Lip Yee Por [1,*], Jing Yang [1], Chin Soon Ku [2] and Abdullah Ayub Khan [3]

[1] Faculty of Computer Science & Information Technology, Universiti Malaya, Kuala Lumpur 50603, Malaysia; yj741655109@163.com
[2] Department of Computer Science, Universiti Tunku Abdul Rahman, Kampar 31900, Malaysia; kucs@utar.edu.my
[3] Department of Computer Science and Information Technology, Benazir Bhutto Shaheed University Lyari, Karachi 75660, Pakistan; abdullah.ayub@bbsul.edu.pk
* Correspondence: porlip@um.edu.my

In today's increasingly connected world, the demand for secure computing and data protection is soaring [1]. To address this urgent need, our Special Issue presents cutting-edge research, innovative insights, and breakthrough developments in the fields of cryptography, information security, and related ICT security challenges.

This all-encompassing Special Issue delves into a wide array of crucial topics to provide an unparalleled understanding of the current state and future possibilities of digital security. Our comprehensive coverage includes state-of-the-art encryption algorithms and techniques, advanced secure communication protocols, blockchain technology, authentication and verification processes, and emerging threats to cybersecurity. Furthermore, the issue sheds light on ground-breaking methods to bolster security within the Internet of Things (IoT), an area of mounting concern due to the rapid proliferation of connected devices.

One of the most significant topics covered in this issue is encryption, a critical component in securing digital communication and protecting sensitive information [2]. We delve into the latest developments in symmetric and asymmetric encryption techniques, showcasing novel algorithms designed to ensure the confidentiality, integrity, and authenticity of digital data. Additionally, we examine post-quantum cryptography, a vital area of research in the face of the impending arrival of quantum computers.

Another vital aspect of our Special Issue is secure communication protocols. As cyber threats continue to evolve, we explore advances in network security, transport layer security, and end-to-end encryption. We also examine the challenges and opportunities presented by secure messaging applications and decentralized systems, such as blockchain technology.

Blockchain technology is transforming industries by enabling secure, transparent, and decentralized data storage and processing [3,4]. This Special Issue offers an in-depth analysis of cutting-edge blockchain applications, including smart contracts, decentralized finance, and digital identity management. We also investigate the potential of blockchain technology to enhance privacy and security in IoT environments.

Authentication and verification are fundamental components of digital security [3,5]. We delve into the latest advances in multi-factor authentication, biometrics, and digital signatures, highlighting how these technologies can be integrated to provide robust security solutions. Furthermore, we explore innovative approaches to user authentication, such as continuous and context-aware authentication methods that leverage machine learning and artificial intelligence.

Emerging threats to cybersecurity are a constant concern in the digital age [6]. Our Special Issue addresses this critical topic by examining new attack vectors, advanced persistent threats, and zero-day vulnerabilities. We also discuss the role of threat intelligence, vulnerability assessment, and incident response in detecting and mitigating cyber threats.

In this Special Issue, we also investigate the transformative potential of trailblazing technologies, such as ChatGPT, to revolutionize ICT technology. ChatGPT, an impressive

Citation: Por, L.Y.; Yang, J.; Ku, C.S.; Khan, A.A. Special Issue on Cryptography and Information Security. *Appl. Sci.* **2023**, *13*, 6042. https://doi.org/10.3390/app13106042

Received: 28 April 2023
Accepted: 10 May 2023
Published: 15 May 2023

Copyright: © 2023 by the authors. Licensee MDPI, Basel, Switzerland. This article is an open access article distributed under the terms and conditions of the Creative Commons Attribution (CC BY) license (https://creativecommons.org/licenses/by/4.0/).

large language model, can generate natural language responses and interact with humans in a conversational manner. This extraordinary technology is poised to reshape numerous telecommunications applications, encompassing chatbots, virtual assistants, and customer service automation.

Additionally, we eagerly welcome papers related to unexplored aspects of ICT security, providing a vital resource for professionals, researchers, and enthusiasts eager to navigate the intricate landscape of digital security. Our Special Issue also highlights the importance of interdisciplinary collaboration, bringing together experts from fields such as computer science, cryptography, engineering, and the social sciences to address the multi-faceted challenges of information security.

Embark on this exciting journey with us as we unveil this Special Issue, offering a comprehensive and insightful overview of the latest breakthroughs in cryptography and information security. Together, let us foster an informed, engaged community of experts and enthusiasts, ready to confront the ever-evolving world of information security and seize the abundant challenges and opportunities that await.

In conclusion, this ground-breaking Special Issue on "Cryptography and Information Security" seeks to empower readers by providing an unparalleled exploration of the digital security landscape. We aim to inspire collaboration and innovation among professionals, researchers, and enthusiasts from various fields, fostering a secure and resilient digital future for all.

Acknowledgments: Thank you to all of the authors and peer reviewers who contributed to the Special Issue on "Cryptography and Information Security".

Conflicts of Interest: The authors declare no conflict of interest.

References

1. Zhang, X.; Shan, C.; Zou, Y. Multi-party Secure Comparison of Strings Based on Outsourced Computation. In Proceedings of the International Conference on Machine Learning for Cyber Security, Guangzhou, China, 2–4 December 2022. [CrossRef]
2. Alexan, W.; Chen, Y.-L.; Por, L.Y.; Gabr, M. Hyperchaotic Maps and the Single Neuron Model: A Novel Framework for Chaos-Based Image Encryption. *Symmetry* **2023**, *15*, 1081. [CrossRef]
3. Wagan, A.A.; Khan, A.A.; Chen, Y.-L.; Yee, P.L.; Yang, J.; Laghari, A.A. Artificial Intelligence-Enabled Game-Based Learning and Quality of Experience: A Novel and Secure Framework (B-AIQoE). *Sustainability* **2023**, *15*, 5362. [CrossRef]
4. Meisami, S.; Meisami, S.; Yousefi, M.; Aref, M.R. Combining Blockchain and IOT for Decentralized Healthcare Data Management. *Int. J. Cryptogr. Inf. Secur.* **2023**, *13*, 35–50. [CrossRef]
5. Binbeshr, F.; Por, L.Y.; Kiah, M.L.M.; Zaidan, A.A.; Imam, M. Secure PIN-Entry Method Using One-Time PIN (OTP). *IEEE Access* **2023**, *11*, 18121–18133. [CrossRef]
6. Oruj, Z. Cyber Security: Contemporary Cyber Threats and National Strategies. *Distance Educ. Ukr. Innov. Norm.-Leg. Pedagog. Asp.* **2023**, *1*, 100–116. [CrossRef]

Disclaimer/Publisher's Note: The statements, opinions and data contained in all publications are solely those of the individual author(s) and contributor(s) and not of MDPI and/or the editor(s). MDPI and/or the editor(s) disclaim responsibility for any injury to people or property resulting from any ideas, methods, instructions or products referred to in the content.

Editorial

Special Issue on Information Security and Cryptography: The Role of Advanced Digital Technology

Abdullah Ayub Khan [1,2,*] and Lip Yee Por [3]

1. Department of Computer Science, Sindh Madressatul Islam University, Karachi 74000, Pakistan
2. Department of Computer Science and Information Technology, Benazir Bhutto Shaheed University Lyari, Karachi 75660, Pakistan
3. Faculty of Computer Science & Information Technology, Universiti Malaya, Kuala Lumpur 50603, Malaysia; porlip@um.edu.my
* Correspondence: abdullah.ayub@bbsul.edu.pk

Citation: Khan, A.A.; Por, L.Y. Special Issue on Information Security and Cryptography: The Role of Advanced Digital Technology. *Appl. Sci.* **2024**, *14*, 2045. https://doi.org/10.3390/app14052045

Received: 27 January 2024
Accepted: 28 February 2024
Published: 29 February 2024

Copyright: © 2024 by the authors. Licensee MDPI, Basel, Switzerland. This article is an open access article distributed under the terms and conditions of the Creative Commons Attribution (CC BY) license (https://creativecommons.org/licenses/by/4.0/).

Information security has become a potential prospect that ensures information cannot be breached throughout the process of delivery while being exchanged over the Internet. In recent times, blockchain technology has played a critical role by providing a modular infrastructure, the main objectives of which are to maintain information integrity, transparency, provenance, and trustworthiness in a distributed environment [1].

In this Special Issue, we introduced the role of advanced digital technology (ADT), especially cryptography, such as public key cryptography and private key cryptography, which includes advancements in hash-re-encryption (SHA-256), NuCypher Threshold Proxy Re-Encryption (NTPRE), and authentication [2,3], in information security. We present a set of papers that have been selected after rigorous peer review within the scope of cryptography, blockchain distributed ledger technology, information security, cyber security, and their related sub-domains involved at various levels of system privacy and security.

In a device-to-device- or system-to-system-level environment, various aspects that disintegrate have been highlighted, along with a description of related impacts on the ecosystem in terms of making compromises, such as recycled passwords, the physical theft of sensitive devices, simplifying access permissions, vulnerabilities, and the use of default passwords [4,5].

Recently, cryptography collaborated with the newly developed distributed ledger technology (DLT), which has been proposed as a secure and protected infrastructure for designing a novel environment of information security in almost every domain of information technology (IT). This Special Issue has presented a new paradigm in computing privacy protection and security-related structures to bring new cryptographic principles to the attention of readers and new researchers [6].

In traditional security adaptations, cybersecurity solutions are immature and often considered as an afterthought; they are critical because there is a need to design a system first and then retrofit solutions with cybersecurity. This collaborative approach promotes a proactive environment, which means the design of the ecosystem is tightly exhibited in terms of the provision of a novel and secure infrastructure with the association of cybersecurity that aims to manage flow controls, from the initial design steps to delivery. The fundamental tasks related to this technology include (i) default security management; (ii) proactive and reactive mechanisms; (iii) embedded-enabling design; (iv) end-to-end lifecycles; (v) a fully functional environment; (vi) integrity and transparency; (vii) a secure channel for transmission; and (viii) connected stakeholder environments.

In the blockchain cryptographic technique (BCT), security protocols are one of the core components for securing data from unauthorized access [7,8]. To secure transactions, two nodes of the chain are interconnected in chronological order in the consortium blockchain network. The three main pillars that make this infrastructure more protected are (i) the peer-to-peer (P2P) network [9]; (ii) cryptographic hash encryption [10]; and (iii) distributed storage [11], often referred to as a ledger in the blockchain domain. However, the working scenario of BCT aims to make the system safer within a point-to-point network space, which is difficult to achieve in traditional environments due to weak approaches to system security. In this recent integration, blockchain uses two types of privacy protection and security solutions, namely hashing and NuCypher mechanisms. For instance, the basic difference between these types is that one encrypts information in a P2P network, and the second ensures secure links as blocks of information travel through the chain over the P2P network.

On the other hand, encryption is generally considered a best practice from a security perspective and has recently been applied to the Internet of Things (IoT) environment for data encryption [12]. This application creates a new paradigm in terms of offering stronger protection against malicious threats over the Internet. Undoubtedly, the IoT is considered a significant prospect that contributes significantly to advanced digital technology. However, currently, the risk of unauthorized access due to the connection of a large number of devices over the network is one of the critical challenges [13,14], along with IoT analytics and the IoT process hierarchy.

Acknowledgments: In this Editorial, we thank all the authors and peer reviewers for making this Special Issue, entitled "Cryptography and Information Security", successful.

Conflicts of Interest: The authors declare no conflict of interest.

List of Contributions:

1. Por, L.Y.; Yang, J.; Ku, C.S.; Khan, A.A. Special Issue on Cryptography and Information Security. *Appl. Sci.* **2023**, *13*, 6042. https://doi.org/10.3390/app13106042.
2. Yang, J.; Chen, Y.-L.; Por, L.Y.; Ku, C.S. A Systematic Literature Review of Information Security in Chatbots. *Appl. Sci.* **2023**, *13*, 6355. https://doi.org/10.3390/app13116355.
3. Cao, Y.; Li, H.; Han, L.; Zhao, X.; Pan, X.; Yao, E. AccFlow: Defending against the Low-Rate TCP DoS Attack in Drones. *Appl. Sci.* **2023**, *13*, 11749. https://doi.org/10.3390/app132111749.
4. Li, Y.; Kang, F.; Shu, H.; Xiong, X.; Zhao, Y.; Sun, R. APIASO: A Novel API Call Obfuscation Technique Based on Address Space Obscurity. *Appl. Sci.* **2023**, *13*, 9056. https://doi.org/10.3390/app13169056.
5. López-García, D.A.; Pérez Torreglosa, J.; Vera, D.; Sánchez-Raya, M. Binary-Tree-Fed Mixnet: An Efficient Symmetric Encryption Solution. *Appl. Sci.* **2024**, *14*, 966. https://doi.org/10.3390/app14030966.
6. Gavrovska, A. Effects on Long-Range Dependence and Multifractality in Temporal Resolution Recovery of High Frame Rate HEVC Compressed Content. *Appl. Sci.* **2023**, *13*, 9851. https://doi.org/10.3390/app13179851.
7. Al-Shatari, M.; Hussin, F.A.; Aziz, A.A.; Eisa, T.A.E.; Tran, X.-T.; Dalam, M.E.E. IoT Edge Device Security: An Efficient Lightweight Authenticated Encryption Scheme Based on LED and PHOTON. *Appl. Sci.* **2023**, *13*, 10345. https://doi.org/10.3390/app131810345.
8. Li, H.; Li, J.; Wang, Y.; Zhou, C.; Yin, M. Leaving the Business Security Burden to LiSEA: A Low-Intervention Security Embedding Architecture for Business APIs. *Appl. Sci.* **2023**, *13*, 11784. https://doi.org/10.3390/app132111784.
9. Yin, J.; Cui, J. Secure Application of MIoT: Privacy-Preserving Solution for Online English Education Platforms. *Appl. Sci.* **2023**, *13*, 8293. https://doi.org/10.3390/app13148293.
10. Lee, M.; Seo, M. Secure and Efficient Deduplication for Cloud Storage with Dynamic Ownership Management. *Appl. Sci.* **2023**, *13*, 13270. https://doi.org/10.3390/app132413270.
11. Shyaa, G.S.; Al-Zubaidie, M. Utilizing Trusted Lightweight Ciphers to Support Electronic-Commerce Transaction Cryptography. *Appl. Sci.* **2023**, *13*, 7085. https://doi.org/10.3390/app13127085.
12. Alhamarneh, R.A.; Mahinderjit Singh, M. Strengthening Internet of Things Security: Surveying Physical Unclonable Functions for Authentication, Communication Protocols, Challenges, and Applications. *Appl. Sci.* **2024**, *14*, 1700. https://doi.org/10.3390/app14051700.

References

1. Khan, A.A.; Shaikh, A.A.; Laghari, A.A. IoT with Multimedia Investigation: A Secure Process of Digital Forensics Chain-of-Custody Using Blockchain Hyperledger Sawtooth. *Arab. J. Sci. Eng.* **2023**, *48*, 10173–10188. [CrossRef]
2. Wu, T.-Y.; Meng, Q.; Chen, Y.-C.; Kumari, S.; Chen, C.-M. Toward a Secure Smart-Home IoT Access Control Scheme Based on Home Registration Approach. *Mathematics* **2023**, *11*, 2123. [CrossRef]
3. Wu, T.-Y.; Meng, Q.; Yang, L.; Kumari, S.; Pirouz, M. Amassing the Security: An Enhanced Authentication and Key Agreement Protocol for Remote Surgery in Healthcare Environment. *Comput. Model. Eng. Sci.* **2023**, *134*, 317–341. [CrossRef]
4. Rana, M.; Mamun, Q.; Islam, R. Lightweight Cryptography in IoT Networks: A Survey. *Future Gener. Comput. Syst.* **2022**, *129*, 77–89. [CrossRef]
5. Mehic, M.; Michalek, L.; Dervisevic, E.; Burdiak, P.; Plakalovic, M.; Rozhon, J.; Mahovac, N.; Richter, F.; Kaljic, E.; Lauterbach, F.; et al. Quantum cryptography in 5g networks: A comprehensive overview. *IEEE Commun. Surv. Tutor.* **2023**, *26*, 302–346. [CrossRef]
6. Tanwar, S.; Kumar, A. Secure Key Issuing Scheme in ID-Based Cryptography with Revocable ID. *Inf. Secur. J. Glob. Perspect.* **2022**, *31*, 676–685. [CrossRef]
7. Alhayani, B.S.A.; Hamid, N.; Almukhtar, F.H.; Alkawak, O.A.; Mahajan, H.B.; Kwekha-Rashid, A.S.; İlhan, H.; Marhoon, H.A.; Mohammed, H.J.; Chaloob, I.Z.; et al. Optimized Video Internet of Things Using Elliptic Curve Cryptography Based Encryption and Decryption. *Comput. Electr. Eng.* **2022**, *101*, 108022. [CrossRef]
8. Binbeshr, F.; Kiah, M.M.; Por, L.Y.; Zaidan, A.A. A systematic review of PIN-entry methods resistant to shoulder-surfing attacks. *Comput. Secur.* **2021**, *101*, 102116. [CrossRef]
9. Kairaldeen, A.R.; Abdullah, N.F.; Abu-Samah, A.; Nordin, R. Peer-to-Peer User Identity Verification Time Optimization in IoT Blockchain Network. *Sensors* **2023**, *23*, 2106. [CrossRef] [PubMed]
10. Singh, M.; Singh, A.K. A comprehensive survey on encryption techniques for digital images. *Multimed. Tools Appl.* **2023**, *82*, 11155–11187. [CrossRef]
11. Li, J.; Zhang, Y.; Lu, S.; Gunawi, H.S.; Gu, X.; Huang, F.; Li, D. Performance Bug Analysis and Detection for Distributed Storage and Computing Systems. *ACM Trans. Storage* **2023**, *19*, 1–33. [CrossRef]
12. Condon, F.; Franco, P.; Martínez, J.M.; Eltamaly, A.M.; Kim, Y.-C.; Ahmed, M.A. EnergyAuction: IoT-Blockchain Architecture for Local Peer-to-Peer Energy Trading in a Microgrid. *Sustainability* **2023**, *15*, 13203. [CrossRef]
13. Nanjappan, M.; Pradeep, K.; Natesan, G.; Samydurai, A.; Premalatha, G. DeepLG SecNet: Utilizing deep LSTM and GRU with secure network for enhanced intrusion detection in IoT environments. *Clust. Comput.* **2024**. [CrossRef]
14. Aboukadri, S.; Ouaddah, A.; Mezrioui, A. Machine Learning in Identity and Access Management Systems: Survey and Deep Dive. *Comput. Secur.* **2024**, *139*, 103729. [CrossRef]

Disclaimer/Publisher's Note: The statements, opinions and data contained in all publications are solely those of the individual author(s) and contributor(s) and not of MDPI and/or the editor(s). MDPI and/or the editor(s) disclaim responsibility for any injury to people or property resulting from any ideas, methods, instructions or products referred to in the content.

Review

Strengthening Internet of Things Security: Surveying Physical Unclonable Functions for Authentication, Communication Protocols, Challenges, and Applications

Raed Ahmed Alhamarneh [1,2,*] and Manmeet Mahinderjit Singh [1,*]

1. School of Computer Sciences, University Sains Malaysia (USM), Minden 11800, Penang, Malaysia
2. College of Applied Sciences, Department of Computer Science and Information Systems, AlMaarefa University, Diriyah, Riyadh 13713, Saudi Arabia
* Correspondence: raedalhamarneh@student.usm.my (R.A.A.); manmeet@usm.my (M.M.S)

Abstract: The spectrum of Internet of Things (IoT) applications is vast. It serves in various domains such as smart homes, intelligent buildings, health care, emergency response, and many more, reflecting the exponential market penetration of the IoT. Various security threats have been made to modern-day systems. Cyberattacks have seen a marked surge in frequency, particularly in recent times. The growing concern centers around the notable rise in cloning attacks, persisting as a significant and looming threat. In our work, an in-depth survey on the IoT that employs physically unclonable functions (PUFs) was conducted. The first contribution analyzes PUF-based authentication, communication protocols, and applications. It also tackles the eleven challenges faced by the research community, proposes solutions to these challenges, and highlights cloning attacks. The second contribution suggests the implementation of a framework model known as PUF3S-ML, specifically crafted for PUF authentication in the Internet of Things (IoT), incorporating innovative lightweight encryption techniques. It focuses on safeguarding smart IoT networks from cloning attacks. The key innovation framework comprises three stages of PUF authentication with IoT devices and an intelligent cybersecurity monitoring unit for IoT networks. In the methodology of this study, a survey relevant to the concerns was conducted. More data were provided previously regarding architecture, enabling technologies, and IoT challenges. After conducting an extensive survey of 125 papers, our analysis revealed 23 papers directly relevant to our domain. Furthermore, within this subset, we identified 11 studies specifically addressing the intersection of communication protocols with PUFs. These findings highlight the targeted relevance and potential contributions of the existing literature to our research focus.

Keywords: hardware; communication protocol; IoT; network security; machine learning; PUF; authentication mechanisms

1. Introduction

In today's digital age of interconnection, technology plays a significant role in transforming and affecting the daily lives of individuals in all dimensions, including traveling, shopping, and household electronics. There are many changes around us because of technology. Sophisticated sensors are embedded in many of the objects that surround us. Each sensor conveys crucial data that allow us to understand the functioning and interaction of these things. By 2025, it is estimated that the number of Internet of Things (IoT) devices will increase to more than 64 billion, approximately eight times the Earth's human population [1]. The IoT is a system of interconnected computing devices [2] that can transfer data (by sensing/acquiring) without human intervention. Unique identifiers are used to distinguish IoT devices. The IoT has revolutionized lives by enabling individuals and businesses to work more intelligently with enhanced control. It automates processes and significantly reduces labor costs and human errors. Nevertheless, challenges persist when deploying IoT networks.

At the forefront of these challenges is the conundrum posed by multiple, heterogeneous IoT frameworks and existing standards. This intricacy necessitates a clarion call for enhanced standardization and a re-evaluation of compliance in device development [3]. The second challenge emanates from the ubiquity of miniature sensors and microcontrollers, defaulting to an "ON" state, potentially laying the groundwork for unauthorized access. However, the paramount concern lies in the realm of security and privacy, where IoT-sensitive data become vulnerable to the prying eyes of intruders and hackers [4]. The specter of data leakage looms large, with attacks stemming from impersonation and interceptions. Impersonation involves hackers masquerading as authorized users, while interception entails seizing communication channels to pilfer sensitive data, exemplified by a hacker infiltrating an intelligent home IoT application to steal personal information. Moreover, identification, authentication, encryption, confidentiality, jamming [5], cloning [6], hijacking [7], and privacy are among the IoT security challenges. Several systems employ encryption to secure their messages from being intercepted by hackers.

To counteract these threats, encryption becomes the linchpin of IoT security, with cryptographic approaches serving as the vanguard. While encryption fortifies message security, its efficacy is not absolute. Malevolent third parties can still dispatch encrypted packets over the network [8], laying bare the need for additional protective measures. Authentication mechanisms emerge as a potent shield [9], with studies [10,11] and proposals abounding to authenticate users or devices within the IoT ecosystem.

One of the technologies adopted to protect IoT devices is PUFs. A PUF is a form of hardware that embraces challenge–response authentication [12]. It changes the input challenge into an output response with the help of a physical system. The scheme adopted to calculate the answer is designed to be exact to the hardware instance (unique) and cannot be replicated (unclonable). PUF authentication is based on users and devices. There are four different types of user authentication (password, token, and biometrics—hard and soft), the machines are cryptographic [13], and the PUFs have authentication protocols. The benefits of PUFs make them good candidates for IoT applications and systems.

This paper embarks on a comprehensive exploration of PUFs in the context of IoT security. Building upon prior reviews, we delve into the characteristics, classifications, and relationships of various PUF technologies. A survey scrutinizes low-power System-on-Chip (SoC) designs, illuminating suitable hardware defenses in mobile and embedded systems operating under power constraints [14]. A retrospective analysis of proposed PUFs between 2001 and 2014 uncovers security issues, motivating further research to bolster PUF strength. In the face of conventional cryptographic key generation methods, this paper advocates protocols leveraging strong PUFs, complemented by resistance to side-channel attacks and a machine learning block for physical attack resilience [15].

Amidst the landscape of the existing literature on this subject, this survey distinguishes itself through its unparalleled scope, depth, and comprehensiveness. While prior works touch on select attributes, our survey encompasses the entirety of PUF design, implementation, and the challenges arising from these attributes. Our conceptual model, PUF3S-ML, not only encapsulates a taxonomy of IoT-enabled PUF authentication but also proposes a framework adept at safeguarding smart IoT networks against cloning attacks (Table 1).

The objectives of the paper are as follows:

- The presentation of a comprehensive PUF design and implementation attributes and a complete survey and taxonomy on PUF authentication revolving around PUF architecture, PUF communication protocols, and security challenges.
- The proposal of a framework model on PUF authentication for the IoT known as PUF3S-ML, capable of protecting smart IoT networks against cloning attacks. The scope of our survey and taxonomy is specifically in the domain of the IoT.

Table 1. Contributions of previous surveys and comparison.

Paper/Article	Type Study	Architectures	Implementation	Communication Protocols	Open Issues	Conceptual Design Framework/Solution to Cloning Attacks	Highlights Cloning Attacks
[16]	Survey	Yes	No	No	Yes	No	No
[17]	Survey	Yes	Yes	No	No	No	No
[18]	Taxonomy	Yes	Yes	No	No	No	No
[19]	Taxonomy	No	Yes	No	Yes	No	No
[20]	Survey	Yes	Yes	No	No	No	No
[21]	Review	Yes	No	No	Yes	No	No
[22]	Survey	Yes	Yes	Yes	Yes	No	No
[23]	Survey	Yes	Yes	No	No	No	No
This paper	Survey and Taxonomy	Yes	Yes	Yes	Yes	Yes	Yes

1.1. Innovative Contributions

In this manuscript, the principal contributions include presenting an extensive taxonomy of IoT-enabled PUF authentication and introducing a conceptual framework for authentication using IoT-enabled PUFs. The significant benefits of this model, PUF3S-ML are as follows:

1.1.1. Detecting Cloning Attacks and Mitigation

Our study is centered on the mitigation of cloning attacks, particularly addressing replay attacks, etc. The model employs unique algorithms during the data processing phase to identify irregularities that may indicate cloning attempts. These algorithms analyze challenge–response pairs (CRPs) and flag bit packets and utilize specific parameters, such as C, R to detect deviations from regular behavior. The model suggests a new approach to thwarting cloning attempts by introducing a lightweight Cipher PRESENT algorithm. This encryption method ensures secure communication and data exchange, adding an additional layer of protection against cloning attacks.

1.1.2. Efficient Resource Utilization

We turn our focus to the imperative aspect of optimizing resource allocation within our proposed model. Efficient resource utilization is paramount for ensuring the overall effectiveness, scalability, and sustainability of the system. Our approach aims to strike a balance between performance and resource consumption, enhancing the model's efficiency.

1.1.3. Reliability and Resilience

Reliability is supported by the presence of a specialized unit of vigilant monitoring mechanisms that examine network behaviors and patterns. In case of any deviations from the norm, alerts are triggered, allowing proactive responses to potential threats or abnormal activities. Following an attack or system crash, the model employs specific strategies to quickly restore the system without significant problems. This involves maintaining data, configurations, and personal files, ensuring a swift return to operational status.

1.1.4. Lightweight Cipher for Secure Communication

Our model incorporates the Lightweight Cipher PRESENT algorithm as a cornerstone for secure communication. This ultra-lightweight block cipher, with options for 80-bit and 128-bit key lengths, strikes an optimal balance between robust encryption and minimal resource consumption. The PRESENT algorithm operates on 64-bit plaintext blocks, providing efficient encryption without compromising the processing speed. Its streamlined design enables swift execution, making it particularly suitable for resource-constrained IoT devices.

1.2. Organization

The outline of this paper is as follows. Section 2 presents a detailed background of IoT design and architecture and the IoT framework. Section 3 presents a survey on PUF authentication revolving around the PUF architecture, PUF communication protocols, and security challenges. Section 4 presents an in-depth analysis of PUF-based authentication and its applications, discusses the challenges involved, and proposes a solution to each problem. Finally, a conceptual framework or model is offered to solve the major issues, revolving around the PUF architecture, PUF communication protocols, and security challenges.

2. Background

In this section, the background of Internet of Things (IoT) will be presented. The description includes the overview, the architecture, the framework, challenges, and security issues. Apart from that, a detailed overview of the authentication process is presented.

2.1. IoT Definition, Benefits, and Type of Applications

There are several definitions of the IoT available in the literature. Based on [24], the IoT is a platform that involves the process of gathering raw data from smart devices and allowing communication between devices and humans. In the context of business, the IoT is defined as technology that involves devices that not only communicate among themselves but also solve issues and challenges [25]. The IoT is also called the "Internet of the Future" [26].

The prime benefits of the Internet of Things are as follows.

1. Cost reduction: The IoT reduces costs by setting priorities, assigning specialized work to specialized people, and improving the production process by reducing internal processes so that they are efficient and effective.
2. Business opportunities: With the Fourth Industrial Revolution, the Internet of Things has become an indispensable entity in the modern world, and companies rely mainly on artificial intelligence and smart networks. IoT solutions have a substantial role in the development of companies and large organizations.
3. Improved safety and security: The IoT provides safety and security solutions as it provides password services to protect against intrusion and illegal access and provides multifactor authentication. Applications of the IoT are countless and are in all walks of life. In Table 2, major applications of the IoT are discussed regarding Industrial Revolution 4.0 and beyond.

Table 2. Applications of the IoT in various domains.

Paper	Domain	Contribution
[27]	Medical field	The authors propose important entities that can possibly influence users' acceptance of IoT-based disease management services.
[28]	Smart city	The authors explain the data security and privacy techniques that can be used in future smart cities. Salient features of smart cities are discussed along with the technology supporting that paradigm shift. The paper also highlights the research challenges in this journey.
[29]	Home automation	In this paper, the authors used a grouping of sensors, microcontrollers, and various communication protocols to detect user conduct at different access points and execute a sensing algorithm.
[30]	Smart industry	In this work, the authors have proposed the use of an Arduino ATmega 2560 board that gathers the temperature and humidity parameters from sensors and records them in an online database. This application is useful in realizing smart industries.
[31]	Commercial applications	In this work, a novel method is given with the aim of systematizing the generation of a quality of service (QoS)-aware service, offering real-time checking that is beneficial in various commercial applications.

2.2. Architecture of IoT

The Internet of Things is made up of four major components [24]:

1. Sensors/devices: these help to collect data from the surrounding environment in a pre-defined manner.
2. Connectivity: this ensures that the stored data are transferred to a cloud infrastructure, and for transportation, either wired or wireless communication is required.
3. Data processing: after the data are collected and made readily available on the cloud, the acquired data are processed via the management system.
4. User interface: the data are accessible to the end-user.

Our view of the IoT structure is demonstrated in Figure 1, which shows the important components of the IoT.

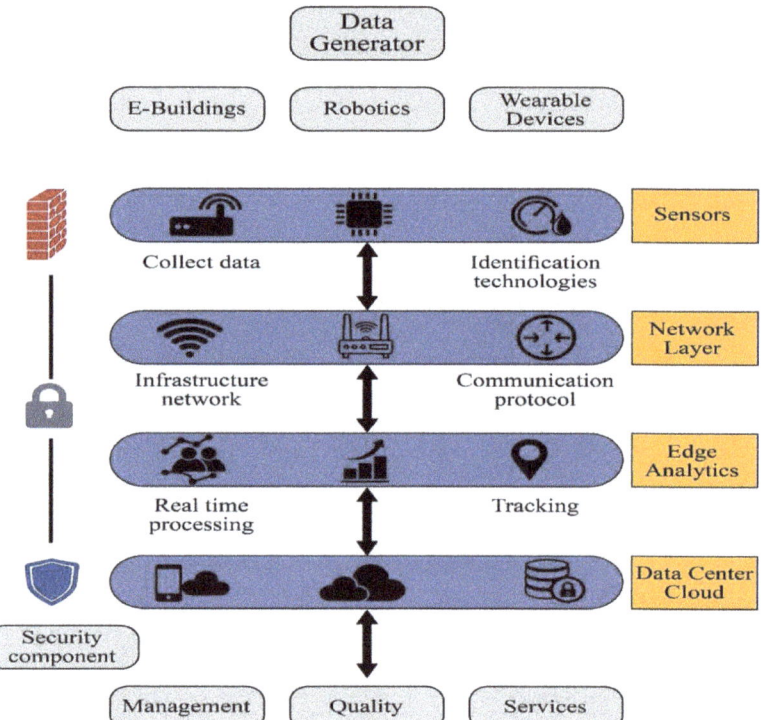

Figure 1. IoT framework.

As shown in Figure 1, the data collection is performed with the help of sensors (which can be of various types). The collected raw data are transmitted via communication channels such as Wi-Fi or wired local area networks (LANs). The transmission involves an internet gateway as an intermediary node between the sensor and the edge analytics. The network layer serves as a communication channel between the sensors and edge analytics. This stage may involve routers, switches, smart cameras, analog-to-digital conversion of the data, etc. Edge analytics are responsible for automated analytical computations. The last stage involves data storage in the data center/cloud. The end-user requires accurate data and integrity for application success. Backup data and cloud computing are essential elements in this stage.

2.3. IoT Challenges

Discussion of IoT technology is imperative because of the rapid development of the technology and many existing issues.

2.3.1. Connectivity Technology

The Internet of Things (IoT) demands the creation of connections across short, medium, and long distances. IoT solutions are expected to fulfill diverse transmission needs, such as responding quickly (ultra-low latency), repeating tasks (recurrence), operating asynchronously, storing and forwarding data, supporting mobility, and facilitating streaming. To meet these requirements effectively, these solutions may need optimization for specific circumstances [32,33].

2.3.2. Platform Technology

IoT systems consist of apps, tools, and data that users can access at each station to perform various tasks. Platforms with fewer restrictions can be customized to enhance connectivity, reduce delays, and optimize overall size. Additionally, these less restrictive IoT platforms offer versatility for different applications [32].

2.3.3. IoT Security

With the steady increase over the last decade in IoT devices, IoT security has become imperative, and security can be categorized as the largest challenge of the IoT. The major security challenges are as follows:

1. Confidentiality: Making the data secure ensures that only authorized individuals have access, thus preventing access by unauthorized personnel [32].
2. Heterogeneity: Many companies around the world are actively working on the IoT, producing products and devices. Due to non-standardization, different protocols and operating systems are being developed, and the configuration of these devices is also different. Thus, there is a need for uniformity and homogeneity [32].
3. Integrity: Data integrity involves accuracy and completeness. When the data are transferred between devices based on a wired or wireless network, messages may be garbled during wireless IoT transmission owing to attenuation, distortion, or noise [32].
4. Availability: Availability is one of the main factors in the elevation and improvement of the IoT based on the hardware or network; however, the IoT is still vulnerable to massive cyberattacks [32].

2.4. Authentication Overview

After the COVID-19 pandemic, IoT device adoption has increased exponentially, but cybersecurity has been a concern for all people and professionals. User authentication refers to the process of establishing a user's identity while using a computer device (for example, a mobile phone) or an online service [13]. Users are required to authenticate themselves to prevent others from gaining access to the system. Identification, the initial stage in verifying a user's identity by asking for their credentials, is a different process. For example, to access a system, a user must provide an ID (username), which serves as the system's unique identifier. The various types of authentication, their definitions, along with their shortcomings are described in Table 3.

Table 3. Types of authentication, definitions, and examples.

	Definition	Example	Major Disadvantages
User	Checks a user's identity by allowing human-to-machine transfer.	Signal sign-on (SSO), multi-factor, three-way authentication.	Vulnerable to spoofing attacks
Device	Detects and checks users accessing a device. This method of authentication uses a device's metadata or an app.	PUF, mobile.	No standardization of IoT device authentication
Software/protocol	Users or devices are authenticated through a software application that verifies access to objects.	Challenged response; mutual authentication; out-of-band management; one-, two-, and three-way authentication; zero-knowledge authentication.	Limited cryptographic authentication

2.5. Types of Authentication

There are five types of authentication, which are presented in Figure 2:

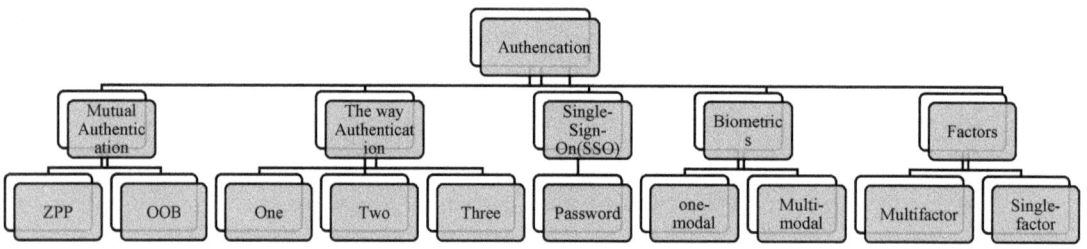

Figure 2. Taxonomy of user authentication methods.

One of the most well-known methods, single sign-on (SSO), allows a valid user to efficiently access a wide range of service providers by employing a unique key [1,34].

1. Factors: An authentication factor is a kind of security identification that is used to authenticate the identity and authorization of a user who is seeking to obtain access, transmit messages, or request data from a secure network, system, or application. There are two types: multifactor and single-factor [35,36].
2. Three-way authentication: There are three different stages of authentication in the general transaction between server and client.
3. Mutual authentication: Multifactor authentication is slightly more complicated since it requires an additional step from the user, such as the well-known out-of-band (OOB) management or zero-knowledge password proof (ZPP) [37].
4. Biometrics: Biometric authentication is the technique of identifying persons based on physiological and behavioral characteristics. There are two types (multi-modal biometrics and single-mode biometrics) [13].

3. Overview of Physical Unclonable Functions

3.1. PUF Definition and Functionality

PUFs are physical, random functions that offer particular physical outputs that are easy to generate but difficult to construct without gaining access to the object. Figure 3 shows the PUF functionality. PUFs work by implementing challenge–response authentication. The input to the PUF module serves as a challenge, and, based on the input and transfer function of the PUF, a digital fingerprint is produced, which is termed as the response. In other words, for a given PUF, there is a specific input known as a "challenge" that produces an output response that is distinctive to the particular PUF and, hence, unclonable.

Figure 3. Challenges and response of PUF [11].

3.2. PUF Implementation

3.2.1. Optical PUF

An optical PUF is a physical one-way function (POWF) comprising translucent matter doped with light-dispersing particles. As the laser beam falls on the matter, a unique and random speckle pattern is generated, and this process is shown in Figure 4. For the case of optical PUFs, the challenge is the light source, and the response is a speckle pattern. As the process of light falling on the material and then generating a speckle pattern is an uncontrolled process, replicating such a pattern is quite difficult.

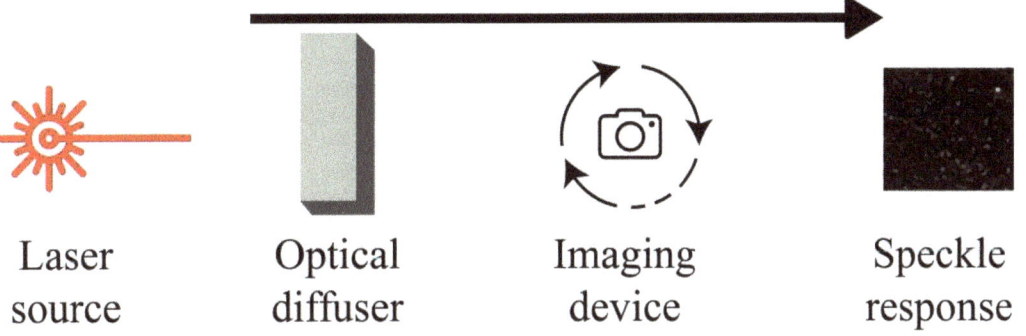

Figure 4. Optical PUF [12].

3.2.2. Ring Oscillator (RO)

Ring oscillator (RO) PUFs, as shown in Figure 5, are built on frequency deviation, while switch-based/arbiter PUFs are based on propagation delay. There are odd numbers of NOT gates in an RO. The output of the oscillator varies between two levels of voltage, and these two levels can be classified as true and false. Such an oscillator operates in a feedback manner where the output of last NOT gate is the feedback to the input to the RO. The advantage of the RO is the ease of implementation.

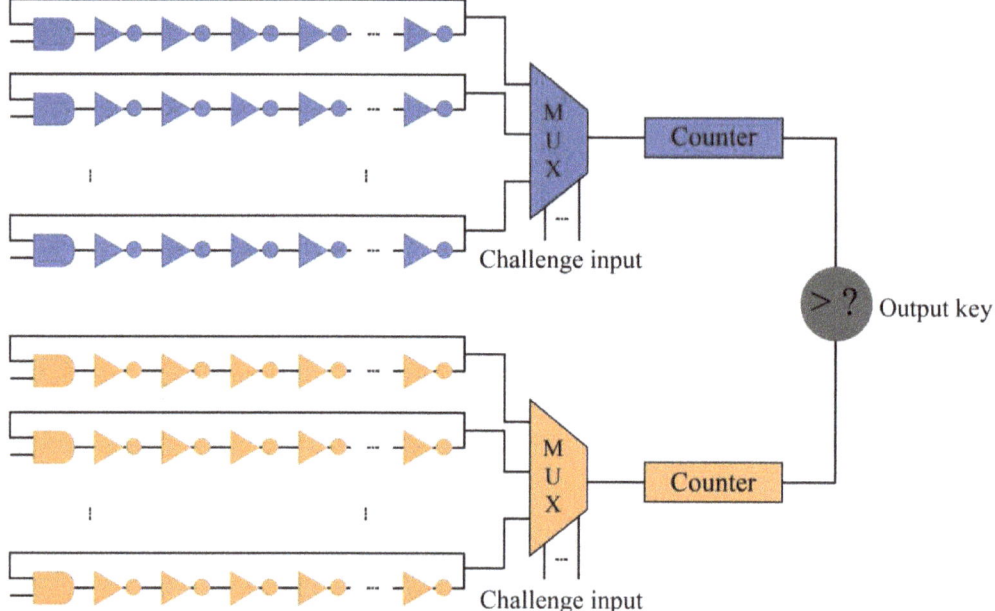

Figure 5. Ring oscillator (RO) [12].

3.2.3. Arbiter PUF

This type of PUF includes multiplexers coupled in succession, as portrayed in Figure 6. In the case of an RO-PUF design, there is an issue with the frequency oscillation, which is dependent on multiple factors. In the arbiter PUF, the transistors in multiplexers are responsible for producing variable delays. The last part of such a PUF is a D flip-flop. The signal from the top multiplexers is used as an input to the D flip-flop. The wave from the bottom multiplexers is given to the clock signal of the D flip-flop.

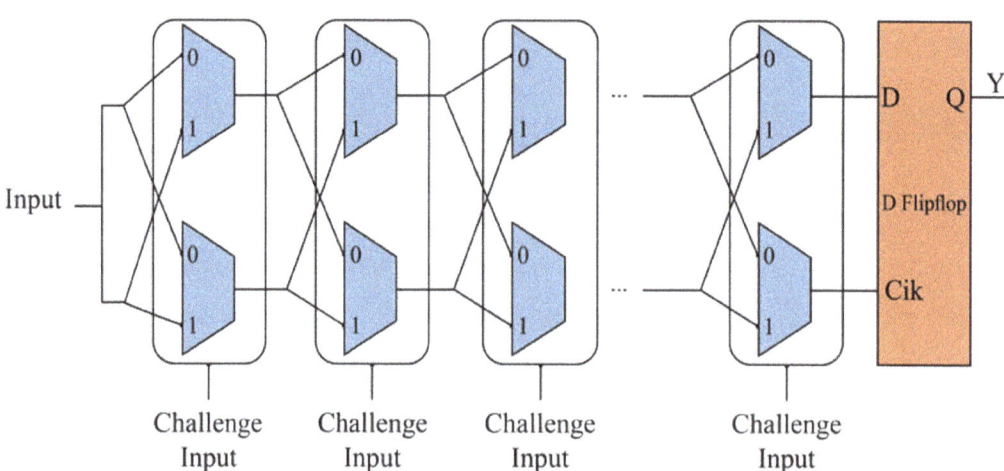

Figure 6. Arbiter PUF [12].

3.2.4. SRAM-PUF (Static Random-Access Memory PUF)

SRAM-PUF utilizes the random variations in the state of memory cells in static RAM. The start-up values of the SRAM cells are sensitive to manufacturing differences and environmental conditions, creating a unique and unpredictable pattern.

3.2.5. Butterfly PUF

Butterfly PUFs exploit the variations in delay paths within a symmetric structure. The structure consists of two paths that resemble a butterfly shape, and the delays through these paths are sensitive to manufacturing variations.

3.3. PUF Types

The following are the various types of PUFs as shown in Figure 7. Broadly speaking, PUFs can be classified into two categories, i.e., all-electronic and hybrid. Due to uniqueness causing randomness to arise, both types of PUFs can be further classified into implicit and explicit categories. If the variations are produced because of an external force/action, then we term such PUFs as explicit, and if the variations are created internally, then PUFs can be classified as implicit. Explicit hybrid PUFs can be optical or RF-based, and implicit hybrid PUFs can be optical or magnetic-based. Explicit, all-electronic PUFs can be based on direct characterization or non-volatile memory, whereas implicit all-electronic PUFs can be classified as a racetrack, volatile, transient, or direct characterization type.

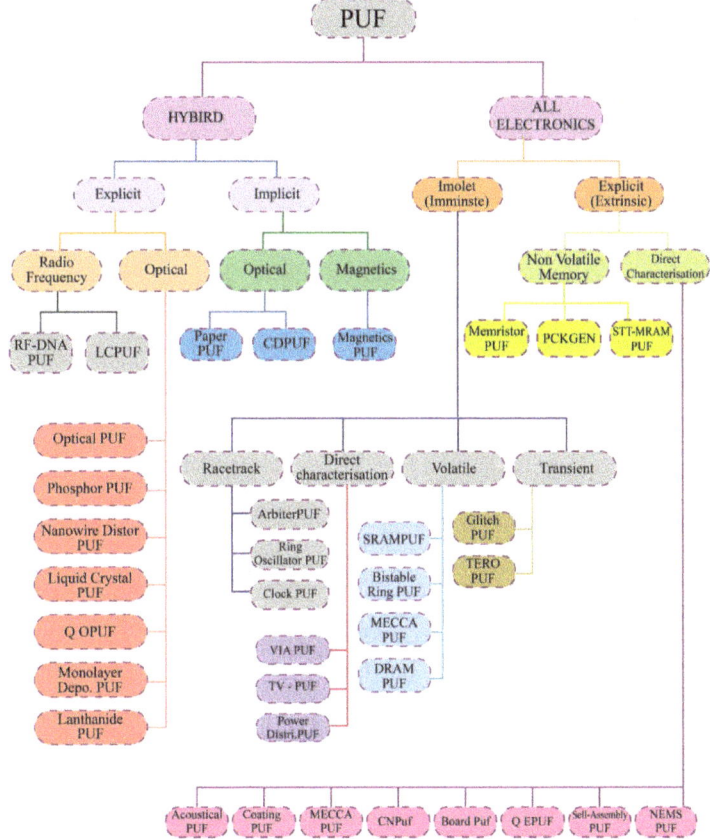

Figure 7. Types of PUFs [38].

Table 4 comprehensively lists the types of PUFs, their brief descriptions, and their limitations. From the table, we can see that different types of PUFs work on different principles. Based on the strength and uniqueness of the principle, different levels of security are provided. Some PUFs are easy to hack, while some PUFs generate a response that is difficult to replicate. The details for each PUF can be found.

Table 4. The relationship between type of PUFs, benefits, and limitations.

Study	Year	Type of PUF	Description	Limitations
[39]	2013	Memristor PUF	Memristors are potential future-generation memory technologies.	Process variation.
[40]	2013	PCKGEN	A phase change memory-based cryptographic key generator (PCKGEN) is a technology used to create updated cryptographic keys whenever it is desired to enhance the security of a system.	Highly hackable.
[41]	2014	STT-MRAM PUF	Spin-transfer torque magnetic random-access memory (STT-MRAM)-based PUF that utilizes orientation of a magnetic layer to generate unique patterns.	Read disturb errors in MLC NAND flash memory.
[42]	2004	Acoustical PUF	In an acoustical PUF (APUF), delay lines are applied to estimate the feasibility of creating an APUF.	Highly hackable.
[43]	2017	NEMS PUF	A PUF utilizing a nano-electromechanical (NEM) switch is termed as a NEMS PUF. A particular property of the NEM-switch-based PUF is its application of stiction.	Highly hackable.
[44]	2007	RF-DNA PUF	RF-DNA PUFs comprise an array of antennas with an analog or digital backend. Every individual antenna can act as a transmitter or receiver of RF waves in a particular frequency band backed by the backend process.	Special requirements.
[45]	2009	LC PUF	Such PUFs are based on resonance peaks in the frequency response of inductor–capacitor circuits.	Increased storage cost for noise issues.
[46]	2002	Optical PUF	The process of light scattering by particles is unrestrained, and the contact between the laser and the particles is quite complex. This attribute can be used for creating unique patterns that can enhance the security of the system.	Building complex physical structures for authentication.
[47]	2008	Phosphor PUF	Phosphor PUFs are made up of phosphorescent particles of arbitrary shape and dimensions that are blended randomly.	Vulnerable to invasive human factors and environmental factors, including scratching, temperature, and humidity.
[48]	2014	Nanowire Distro PUF	Fingerprint patterns can be physically validated in an easy and straightforward way by using an optical microscope.	Weak for spoofing attack.
[49]	2017	Liquid Crystal PUF	A liquid crystal PUF uses μm scale diameter shells of cholesteric liquid crystals (CLCs) at the surface of the physical object to be verified.	The challenge of the PUF is the number or position of the liquid crystal in the array, and the response is the frequency of reflected light.

Table 4. Cont.

Study	Year	Type of PUF	Description	Limitations
[50]	2017	Q-OPUF	A Q-OPUF uses nanometer-scale imperfections in pieces of 2D materials to achieve the functionality of a PUF.	Defect-free fabrication of monolayers is not possible, which results in bandgap alteration.
[51]	2017	Monolayer Deposition PUF	The monolayer deposition PUF assesses the existence or deficiency of monolayer matter in different positions along with a growth substrate.	This technique examines only the variation in physical position on layers.
[52]	2018	Lanthanide PUF	The lanthanide PUF explores the locations of zeolites doped with lanthanide (III) ions through a substrate via a photoluminescence dimension.	The random pattern generated by this method is difficult to replicate.
[53]	1993	Paper PUF	The paper PUF utilizes the distinctive marks of physical fibers such as currency to generate fingerprints.	Unique fingerprint can be established just by scanning the fiber/paper.
[54]	2009	CD PUF	The CD PUF utilizes the distinctive marks of the compact disk medium. It works by determining the length of the lands and pits of the CD.	A photodetector can be used for the determination of pits and lands.
[55]	1994	Magnetics PUF	The magnetic PUF uses randomness in ferromagnetic particle arrangement to generate unique magnetic swipe cards.	The inherit randomness in ferromagnetic particle arrangement is used to distinguish cards present in the database.
[56]	2014	Ring Oscillator PUF	A ring oscillator PUF works by analyzing the changes in the delay, which results in frequency of a signal propagating across an oscillator circuit formed of logic gates.	Simple circuitry. Can be implemented with the help of basic logic gates.
[57]	2004	Arbiter PUF	An arbiter PUF determines a system by analyzing the variations in the travel time of two electrical signals traveling through symmetrical paths.	Built from the on/off technique of the routing switches, giving a binary response depending on the faster path after this switching.
[58]	2013	Clock PUF	This type of PUF measures the changes in clock signal traveling velocity among signal lines, centered on the fabrication variation in these signal lines.	Now, due to the improvement in the design process, clock skew variations are almost negligible.
[59]	2015	VIA PUF	Such PUFs employ direct categorization of electronic modules. The VIA PUF uses the probability of physical connection between the electrical layers.	Approximately 50% uniformity and uniqueness can be achieved.
[60]	2000	TV-PUF	The main idea of the threshold voltage (TV)-PUF is to quantify the discrepancy in threshold voltage of ICs at the point of production.	Number of transistors required.
[61]	2009	Power Distribution PUF	The power distribution PUF works by defining the disparity in resistance of the power distribution system during the process of manufacturing an IC.	Additional components are added to each branch.
[62]	2007	SRAM-PUF	The static random-access memory (SRAM) PUF operates by finding the differences of transistor branches within SRAM.	Complexity of implementation as a fuzzy extractor on an FPGA is not known.

Table 4. Cont.

Study	Year	Type of PUF	Description	Limitations
[63]	2011	Bistable Ring PUF	Based on the variation in a series of logic gates.	The BR-PUF oscillates for a relatively significant period before it stabilizes.
[64]	2011	MECCA PUF	A memory cell-based chip authentication (MECCA) PUF comprises an arrangement of SRAM elements just like the SRAM-PUF and is based on the essential transistor deviation.	Additional hardware required.
[65]	2015	DRAM PUF	Analyzing difference in the elements' dynamic random-access memory (DRAM) cells.	Performance is temperature-dependent.
[66]	2010	Glitch PUF	The glitch PUF works by analyzing the complicated variation in glitches that are created because of the delay-based circuits.	N/A
[56]	2014	TERO-PUF	A new silicon PUF based on a transient effect ring oscillator.	N/A
[67]	2006	Coating PUF	Such PUFs work by measuring the capacitance across a pair of comb-shaped sensors in the top layer of an integrated circuit.	Eliminating/reducing the resistance in this type of construction against side-channel attacks is challenging.
[68]	2014	CNPUF	Carbon nanotube field-effect transistors (CNFETs) have excellent electrical properties. These distinguished physical features that can be used to create a CNPUF.	There is a trade-off between power consumed and security.
[69]	2015	Q-EPUF	The Q-EPUF PUF uses fluctuations in tunneling widths through quantum wells in resonant tunneling diodes.	N/A
[70]	2016	Self-Assembly PUF	These PUFs use the physical phenomenon of molecular self-assembly.	Limited semiconducting purity and non-ideal assembly.

3.4. PUF Attack

PUF attacks aim to compromise the integrity and security of systems relying on PUF, thereby diminishing their effectiveness. Referred to as "PUF attacks" by researchers and academics, these incursions strategically exploit weaknesses in the implementation or design of security measures based on PUFs. PUFs capitalize on the inherent uniqueness and unpredictability arising from variations in device production, making them resistant to traditional cloning methods. As these attacks pose a potential threat to the integrity of PUFs, it is crucial to understand the diverse tactics employed. PUF attacks manifest in various forms, each targeting specific elements of the PUF architecture. Examples of these attacks include:

Cloning Attacks: In a modeling attack, an adversary tries to create a mathematical model or replica of the PUF. This model could be based on measurements or observations of the PUF's responses to various challenges. If the attacker successfully models the PUF, they may be able to simulate its behavior and bypass security measures [71].

Side-Channel Attacks: Side-channel attacks involve analyzing unintended information leakage from the PUF, such as power consumption or electromagnetic radiation. By monitoring these side channels, attackers may gain insights into the PUF's behavior and potentially extract sensitive information [72].

Fault Injection Attacks: Attackers intentionally inject faults into the PUF or surrounding circuitry to disrupt normal operation. Techniques like voltage glitching or laser attacks may be employed to manipulate PUF responses and compromise their security [73].

4. Analysis and Discussion

PUFs are adopted in applications and cryptographic-based systems; however, PUFs fail to provide proper protection because they can be completely broken using computational models and other non-invasive methodologies [12]. Since the PUF is one of the main components of cryptography, it can achieve all goals of security protection for various companies, businesses, and other essential organizations. Some research has mentioned how PUFs are suitable for hardware security and protocol authentication. PUF entities, namely, the authentication, protocol, classification, and model, are shown in Figure 8.

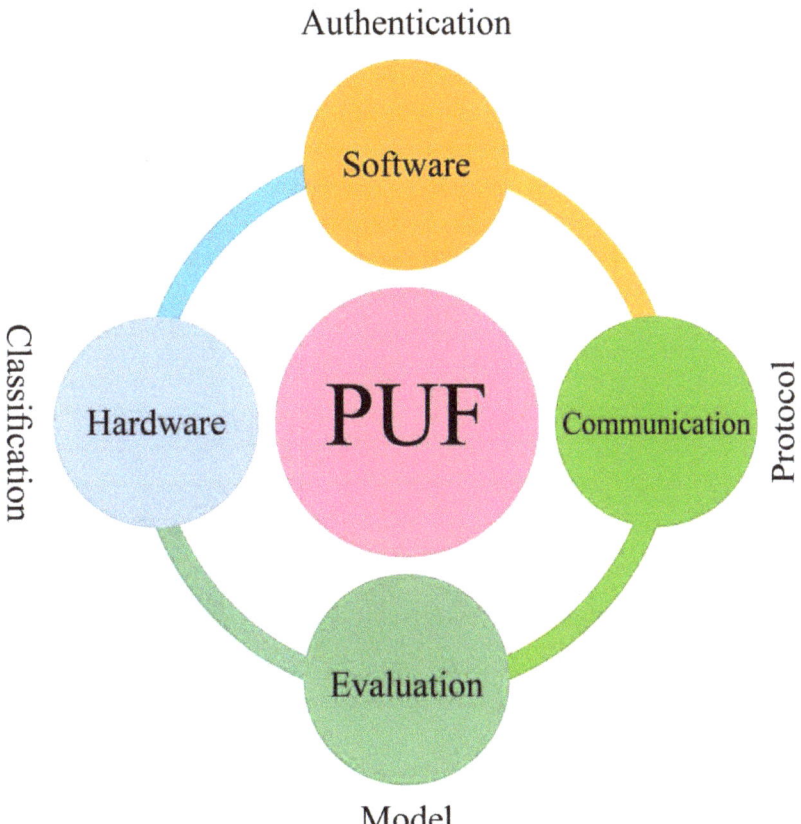

Figure 8. PUF entities.

4.1. Analysis of PUF-Based Authentication and Its Applications

We explain all the terms in Table 5 before describing Table 6. A detailed analysis of PUF-based authentication and its applications is given in Table 6. This table describes the differences between protocols in PUF-based authentication protocols.

Table 5. An explanation of terms of PUF-Based Authentication and Its Applications.

Symbol	Explanation	Symbol	Explanation
PKI	Public Key Infrastructure	CRPs	Challenge–response pairs
T2M	Things-to-Machine	T2T	Things to Things
AES	The Advanced Encryption Standard	ECC	Elliptic-curve cryptography
XOR	Exclusive OR Gate	LBRAPS	Lightweight blockchain-enabled RFID-based authentication protocol

Table 6. Summary of the differences of PUF-based authentication protocols.

Protocol	PUF	Authentication Schema	Secure Storage of Keys	Storage of CRPs	Encryption Methods	Platform Used	Major Issues	Major Advantages
[8]	Unspecified	T2T	No	Yes	Hash	-	High storage cost	Secure communication
[10]	SARAM-PUF	T2T	No	Yes	Hash	Arduino Mega Raspberry	Ineffective spoofing attack	Low cost
[11]	APUF	T2T	Yes	Yes	AES, hash	Simulation	Limited machine learning attack	Low computational complexity
[74]	XOR-PUF	T2T	No	Yes	-	Simulation	Limited resources	Tempo-blocking free
[75]	Unspecified	T2T	No	Yes	PKI	Artix-7 FPGA	Limited resources	Verifier database without CRPs
[76]	APUF	T2T	No	Yes	ECC	Xilinx zynq:7000 zc706	Limited database security	Strong logic control
[77]	XOR-PUF	T2M	No	No	Hash	Simulation	Infective spoofing attack	Verifying without CRPs
[78]	Unspecified	T2T	No	Yes	Hash	Arduino Mega 2560/due	High cost of storing eCRPs	Automated authenticate
[79]	SRAM-PUF	T2T	No	Yes	Hash	Arduino Mega 2560/due	Unstable cell in SRAM	Effects of memory storage
[80]	Unspecified	T2T	No	No	Hash	-	Limited encryption	Low-cost devices using PUFs
[81]	Unspecified	T2M	No	Yes	Hash	Zolertia Zoul Remote	Limited encryption	Less constrained resources
[82]	Unspecified	T2T	No	Yes	-	-	Limited encryption	Prevents machine learning attack
[83]	RO-PUF	T2T	No	Yes	Hash	FPGA platform	Limited evaluation and attack	Improved CRO PUF circuits with latch structure.
[84]	Unspecified	T2T	No	No	Hash + XOR	(AVISPA) simulation tool + BAN logic	Communication cost is undesirable	Light weight
[14]	SRAM	T2T	Yes	No	-	MSP430 controllers	Time is not mentioned	Secure channel
[85]	Unspecified	T2T	No	Yes	Elliptic curve	CC2538 SoC model	Storage cost	Secure channel
[86]	Unspecified	T2T	No	No	XOR	-	Benchmark not clear	-
[87]	Unspecified	T2T	No	Yes	XOR+hash	-	Limited encryption	Light weight

Table 6. Cont.

Protocol	PUF	Authentication Schema	Secure Storage of Keys	Storage of CRPs	Encryption Methods	Platform Used	Major Issues	Major Advantages
[18]	SPUF	T2T	Yes	Yes	-	Xilinx XC7A35-T FPGA	Limited encryption	Does not utilize cryptography
[88]	Unspecified	T2T	No	Yes	XOR, hash, and ECC	Xilinx FPGA Zynq-7	Limited encryption	Good resistance
[89]	APUF	T2T	No	No	-	-	-	Very high resilience
[90]	Unspecified	T2T	No	No	Hash	-	Easy to attack session key	Good communication overhead
[91]	Unspecified	T2T	Yes	Yes	Hash	-	Does not support PUF interference attack caused by noise	Covers various types of cryptographic protocols
[92]	Unspecified	T2T	Yes	Yes	LBRAPS	-	-	Vulnerable to secret disclosure attack and desynchronization attack
[17]	Unspecified	T2T	Yes	Yes	-	NodeMCU v3 and Raspberry Pi 3B	Too many stages in authentication	Good resistance
[93]	XOR-PUF	T2T	Yes	Yes	XOR	Xilinx XC5LVX110T	Excessive storage space to store e-CRPs	Good resistance
[94]	Unspecified	T2T	Yes	Yes	Hash, XOR	-	Excessive storage space	Integrity
[95]	Unspecified	T2T	Yes	Yes	Hash, XOR	-	-	Evaluates PUF attributes
[96]	Unspecified	T2T	Yes	Yes	EC, Hash	-	Many parameters	-

Table 6 also shows the differences between researchers working on PUF-based authentication protocols. This extensive and detailed table delineates various aspects, including authentication schema, secure storage of keys, storage of CRPs, encryption methods, platform used, issues, and the advantages of each protocol. We can observe that Things to Things (T2T) is the most popular authentication scheme used in PUFs. The most popular encryption method used in a hash function is primarily used because of its simplicity and low computational power, and the advanced encryption key (AES) is also a popular technique. A range of platforms are used in order to evaluate the performance of the protocols. Simulation software, field-programmable gate arrays (FPGAs), and Arduino are popular choices to evaluate the performance of the protocols.

One of the most important characteristics that must be studied further by the research community is "Secure store key". These keys are vulnerable to attacks and hacking, especially those which are stored in memory. Although secure keys have been designed [11], the developed keys are still weak because the method functions are not strong enough for decryption. We believe the authors used traditional methods, which mean that they are always displayed and thus vulnerable to machine learning attacks. Another major concern for users is trust in the data regarding their origin and location. This is especially true for IoT devices, which are typically low-cost. A lightweight protocol for data provenance in the IoT was given [74]. PUFs are used to give physical security and uniquely identify IoT devices. Channel impairments and characteristics are used to uniquely identify the communication link between the server and the IoT device.

Next, the key agreement between two constrained IoT devices is essential to establish trust between the devices, and PUFs can play a role in this regard as well. The existing key agreement protocols are exposed to man-in-the-middle, impersonation, and replay attacks, as has been demonstrated [8]. Also, a proposed alternative scheme offers identity-based authentication and repudiation. Another challenge with PUFs is that they are prone to attacks if several PUFs' challenge–response pairs (CRPs) are subjected to an intrusion attack. A PUF-based, insubstantial, reliable authentication mechanism using binary string shuffling was proposed [85]. The key feature of this technique is that it is inexpensive yet secure. The server authentication is carried out before the underlying PUF becomes exposed, thus preventing it from being brute-forced.

Finally, most researchers, such as [76,77], when designing PUFs with IoT devices/servers use five methods of encryption that still suffer from cyberattacks, which are as follows:

1: XOR gate encryption;
2: Hash function methods;
3: Block cipher methods;
4: Elliptic-curve methods;
5: AES methods.

The significant vulnerability of these methods is a cloning cyberattack that puts the network/system under attack, so we must develop a smart framework with PUF technology that is able to keep IoT ecosystems safe. Any novel method must be strong and lightweight to face these challenges.

4.2. Analysis of PUF-Based Authentication and Its Communication Protocol

We explain all the terms in Table 7 to presenting Table 8. A detailed analysis of PUF-based authentication and its communication protocol follows.

Table 7. An explanation of terms of PUF-Based Authentication and Its Communication Protocol.

Symbol	Explanation	Symbol	Explanation
CoAP	Constrained Application Protocol	AMQP	Advanced Message Queuing Protocol
MQTT	Message Queuing Telemetry Transport	HTTP	Hypertext Transfer Protocol
DDS	Data Distribution Service	UDP-based	User Datagram Protocol
XMPP	Extensible Messaging and Presence Protocol	Modbus-TCP	Modbus Communication Protocol

Table 8. PUF-based authentication and its communication protocols.

Study	Current IoT Protocols	Objectives	Results	Analyzer Tools (Hardware + Software)	Metrics	Major Disadvantages
[97]	CoAP, MQTT, AMQP	Design and build an application layer framework to assess and discover how these protocols work. Experiments were performed on a realistic testbed with wired, Wi-Fi, and 2/3/4G networks.	CoAP performs reliably during connection and is less network-dependent.	Wireshark, RabbitMQ, Eclipse Mosquitto, Libcoap Server, Python	Number of messages, number of packets, bandwidth utilization	Limited client/server approach.

Table 8. Cont.

Study	Feature: Current IoT Protocols	Objectives	Results	Evaluation Methods: Analyzer Tools (Hardware + Software)	Metrics	Major Disadvantages
[98]	MQTT, CoAP, AMQP, HTTP	Review MQTTSN, MQTT, CoAP, AMQP, DDS, and XMPP data protocols of the IoT and evaluate these protocols with demanding issues such as caching, security, support to QoS, and resource discovery.	In system control, instant messaging, and VoIP for communication, XMPP exhibits superior results due to its XML stanza-based transmission and lightweight carrying of messages with lower propagation delay.	Contiki	Network message size, packet loss rate, latency bandwidth consumption	Missed performance metrics.
[99]	MQTT, CoAP, DDS, custom UDP-based	Provide a quantitative comparison of the performance of IoT protocols.	DDS demonstrates greater bandwidth utilization than MQTT and superior operation regarding data latency and reliability.	NetEM, Wireshark, Hacks, eHealth sensor, Raspberry Pi, central Server	Bandwidth consumption, system latency, system packet loss	Missed performance metrics.
[100]	AMQP, MQTT	Focus on two protocols, AMQP and MQTT, which are the foundation for the effective functioning of the entire IoT system.	MQTT is an efficient protocol and use of the transmission line. AMQP is a recent, advanced, reliable, and superior security protocol.	Python, laptop with 2GB RAM, NetEm, Fanout Exchange	Packet transmission time	Insufficient metrics.
[101]	HTTP, MQTT, AMQP, CoAP, XMPP	Present a comprehensive review of the existing messaging protocols that can be used in deploying IoT systems.	Basic protocol characteristics that need to be studied when making and deploying IoT systems.	No	No	No metrics for security.
[102]	MQTT, AMQP, XMPP DDS, HTTP, CoAP	Present potential protocol candidates and compare between them in performance metrics.	The two most mature choices to consider, which are also favored by developers, are MQTT and RESTful HTTP.	No	Latency, bandwidth consumption and throughput, energy consumption security	No metrics for security.
[103]	WebSocket, CoAP, and MQTT	Construct a conceptual model for obtaining and evaluating WebSocket, CoAP, and MQTT protocols.	MQTT with QoS demonstrates the second-best overhead. WebSocket demonstrates almost the same throughput as MQTT with QoS 0.	Raspberry Pi model B, Wireshark	Packet loss	No metrics for security.
[104]	MQTT, CoAP, Modbus-TCP	Design a new scheme for communication protocols of IoT devices and incorporate the formats of the data gathered by numerous IoT devices.	A new model was assessed with three key performance indicators, and the proposed IoT-CPCS method can enhance the application affinity of the IoT to facilitate wider promotion.	WireShark, Amazon AWS platform, Python 3.7	Conversion time, average latency, system throughput	KPI for security was not included.

Table 8. Cont.

Study	Feature / Current IoT Protocols	Objectives	Results	Evaluation Methods			Major Disadvantages
				Analyzer Tools (Hardware + Software)	Metrics		
[105]	CoAP, MQTT, XMPP, TLS	Investigate three IoT communication protocols: MQTT/TLS, CoAP/DTLS, and XMPP/TLS.	Overhead and latency both increased at least threefold for each protocol.	Arduino Uno Rev3, WireShark, Raspberry Pi 3 Model B	Packet overhead, latency, scalability		Increased latency time.
[106]	MQTT, AMQP, CoAP, XMPP	Present the functions of the IoT and its applications in various domains such as smart cities, health care, environmental, Industry 4.0, and beyond and infrastructural applications.	This paper reviews modern IoT technologies and use cases, future-generation protocol. IoT disputes were examined to enhance R&D in the fields.	N/A	Application focus area		Few metrics.

Eleven studies discussing PUF-based authentication and communication protocols were reviewed and analyzed. The detailed analysis is shown in Table 5. Table 5 describes the IoT protocols that are being developed or adopted in the literature. AMQP and MQTT are the most widely adopted protocols that are being used in the literature and are being deployed and tested for wired as well as wireless technologies. Wireshark and Raspberry Pi are the two popular choices in terms of hardware testbeds to observe the performance of the proposed protocols. Based on further analysis, it can be found that the above-mentioned researchers did not use or suggest a method for assessing the challenges facing security. This is a drawback, as a real assessment of security is necessary. Most researchers, such as [39,40], have used MQTT because it is lightweight and the mechanism is simple in a network. Chaudhary et al. designed a new protocol [87] and a new schema, which was different in metrics and key performance indicators (KPIs) [42].

4.3. PUF with MQTT Communication Protocols

MQTT is a robust standard messaging protocol, and it has been adopted widely because of it is lightweight and low cost. Nevertheless, authentication is still a major issue where authentication criteria are provided. In other words, it uses username/password verification, which cannot provide necessary security [107]. To address this issue, in [107], it was proposed that each client/end-device must generate a unique output/response using a PUF. This response is applied as encryption/decryption key and identification of devices. Each broker is allowed a node in the blockchain that ensures that only permitted brokers can add a block for data/device validation values like device ID and PUF response. The system comprises chains. One records the devices' PUF response and device ID (Chain A). The second one saves the data transmitted among the devices.

A secure MQTT PUF-based key exchange protocol was proposed in [108], allowing smart health device verification [28]. The protocol was designed with one handshake process and three authentication processes to handle replay and eavesdropping attacks. A new method was built with a PUF called the OSCORE Security Protocol using a key exchange on PUF-based SRAM [109]. A key exchange solution to OSCORE key material based on the PUF-based verification principle, which is unique in its features, is also proposed.

4.4. PUF-Based Authentication Challenges and Solutions
4.4.1. Challenge 1: Delay Gates

In electronics and digital circuits, the propagation delay, also called the gate delay, is the amount of time between when the input to a logic gate becomes stable and valid to change and when the output of that logic gate becomes constant and rational to change [110].

The time that passes during normal operation when the PUF unit receives the input and when it begins producing output is referred to as the stabilization time. The critical and emergency systems at this location cannot tolerate this kind of delay. It is a very significant research challenge for scholars to design novel PUFs that can affect the initiation and handling times [111]. Recent studies have shown that unbalanced ternary logic gates and arithmetic circuits can help reduce the delay [112,113].

4.4.2. Challenge 2: Bit Size of PUF

PUFs are thought to be safer when the pattern of outputs (the number of different responses) is larger. The 192-bit response is more secure because it has more bits than one with 128 bits. However, the length of each bit is shortened because some bits of the response are different (random). Therefore, there is a need to utilize mismatch size to produce an additional stable bit so that PUFs become safer.

4.4.3. Challenge 3: Power Efficiency

Power consumption is a major challenge for PUFs. The authentication process, stages of logical gates, and growth of CRPs consume previous components with too low power. However, some resistors employing PUFs require more power. In addition, using modern encryption and complex authentication lead to increased power consumption. There is a need to design ultra-low-power and aging-tolerant PUFs. In addition to that, performance optimization is a solution to improve power efficiency.

4.4.4. Challenge 4: Cost Efficiency

The cost of production in the design, structure, and authentication process should account for negligible resources of all kinds, including memory, energy consumption, and communication bandwidth. Cost reduction in design and structure is generally associated with the maturity of the product. However, lightweight authentication algorithms can be designed to improve cost efficiency. This will assist the further penetration of PUFs in the consumer market.

4.4.5. Challenge 5: Memory Consumption

Conventional security protocols cannot be implemented on IoT devices as they have small ROM, RAM, and processing power. Apart from that, they have power constraints. Therefore, there is a need for the development of power—as well as memory-efficient algorithms. A lightweight PUF-based authentication system was proposed and tested on a wireless sensor network [81]. The performance analysis shows that the proposed algorithm saves up to 45% power and uses 12% less memory compared to datagram transport layer security (DTLS) handshake authentication.

4.4.6. Challenge 6: Eavesdropping

It is challenging to implement intricate security algorithms on cost-sensitive devices because they have limited computational capacity. As a result of this restriction, the likelihood of espionage and other intrusions increases. In [114], the authors introduced the concept of PUF sensors, which work on authenticated sensing protocols, thus reducing the chances of eavesdropping and man-in-the-middle attacks. An experimental demonstration of this concept was carried out with the help of a ring oscillator PUF.

4.4.7. Challenge 7: Black Box Adversaries

PUFs can simply be treated as black boxes with the challenge considered as an input of the transfer function and the response considered as the output of the transfer function. To detect these adversaries, sensors are used, and the solution to avoid this adversary is physical protection [115].

4.4.8. Challenge 8: Distributed Denial-of-Service (DDoS) Attack

A distributed denial-of-service (DDoS) attack is an attempt to disturb the regular traffic flow of a particular server by overcrowding the infrastructure with a flood of Internet traffic. The SOM algorithm with the addition of the packet-per-flow feature can be the answer to the various weaknesses of other methods [116].

4.4.9. Challenge 9: Secret Key Two-Pair CRPs and ID for Devices Stored in Memory

Regarding spoofing and splicing/relocation attacks, a partial solution was provided in [79,82] via authentication of the protocol without CRPs. A stored key method was used in conjunction with encryption methods such as hash functions and Advanced 5.9 Encryption Standard (AES) [11].

4.4.10. Challenge 10: Limited Encryption Methods

Several works [16,19,26,79,117] have emphasized that PUF authentication protocols still require lightweight and strong methods, i.e., less power and less memory usage are required. However, all protocols used are still vulnerable to cyberattacks, as they use the hash function and some notations like the concatenation of a random number generator. The solution to this existing problem is the usage of a neural network method for encryption, which is lightweight.

4.4.11. Challenge 11: Noise

PUFs offer a lightweight replacement for high-cost encryption methods and secure key storage. Noise can flip one or more of the PUF output bits, which means the server will not accept a valid client. This is called a "false negative authentication". Environmental effects such as temperature, voltage variation, and temporal effects (aging) can introduce noise. Machine learning and artificial intelligence can play a role in overcoming noise issues in PUFs.

5. Proposed Framework of IoT-Enabled Authentication PUF

Our framework adopts the IoT layer shown in Figure 9, which consists of five layers that fit into the model attack; we explain each layer and the significant components related to the layer.

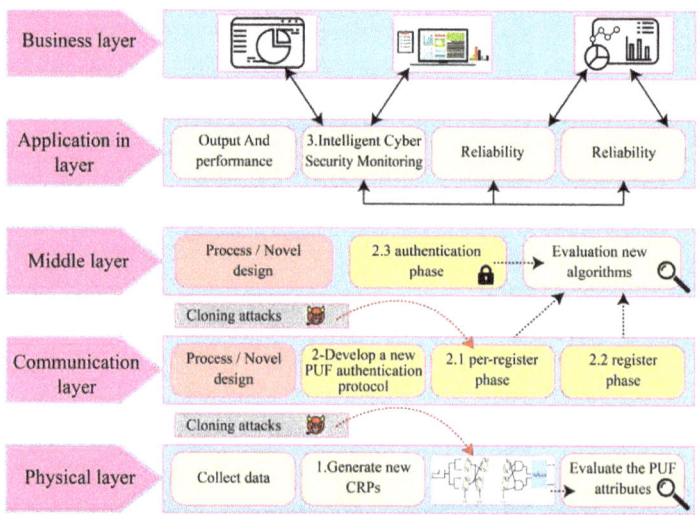

Figure 9. Framework of IoT-enabled authentication PUF.

5.1. Physical Layer

For this layer, during data collection, we collected all CRPs to evaluate a new design for a PUF that is a hybrid of NAND gate and multiplexers. Moreover, we used the JK flip-flop that results in the output Q for a normal situation and Q' for a cloning attack. The output is 0 or 1, which can be used to evaluate the PUF's attributes. The results are aggregated and compared with ideal values.

5.2. Communication Layer

In the second phase, known as the data processing phase, there are three distinct stages. Specifically, two of these stages operate within this layer, while the remaining stage is situated in the middle layer. Each stage has an algorithm; these algorithms are unique and provide solutions to an attack. We divided this phase into three stages:

Stage 1: preregister stage. We proposed an algorithm that checks all packets from IoT devices. If any spoofing station scans/reads the packet, the target station drops the packet (it is read only once). In addition, the algorithm collects all details of a network (IP, MAC, Flage bit, and latency time) as the input. A temporary database is created to store the details

(IP, MAC, response times for a packet) as the output. The main outcome of this algorithm is creating a temporary database with these parameters, as illustrated in Figure 10.

Figure 10. Process of pre-register.

Stage 2: In this stage, we wrote unique algorithms that regard temporary databases and CRPs as the input. They allow IoT devices to access the network/server to be trusted devices through CRPs. They must check whether the devices are legitimate using ID/IP devices, MAC addresses, and latency time. This phase must be used to increase security and protection. Moreover, two parameters, C and R, are used to create a trusted database on the server/cloud. This provides a solution to cloning attacks where C and R are collected and used to build mathematical methods. We can detect attacks from non-regular behavior stations, record response time, and scan packets a second time. In this case, we suggest a new thrust reverser method for a PUF, sending dummy CRPs to an attacker. At the end of this stage, we can register devices (D) in a network and build a trusted database. Figure 11 illustrates the process of registration with a focus on the registration process and the associated parameters

Figure 11. Process of registration.

5.3. Middle Layer

Stage 3: This stage is important for network communication with the connection of other stations/devices. The third algorithm participants communicate using a trusted database as the input. The device (Dj) sends R to confirm with the trusted database in the server. We utilized Cipher PRESENT algorithms because they are lightweight. PRESENT is an ultra-lightweight block cipher consisting of 31 rounds in this algorithm. This lightweight cipher takes a plaintext block of 64 bits as the input and outputs a ciphertext block of the same length. The algorithm of PRESENT supports two key sizes of length 80 bits and 120 bits, named PRESENT-80 with an 80-bit key length and PRESENT-128 with a 128-bit key length. At the end of the algorithm, which can exchange data/files using intelligent cybersecurity monitoring, this component is responsible for detecting cloning attacks with the PUF3S-ML model. We used the best-fitting algorithms with a dataset from a model that can classify attacks. Figure 12 presents the authentication process with parameters.

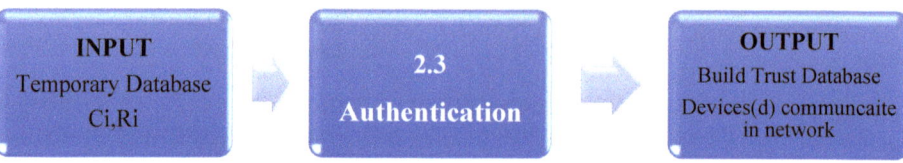

Figure 12. Process of authentication.

5.4. Application Layer

Reliability is a well-established analysis method reserved for a typical attack. As its name indicates, reliability is the main reference point for the detection model, but the consequences of failure are also evaluated, which means that the framework runs and adapts to PUF3S-ML. Also, for resilient preservation that integrates with the innovative PUF technology, we designed a novel model for our deployment methods in Figure 13.

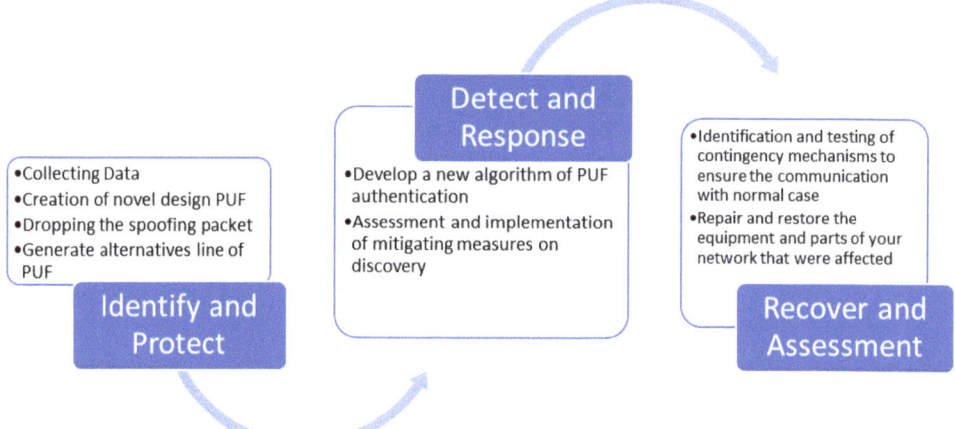

Figure 13. Framework reliability and resilience.

In the first phase, we must understand all target attacks on IoT devices in the smart network, understanding the environments of networks and focusing on generating CRPs with complete safety within the novel structure of PUFs that can protect IoT devices from attack.

In the second phase, we must take action after protecting our model from attack through the new design; it consists of three steps, and each step has unique algorithms and PUF-based authentication that provide solutions. In addition, intelligent cybersecurity monitoring is used to detect and classify all targeted attacks. In this component, we included machine learning algorithms that can analyze all data before, during, and after an attack. Using our responses in this model, when an attack happens and the PUF design is a failure, the structure must be renewed and made more robust and resilient.

The last phase connects two-layer application and business layers. Recovery is the core of these phases. After the attacks are closed, the data, configurations, and profiles are stored effectively, and the database is strong and updated. The new structure can work again without any issues or repair requirements. In this phase, a dashboard and the actual value of the network, the number of attacks, and the type of attack are provided.

5.5. Business Layer

All network values are monitored and compared with typical values, such as bandwidth, latency (delay), bandwidth—delay product throughput, and jitter. At the end of this stage, a thorough report is built and sent to users and administrators.

6. Conclusions

In the age of wireless communication, the connectivity between devices and their seamless communication plays a pivotal role in shaping a more interconnected world. However, this interconnectedness introduces vulnerabilities in the transmission of sensitive data across shared channels as the data are susceptible to potential intruders and cyberthreats.

This paper delves into a comprehensive survey of IoT networks integrating PUFs and examines the means of fortifying security against cyberattacks. Regarding the limitations of traditional security protocols for such networks, this study highlights the necessity of developing specifically tailored lightweight algorithms to meet the demands of IoT devices. By exploring the IoT field, its advantages, architectural applications, and associated challenges, this paper extensively researches the functionality and varied types of PUFs. It meticulously examines PUF-based authentication, communication protocols, and their diverse applications. Furthermore, it addresses eleven crucial challenges encountered in this domain along with proposed solutions.

This survey uniquely contributes to the literature by providing a comprehensive analysis encompassing eleven studies concerning PUF-based authentication and communication protocols. Notably, MQTT and AMQP emerge as widely adopted technologies, having undergone rigorous testing across both wired and wireless platforms. Innovative solutions are proposed to tackle the challenges related to PUFs, address propagation delay, bit stability, power consumption, cost efficiency, encryption methods, and security concerns such as DDoS attacks. This study focuses on revolution around three key aspects: authentication, encryption, and PUFs within communication protocols. The aim is to fortify security within IoT systems.

In summary, the proposed PUF-based authentication and communication protocols offer a multifaceted solution to an array of challenges faced in this domain. They strive to enhance security, reliability, and efficiency within IoT networks. By highlighting the importance of tailored algorithms and robust security measures, this study contributes to the ongoing discourse surrounding the integrity and resilience of IoT systems.

Author Contributions: Conceptualization, R.A.A. and M.M.S.; methodology, R.A.A. and M.M.S.; investigation, R.A.A.; resources, R.A.A.; data curation, R.A.A.; writing—original draft preparation, M.M.S.; writing—review and editing, M.M.S.; supervision, M.M.S. All authors have read and agreed to the published version of the manuscript.

Funding: This work was supported by the Ministry of Higher Education Malaysia under the Fundamental Research Grant Scheme with project Code: FRGS/1/2020/ICT07/USM/02/2. The authors also would like to express sincere gratitude to AlMaarefa University, Riyadh, Saudi Arabia, for providing funding to conduct this research.

Informed Consent Statement: Not applicable.

Conflicts of Interest: The authors declare no conflicts of interest. The funders had no role in the design of the study; in the collection, analyses, or interpretation of data; in the writing of the manuscript; or in the decision to publish the results.

References

1. Al-Naji, F.H.; Zagrouba, R. A survey on continuous authentication methods in Internet of Things environment. *Comput. Commun.* **2020**, *163*, 109–133. [CrossRef]
2. Mrabet, H.; Belguith, S.; Alhomoud, A.; Jemai, A. A survey of IoT security based on a layered architecture of sensing and data analysis. *Sensors* **2020**, *20*, 3625. [CrossRef]
3. Ali, O.; Ishak, M.K.; Bhatti, M.K.; Khan, I.; Kim, K.-I. A comprehensive review of Internet of Things: Technology stack, middlewares, and Fog/Edge computing interface. *Sensors* **2022**, *22*, 995. [CrossRef]
4. Adat, V.; Gupta, B.B. Security in Internet of Things: Issues, challenges, taxonomy, and architecture. *Telecommun. Syst.* **2018**, *67*, 423–441. [CrossRef]
5. Dubey, A.K.; Meena, D.C.; Gaur, S. A survey in hello flood attack in wireless sensor networks. *Int. J. Eng. Res. Technol.* **2014**, *3*, 1882–1887.
6. Elhoseny, M.; Thilakarathne, N.N.; Alghamdi, M.I.; Mahendran, R.K.; Gardezi, A.; Weerasinghe, H.; Welhenge, A.M. Security and privacy issues in medical Internet of Things: Overview, countermeasures, challenges and future directions. *Sustainability* **2021**, *12*, 11645. [CrossRef]
7. Attkan, A.; Ranga, V. Cyber-physical security for IoT networks: A comprehensive review on traditional, blockchain and artificial intelligence based key-security. *Complex Intell. Syst.* **2022**, *8*, 3559–3591. [CrossRef]
8. Braeken, A. PUF based authentication protocol for IoT. *Symmetry* **2018**, *10*, 352. [CrossRef]
9. Baig, A.F.; Eskeland, S. Security, privacy, and usability in continuous authentication: A survey. *Sensors* **2021**, *21*, 5967. [CrossRef] [PubMed]
10. Mahmod, M.J.a.; Guin, U. A robust, low-cost and secure authentication scheme for IoT applications. *Cryptography* **2020**, *4*, 8. [CrossRef]
11. Mostafa, A.; Lee, S.J.; Peker, Y.K. Physical unclonable function and hashing are all you need to mutually authenticate IoT devices. *Sensors* **2020**, *20*, 4361. [CrossRef]
12. Joshi, S.; Mohanty, S.P.; Kougianos, E. Everything you wanted to know about PUFs. *IEEE Potentials* **2017**, *36*, 38–46. [CrossRef]
13. Shah, S.W.; Kanhere, S.S. Recent trends in user authentication—A survey. *IEEE Access* **2019**, *7*, 112505–112519. [CrossRef]
14. Badr, Y.; Zhu, X.; Alraja, M.N. Security and privacy in the Internet of Things: Threats and challenges. *Serv. Oriented Comput. Appl.* **2021**, *15*, 257–271. [CrossRef]
15. Chatterjee, U.; Chatterjee, S.; Mukhopadhyay, D.; Chakraborty, R.S. Machine learning assisted PUF calibration for trustworthy proof of sensor data in IoT. *ACM Trans. Des. Autom. Electron.Syst.* **2020**, *25*, 32. [CrossRef]
16. Babaei, A.; Schiele, G. Physical Unclonable Functions in the Internet of Things: State of the Art and Open Challenges. *Sensors* **2019**, *19*, 3208. [CrossRef] [PubMed]
17. Kulkarni, S.; Vani, R.M.; Hunagund, P.V. A study on physical unclonable functions based security for Internet of Things applications. In *Intelligent Data Communication Technologies and Internet of Things*; Springer: Berlin, Germany, 2019; pp. 607–614. [CrossRef]
18. Garcia-Bosque, M.; Díez-Señorans, G.; Sánchez-Azqueta, C.; Celma, S. Introduction to physically unclonable fuctions: Properties and applications. In Proceedings of the 2020 European Conference on Circuit Theory and Design (ECCTD), Sofia, Bulgaria, 7–10 September 2020. [CrossRef]
19. El-Hajj, M.; Fadlallah, A.; Chamoun, M.; Serhrouchni, A. A taxonomy of PUF schemes with a novel arbiter-based PUF resisting machine learning attacks. *Comput. Netw.* **2021**, *194*, 108133. [CrossRef]
20. Al-Meer, A.; Al-Kuwari, S. Physical unclonable functions (PUF) for IoT devices. *arXiv* **2022**, arXiv:2205.08587. [CrossRef]
21. Gebali, F.; Mamun, M. Review of physically unclonable functions (PUFs): Structures, models, and algorithms. *Front. Sens.* **2022**, *2*, 751748. [CrossRef]
22. Shamsoshoara, A.; Korenda, A.; Afghah, F.; Zeadally, S. A survey on physical unclonable function (puf)-based security solutions for internet of things. *Comput. Netw.* **2020**, *183*, 107593. [CrossRef]
23. Mall, P.; Amin, R.; Das, A.K.; Leung, M.T.; Choo, K.-K.R. PUF-based Authentication and Key Agreement Protocols for IoT, WSNS, and Smart Grids: A Comprehensive Survey. *IEEE Internet Things J.* **2022**, *9*, 8205–8228. [CrossRef]
24. Gillis, A.S. What Is the Internet of Things (IoT)? Available online: https://www.techtarget.com/iotagenda/definition/Internet-of-Things-IoT (accessed on 22 April 2023).
25. Rashidah Funke, O.; Burhan Ul Islam, K.; Aisha Hassan Abdalla, H.; Khairul Azami, S.; Zuhani Ismail, K.; Hamdan, D. The Internet of Things vision: A comprehensive review of architecture, enabling technologies, adoption challenges, research open issues and contemporary applications. *J. Adv. Res. Appl. Sci. Eng. Technol.* **2022**, *26*, 51–77. [CrossRef]
26. Wazid, M.; Das, A.K.; Lee, J.-H. User authentication in a tactile internet based remote surgery environment: Security issues, challenges, and future research directions. *Pervasive Mob. Comput.* **2019**, *54*, 71–85. [CrossRef]
27. Kim, S.; Kim, S. User preference for an IoT healthcare application for lifestyle disease management. *Telecommun. Policy* **2018**, *42*, 304–314. [CrossRef]

28. Gharaibeh, A.; Salahuddin, M.A.; Hussini, S.J.; Khreishah, A.; Khalil, I.; Guizani, M.; Al-Fuqaha, A. Smart cities: A survey on data management, security, and enabling technologies. *IEEE Commun. Surv. Tutor.* **2017**, *19*, 2456–2501. [CrossRef]
29. Jose, A.C.; Malekian, R. Improving smart home security: Integrating logical sensing into smart home. *IEEE Sen. J.* **2017**, *17*, 4269–4286. [CrossRef]
30. Swain, K.B.; Santamanyu, G.; Senapati, A.R. Smart industry pollution monitoring and controlling using LabVIEW based IoT. In Proceedings of the 2017 Third International Conference on Sensing, Signal Processing and Security (ICSSS), Chennai, India, 4–5 May 2017; pp. 74–78. [CrossRef]
31. Alodib, M. QoS-Aware approach to monitor violations of SLAs in the IoT. *J. Innov. Digit. Ecosyst.* **2016**, *3*, 197–207. [CrossRef]
32. Cheruvu, S.; Kumar, A.; Smith, N.; Wheeler, D.M. *Demystifying Internet of Things Security*, 1st ed.; Apress: Berkeley, CA, USA, 2020. [CrossRef]
33. Kumar, C.; Prakash, S. Chapter 6—Routing protocols: Key security issues and challenges in IoT, ad hoc, and sensor networks. In *Security and Privacy Issues in IoT Devices and Sensor Networks*; Sharma, S.K., Bhushan, B., Debnath, N.C., Eds.; Academic Press: Cambridge, MA, USA, 2021; pp. 105–132. [CrossRef]
34. Singh, S.; Pandey, N.; Datta, M.; Batra, S. Stress, internet use, substance use and coping among adolescents, young-adults and middle-age adults amid the 'new normal' pandemic era. *Clin. Epidemiol. Glob. Health* **2021**, *12*, 100885. [CrossRef] [PubMed]
35. Dasgupta, D.; Roy, A.; Nag, A. *Advances in User Authentication*, 1st ed.; Springer: Cham, Switzerland, 2017. [CrossRef]
36. Shepherd, J. What Is Authentication? The Ultimate Authentication Playbook. Available online: https://www.okta.com/uk/blog/2019/02/the-ultimate-authentication-playbook/ (accessed on 15 February 2023).
37. Melki, R.; Noura, H.N.; Chehab, A. Lightweight multi-factor mutual authentication protocol for IoT devices. *Int. J. Inf. Secur.* **2020**, *19*, 679–694. [CrossRef]
38. McGrath, T.; Bagci, I.E.; Wang, Z.M.; Roedig, U.; Young, R.J. A PUF Taxonomy. *Appl. Phys. Rev.* **2019**, *6*, 011303. [CrossRef]
39. Koeberl, P.; Ünal, K.; Sadeghi, A.R. Memristor PUFs: A new generation of memory-based physically unclonable functions. In Proceedings of the 2013 Design, Automation & Test in Europe Conference & Exhibition (DATE), Grenoble, France, 18–22 March 2013; pp. 428–431. [CrossRef]
40. Zhang, L.; Kong, Z.H.; Chang, C.H. PCKGen: A phase change memory based cryptographic key generator. In Proceedings of the 2013 IEEE International Symposium on Circuits and Systems (ISCAS), Beijing, China, 19–23 May 2013; pp. 1444–1447. [CrossRef]
41. Zhang, L.; Fong, X.; Chang, C.H.; Kong, Z.H.; Roy, K. Highly reliable memory-based physical unclonable function using spin-transfer torque MRAM. In Proceedings of the 2014 IEEE International Symposium on Circuits and Systems (ISCAS), Melbourne, VIC, Australia, 1–5 June 2014; pp. 2169–2172. [CrossRef]
42. Vrijaldenhoven, S. Acoustical Physical Uncloneable Functions. Master's Thesis, Eindhoven University of Technology, Eindhoven, The Netherlands, 2004.
43. Hwang, K.-M.; Park, J.-Y.; Bae, H.; Lee, S.-W.; Kim, C.-K.; Seo, M.; Im, H.; Kim, D.-H.; Kim, S.-Y.; Lee, G.-B.; et al. Nano-electromechanical switch based on a physical unclonable function for highly robust and stable performance in harsh environments. *ACS Nano* **2017**, *11*, 12547–12552. [CrossRef]
44. DeJean, G.; Kirovski, D. RF-DNA: Radio-frequency certificates of authenticity. In Proceedings of the Cryptographic Hardware and Embedded Systems, CHES 2007, Vienna, Austria, 10–13 September 2007; pp. 346–363. [CrossRef]
45. Guajardo, J.; Škorić, B.; Tuyls, P.; Kumar, S.S.; Bel, T.; Blom, A.H.M.; Schrijen, G.-J. Anti-counterfeiting, key distribution, and key storage in an ambient world via physical unclonable functions. *Inf. Syst. Front.* **2009**, *11*, 19–41. [CrossRef]
46. Pappu, R.; Recht, B.; Taylor, J.; Gershenfeld, N. Physical one-way functions. *Science* **2002**, *297*, 2026–2030. [CrossRef]
47. Chong, C.N.; Jiang, D.; Zhang, J.; Guo, L. Anti-counterfeiting with a random pattern. In Proceedings of the 2008 Second International Conference on Emerging Security Information, Systems and Technologies, Cap Esterel, France, 25–31 August 2008; pp. 146–153. [CrossRef]
48. Kim, J.; Yun, J.M.; Jung, J.; Song, H.; Kim, J.-B.; Ihee, H. Anti-counterfeit nanoscale fingerprints based on randomly distributed nanowires. *Nanotechnology* **2014**, *25*, 155303. [CrossRef]
49. Lenzini, G.; Ouchani, S.; Roenne, P.; Ryan, P.Y.A.; Geng, Y.; Lagerwall, J.; Noh, J. Security in the shell: An optical physical unclonable function made of shells of cholesteric liquid crystals. In Proceedings of the 2017 IEEE Workshop on Information Forensics and Security (WIFS), Rennes, France, 4–7 December 2017; pp. 1–6. [CrossRef]
50. Cao, Y.; Robson, A.J.; Alharbi, A.; Roberts, J.; Woodhead, C.S.; Noori, Y.J.; Bernardo-Gavito, R.; Shahrjerdi, D.; Roedig, U.; Fal'ko, V.I.; et al. Optical identification using imperfections in 2D materials. *2D Mater.* **2017**, *4*, 045021. [CrossRef]
51. Alharbi, A.; Armstrong, D.; Alharbi, S.; Shahrjerdi, D. Physically unclonable cryptographic primitives by chemical vapor deposition of layered MoS2. *ACS Nano* **2017**, *11*, 12772–12779. [CrossRef]
52. Carro-Temboury, M.R.; Arppe, R.; Vosch, T.; Sørensen, T.J. An optical authentication system based on imaging of excitation-selected lanthanide luminescence. *Sci. Adv.* **2018**, *4*, e1701384. [CrossRef] [PubMed]
53. National Research Council. *Counterfeit Deterrent Features for the Next-Generation Currency Design*; The National Academies Press: Washington, DC, USA, 1993; p. 144. [CrossRef]
54. Hammouri, G.; Dana, A.; Sunar, B. CDs have fingerprints too. In Proceedings of the Cryptographic Hardware and Embedded Systems, CHES 2009, Lausanne, Switzerland, 6–9 September 2009; pp. 348–362. [CrossRef]
55. Indeck, R.S.; Muller, M.W. Method and Apparatus for Fingerprinting Magnetic Media. U.S. Patent 5365586A, 15 November 1994.

56. Bossuet, L.; Ngo, X.T.; Cherif, Z.; Fischer, V. A PUF based on a transient effect ring oscillator and insensitive to locking phenomenon. *IEEE Trans. Emerg. Top. Comput.* **2014**, *2*, 30–36. [CrossRef]
57. Lee, J.W.; Daihyun, L.; Gassend, B.; Suh, G.E.; Dijk, M.v.; Devadas, S. A technique to build a secret key in integrated circuits for identification and authentication applications. In Proceedings of the 2004 Symposium on VLSI Circuits. Digest of Technical Papers (IEEE Cat. No.04CH37525), Honolulu, HI, USA, 17–19 June 2004; pp. 176–179. [CrossRef]
58. Yao, Y.; Kim, M.; Li, J.; Markov, I.L.; Koushanfar, F. ClockPUF: Physical unclonable functions based on clock networks. In Proceedings of the 2013 Design, Automation & Test in Europe Conference & Exhibition (DATE), Grenoble, France, 18–22 March 2013; pp. 422–427. [CrossRef]
59. Jeon, D.; Baek, J.H.; Kim, D.K.; Choi, B.D. Towards zero bit-error-rate physical unclonable function: Mismatch-based vs. Physical-based approaches in standard CMOS technology. In Proceedings of the 2015 Euromicro Conference on Digital System Design, Madeira, Portugal, 26–28 August 2015; pp. 407–414. [CrossRef]
60. Lofstrom, K.; Daasch, W.R.; Taylor, D. IC identification circuit using device mismatch. In Proceedings of the 2000 IEEE International Solid-State Circuits Conference. Digest of Technical Papers (Cat. No.00CH37056), San Francisco, CA, USA, 9 February 2000; pp. 372–373. [CrossRef]
61. Helinski, R.; Acharyya, D.; Plusquellic, J. A physical unclonable function defined using power distribution system equivalent resistance variations. In Proceedings of the 2009 46th ACM/IEEE Design Automation Conference, San Francisco, CA, USA, 26–31 July 2009; pp. 676–681. [CrossRef]
62. Guajardo, J.; Kumar, S.S.; Schrijen, G.-J.; Tuyls, P. FPGA intrinsic PUFs and their use for IP protection. In Proceedings of the Cryptographic Hardware and Embedded Systems, CHES 2007, Vienna, Austria, 10–13 September 2007; pp. 63–80. [CrossRef]
63. Chen, Q.; Csaba, G.; Lugli, P.; Schlichtmann, U.; Rührmair, U. The bistable ring PUF: A new architecture for strong physical unclonable functions. In Proceedings of the 2011 IEEE International Symposium on Hardware-Oriented Security and Trust, San Diego, CA, USA, 5–6 June 2011; pp. 134–141. [CrossRef]
64. Krishna, A.R.; Narasimhan, S.; Wang, X.; Bhunia, S. MECCA: A robust low-overhead PUF using embedded memory array. In Proceedings of the Cryptographic Hardware and Embedded Systems, CHES 2011, Nara, Japan, 28 September–1 October 2011; pp. 407–420. [CrossRef]
65. Tehranipoor, F.; Karimian, N.; Xiao, K.; Chandy, J. DRAM based intrinsic physical unclonable functions for system level security. In Proceedings of the 25th edition on Great Lakes Symposium on VLSI, Association for Computing Machinery, Pittsburgh, PA, USA, 20–22 May 2015; pp. 15–20. [CrossRef]
66. Anderson, J.H. A PUF design for secure FPGA-based embedded systems. In Proceedings of the 2010 15th Asia and South Pacific Design Automation Conference (ASP-DAC), Taipei, Taiwan, 18–21 January 2010; pp. 1–6. [CrossRef]
67. Tuyls, P.; Schrijen, G.J.; Skoric, B.; van Geloven, J.; Verhaegh, N.; Wolters, R. Read-proof hardware from protective coatings. In *Cryptographic Hardware and Embedded Systems (CHES)*; Springer: Berlin, Germany, 2006.
68. Konigsmark, S.T.C.; Hwang, L.K.; Chen, D.; Wong, M.D.F. CNPUF: A carbon nanotube-based physically unclonable function for secure low-energy hardware design. In Proceedings of the 2014 19th Asia and South Pacific Design Automation Conference (ASP-DAC), Singapore, 20–23 January 2014; pp. 73–78. [CrossRef]
69. Roberts, J.; Bagci, I.E.; Zawawi, M.A.M.; Sexton, J.; Hulbert, N.; Noori, Y.J.; Young, M.P.; Woodhead, C.S.; Missous, M.; Migliorato, M.A.; et al. Using quantum confinement to uniquely identify devices. *Sci. Rep.* **2015**, *5*, 16456. [CrossRef] [PubMed]
70. Hu, Z. Physically unclonable cryptographic primitives using self-assembled carbon nanotubes. *Nat. Nanotechnol.* **2016**, *11*, 559. [CrossRef] [PubMed]
71. Duan, S.; Sai, G. Bti aging-based physical cloning attack on SRAM PUF and the countermeasure. *Analog Integr. Circuits Signal Process.* **2023**, *117*, 45–55. [CrossRef]
72. Delvaux, J.; Verbauwhede, I. Side channel modeling attacks on 65nm ARBITER PUFs exploiting CMOS device noise. In Proceedings of the 2013 IEEE International Symposium on Hardware-Oriented Security and Trust (HOST), Austin, TX, USA, 2–3 June 2013.
73. Delvaux, J.; Verbauwhede, I. Fault injection modeling attacks on 65 nm arbiter and Ro sum PUFs via environmental changes. *IEEE Trans. Circuits Syst. I Regul. Papers* **2014**, *61*, 1701–1713. [CrossRef]
74. Aman, M.N.; Chua, K.C.; Sikdar, B. A lightweight mutual authentication protocol for IoT systems. In Proceedings of the 2017 IEEE Global Communications Conference, Singapore, 4–8 December 2017; pp. 1–6. [CrossRef]
75. Chatterjee, U.; Go1vindan, V.; Sadhukhan, R.; Mukhopadhyay, D.; Chakraborty, R.S.; Mahata, D.; Prabhu, M.M. Building PUF based authentication and key exchange protocol for IoT without explicit CRPs in verifier database. *IEEE Trans. Dependable Secure Comput.* **2019**, *16*, 424–437. [CrossRef]
76. Qureshi, M.A.; Munir, A. PUF-RLA: A PUF-based reliable and lightweight authentication protocol employing binary string shuffling. In Proceedings of the 2019 IEEE 37th International Conference on Computer Design (ICCD), Abu Dhabi, United Arab Emirates, 17–20 November 2019; pp. 576–584. [CrossRef]
77. Nimmy, K.; Sankaran, S.; Achuthan, K. A novel lightweight PUF based authentication protocol for IoT without explicit CRPs in verifier database. *J. Ambient Intell. Hum. Comput.* **2023**, *14*, 6227–6242. [CrossRef]
78. Lounis, K.; Zulkernine, M. T2T-MAP: A PUF-based thing-to-thing mutual authentication protocol for IoT. *IEEE Access* **2021**, *9*, 137384–137405. [CrossRef]

79. Farha, F.; Ning, H.; Ali, K.; Chen, L.; Nugent, C. SRAM-PUF-based entities authentication scheme for resource-constrained IoT devices. *IEEE Internet Things J.* **2021**, *8*, 5904–5913. [CrossRef]
80. Clupek, V.; Zeman, V. Robust mutual authentication and secure transmission of information on low-cost devices using Physical unclonable functions and Hash functions. In Proceedings of the 2016 39th International Conference on Telecommunications and Signal Processing (TSP), Vienna, Austria, 27–29 June 2016; pp. 100–103. [CrossRef]
81. Yilmaz, Y.; Gunn, S.R.; Halak, B. Lightweight PUF-based authentication protocol for IoT devices. In Proceedings of the 2018 IEEE 3rd International Verification and Security Workshop (IVSW), Costa Brava, Spain, 2–4 July 2018; pp. 38–43. [CrossRef]
82. Nozaki, Y.; Yoshikawa, M. Secret sharing schemes based secure authentication for physical unclonable function. In Proceedings of the 2019 IEEE 4th International Conference on Computer and Communication Systems (ICCCS), Singapore, 23–25 February 2019; pp. 445–449. [CrossRef]
83. Huang, Z.; Wang, Q. A PUF-based unified identity verification framework for secure IoT hardware via device authentication. *World Wide Web* **2020**, *23*, 1057–1088. [CrossRef]
84. Son, S.; Park, Y.; Park, Y. A secure, lightweight, and anonymous user authentication protocol for IoT environments. *Sustainability* **2021**, *13*, 9241. [CrossRef]
85. Li, S.; Zhang, T.; Yu, B.; He, K. A provably secure and practical PUF-based end-to-end mutual authentication and key exchange protocol for IoT. *IEEE Sens. J.* **2021**, *21*, 5487–5501. [CrossRef]
86. Mahalat, M.H.; Saha, S.; Mondal, A.; Sen, B. A PUF-Based Lightweight Protocol for Secure WIFI Authentication of IoT Devices. In Proceedings of the 2018 8th International Symposium on Embedded Computing and System Design (ISED), Cochin, India, 13–15 December 2018. [CrossRef]
87. Yoon, S.; Kim, B.; Kang, Y.; Choi, D. PUF-based authentication scheme for IoT devices. In Proceedings of the 2020 International Conference on Information and Communication Technology Convergence (ICTC), Jeju, Republic of Korea, 21–23 October 2020; pp. 1792–1794. [CrossRef]
88. Adeli, M.; Bagheri, N.; Martín, H.; Peris-Lopez, P. Challenging the security of "A PUF-based hardware mutual authentication protocol". *J. Parallel Distrib. Comput.* **2022**, *169*, 199–210. [CrossRef]
89. Idriss, T.A.; Idriss, H.A.; Bayoumi, M.A. A lightweight PUF-based authentication protocol using secret pattern recognition for constrained IoT devices. *IEEE Access* **2021**, *9*, 80546–80558. [CrossRef]
90. Muhal, M.A.; Luo, X.; Mahmood, Z.; Ullah, A. Physical unclonable function based authentication scheme for smart devices in Internet of Things. In Proceedings of the 2018 IEEE International Conference on Smart Internet of Things (SmartIoT), Xi'an, China, 17–19 August 2018; pp. 160–165. [CrossRef]
91. Song, J.; Xiao, M.; Zhang, T.; Zhou, H. Proving authentication property of PUF-based mutual authentication protocol based on logic of events. *Soft Comput.* **2022**, *26*, 841–852. [CrossRef]
92. Trinh, C.; Huynh, B.; Lansky, J.; Mildeova, S.; Safkhani, M.; Bagheri, N.; Kumari, S.; Hosseinzadeh, M. A novel lightweight block cipher-based mutual authentication protocol for constrained environments. *IEEE Access* **2020**, *8*, 165536–165550. [CrossRef]
93. Wu, T.-Y.; Kong, F.; Wang, L.; Chen, Y.-C.; Kumari, S.; Pan, J.-S. Toward smart home authentication using PUF and edge-computing paradigm. *Sensors* **2022**, *22*, 9174. [CrossRef] [PubMed]
94. Chen, Z.; Li, B.; Zhang, Y.; Gu, M.; Yuan, P.; Cheng, X. Lightweight and modeling attack resistant PUFs authentication based on portion mapping. In Proceedings of the 2020 IEEE 5th International Conference on Signal and Image Processing (ICSIP), Nanjing, China, 23–25 October 2020; pp. 975–979. [CrossRef]
95. Zerrouki, F.; Ouchani, S.; Bouarfa, H. Towards a foundation of a mutual authentication protocol for a robust and resilient PUF-based communication network. *Procedia Comput. Sci.* **2021**, *191*, 215–222. [CrossRef]
96. Gaba, G.S.; Hedabou, M.; Kumar, P.; Braeken, A.; Liyanage, M.; Alazab, M. Zero knowledge proofs based authenticated key agreement protocol for sustainable healthcare. *Sustain. Cities Soc.* **2022**, *80*, 103766. [CrossRef]
97. Chaudhary, A.; Peddoju, S.K.; Kadarla, K. Study of Internet-of-Things messaging protocols used for exchanging data with external sources. In Proceedings of the 2017 IEEE 14th International Conference on Mobile Ad Hoc and Sensor Systems (MASS), Orlando, FL, USA, 22–25 October 2017; pp. 666–671. [CrossRef]
98. Anusha, M.; Babu, E.S.; Reddy, L.S.M.; Krishna, A.V.; Bhagyasree, B. Performance analysis of data protocols of Internet of Things: A qualitative review. *Int. J. Pure Appl. Math.* **2017**, *115*, 37–47.
99. Chen, Y.; Kunz, T. Performance evaluation of IoT protocols under a constrained wireless access network. In Proceedings of the 2016 International Conference on Selected Topics in Mobile & Wireless Networking (MoWNeT), Cairo, Egypt, 11–13 April 2016; pp. 1–7. [CrossRef]
100. Uy, N.Q.; Nam, V.H. A comparison of AMQP and MQTT protocols for Internet of Things. In Proceedings of the 2019 6th NAFOSTED Conference on Information and Computer Science (NICS), Hanoi, Vietnam, 12–13 December 2019; pp. 292–297. [CrossRef]
101. Al-Masri, E.; Kalyanam, K.; Batts, J.; Kim, J.; Singh, S.; Vo, T.; Yan, C. Investigating messaging protocols for the Internet of Things (IoT). *IEEE Access* **2020**, *8*, 94880–94911. [CrossRef]
102. Dizdarevic, J.; Carpio, F.; Jukan, A.; Masip-Bruin, X. A survey of communication protocols for Internet of Things and related challenges of Fog and cloud computing integration. *ACM Comput. Surv.* **2018**, *51*, 116. [CrossRef]

103. Sarafov, V. Comparison of IoT data protocol overhead. In Proceedings of the Seminars of Future Internet (FI) and Innovative Internet Technologies and Mobile Communication (IITM), Winter Semester 2017/2018, Munich, Germany, 1 August 2017–26 February 2018; pp. 7–14.
104. Yang, S.-J.; Wei, T.-C. Design issues for communication protocols conversion scheme of IoT devices. *J. Internet Technol.* **2021**, *22*, 657–667.
105. Kondoro, A.; Ben Dhaou, I.; Tenhunen, H.; Mvungi, N. Real time performance analysis of secure IoT protocols for microgrid communication. *Future Gen. Comput. Syst.* **2021**, *116*, 1–12. [CrossRef]
106. Hassan, R.; Qamar, F.; Hasan, M.K.; Aman, A.H.M.; Ahmed, A.S. Internet of Things and its applications: A comprehensive survey. *Symmetry* **2020**, *12*, 1674. [CrossRef]
107. Tabassum, K.A.; Hossain, A.; Rahman, M.H. Trident: A M2M Communication Solution for IoT Devices Using Blockchain Fused MQTT and PUF Based Authentication Scheme. Bachelor's Thesis, Islamic University of Technology, Gazipur, Bangladesh, 2021.
108. Pahlevi, R.R.; Sukarno, P.; Erfianto, B. Secure MQTT PUF-based key exchange protocol for smart healthcare. *Jurnal Rekayasa Elektrika* **2021**, *17*, 107–114. [CrossRef]
109. Díaz, J.P.; Almenares, F. A PUF-based authentication mechanism for OSCORE. In Proceedings of the 18th ACM Symposium on Performance Evaluation of Wireless Ad Hoc, Sensor, & Ubiquitous Networks, Association for Computing Machinery, Alicante, Spain, 22–26 November 2021; pp. 65–72.
110. Yamamoto, D.; Sakiyama, K.; Iwamoto, M.; Ohta, K.; Takenaka, M.; Itoh, K. Variety enhancement of PUF responses using the locations of random outputting RS latches. *J. Cryptogr. Eng.* **2013**, *3*, 197–211. [CrossRef]
111. Ning, H.; Farha, F.; Ullah, A.; Mao, L. Physical unclonable function: Architectures, applications and challenges for dependable security. *IET Circuits Devices Syst.* **2020**, *14*, 407–424. [CrossRef]
112. Jooq, M.K.Q.; Moaiyeri, M.H.; Tamersit, K. Ultra-compact ternary logic gates based on negative capacitance carbon nanotube FETs. *IEEE Trans. Circuits Syst. II Express Briefs* **2021**, *68*, 2162–2166. [CrossRef]
113. Vijay, V.; Pittala, S.C.; Koteshwaramma, K.C.; Shaik, A.S.; Chaitanya, K.; Birru, S.G.; Medapalli, S.R.; Thoranala, V.R. Design of unbalanced ternary logic gates and arithmetic circuits. *J. VLSI Circuits Syst.* **2022**, *4*, 20–26. [CrossRef]
114. Gao, Y.; Ma, H.; Abbott, D.; Al-Sarawi, S.F. PUF sensor: Exploiting PUF unreliability for secure wireless sensing. *IEEE Trans. Circuits Syst. I Regul. Papers* **2017**, *64*, 2532–2543. [CrossRef]
115. Halak, B. *Physically Unclonable Functions*, 1st ed.; Springer: Cham, Switzerland, 2018. [CrossRef]
116. Sanmorino, A.; Gustriansyah, R. An alternative solution to handle ddos attacks. *J. Theor. Appl. Inf. Technol.* **2018**, *96*, 657–667.
117. Hertz, J. An Introduction to Physically Unclonable Functions. 2021. Available online: https://www.allaboutcircuits.com/technical-articles/an-introduction-to-physically-unclonable-functions/ (accessed on 1 March 2022).

Disclaimer/Publisher's Note: The statements, opinions and data contained in all publications are solely those of the individual author(s) and contributor(s) and not of MDPI and/or the editor(s). MDPI and/or the editor(s) disclaim responsibility for any injury to people or property resulting from any ideas, methods, instructions or products referred to in the content.

Article

Binary-Tree-Fed Mixnet: An Efficient Symmetric Encryption Solution

Diego Antonio López-García [1,*,†], Juan Pérez Torreglosa [2,†], David Vera [3,†] and Manuel Sánchez-Raya [1,†]

1. Department of Electrical Engineering, Computing and Automatics, Escuela Técnica Superior de Ingeniería, Universidad de Huelva, Campus El Carmen, Avda. de las Fuerzas Armadas, s/n, 21007 Huelva, Spain; msraya@uhu.es
2. Department of Electrical Engineering, Escuela Técnica Superior de Ingeniería, Universidad de Huelva, Campus El Carmen, Avda. de las Fuerzas Armadas, s/n, 21007 Huelva, Spain; juan.perez@die.uhu.es
3. Department of Electrical Engineering, Escuela Politécnica Superior de Linares, Universidad de Jaén, Avda. de la Universidad s/n, 23700 Linares, Spain; dvera@ujaen.es
* Correspondence: diego.lopez@diesia.uhu.es
† These authors contributed equally to this work.

Abstract: Mixnets are an instrument to achieve anonymity. They are generally a sequence of servers that apply a cryptographic process and a permutation to a batch of user messages. Most use asymmetric cryptography, with the high computational cost that this entails. The main objective of this study is to reduce delay in mixnet nodes. In this sense, this paper presents a new scheme that is based only on symmetric cryptography. The novelty of this scheme is the use of binary graphs built by mixnet nodes. The root node collects user keys and labels without knowing their owners. After feeding each node by its graph, they can establish a random permutation and relate their keys to the incoming batch positions through labels. The differences with previous symmetric schemes are that users do not need long headers and nodes avoid the searching process. The outcomes are security and efficiency improvements. As far as we know, it is the fastest mixnet system. Therefore, it is appropriate for high-throughput applications like national polls (many users) or debates (many messages).

Keywords: mixnets; symmetric encryption; anonymous channel; e-voting

1. Introduction

Anonymity is a service required in several applications like e-voting, journalism, surveys, etc. Additionally, it is a desirable feature in order to mitigate the threats of communications surveillance. For these reasons, many anonymous communication systems have been proposed [1,2]. These can be classified by their strategies [3].

One of them is to build a broadcast channel where all users participate. These schemes are known as DC-nets (Dinning Cryptographers Network) [4] and have some variants, such as Dissent (Dining Cryptographers Shuffled Send Network) [5] or BAR (Broadcast Anonymous Routing) [6]. These protocols offer a high level of privacy, but they lack flexibility, require all participants' cooperation, and allow only one user to communicate in one protocol round, which implies low throughput.

Another technique is hiding the transmission path by multiple hops. For example, Tor (The Onion Router) [7], Herd [8], Hornet [9], TresMep (Tracking-resistant Communication Mechanism with Dynamic Paths) [10], Misty Clouds [11], dPHI (dependable Path-HIdden lightweight anonymity protocol) [12], and Nym [13] belong to this category. These onion routing systems are suitable for low-latency communications in environments where messages arrive at different times in an almost constant flow. Nevertheless, they are vulnerable to traffic analysis [14,15] and attacks from adversary nodes [16,17].

The third approach is the use of mixnets. They are sequences of nodes that work with batches of messages. Each node makes a cryptographic operation and shuffles the batch,

thus breaking the relationship between incoming and outgoing messages [18]. Mixnets have evolved and diversified widely in recent years. They started with [19], where users have to encrypt their messages with the public keys of the nodes. Then, each one decrypts the batch with its private key. These were followed by the so-called "encryption mixnets" [20]. Taking advantage of the properties of the ElGamal cryptosystem, this new category provides greater privacy and less delay for users and nodes.

An effort to improve efficiency is the combination of asymmetric and symmetric encryption. This gave rise to hybrid mixnets [21–23]. Instead of encrypting the entire message with public keys, what is encrypted with these is a symmetric one. Then, the message encrypted with the latter is appended. This solution reduces the high computational effort of asymmetric encryption to the few bits of a symmetric key. However, this does not bypass exponential calculations and must add symmetric decryption to the process.

A better idea is cMIX (fixed cascade mixnet), proposed in [24], where operations in users and nodes are reduced to a set of modular multiplications. Although the latency in the production phase is small, each message must traverse the mixnet twice. Moreover, it requires a precomputation phase where a set of asymmetric cryptographic operations must be carried out. Another solution is the use of alternative encryption methods like lattice-based ones [25], which can be six times faster than traditional mixnets [26]. However, these methods are relatively new and require deeper research [27,28].

The first pure symmetric mixnet was SEBM (Symmetric-Key-Encryption-Based Mixnet) [29], improved with ESEBM (Enhanced SEBM) [30]. In these schemes, nodes generate keys and an identifier linked to it in an internal table. These values are propagated, shuffled, and blinded from the last node in a predefined sequence to the first one, which delivers them to users. Then, users send their encrypted messages to the mixnet, which is composed in another different sequence. There is no need for asymmetric operations in any step, which provides this scheme the highest speed. However, each message entails a vector of identifiers that must be found in a table at each step. Moreover, depending on the place each node occupies in the mixnet, several vulnerabilities arise. Some of them could be exploited by just one adversary.

The purpose of this work has been overcoming the drawbacks of ESEBM and improving its throughput. In this regard, the new scheme presented here, called binary-tree-fed mixnets or BTFM, does not require any identifiers and eliminates the need of searching in tables. The outcome is a faster mixnet without overloading messages with superfluous headers. Additionally, it can stand with a higher number of adversaries. The major contribution is a starting phase where keys are established by means of a binary graph. Then, the production phase is faster than in any other mixnet. This new idea of working with binary graphs solves the problem of how to share keys anonymously without using asymmetric encryption and is a new tool to apply independently in other contexts.

In summary, the main contributions of this paper are

1. A new tool for sharing keys anonymously without asymmetric encryption. Users can send keys or messages to a server while preserving their privacy. This is achieved using a binary graph where only permutations and XOR operations are required.
2. The development of a new mixnet scheme, BTFM, which is based solely on symmetric encryption. Its main attributes are improvements in performance and security.
3. The discovery of some vulnerabilities in a previous symmetric encryption mixnet scheme, ESEBM.
4. A security study of BTFM, where the minimum threshold of adversaries necessary to violate privacy is determined.
5. The comparison of BTFM with previous schemes, carried out through a series of experiments.

The paper is structured as follows. The next section is devoted to ESEBM, describes it, and shows some vulnerabilities. Then, BTFM is detailed in Section 3. The security analysis follows in Section 4. Section 5 shows and discusses the results of some experiments. The last section presents our conclusions.

2. Vulnerabilities of ESEBM

ESEBM is an evolution of SEBM [29] and is explained in detail in [30]. To date, no weaknesses in its security have been published. This is precisely the objective of this section. In this mixnet, nodes form groups to generate concealing patterns that are delivered to users. Figure 1 shows an example of an ESEBM mixnet with nine nodes. They form three groups labeled as A, B, and C. Notice that members of these groups are scattered in the mixnet. The only rule is that priority in the group must be respected on the mixnet.

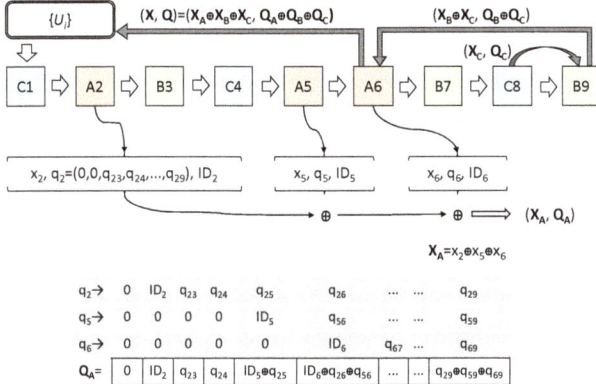

Figure 1. Example of ESEBM. Mixnet of 9 servers distributed in three groups. Each node builds its concealing patterns x_i and q_i, which are stored in a table with an identifier ID_i. Then, they are combined by groups (like (X_A, Q_A) for group A), and then by mixnet (X, Q), which are sent to users.

Concealing patterns are random numbers intended to hide user messages. These concealing patterns are built by XORing binary strings generated by each node. Users encrypt their messages by an XOR operation with the patterns and send the result to the first node of the mixnet. Then, each node of the mixnet must remove its binary string. For each node to know which string to apply to which message, it needs a separate identifier. These identifiers could be used to trace senders and therefore must be hidden too. This is the purpose of vector q in Figure 1.

In ESEBM, each node generates a binary string (x_2 in node $A2$), a vector (q_2), and an identifier (ID_2). These values are stored in a table. Then, inside each group, this tuple is passed to the next node, which performs an XOR operation and sends the result to the next one, and so on until reaching the last node of the group ($A6$). This one, the collector node, obtains two values: the aggregated keys (X_A) and the concealed identifiers (vector Q_A).

Each collector node ($A6, B9$, and $C8$) shuffles many pairs obtained this way. Then, the batch is passed from collector node to collector node, creating an XOR operation. The last node, ($A6$), the delivery node, delivers the result to users, which is

$$X = X_A \oplus X_B \oplus X_C = x_1 \oplus x_2 \oplus ... \oplus x_9 \quad (1)$$

$$Q = ID_1, ID_2 \oplus q_{12}, ID_3 \oplus q_{13} \oplus q_{23}, ..., ID_9 \oplus q_{19}...q_{89} \quad (2)$$

When a user sends a message m to the mixnet, it follows the format $m \oplus X, Q$. The first node of the mixnet, $C1$, recognizes the identifier ID_1, which is disclosed in the first position of Q. It must be in its table, in the same row as x_1 and q_1. Then, $C1$ creates an XOR operation with these values. The result is an encrypted message without the string x_1 and a vector Q without the concealing values of q_1. The next node $A2$ will find its identifier ID_2 unveiled and will create the same process. At the end, all the strings x_i will be removed and the message shown in plain text.

The only node that knows the complete key X and the user is the delivery node ($A6$). In order to prevent that, the user sends blinding factors to each member of this last group. These factors (b_i) are combined with the strings by each node (x_i for $i = 2, 5, 6$ in the example). Therefore, the user receives the pair $(X \oplus B, Q)$, where B is an XOR of blinding factors b_i to be removed by the user before sending m. The delivery node can store in its internal table the aggregated key of the remaining groups ($X_B \oplus X_C, Q_B \oplus Q_C$) and the user but cannot know its group key (X_A). Collector nodes can store its keys (pair X_B, Q_B for node $B9$; pair X_C, Q_C for node $C8$). With this scheme, there are feasible attacks such as the following:

1. *Collusion of last group with the first node of the mixnet*. If all members of the last group ($A2$ and $A5$) reveal their passwords (x_2, x_5) to the last member ($A6$), the latter will have the password of its group (X_A) and also that of the rest of the groups (X_B, X_C). That is, it has the complete key. It also knows which user it gave that key to; that is, it has the link with the user. Therefore, it is able to decrypt any message of this user delivered to the first member of the mixnet. In the example (Figure 1), it means a collusion of four nodes: $C1, A2, A5,$ and $A6$.
2. *Collusion of the delivery node with the remaining nodes in the mixnet*. The delivery node ($A6$) can associate its key and ID with the receiving user. This node, by passing the message through it, can therefore identify the user and transmit this knowledge to the following nodes. The last one reveals the message in plain text and it will know its author. This case corresponds with the collusion of four nodes in the example: $A6, B7, C8,$ and $B9$.
3. *Collusion of the delivery node, the nodes of the groups that have performed a partial decryption, and nodes in between*. The delivery node knows the full key of the remaining groups ($X_B \oplus X_C$). When the message arrives within the mixnet (to $A6$), its key (x_6) is applied and the message is clean of the keys of the last group (X_A), but it may already have the keys of some nodes of the following groups applied (x_1 from $C1$, x_3 from $B3$, and x_4 from $C4$). These nodes can collude and share these keys with the delivery node, but it also needs to know where the message is within the batch. Namely, the permutations of previous nodes are also required. (If any of the following groups have already fully operated on the mixnet, then only collusion from the collector node of that group would be required.) For this example, it means a collusion of the following six nodes: $C1, A2, B3, C4, A5,$ and $A6$.
4. *Collusion of collection nodes*. The delivery node can relate the user to the message. If all collection nodes collaborate, they can know the aggregate key of each group for that message. From the added key, they can know their particular key. The last member of the mixnet, who is necessarily a group leader, will know the author when he has to use that key. In the example, only three nodes are required: $A6, C8,$ and $B9$.

ESEBM does not establish how many groups to define and how to scatter groups in the mixnet. Therefore, each vulnerability requires more or fewer adversaries depending on this distribution. Table 1 shows the list of vulnerabilities with the adversaries required in each one. The last two columns depict the maximum and minimum number of adversaries needed in each attack considering the best and worst distribution for each case. Notice that two vulnerabilities requires only one adversary in the worst case (delivery node at the end in type 2 and last group placed at the beginning in type 3). This problem is solved in the new scheme.

Table 1. Adversaries required in ESEBM for n nodes = k groups $\times$ m members.

Vulnerability	Example	Max.	Min.
1. Last group and first node	C1, A2, A5, A6.	$m + 1$	m
2. Delivery node and following ones	A6, B7, C8, B9	$(k-1)m + 1$	1
3. Delivery node and previous ones	C1...A6	$n - m + 1$	1
4. Collector nodes	A6, C8, B9	k	k

3. Binary-Tree-Fed Mixnets

The new mixnet scheme, BTFM, is detailed below. With the intention of facilitating its understanding, first, an example is shown and then the formal description of the method is undertaken.

3.1. Overview

The presented scheme consists of three stages. The first one allows mix nodes to share secret keys with users but preserve privacy. The second stage configures a fixed permutation on each node of the mixnet. The last stage is the production mode, where users can continuously send messages.

In the first stage, each node is placed at the root of a binary node tree. For each root, the remaining nodes form the branches of the tree. Each user links with each node of the last level (nodes without children), called leaf nodes. Through those links, users send fragments of a key and a label they want to share with the root node. Therefore, each leaf node has a key fragment but needs all the other nodes to unveil the key. All the leaf nodes agree on a permutation and shuffle their fragments with it. Each pair of leaf nodes delivers the batch to its parent node in the next level. Each parent node creates an XOR operation with the key fragments at the same position of the batch. In this level, all the nodes agree on a permutation, which is applied to the result. The process is repeated in each level. When it reaches the root node, all the fragments will build the complete key.

Figure 2 shows a case of a mixnet of seven nodes in which a generic user U_i is feeding with a key K_{iG} and a label L_{iG} node G. This couple is divided into four parts: $K_{iG} = a_i \oplus b_i \oplus c_i \oplus d_i$ and $L_{iG} = a'_i \oplus b'_i \oplus c'_i \oplus d'_i$. User U_i sends to node A the couple (a_i, a'_i), to node B the couple (b_i, b'_i), and similarly to nodes C and D. Notice that, at this moment, only a collusion of A, B, C and D is able to unveil the key K_{iG}. These four nodes agree on the permutation π_1. The four nodes create this permutation for the batch of all users including U_i and deliver the result to the parent node. In the case of nodes A and B, the parent node is E, which receives the two batches and creates an XOR operation. As the permutation is the same, the first two fragments of the user key will be at the same position in its batch and E will compute $(a_i \oplus b_i, a'_i \oplus b'_i)$. Nodes E and F agree on a permutation: π_2. Both of them shuffle their results following it. Then, the result reaches node G, which will be able to build the complete couple $(a_i \oplus b_i \oplus c_i \oplus d_i, a'_i \oplus b'_i \oplus c'_i \oplus d'_i)$, that is, (K_{iG}, L_{iG}).

In the second stage, each user sends a vector with the encrypted labels. In the example of Figure 2, it is $(L_{iA}, L_{iB} \oplus K_{iA}, L_{iC} \oplus K_{iA} \oplus K_{iB}, ..., L_{iG} \oplus K_{iA}...K_{iF})$, assuming that the mixnet sequence is $A, B, C, ..., G$. Each node chooses a permutation and sets it. Each node receives a batch of vectors whose first element is a label stored in the previous stage. This process can be observed in Figure 3. Then, each node finds the label in its table and links the corresponding key to the input position of the batch. Next, it removes its label from the vector and applies this key to the remaining values, which is sent to the next node. In the example, B receives $(L_{iB}, L_{iC} \oplus K_{iB}, L_{iD} \oplus K_{iB} \oplus K_{iC}, ..., L_{iG} \oplus K_{iB}...K_{iF})$. Then, at each position i of the batch, it looks for L_{iB} in its table and finds K_{iB} in the same row. Now, B knows which key K_{iB} to apply to which incoming batch position in the next stage. This node then removes key K_{iB} from each element of the label vector, performs its permutation, and sends $(L_{iC}, L_{iD} \oplus K_{iC}, ..., L_{iG} \oplus K_{iC}...K_{iF})$ to the following node (C). When this stage ends, nodes have set an unknown permutation and associated keys that are shared only with users. Then, in the third stage, users only perform an XOR operation of any message with the key $K_i = K_{iA} \oplus K_{iB} \oplus ... \oplus K_{iG}$ and send it to the mixnet.

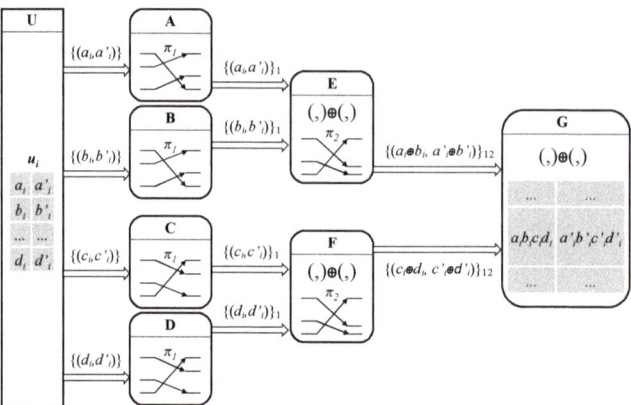

Figure 2. Each user u_i shares a pair label–key with a node G by means of binary trees. Key is composed of XORing a_i, b_i, c_i, and d_i; label a'_i, b'_i, c'_i, and d'_i.

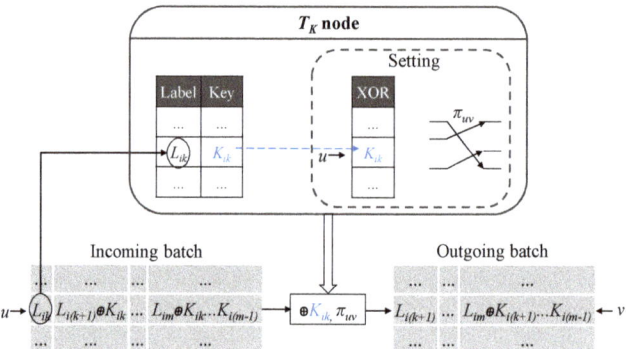

Figure 3. Setting stage: user keys (K_{ik}) are linked to the incoming batch positions (u) and a random permutation (π_{uv} is established).

3.2. Formal Description

Let $U = \{U_i | i = 1, 2...n\}$ be a set of n users. Let $T = \{T_j | j = 1, 2...m\}$ be a set of nodes. The elements of these sets can establish communication links among them. The scheme follows three stages:

1. STAGE 1: FEEDING. The value k is computed from $k = \lfloor log_2(m+1) \rfloor$. That is, k is the highest number that accomplishes $2^k - 1 \leq m$. Then, each user U_i generates 2^k random numbers per node. A half builds the keys with each node: $K_{ij} = K_{ij1} \oplus K_{ij2}...K_{ij\alpha}$, where $j = 1, 2...m$ corresponds to different nodes and $\alpha = 2^{k-1}$. The other half are fragments of the labels: $L_{ij} = L_{ij1} \oplus L_{ij2}...L_{ij\alpha}$. Next, for each node T_j, a perfect binary tree of k levels is established by selecting other nodes randomly until the tree is completed. Nodes collaborate to ensure this randomness against adversaries [31]. The tree is a subset of T with $2^k - 1$ elements, where T_j is the root at the first level. Each node of the tree has two children nodes, occupying the next level. The exception is at the last level, which has $\alpha = 2^{k-1}$ nodes that have no children. To these leaf nodes, each user U_i sends the pair (K_{ijl}, L_{ijl}), where $l = 1, 2, ...\alpha$ corresponds to each leaf node. All the nodes in the same level agree on a random permutation π_h, $h = 1, 2...k$. Nodes at the last level receive the pairs from users in a batch. Next, they create the same permutation π_k and send the result to their parent node. From the level $k - 1$ to the root, each node creates an XOR operation between the pairs received in the same position of the batches. Then, they create the permutation of their level and send the

result to their parent node. The root node creates the XOR operation to obtain the pair (K_{ij}, L_{ij}), which is stored in a table.

2. STAGE 2: SETTING. A random sequence of $T_1, T_2, ..., T_m$ defines the mixnet. Users send to the first node the vector $(L_{i1}, L_{i2} \oplus K_{i1}, L_{i3} \oplus K_{i1} \oplus K_{i2}, ..., L_{im} \oplus K_{i1}...K_{i(m-1)})$. Each node T_j of the mixnet looks for the first element L_{ij} of the vector in its table, where it must be next to the key K_{ij}. Then, it removes the first element of the vector and applies XOR to the remaining elements with K_{ij}. Next, the node establishes a permutation on the input batch and sends the result. From now on, the key K_{ij} will be applied with any value that comes in the same batch position.

3. STAGE 3: MIXING. Users compute $K_i = K_{i1} \oplus K_{i2} \oplus ... \oplus K_{im}$. Then, they can anonymously publish any message m_i by sending $K_i \oplus m_i$ to the first node of the mixnet. The first node processes the batch of encrypted messages, which will remove its partial key K_{i1}. The next nodes do the same until the last one, which shows a batch of decrypted messages.

4. Security Analysis

The nodes of any mixnet can collude among themselves and/or with some users to break the anonymity of others. This section studies this problem. Firstly, some hypotheses are established regarding the limits of these adversaries. Based on these, the strength of the system is determined, indicating the minimum number of conspirators to violate it. Finally, the properties of this scheme are reviewed.

4.1. Security Model

In order to obtain a security measure of the scheme, some starting assumptions must be established:

1. The bit length of keys (k_{ij}) and labels (L_{ij}) is large enough to reduce the probability of guessing them from their XOR encryption forms to a negligible value.
2. Peer-to-peer communications are safe; in other words, adversaries cannot prevent (DoS), decrypt (confidentiality), impersonate (authentication), or tamper with (integrity) these communications.
3. Adversaries can only gather information from their role in the process or from other adversaries.

4.2. Analysis

The objective of adversaries is to link the decrypted message with its author. If the first node is an adversary, it will only need the key because it knows the sender. If the last node is an adversary, it will only need the authorship because the message is decrypted. Intermediate nodes will need the two kinds of information.

Definition 1. *"Binary-tree cut" is defined as a set of nodes of which at least one participates in any connected path between root and leaves.*

Proposition 1. *The nodes capable of learning user keys must necessarily constitute a cut.*

Proof. The information needed to deduce the key is initially the set of fragments. All the leaf nodes could reconstruct the key, and it is also true that the set defined by them is a cut. If instead of the initial fragments any aggregation of them is available, it can also be reconstructed as long as all the fragments have participated. For a fragment not to have participated, it must happen that, on the path that joins it to the root, there is no node of the cut, which is precisely the definition of cut. □

Figure 4 shows two examples of binary-tree cuts. Although being a cut is a necessary condition, it is not sufficient. Notice that the cut in Figure 4a has no node of the third level (i, j, k, l); therefore, the elements of the cut are unaware of the permutation carried out at said level and cannot associate the keys to the users. However, the cut in Figure 4b is capable.

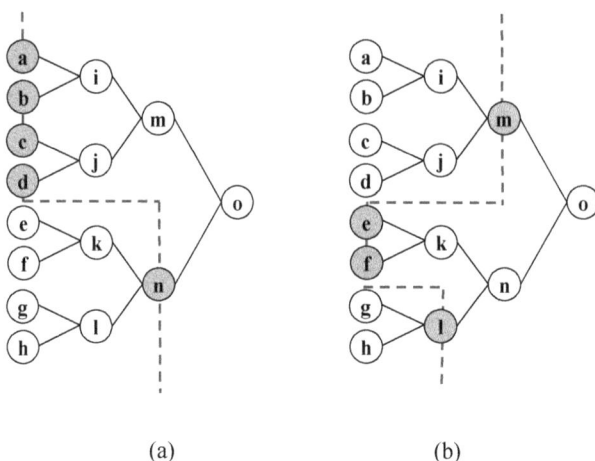

Figure 4. Binary-tree cuts: (**a**) permutation of third level (node *i*) is not known for the cut, so they cannot build the key; (**b**) cut able to break privacy.

Proposition 2. *For a cut to reveal the keys and associate them with their users, it must have at least one node at each level between the level of the leaves and the lowest level (closest to the root) of the cut.*

Proof. To construct the keys, in addition to the fragments or aggregations of these, the permutations carried out on them must be known. Only the nodes at each level know their permutation. That is, the collaboration of at least one of the nodes at each level is needed between the extreme nodes of the cut. If the top of the cut is a level that does not correspond to the leaf nodes, then a batch of keys can be obtained, but they cannot be associated with users. The first permutation is only known to the leaf nodes. Therefore, it is necessary to incorporate the information of all the permutations from these to the cut. □

Theorem 1. *The minimum number of adversaries to learn keys in a binary tree of k levels is k.*

Proof. Given Proposition 1, the minimum number of levels of a cut capable of revealing the keys would be the one constituted by the leaf nodes, whose number is 2^{k-1}. Furthermore, it is the only cut possible with this single level given Proposition 2. The fragment information that exists in two leaf nodes is obtained aggregated in their parent nodes. Therefore, if we now consider a cut that includes the next level, each pair of leaf nodes can be replaced by its parent node by reducing the cut by one. It is not possible to conduct it with all of them because at least one leaf node must remain to report the permutation of its level. In this way, different cuts of size $2^{k-2} + 1$ can be established, that is, the nodes of the next level plus a leaf node. This number would be the minimum because with one less node there would always be a lack of information.

Now consider a cut A that reaches level r formed by a sequence of nodes from a leaf node to r (minimum number of nodes to know all the permutations) and the rest of the nodes of level r (those that make up the minimum number to build the keys). That is, $|A| = 2^{r-1} + k - r$ (for example, nodes a, i, m, and n in Figure 4 for the case $k = 2$ and $r = 2$). Suppose there is a cut B with a smaller number of nodes ($|B| < |A|$). This cut B must necessarily exclude nodes from cut A as it is smaller in number. If the excluded node is one of level r, then it must be replaced with any combination of its descendants, a number never less than two. Therefore, for this change to allow the size of B to be reduced, the level would have to be decreased, thus reducing the number of nodes necessary to know the permutations. However, reducing a level implies multiplying by two the minimum number of nodes necessary to know the key (those of the level) while only reducing those necessary to know the permutation by one unit. Therefore, B can never be less than A. Its size, $|A| = 2^{r-1} + k - r$, reaches the minimum value for $r = 1$; that is, the root node is enough to know the key to which any sequence up to a leaf node must be added. Therefore, there is one node per level. □

This result can be applied to labels as they follow the same process as keys. At the second stage, the mixnet is constituted with a random sequence of all the nodes. Then, each node chooses a random permutation to apply to the batches. Users then send their encrypted labels to the mixnet. Nodes learn the position to apply each key through the labels. If a node knows the owner of a key (for example, when this node is the root node in a successful attack of k adversaries on stage 1), it can identify the owner of any message when it reaches that node and share that information with the following node. However, this node cannot disclose the message without the remaining keys. Therefore, any successful collusion in stage 2 will need the collaboration of all the existing nodes between this attacking node and the end of the mixnet. The easiest case is when the attacking node is precisely the last in the mixnet. In this case, no additional node is required for the attacker and therefore no more adversaries than k are needed. In stage 3, the same reasoning can be applied as in stage 2 since it is very similar (messages are encrypted instead of labels). Thus, the minimum number of adversaries to break privacy is, again, k.

4.3. Properties

Mixnets are usually compared based on a number of commonly known features [2]. The main one is anonymity, and both schemes (ESEBM and BTFM) provide it. However, ESEBM shows cases (2 and 3 in Table 1) where only one adversary can break privacy. In comparison, BTFM offers a higher minimum adversary threshold ($\lfloor log_2(m+1) \rfloor$). On the other hand, it is enough to have a single honest node in asymmetric mixnets to ensure privacy.

When considering the other characteristics, there are some that no symmetric mixnet can meet. As far as we know, verifiability, robustness, and fault tolerance can only be accomplished by asymmetric encryption techniques. Nevertheless, scalability, throughput, and latency are vastly surpassed by symmetric mixnets, as indicated in experiments. In this area, BTFM shows better results than ESEBM, especially when processing huge amounts of messages, as described in the next section.

5. Results and Discussion

This section describes a series of experiments aimed at assessing the differences regarding BTFM with other schemes. Firstly, it is compared with asymmetric systems (RSA and cMIX) and then with ESEBM. The first graph meets the objective of contextualizing purely symmetric systems with respect to traditional schemes (RSA), including one of the most advanced in terms of speed, such as cMIX. The following charts show cases in which BTFM and ESEBM clearly differ in delay and header size.

The following results have been obtained using a CPU i5-3230M, at 2.6 GHz and 16 GB of RAM. The software has been developed on Java 1.8.0_121 in a Windows 10 OS. The message length has been chosen to be 1024 bits. It must be the same for any key. However, for labels (q_{ij} in ESEBM and L_{ij} in BFTM), an integer (32 bits) has been selected. Network delays are not considered. With this scenario, a mixnet of ten nodes throws an average node delay shown in Figure 5. The batch size varies from 1000 to 10,000 users. Each line corresponds to one of the four schemes: a decryption mixnet based on RSA, cMIX (modular products), ESEBM, and BTFM. As can be seen, symmetric mixnets are very similar with the lowest latency. However, RSA and cMIX present a significantly higher delay. In fact, for 10,000 users, RSA is 91 times slower than BTFM, cMIX 30 times, and ESEBM 1.6 times.

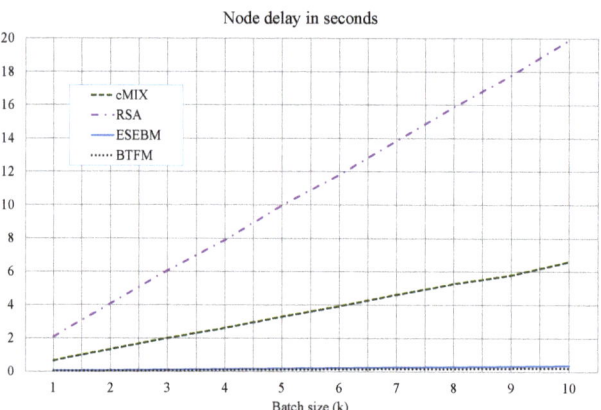

Figure 5. Node delay comparison among RSA, cMIX, ESEBM, and BTFM mixnets.

In order to appreciate the differences between BTFM and ESEBM, the batch size must be increased. The considerable reduction offered by BTFM can be seen in Figure 6. In the first case (100 K users), BTFM takes almost half (50.8%) the time of ESBM. This difference increases as the number of users grows, to the point that with 550 K users it reaches 23.6%. That is, BTFM is 4.2 times faster than ESEBM in this case. A deeper look reveals that the XORing time is very reduced in both schemes (4.2% of total time in BTFM and 1.6% in ESEBM). Permutation and serialization operations are the most time-consuming.

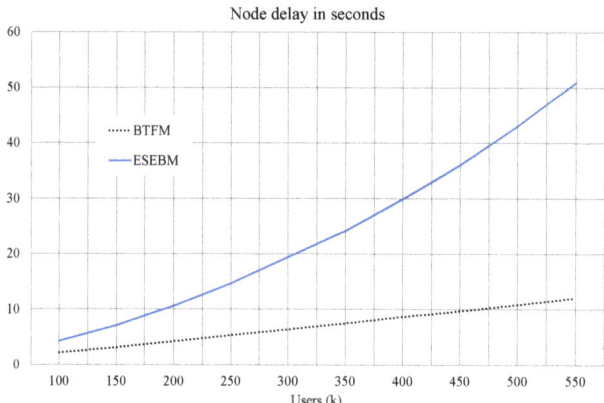

Figure 6. Delay in an ESEBM node (continuous line) and in a BTFM node (dots).

In ESEBM, the batch size is significantly larger than in BTFM because a label vector proportional to the size of the mixnet must be added. Figure 7 shows this exceedance of the BTFM batch in two ways: megabytes in columns and percentages in a line. The mixnet size, from 10 nodes to 100, is represented on the abscissa. In ordinates, the same number represents the percentage and the overload megabytes. This chart corresponds to 250 K users. However, if the number of users with the same mixnet size is varied, horizontal lines are observed. That is, the percentage that represents the excess of the batch size remains constant with respect to users. Regarding the nodes, the worst case (100 nodes) presents an overload of 100.1 MB (39.6%).

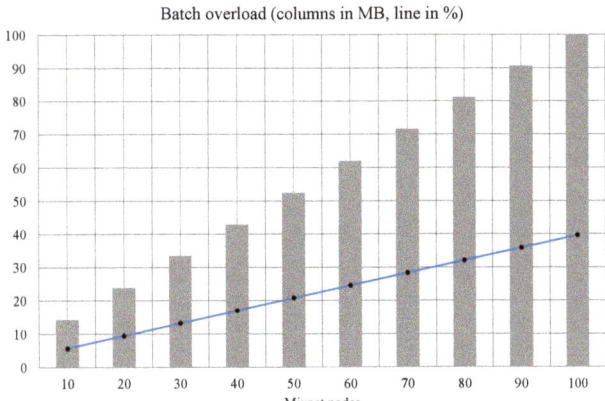

Figure 7. Excedance of an ESEBM batch over BTFM.

Overall, in light of these experiments, the performance of BTFM stands out from other systems. It is overwhelmingly superior to asymmetric encryption systems (up to 30 times faster), it slightly improves ESEBM in low-demand environments (batches of 10.000 users), and clearly surpasses it when demand increases (doubles it from 100,000 users). Furthermore, messages do not increase in size by aggregating headers as in ESEBM, which implies a reduction in the time to send batches between nodes.

6. Conclusions

This section offers an overview of this work. The main contributions are reviewed, the advantages and limitations of this new scheme are highlighted, and future lines of research are discussed.

In the context prior to this article, ESEBM was the fastest mixnet to date. It represented a qualitative leap over previous schemes by reducing the computing time in the nodes by two orders of magnitude. Its greatest merit is perhaps to have demonstrated that it is possible to do without asymmetric encryption. However, ESEBM has certain weaknesses and needs to use long message headers. The challenge driving this work was to further improve performance by leveraging the pure symmetric encryption approach. The solution comes from two simple ideas: fragmenting the keys to hide them from the nodes (stage 1) and using labels to enable free permutation in stage 2. The former originated the key sending method of the binary graph, and the latter enables the nodes to reduce the operations to be performed to a minimum (stage 3), thus maximizing their performance.

Among the contributions, the new technique of sending keys through a binary graph from stage 1 stands out. Through this, a set of entities can establish a symmetric key with another anonymously, all this using only XOR operations and permutations. Although it has been applied to mixnets, it could be used in other environments. For example, a group of authorized users could establish label–key pairs in this way with a server. They could then contact it using any anonymous channel [1]. By identifying themselves only with the tag and demonstrating knowledge of the key, the server would know that they belong to the authorized group but would not be able to identify any user in particular. From here, users could interact anonymously and securely with the server. This technique would be similar to blind signature but with the advantage of requiring less computational cost and without the weakness inherent to any asymmetric key cryptosystem.

The main contribution is BTFM. It is a new mixnet scheme inside a very rare category, symmetric encryption mixnets, which includes only two more: SEBM and ESEBM. While these types of mixnets lack robustness, fault tolerance, and verifiability, they instead offer a qualitative leap in performance, reducing delay. In this respect, BTFM shows better rates than ESEBM (4 times faster). The reason is that BTFM minimizes the processing of each node. As far as we know, there is no mixnet faster than BTFM.

This new scheme can be used in any scenario where a mixnet is the solution. Nevertheless, the requisite of a complex starting phase leads to environments where the same users send messages continuously, like in forums or meetings. In this context, using the same key multiple times could be a weakness when just an XOR operation is performed. However, the same scheme is valid with other symmetric encryption algorithms like AES (Advanced Encryption Standard) in the production phase. Other applications appropriate for BTFM are those requiring high throughput, such as elections or nationwide surveys.

Another contribution of this article has been the revelation of ESEBM vulnerabilities. A comparison with BTFM yields a tougher constraint on adversaries being successful. Therefore, BTFM improves ESEBM in speed and security. The drawback is that BTFM must be applied to batches of users acting at the same time. ESEBM can better deal with an asynchronous demand. For both, it remains an open question to provide verifiability and robustness to overcome traditional schemes. In this sense, it would be interesting as a line of research to study the combination with asymmetric encryption techniques only for verifiability, trying to maintain the same performance when all nodes are honest. Another challenge for future work is to increase the minimum threshold of adversaries to break anonymity.

Author Contributions: Conceptualization, D.A.L.-G.; Methodology, D.A.L.-G.; Literature review, D.A.L.-G., J.P.T., D.V. and M.S.-R.; Software, D.A.L.-G., J.P.T., D.V. and M.S.-R.; Validation, J.P.T., D.V. and M.S.-R.; Writing—original draft preparation, D.A.L.-G.; writing—review and editing, D.A.L.-G., J.P.T., D.V. and M.S.-R. All authors have read and agreed to the published version of the manuscript.

Funding: This research received no external funding.

Institutional Review Board Statement: Not applicable.

Informed Consent Statement: Not applicable.

Data Availability Statement: Datasets at https://www.uhu.es/diego.lopez/research/dataBTFM.xls (accessed on 21 December 2023).

Conflicts of Interest: The authors declare no conflicts of interest.

References

1. Shirazi, F.; Simeonovski, M.; Asghar, M.R.; Backes, M.; Diaz, C. A survey on routing in anonymous communication protocols. *ACM Comput. Surv. (CSUR)* **2018**, *51*, 1–39. [CrossRef]
2. He, Y.; Zhang, M.; Yang, X.; Luo, J.; Chen, Y. A Survey of Privacy Protection and Network Security in User On-Demand Anonymous Communication. *IEEE Access* **2020**, *8*, 54856–54871. [CrossRef]
3. Ren, J.; Wu, J. Survey on anonymous communications in computer networks. *Comput. Commun.* **2010**, *33*, 420–431. [CrossRef]
4. Chaum, D. The dining cryptographers problem: Unconditional sender and recipient untraceability. *J. Cryptol.* **1988**, *1*, 65–75. [CrossRef]
5. Corrigan-Gibbs, H.; Ford, B. Dissent: Accountable anonymous group messaging. In Proceedings of the 17th ACM Conference on Computer and Communications Security, Chicago, IL, USA, 4–8 October 2010; pp. 340–350.
6. Kotzanikolaou, P.; Chatzisofroniou, G.; Burmester, M. Broadcast anonymous routing (bar): Scalable real-time anonymous communication. *Int. J. Inf. Secur.* **2017**, *16*, 313–326. [CrossRef]
7. Dingledine, R.; Mathewson, N.; Syverson, P. F. Tor: The second-generation onion router. *USENIX Secur. Symp.* **2004**, *4*, 303–320.
8. Blond, S.L.; Choffnes, D.; Caldwell, W.; Druschel, P.; Merritt, N. Herd: A scalable, traffic analysis resistant anonymity network for voip systems. In Proceedings of the 2015 ACM Conference on Special Interest Group on Data Communication, London, UK, 17–21 August 2015; pp. 639–652.
9. Chen, C.; Asoni, D.E.; Barrera, D.; Danezis, G.; Perrig, A. Hornet: High-speed onion routing at the network layer. In Proceedings of the 22nd ACM SIGSAC Conference on Computer and Communications Security, Denver, CO, USA, 12–16 October 2015; pp. 1441–1454.
10. Tian, C.; Zhang, Y.; Yin, T.; Tuo, Y.; Ge, R. Achieving dynamic communication path for anti-tracking network. In Proceedings of the 2019 IEEE Global Communications Conference (GLOBECOM), Big Island, HI, USA, 9–13 December 2019; pp. 1–6.
11. Al-Muhtadi, J.; Qiang, M.; Saleem, K.; AlMusallam, M.; Rodrigues, J.J. Misty clouds—A layered cloud platform for online user anonymity in Social Internet of Things. *Future Gener. Comput. Syst.* **2019**, *92*, 812–820. [CrossRef]

12. Alexander, B.; Becker, G.T. dPHI: An improved high-speed network-layer anonymity protocol. *Proc. Priv. Enhancing Technol.* **2020**, *3*, 304–326.
13. Kramer, A.; Rezabek, F.; von Seck, R. Recent Advancements in Privacy Preserving Network Layer Approaches. In *Proceedings of the Seminar Innovative Internet Technologies and Mobile Communications (IITM)*; Winter Semester 2022/2023. Chair of Network Architectures and Services (NET 2023-06-1); Technical University of Munich: Munich, Germany, 2023; pp. 19–24.
14. Montieri, A.; Ciuonzo, D.; Aceto, G.; Pescapé, A. Anonymity services tor, i2p, jondonym: Classifying in the dark (web). *IEEE Trans. Dependable Secure Comput.* **2018**, *17*, 662–675. [CrossRef]
15. Kwon, A.; AlSabah, M.; Lazar, D.; Dacier, M.; Devadas, S. Circuit fingerprinting attacks: Passive deanonymization of tor hidden services. In Proceedings of the 24th USENIX Security Symposium (USENIX Security 15), Washington, DC, USA, 12–14 August 2015; pp. 287–302.
16. Evans, N.S.; Dingledine, R.; Grothoff, C. A practical congestion attack on tor using long paths. In Proceedings of the 18th USENIX Security Symposium (USENIX Security 09), Montreal, QC, Canada, 10–12 August 2009; pp. 33–50.
17. Winter, P.; Ensafi, R.; Loesing, K.; Feamster, N. Identifying and characterizing sybils in the tor network. In Proceedings of the 25th USENIX Security Symposium (USENIX Security 16), Austin, TX, USA, 10–12 August 2016 ; pp. 1169–1185.
18. Sampigethaya, K.; Poovendran, R. A survey on mix networks and their secure applications. *Proc. IEEE* **2006**, *94*, 2142–2181. [CrossRef]
19. Chaum, D. Untraceable electronic mail, return addresses, and digital pseudonyms. *Commun. ACM* **1981**, *24*, 84–88. [CrossRef]
20. Park, C.; Itoh, K.; Kurosawa, K. Efficient anonymous channel and all/nothing election scheme. In *Advances in Cryptology—EUROCRYPT'93: Workshop on the Theory and Application of Cryptographic Techniques Lofthus, Norway, 23–27 May 1993 Proceedings 12*; Springer: Berlin/Heidelberg, Germany, 1994; pp. 248–259.
21. Goldschlag, D.;Reed, M.; Syverson, P. Hiding routing information. In *International Workshop on Information Hiding*; Springer: Berlin/Heidelberg, Germany, 1996; pp. 137–150.
22. Jakobsson, M.; Juels, A. An optimally robust hybrid mix network. In Proceedings of the Twentieth Annual ACM Symposium on Principles of Distributed Computing, Newport, RI, USA, 26–29 August 2001 ; pp. 284–292.
23. Huszti, A.; Kovács, Z. Bilinear pairing-based hybrid mixnet with anonymity revocation. In Proceedings of the 2015 International Conference on Information Systems Security and Privacy (ICISSP), Angers, France, 9–11 February 2015 ; pp. 238–245.
24. Chaum, D.; Das, D.; Javani, F.; Kate, A.; Krasnova, A.; De Ruiter, J.; Sherman, A.T. cMix: Mixing with minimal real-time asymmetric cryptographic operations. In *Applied Cryptography and Network Security: 15th International Conference, ACNS 2017, Kanazawa, Japan, 10–12 July 2017, Proceedings 15*; Springer: Berlin/Heidelberg, Germany, 2017; pp. 557–578.
25. Aranha, D.F.; Baum, C.; Gjøsteen, K.; Silde, T. Verifiable mix-nets and distributed decryption for voting from lattice-based assumptions. In Proceedings of the 2023 ACM SIGSAC Conference on Computer and Communications Security, Copenhagen, Denmark, 26–30 November 2023 ; pp. 1467–1481.
26. Ahmad, M.; Kamal, A.; Ahmad, K.A.B.; Khari, M.; Crespo, R.G. Fast hybrid-MixNet for security and privacy using NTRU algorithm. *J. Inf. Secur. Appl.* **2021**, *60*, 102872. [CrossRef]
27. Rabas, T.; Bucek, J.; Lórencz, R. SPA Attack on NTRU Protected Implementation with Sparse Representation of Private Key. In Proceedings of the 9th International Conference on Information Systems Security and Privacy (ICISSP 23), Lisbon, Portugal, 22–24 February 2023; pp.135–143.
28. Esser, A.; May, A.; Verbel, J.; Wen, W. Partial key exposure attacks on BIKE, Rainbow and NTRU. In Proceedings of the 42nd Annual International Cryptology Conference, Santa Barbara, CA, USA, 13–18 August 2022; Springer: Cham, Switzerland , 2022; pp. 346–375.
29. Tamura, S.; Kouro, K.; Sasatani, M.; Alam, K.M.R.; Haddad, H.A. An information system platform for anonymous product recycling. *J. Softw.* **2008**, *3*, 46–56. [CrossRef]
30. Haddad, H.; Tamura, S.; Taniguchi, S.; Yanase, T. Development of anonymous networks based on symmetric key encryptions. *J. Netw.* **2011**, *6*, 1533. [CrossRef]
31. Awerbuch, B.; Scheideler, C. Robust random number generation for peer-to-peer systems. *Theor. Comput. Sci.* **2009**, *410*, 453–466. [CrossRef]

Disclaimer/Publisher's Note: The statements, opinions and data contained in all publications are solely those of the individual author(s) and contributor(s) and not of MDPI and/or the editor(s). MDPI and/or the editor(s) disclaim responsibility for any injury to people or property resulting from any ideas, methods, instructions or products referred to in the content.

Article

Secure and Efficient Deduplication for Cloud Storage with Dynamic Ownership Management

Mira Lee and Minhye Seo *

Department of Cyber Security, Duksung Women's University, Seoul 01369, Republic of Korea; dsu2007@duksung.ac.kr
* Correspondence: mhseo@duksung.ac.kr

Abstract: Cloud storage services have become indispensable in resolving the constraints of local storage and ensuring data accessibility from anywhere at any time. Data deduplication technology is utilized to decrease storage space and bandwidth requirements. This technology has the potential to save up to 90% of space by eliminating redundant data in cloud storage. The secure data sharing in cloud (SeDaSC) protocol is an efficient data-sharing solution supporting secure deduplication. In the SeDaSC protocol, a cryptographic server (CS) encrypts clients' data on behalf of clients to reduce their computational overhead, but this essentially requires complete trust in the CS. Moreover, the SeDaSC protocol does not consider data deduplication. To address these issues, we propose a secure deduplication protocol based on the SeDaSC protocol that minimizes the computational cost of clients while leveraging trust in the CS. Our protocol enhances data privacy and ensures computational efficiency for clients. Moreover, it dynamically manages client ownership, satisfying forward and backward secrecy.

Keywords: deduplication; cloud storage; data sharing; message-locked encryption; dynamic ownership update

1. Introduction

In the era of the fourth industrial revolution, digital technology permeates every aspect of our lives, generating vast amounts of client data in real time. The collected data are used in extensive big data analyses, applied in diverse areas including pattern recognition and predictive analytics. Companies leverage client data to formulate effective business strategies, while individuals enjoy personalized services tailored precisely to their needs.

- Social media: Social media platforms generate a wide range of data daily, including posts, photos, and videos. And, they captures client activities and interests for the purpose of delivering personalized content and targeted advertising.
- Search the Internet: Search engines such as Google (90.82%), Yahoo (3.17%), and Bing (2.83%) analyze clients' search terms and click behavior to improve search results, providing personalized information and advertisements [1].
- Internet of Things: Internet of Things (IoT) devices gather diverse environmental data such as temperature, humidity, and location in smart cities and homes. The collected data are used to improve the client convenience and energy efficiency.

As a large volume of data is rapidly generated and accumulated, discussions have arisen about efficient methods to manage these data, and one of them is cloud services. Cloud services provide a virtual server environment that grants clients access to intangible IT resources, including software and storage, with costs incurred only for actual usage. This not only reduces expenses linked to local equipment management but also mitigates the risk of data loss. Furthermore, cloud services offer the convenience of seamless data access,

Citation: Lee, M.; Seo, M. Secure and Efficient Deduplication for Cloud Storage with Dynamic Ownership Management. *Appl. Sci.* **2023**, *13*, 13270. https://doi.org/10.3390/app132413270

Academic Editors: Lip Yee Por and Abdullah Ayub Khan

Received: 24 October 2023
Revised: 5 December 2023
Accepted: 12 December 2023
Published: 15 December 2023

Copyright: © 2023 by the authors. Licensee MDPI, Basel, Switzerland. This article is an open access article distributed under the terms and conditions of the Creative Commons Attribution (CC BY) license (https://creativecommons.org/licenses/by/4.0/).

enabling clients to manage and retrieve their data from anywhere with an Internet connection. The advent of cloud services has effectively transcended the physical limitations of local computing power and storage.

Deduplication technology is widely employed in cloud storage to minimize service space and lower bandwidth requirements. Deduplication refers to not storing uploaded data twice if they already exist in cloud storage. Instead, the information of the client who uploads the data is linked to the identical data in the cloud storage. Clients who own the same data can access and retrieve them within storage [2]. Data deduplication has the potential to save up to 90% of storage space while providing the same advantages as storing data multiple times [3].

It is important for clients to take into account various security concerns while utilizing the service. Individual clients may express concerns about potential leaks of personal information, while corporate clients may worry about service interruptions or the disclosure of confidential data. To address these security concerns, clients should have the option to directly encrypt and upload their data. However, when clients encrypt and upload data, there is a high likelihood that they might use different secret keys. Encrypting the same data with different secret keys will result in different ciphertexts. When cloud storage attempts to check for data duplicates, it becomes difficult to confirm if different ciphertexts are derived from the same plaintext. Consequently, data deduplication becomes unfeasible. A solution to this problem is the introduction of a new encryption approach for data deduplication, called convergent encryption (CE) [4]. In CE, encryption keys are derived directly from the data themselves. More specifically, the hash value of the data is used as the encryption key, which generates the same encryption key (and thereby the same ciphertext) from the same data. Consequently, it becomes feasible to deduplicate encrypted data for multiple clients sharing the same data.

There are various ways to use cloud storage securely. If the clients uploads the data directly, then the client should encrypt their own data during upload and go through extra steps by themselves. To alleviate this burden, a novel approach was proposed [5], employing a trusted third party called a cryptographic server (CS). In this protocol, the CS receives data from clients and handles the encryption on their behalf, thereby enhancing client convenience. Nonetheless, this protocol comes with several limitations:

- The protocol lacks data deduplication functionality, resulting in an inefficient usage of cloud storage space.
- The protocol requires trust in the CS as it exposes the client's plaintext to the CS.
- The protocol does not consider specifically updating ownership information concerning stored data in cloud storage.

In the context of cloud storage, data ownership refers to the right of a client to access data stored in the cloud. Clients acquire ownership by uploading data to cloud storage. Furthermore, after storing their data in the cloud, clients can request modifications or deletions. In cases where a client requests data modification or deletion, the cloud storage can remove the client's information from the group that owns the data. Particularly, the reason for removing the client from the data owner group when a modification request occurs is because cloud storage recognizes the original and modified data as distinct entities. Therefore, to prevent the client from accessing the data before modification, cloud storage needs to delete the client's information from the group, necessitating a change in the client's ownership status. Data deduplication requires changing ownership information, which is called a dynamic ownership update. Such changes typically occur in two scenarios: firstly, when clients delete or modify their stored data, leading to a revocation of ownership; and, secondly, when ownership is acquired by uploading data already existing in cloud storage. Dynamic ownership updates in deduplication guarantee that revoked clients cannot access the data and newly added clients are prevented from gaining access to old data [6]. These ownership updates can occur frequently in cloud services, necessitating effective ownership management.

1.1. Contributions

In this paper, we propose a secure and efficient deduplication protocol for cloud storage. Our proposed protocol offers the following advantages:

- **Efficient alleviation of client's computational costs.** Our study focuses on scenarios where clients upload data directly to cloud storage services, necessitating the encryption of data for secure storage. Our proposed deduplication protocol is based on the secure data sharing in cloud (SeDaSC) protocol [5], which aims to enhance the computational efficiency for clients utilizing cloud services. Similar to the SeDaSC protocol, ours also integrates a third party called a cryptographic server (CS). The CS encrypts data and the CS executes the data deduplication process. And, our proposed protocol demonstrates efficiency in terms of client-side computational cost compared to existing server-side deduplication protocols.
- **Strong assurance of data privacy.** In the SeDaSC protocol [5], as clients transmit plaintext to the CS, there is a requirement for trust in the CS, leading to potential privacy infringements. Our protocol prevents the exposure of data to the CS by having clients blind encrypt the data before transmitting them to the CS. The CS then performs CE on the blind encrypted data, enabling deduplication on the encrypted data in cloud storage. Essentially, our protocol ensures privacy for both the CS and cloud storage.
- **Reduced third-party dependency.** Given that the CS in the SeDaSC protocol has access to data in plaintext, the security of the protocol relies heavily on placing strong trust in the CS. To reduce dependency on the CS, Areed et al. proposed a method where the client employs convergent encryption even when a CS is in place [7]. However, this approach negates the advantage of the CS in reducing the client's computational overhead. In our protocol, the CS still performs convergent encryption, but the client has the capability to reduce its level of trust in the CS by providing data that are blindly encrypted.
- **Secure data management in cases of dynamic ownership changes.** Existing deduplication protocols using a CS [5,7] do not specifically consider changes in ownership of data (stored in cloud storage) that may occur due to clients modifying or deleting data. Ref. [5] states that, upon revocation of ownership, clients cannot access the data stored in cloud storage. However, the method mentioned assumes that, without proper authentication of being the rightful owner, the client cannot decrypt the data as they possess only encryption key fragments. Hence, the mentioned process differs in dynamically managing ownership to acquire security elements. Clients' ownership changes are common scenarios in cloud services and data deduplication. Our protocol allows for secure deduplication even in situations where ownership changes occur frequently. By providing dynamic ownership updates, our protocol enhances security, ensuring both forward and backward secrecy.

1.2. Organization

The following sections of the paper are structured as follows. In Section 2, we overview the existing research on secure deduplication protocols. Section 3 describes the background ideas and concepts employed in our proposal. Section 4 discusses the system architecture and security requirements. Section 5 details the construction of our proposed protocol, including its security analysis. Section 6 focuses on the computational analysis of the proposed protocol. Finally, Section 7 concludes the paper.

2. Related Work

The research on secure data deduplication can be divided into server-side deduplication and client-side deduplication depending on the subject that checks and removes data redundancy.

2.1. Server-Side Deduplication

Server-side deduplication is a technology in which cloud storage is the subject of deduplication. When a client uploads data to a server (cloud storage), the server checks whether the data are duplicated. This method is safe for poison attack because the server validates the data collectively before storing them. But, the client always uploads data regardless of whether the data are duplicated, so network traffic increases. Even so, it is difficult for the server to check whether encrypted data are duplicated. If clients with the same data have different encryption keys, different ciphertexts will be generated. To solve this problem, deterministic encryption algorithms have been proposed that use values derived from messages as encryption keys.

In 2002, Douceur et al. introduced convergent encryption (CE), a scheme where the hash value of data is used as an encryption key [4]. In this approach, clients encrypt the result of a cryptographic hash function applied to plaintext using a key, and then upload it to cloud storage. When clients share the same data, they produce an identical hash value. And, if the hash value is used as the encryption key, it can generate the same ciphertext. This characteristic allows for the deduplication of encrypted data. However, since the encryption key is derived from the plaintext, CE is vulnerable to dictionary attack, particularly when the entropy of the plaintext data is low. CE inherently suffers from vulnerabilities to precomputation attacks, where an attacker with encrypted data can make educated guesses about the plaintext data. Bellare et al.'s proposed protocol addresses this issue by utilizing a key server to offer a data deduplication method that is secure against exhaustive brute force attack [8]. The client generates cryptographic keys with the key server through the RSA-OPRF protocol. The client cannot know the key server's private key, and the key server remains unaware of the client's CE key.

Before the introduction of CE, the deduplication of encrypted data was not feasible. This was because different clients would generate different ciphertexts for the same data as their encryption keys were different. Starting with the proposed CE [4] in 2002, the MLE [9] was proposed to generate encryption keys from messages. MLE is recognized as the most suitable approach for server-side deduplication. Subsequently, research in server-side deduplication has gained momentum, with a focus on applying it in various environments. In 2013, Puzio et al. proposed a block-level deduplication protocol that solved the client's key management problem [10]. Block-level deduplication is a method of separating a file into several blocks and encrypting each. In the proposed protocol, the client divides the file into blocks, encrypting each block with CE. In this process, the CE key for the second and subsequent blocks is encrypted with the key of the previous block. Once all the steps are completed, the client stores only the key for the first CE and generates a signature value for each block, which is then uploaded. But, block-level deduplication has the disadvantage of having to remember many random numbers because each file is encrypted with a different key. To address this, the proposed protocol allows clients to remember only the first key, reducing the burden on clients. In 2016, Scanlon proposed a data deduplication approach to reduce digital forensics backlogs [11]. Digital forensic backlogs occur when a significant volume of cases require expert analysis, making it difficult to address each case individually. To solve this problem, he proposed a method of data deduplication and storing data. The proposed method attempted to solve the chronic volume challenge of digital forensics using a centralized data deduplication system. In 2017, Kim et al. proposed the hybrid email deduplication system (HEDS) [12]. This system utilizes single-instance store (SIS) to remove multiple copies at the file level. As a result, the email server stores unique emails and links duplicate emails through pointers. In 2017, Shin et al. proposed a data deduplication protocol based on decentralized server-aided encryption with multiple key servers [13]. Server-aided encryption refers to the help of a server when a client wants to retrieve data. In this context, the server referred to here is a key server. When a client sends a query, the key server encrypts this query before sending it to the cloud. Importantly, the key server does not understand the client's query, ensuring confidentiality even in a multi-user environment. The proposed protocol does not involve secret key sharing among key servers and is a decentralized architecture, making it scalable and suitable for widespread deduplication across various key servers. In 2020, Yuan et al. presented a blockchain-based public auditing protocol that allows for automatic penalties against malicious cloud service providers (CSPs) [14]. The proposed protocol offers compensation to clients when their data integrity is compromised and provides a means to penalize malicious CSPs. To ensure secure and consistent data encryption, the protocol uses MLE [9] with hash and CE with tag check.

In this way, various methods employing server-side deduplication have been proposed to address different scenarios. Some of these studies have focused on scenarios involving a large number of clients or substantial data storage requirements. In 2016, Hur et al. proposed a secure server-side deduplication that remains secure even in environments where the ownership of outsourced data changes frequently [6]. In practical scenarios, when providing cloud storage services, changes in data ownership are likely to occur frequently. For example, a client who previously owned data but had their ownership revoked should no longer have access to data stored in cloud storage. The proposed protocol updates the encryption key each time ownership for data changes, satisfying both forward and backward secrecy. Additionally, the updated encryption keys are selectively distributed to valid owners, and the method strictly manages data access by the owners. In 2021, Areed et al. proposed a data deduplication protocol for secure data sharing [7] based on a deduplication method for authenticated clients [4]. In this proposed approach, the cryptographic server (CS) generates the CE key on behalf of the client and sends it to the client. The client encrypts the plaintext using the encryption key received from the CS and sends it back to the CS. The CS accesses an access control list (ACL) to confirm data duplication and decide on storage eligibility. This protocol successfully addresses privacy issues [4] but has the limitation of increasing the computational load on the client during this process. Therefore, it appears that there are no existing papers that address the changing environment efficiently and securely, as proposed in this paper. In 2022, Ma et al. introduced a novel server-side deduplication scheme for encrypted data employing hybrid clouds [15]. This approach involves storing data in the public cloud while ownership information and hash code sets for data are stored in the private cloud.

2.2. Client-Side Deduplication

Client-side deduplication is a method in which the client is the subject of deduplication. The client calculates the tag value of the data and transmits it to the server (cloud storage). The server checks whether there is a client's tag matching in the tag list of the stored data. The server sends the search results to the client. The main feature of the client-side deduplication approach is that clients do not need to encrypt data in the process of verifying that they exist on the server [16]. So, the amount of network transmission is low. However, it is necessary to determine whether the entire data are duplicated by the relatively small tag. Therefore, stored data are vulnerable to poison attack.

In 2011, Halevi et al. proposed a method for proving data ownership using hash tree structures, known as proofs of ownership (PoWs) [17]. In this approach, both the client and cloud construct Merkle trees for their respective data blocks. To build a Merkle tree, data are divided into multiple blocks and arranged as leaf nodes. The leaf nodes are used to create parent nodes until a single root node is generated. Clients can then use this Merkle tree to prove data ownership to the cloud by providing the correct sibling path when requested. But, this approach is sensitive to data size. As data grow, the size of the Merkle tree also increases. And, the cloud must maintain plaintext data to construct the same Merkle tree as the client, which compromises data confidentiality. In 2012, Pietro et al. introduced a secure proof of ownership (s-PoW) that is less dependent on data size [18]. In this method, clients respond to the cloud's request for a specified number of random bit positions. Nevertheless, the cloud still needs to store plaintext data for the client's ownership proof challenge. Additionally, the s-PoW exposes plaintext bits during the ownership proof challenge. In 2014, Blasco et al. proposed a PoW using bloom filters (bf-PoW) [19]. A bloom filter is a probabilistic data structure used to check membership of elements. In this approach, cloud storage uses bloom filters to verify client ownership. However, the bf-PoW is dependent on the size of the data and exposes plaintext bits when issuing ownership proof challenges.

Client-side deduplication aims to reduce network traffic by not sending the entire data. However, during responding to the cloud storage's challenge to prove ownership, a plaintext issue is exposed. Some proposed solutions aimed to prove ownership using encrypted data. In 2012, Ng et al. proposed a method for proving ownership when ciphertext is stored in cloud storage [2]. The initial uploader stores the plaintext hash value and ciphertext in the cloud storage. Subsequent uploaders verify ownership using the plaintext hash value. However, if the initial client uploads poisoned ciphertext to the cloud storage, subsequent uploaders might lose the original data. In 2013, Xu et al. introduced a secure ownership proof method against exhaustive brute force attack, called hash function client-side deduplication (UH-CSD) [19]. The initial client encrypts plaintext (m) with a random key (K) to produce C_m, and also encrypts the K with m to create C_K. And, the ciphertexts are stored in the cloud storage. Subsequent clients verify ownership, receive C_K from the cloud storage, and calculate a new C_m, which is then stored in the cloud storage. However, it is vulnerable to poison attack due to the difficulty in proving the relationship between plaintext and ciphertext. In 2015, Manzano et al. proposed a CE-based PoW method (ce-PoW) [19]. Clients split plaintext into chunks and compute CE results. Clients challenge the storage with k random chunk challenges to prove ownership. However, the client's calculation and management of CE results for each chunk make the process inefficient. In 2019, Li et al. introduced a client-side encrypted deduplication (CSED) protocol based on MLE [20]. This approach employs a dedicated key server in the MLE key generation process to thwart indiscriminate attacks. Moreover, CSED integrates a bloom-filter-based PoW system to combat illegal content distribution. In 2020, Guo et al. proposed a randomized secure user-to-user deduplication method designed to enhance storage performance in cloud computing services [21]. Clients owning identical copies of data can share the same random value through ElGamal key exchange. In 2021, Al-Amer et al. presented a reinforced PoW protocol [22]. In the proposed method, the cloud storage requests the bit positions of the CE ciphertext. The client must respond with the appropriate blocks for proof of ownership. In 2023, Ha et al. introduced a novel approach called client-side deduplication with encryption key updates [23]. This technique extends the server-assisted encryption method by introducing features like uptable encryption and dynamic proof of ownership. The uptable encryption offers a mechanism to update encrypted data, simplifying the process of modifying existing information or adding new data without the need to decrypt and re-encrypt the entire dataset.

Data deduplication allows for the efficient utilization of storage space, and client-side deduplication helps to conserve network bandwidth. Some approaches store ciphertext in the cloud storage for data confidentiality, while proof of ownership is conducted with plaintext. Nevertheless, these methods still remain vulnerable to poison attacks due to the inability to establish a clear relationship between ciphertext and plaintext. Recently, techniques have emerged that use plaintext transformed into MLE keys for proof of ownership. Client-side deduplication research has mainly focused on ownership proof and encryption-based deduplication. However, research that significantly reduces client-side computational overhead, as our proposed method does, has been lacking.

3. Preliminaries and Background

3.1. Encryption for Secure Deduplication

Clients are required to encrypt and store their data for security purposes. However, if each client encrypts data using their individual secret key, even identical data will produce distinct ciphertexts based on the client. As a result, cloud storage recognizes each ciphertext as a unique object, making data deduplication impossible. To address this issue, a proposed encryption method aims to enable clients with identical plaintext to utilize the same secret key.

3.1.1. Convergent Encryption

Douceur et al. proposed a convergent encryption (CE) technique for secure data deduplication in cloud storage [4]. CE is a technique that encrypts data with hash values. With CE, one does not need to share keys in advance because one has the same hash value for the same data. When plaintext data m is added to the hash function and the output string is $h(m)$, the encryption key at CE becomes $h(m)$. Encrypting plaintext m using encryption key $h(m)$ creates ciphertext C. Existing data m can be obtained by decrypting the ciphertext C using the encryption key $h(m)$. The hash values of the same data match according to the nature of the hash function, which is a one-way function. In other words, even if the owner is different, if the data are the same, the same hash value can be generated, and if the same encryption key is used, the same ciphertext can be generated. Cloud storage clients can generate ciphertexts using hash values derived from data without the need for key sharing.

- KeyGen(h, m). Given a cryptographic hash function h and plaintext m as input, a convergent key $K = h(m)$ is output.
- Encrypt(K, m). Given convergent key K and plaintext m as input, it produces encrypted data C.
- Decrypt(K, C). Given convergent key K and ciphertext C as input, it produces decrypted data m.

3.1.2. Message-Locked Encryption

Bellare et al. introduced message-locked encryption (MLE) as a technology for ensuring data integrity in the context of secure data deduplication [9]. MLE is a generic term for encryption techniques that generate encryption keys based on the data themselves. Prior to the introduction of MLE, various encryption methods, including those based on CE, were proposed for data deduplication. However, since the publication of their paper, there has been active research in the field of secure data deduplication, with a particular focus on using cryptographic hash functions to verify data integrity. Currently, there are prominent encryption methods used for secure data deduplication under the MLE umbrella, including CE, hash and CE without tag check (HCE1), hash and CE with tag check (HCE2), and randomized convergent encryption (RCE). In this paper, the MLE technique employed is HCE2.

HCE2 is a technique that builds upon CE and uses keys derived from the data to encrypt and verify integrity through tag consistency. When plaintext data m is hashed, resulting in the string $h(m)$, HCE2 uses $h(m)$ as the encryption key. Using $h(m)$ to encrypt m produces ciphertext C, and decrypting C allows for the recovery of m. In contrast to CE, MLE employs C as the input to a hash function to generate T, which represents the tag. T serves to ensure the integrity of the ciphertext. In summary, HCE2, as a representative MLE encryption method, is used to achieve data deduplication with integrity verification by deriving encryption keys from data and utilizing tag consistency. This approach is a crucial component of the broader field of secure data deduplication.

- KeyGen(h, m). Given a cryptographic hash function h and plaintext m as input, an encryption key for MLE $K = h(m)$ is output.
- Encrypt(K, m). Given an encryption key K and plaintext m as input, it produces encrypted data C.
- Decrypt(K, C). Given an encryption key K and ciphertext C as input, it produces decrypted data m.
- TagGen(h, C). Given a cryptographic hash function H and ciphertext C as input, it produces an integrity verification tag T, which corresponds to ciphertext C.

3.2. Proofs of Ownership

Halevi et al. proposed a protocol for legitimate data ownership proof. The proposed protocol is a Merkle-tree-based ownership proof protocol [17]. It allows individuals to assert ownership of data that they actually possess by presenting a portion of them to cloud storage. Proof of ownership (PoW) is a protocol used to verify whether a client has legitimate rights to access data stored in the cloud storage. When a client requests to download data, the cloud storage checks the ownership of the client. To establish the legitimacy of ownership, the client must respond appropriately to a challenge presented by the cloud storage. This response enables the cloud storage to determine whether the client has the necessary access rights to the data.

The client uses the following algorithm to encrypt the data and generate the tag value for PoW.

- KeyGen(h, m). Given a cryptographic hash function h and plaintext m as input, an encryption key $K = h(m)$ is produced.
- Encrypt(K, m). Given an encryption key K and plaintext m as input, it produces encrypted data C.
- TagGen(h, C, b). Given a cryptographic hash function h, ciphertext C, and the Merkle tree leaf size parameters b as input, it produces a Merkle tree MK and integrity verification tag $T = MT_b(C)$.

The client stores the previously generated values K, T, and MT. It then sends T and the number of lowest-level leaf nodes to the cloud storage server. If the server finds a matching tag for T, it will request ownership proof from the client. In response, the client should provide the requested node and sibling path. However, if no matching tag exists, the cloud storage will request the client to upload encrypted data.

- Decrypt(K, C). Given an encryption key K and ciphertext C as input, it produces decrypted data m.

The client transmits T and the number of lowest-level leaf nodes to the cloud storage server. If the cloud storage server finds a matching tag, it will request ownership proof from the client. In response, the client must provide the appropriate node and sibling path as requested by the cloud storage. Upon successful ownership proof, the cloud storage will send encrypted data to the client. The client can then decrypt the data using the decryption algorithm mentioned above.

3.3. Secure Data Sharing in Cloud (SeDaSC) Protocol

Ali et al. introduced the SeDaSC protocol, which aims to reduce client computational overhead when sharing data among authenticated clients in a cloud [5]. In the SeDaSC protocol, the client uploads plaintext data, and a cryptographic server (CS) is responsible for several key operations, while the client does not engage in encryption operations directly. However, it is crucial to fully trust the CS since it has access to plaintext data. The detailed process is outlined below:

1. **Upload.** The client uploads plaintext data. The CS generates an encryption key for the uploaded data. Using the encryption key, the CS encrypts the plaintext and stores the data's information and client's information in an access control list (ACL). The CS then splits the generated encryption key into two parts, securely storing one part and transmitting the other part to the client. To further enhance security, the CS overwrites and deletes the initial encryption key. The encrypted data are finally stored in the cloud. The purpose of storing client information in the ACL is to verify the legitimate ownership of data when a download request is made. Splitting the encryption key into two parts prevents any single entity from decrypting the data independently. If it is an initial upload, a key generation process is performed.

    - KeyGen($1^\lambda, h$). Given security parameters 1^λ and a 256-bit cryptographic hash function h as input, a symmetric key $K = h(\{0,1\}^{256})$ is produced.

- Encrypt(m, SKA, K). Taking plaintext m, symmetric key algorithms SKA, and symmetric key K as input, it produces encrypted data $C = SKA(K, m)$.
- KeyGen for Client i (K). Given symmetric key K as input, it generates the key of CS, $K_i = \{0, 1\}^{256}$, and the key of client i, $K'_i = K \oplus K_i$.

2. **Download.** The client requests decryption of data stored in the cloud, sending the encrypted data to the CS. The CS uses the information stored in the ACL, along with the symmetric key provided by the client, to recover the encryption key. Since each client has a different (K_i, K'_i) pair, the impersonation of other clients is prevented. If the client sends the correct symmetric key to the CS, it can receive the decrypted data. Alternatively, the client can request the CS to perform both download and decryption. In this case, the client sends the group ID and symmetric key K'_i to the CS, which retrieves and decrypts the data from the cloud before transmitting them to the client.

- Decrypt(C, K_i, K'_i, ACL, SKA). Given encrypted data C, CS's key K_i, client i's key K'_i, access control list ACL, and symmetric key algorithms SKA as input, it recovers the encryption key $K = K_i \oplus K'_i$ and decrypts the data to produce plaintext $m = SKA(C, K)$.

Areed et al. used CE, which uses the hash value of plaintext data as an encryption key, to prevent the CS from accessing plaintext [7]. In CE, the CS generates a file key based on the hash value received from the client and the number of clients to share data and divides the file key into half with the client. The client encrypts the data and sends the received half key to the cloud. The proposed protocol prevents the CS from accessing plaintext through CE. In addition, it proposed a communication method that can be used universally compared to existing protocols that consider only authenticated clients. However, the amount of computation increases as the client performs encryption directly. When the CS generates a file key, it does not check the relationship between plaintext data and hash values. Therefore, the cloud cannot confirm the relationship between plaintext data and encrypted data. Because the cloud does not check the integrity of the data, it is vulnerable to poison attacks that store certified plaintext and other data, such as server-side deduplication technology. Therefore, it is difficult to say that the limitations of SeDaSC have been completely solved.

4. System Model
4.1. Entity

The system model of our proposed secure deduplication protocol is described in Figure 1. The entities in the system model are as follows:

- Client: A client is a person who has ownership by uploading data to cloud storage. Since the data were deduplicated and stored, only the initial client's data are stored in the storage. The client refers to both the initial and subsequent uploaders that have ownership.
- Cryptographic server (CS): The CS acts as an intermediary between the client and cloud storage. The CS configures the access control list (ACL) with the hash value received from the client. The ACL manages data information stored in the cloud storage and client information that owns it. The CS controls the client's data access rights based on the ACL. If data need to be stored in cloud storage, CS encrypts the data and sends them to cloud storage.
- Cloud storage: Cloud storage stores data from clients. Cloud storage generates a group key for the data in which the storage request is made to manage the dynamic ownership update. The key is generated independently of a key shared in the previous owner group. The data in which the storage request occurs are re-encrypted with the generated key and stored in the storage. It is assumed that cloud storage is unreliable.

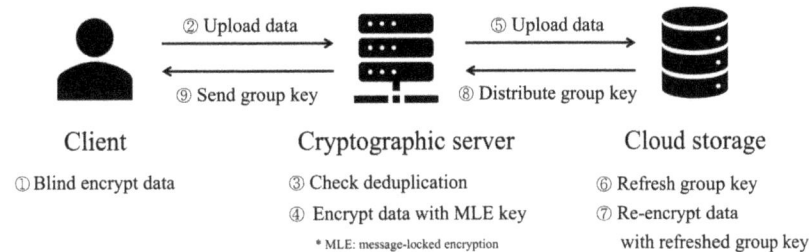

Figure 1. System model.

4.2. Security Requirements

The provided points outline essential security and privacy requirements for the proposed protocol. These requirements collectively emphasize the importance of maintaining data privacy and integrity and ensuring secure ownership transitions in the proposed protocol. The detailed requirements are as follows:

- Data privacy: Data privacy means that the actual content of the data should be protected from unauthorized access, ensuring that sensitive information within the data remains confidential. The original data remain inaccessible to cloud storage, the CS, and unauthorized clients.
- Data integrity: Data integrity involves ensuring that the data stored in the system remain unaltered and reliable. Both the cloud storage and the CS must have mechanisms in place to verify the purity and correctness of the data before storing them or transferring ownership.
- Forward security: Forward security is a concept where clients whose ownership has expired must be prevented from accessing data stored on the cloud storage. This ensures that, even after losing ownership rights, clients cannot access data that they previously owned. It aims to prevent unauthorized access, protect the integrity of data, maintain a clear separation of ownership, and ensure that clients cannot access data outside their current ownership scope.
- Backward security: Backward security is a concept where clients who have uploaded data to the cloud storage should not be able to access data that were stored before they gained ownership. In other words, even after acquiring ownership rights to certain data, clients should not have access to the historical data records from previous owners.

5. The Proposed Secure Deduplication Protocol

In this section, we propose a secure deduplication protocol based on the secure data sharing in cloud (SeDaSC) protocol [5]. The proposed protocol has the following key characteristics. First, our protocol ensures both computational efficiency for the client and data privacy. By building upon SeDaSC, we alleviate the client from complex operations, entrusting these tasks to a cryptographic server (CS). In the initial SeDaSC protocol, there was a challenge in terms of exposing plaintext to the CS. However, our proposed protocol addresses this concern by introducing message-locked encryption (MLE), making it possible to deduplicate encrypted data. Within our proposal, we employ hash and convergent encryption with tag check (HCE2) within the context of MLE. Second, our protocol includes a feature for dynamic ownership updates. When owners upload or revoke their data, the cloud storage re-encrypts the data using a group key, which is shared by clients who own the same data. This group key is generated by the cloud storage when the owner group changes, and then it is distributed by both the CS and the cloud storage. Table 1 provides a description of the notation used in this paper.

Table 1. Notations.

Notation	Description
m	The plaintext
$h(\cdot)$	The cryptographic hash function
M	The blind-encrypted data
C	The ciphertext
r_i	The random value of client i
ACL	The access control list of CS
CTL	The ciphertext list of cloud storage
$E(\cdot)$	The symmetric encrypt function
SK_C	The secret key of cloud storage
i, j, n	The client identification name
session I, J, N	The session identification in progress
GK_N	The group key for session N
RC_N	The re-encrypted data for session N
RGK	The distribution group key
RGK_{adder}, RGK_{other}	
$CRGK_n$	The distribution group key for client n

5.1. Initial Data Upload

The client can gain ownership of data in the cloud storage by successfully uploading them. There are two types of data uploads: initial uploads, which involve data not yet stored in the cloud, and subsequent uploads, which pertain to data that are already present.

The detailed process of the initial upload is as follows:

Step 1. Upload pre-work. Client i must blind encrypt and send data to CS.

- The client i calculates the hash value $h(m)$ of the message m.
- The client calculates $m \oplus h(m) = M$ and a hash value $h(M)$. M is a blind encrypted value sent to the CS. Not only is it generated faster than the encryption operation, but also the characteristics of the plaintext are not revealed to the CS.
- The client randomly selects r_i. This will be used to prove the client themselves.
- The client stores $h(m)$, $h(M)$, and r_i. The $h(m)$ is used to recover m from M when data downloading. The $h(M)$ is used to identify the desired data when requesting an ownership update or data download. The r_i is used to identify the client.
- The client sends an upload request, M, and r_i to the CS.

Step 2. Deduplicate data. The CS determines whether the received data are duplicated and processes the data according to the case.

- The CS calculates the hash value $h(M)$ of the received M.
- The CS checks whether $h(M)$ and r_i exist in the ACL. The initial upload means no data in the cloud storage. In this case, no information exists in the ACL.
- The CS stores $h(M)$ and r_i in ACL. Also, since there are no data in the cloud storage, CS must encrypt M and send it to the cloud storage.
- The CS encrypts M with the hash value $h(M)$. Encrypting data with a hash value is called MLE. Hash values are always the same for the same data. Thus, MLE can generate the same ciphertext for the same data.
- The CS sends a store request, $h(M)$, and $C = E(M)$ to the cloud storage.

Step 3. Re-encrypt data. Cloud storage generates a group key and re-encrypts the data.

- The cloud storage generates a group key, denoted as GK_I, by encrypting the results of XOR operations on $h(M)$ and session I with the cloud storage's SK_C.

- The cloud storage performs an XOR operation on the ciphertext C and the group key GK_I. The C is received from the CS. The result of the XOR operation is a re-encrypted ciphertext RC_I for session I.

Whenever an ownership update occurs, the cloud storage refreshes a group key GK_N and a re-encrypted ciphertext RC_N for the session N.

- The cloud storage stores $h(M)$, GK_I, and RC_I in a ciphertext list of cloud storage (CTL).
- The cloud storage generates an RGK to distribute the refreshed group key. Since there are no owners in the previous session, the RGK generates only GK_I.
- The cloud storage sends the generated RGK to the CS and requests it to be sent to the data owner.

Step 4. Send refreshed group key. The CS sends the group key to the legitimate client. The CS must send the group key to the client based on $h(M)$ and r_i stored in the ACL. And, the client keeps the group key.

- The CS generates the $CRGK_i$ by XOR operation on the client's random value r_i in ACL and the RGK received from the cloud storage. The r_i is the random value of the client i stored as owning $h(M)$ in the ACL.

The $CRGK_n$ should be generated through the RGK and random value of the client that has ownership of $h(M)$ among the clients stored in the ACL. If an owner is added, the $CRGK_n$ should be sent to all clients, and if the owner's ownership is deleted, the $CRGK_n$ should be passed to the remaining clients in the group. The clients can prove their ownership by recovering GK_N from the $CRGK_n$ using r_n. The client recovers and stores GK_I from the $CRGK_i$ received from the CS. The client may use GK_I when downloading data in the future.

5.2. Subsequent Data Upload

In the case of the initial data upload, the data are not yet stored in the cloud storage. This process involves generating the CS's ACL and the cloud storage's CTL. In contrast, subsequent data uploads involve data already present in the cloud storage. In this scenario, client information needs to be added to both the CS's ACL and the cloud storage's CTL. Additionally, the cloud storage conducts dynamic ownership updates, which entail refreshing the group key and re-encrypting data when ownership update occurs.

The detailed process of subsequent uploads is as follows:

Step 1. Upload pre-work.

- The client j calculates the hash value $h(m)$ of the message m.
- The client calculates $m \oplus h(m) = M$ and a hash value $h(M)$ to be sent to the CS.
- The client randomly selects r_j to be used to prove oneself.
- The client j stores $h(m)$, $h(M)$, and r_j.
- The client j sends an upload request, M, and r_j to the CS.

Step 2. Deduplicate data.

- The CS calculates the hash value $h(M)$ of the received M.
- The CS checks whether $h(M)$ and r_j exist in the ACL. For subsequent uploads, they are divided into two cases.
    1. The first case is that client j uploaded the same data before, but the client does not remember it and re-uploads the data. In this case, $h(M)$ and r_j will exist in the ACL of the CS. If so, the CS notifies the client j that the data are already saved.
    2. The second case is that information about $h(M)$ exists in the CS's ACL but the client j is not registered as the owner. In this case, an update of

the ownership group shall be made. The CS stores the client j's random value r_j in the ACL. And, the CS send a group key update request to the cloud storage.

The process of adding ownership in subsequent uploads is described in Section 5.4.

5.3. Data Download

The clients can download data stored in cloud storage at their convenience, whenever they wish. The detailed process of data download is as follows.

Step 1. Request download. The client sends a download request to the CS.

- Client i sends a download request with $h(M)'$, r_i, and GK'_N to the CS to download the data.

$h(M)'$ indicates that the data client wants to download. r_i serves as proof of the client i's identity, and GK'_N signifies the client's involvement in session N. The use of a small quotation mark ($'$) on the values sent by the client visually indicates whether they match the values stored in the CS and the cloud storage.

Step 2. Check ownership. The client sends a download request to the CS.

- The CS checks whether $h(M)'$ and r_i are stored in the ACL. If both $h(M)'$ and r_i exist, the CS will normally perform the download process. However, without $h(M)'$ or r_i, CS will send an error message to the client. This is because the client cannot prove ownership to the CS, or the data do not exist in the cloud storage.
- The CS sends a download request, $h(M)'$, and GK'_N to the cloud storage. $h(M)'$ is for identifying data stored in the CTL of the cloud storage, and GK'_N is a group key for session N used to decrypt the re-encrypted data.

Step 3. Cloud storage's decryption. The cloud storage decrypts the re-encrypted data and sends them to the CS.

- The cloud storage checks whether $h(M)'$ is stored in the CTL. If $h(M)'$ exists, the cloud storage calculates ciphertext C' by performing an XOR operation on the group key GK'_N and re-encrypted data RC_N. The GK'_N is received from the CS, and the RC_N is stored in the CTL of the cloud storage.
- The cloud storage sends C' to the CS.

Step 4. CS's decryption. The CS decrypts the ciphertext and sends to the client.

- The CS decrypts the ciphertext C' as $h(M)'$ to obtain M', and the CS computes the hash value $h(M')$ of the message M'.
- The CS checks whether $h(M)$ and calculated $h(M')$ are the same. The $h(M)$ is a value stored in the CS's ACL. If the two values are the same, it means that they have been decoded normally and will be transmitted to the client. In other cases, it means that an error occurred during the decoding process, and the client will be notified of this error.
- The CS sends M' to the client i.

Step 5. Client's decryption. The client recovers plaintext m from M.

- The client recovers the plaintext m' by performing an XOR operation on $h(m)$ and M'. The hash value $h(m)$ is stored in the client, and the M' is received from the CS.

If there is no error message received from the CS, m and m' will be the same data.

5.4. Ownership Update

The ownership updates occur in subsequent uploads, i.e., when another client attempts to upload the same data while data are already stored in the cloud storage. During an ownership update, the group key is refreshed and distributed to the clients. Suppose that the session prior to the data upload of the client j is session I. When a client j successfully uploads data, it initiates a new session, which is now referred to as session J.

Step 1. Upload pre-work. The same as **Step 1** of the subsequent upload in Section 5.2.

Step 2. Deduplicate data.

- The CS calculates the hash value $h(M)$ of the received M.
- The CS checks whether $h(M)$ and r_j exist in the ACL.

If information about $h(M)$ exists in the ACL of the CS, but client j is not registered as the owning client, an ownership update should be made.

- The CS stores the random value r_j of client j in the ACL.
- The CS sends a data re-encrypting request with $h(M)$ to the cloud storage. The hash value, denoted as $h(M)$, plays a crucial role in identifying the specific data requested for updating in the cloud storage.

Step 3. Re-encrypt data.

- The cloud storage generates a group key, denoted as GK_J, by encrypting the results of XOR operations on $h(M)$ and session J with the cloud storage's SK_C. In this context, the encryption with the cloud storage's secret key is achieved through symmetric key encryption. The hash value $h(M)$ is received from the CS.
- The cloud storage generates re-encrypted data, denoted as RC_J, by conducting an XOR operation on RC_I, GK_I, and GK_J. Accordingly, the re-encrypted data RC_J take the form of $C \oplus GK_J = RC_J$.

The previous group key, denoted as GK_N, serves to decrypt the ciphertext C within RC_N. Essentially, the cloud storage stores only RC_N for efficient storage space utilization. Whenever an ownership update occurs, the cloud storage recovers the original ciphertext C using the group key GK_N from RC_N stored in the CTL. In addition, the cloud creates re-encryption data, RC_{N+1}, through an XOR operation on ciphertext C and GK_{N+1}. Importantly, a new group key is generated independently of any prior session. This independence arises because when the cloud storage generates a session value, it remains disconnected from previous sessions, ensuring that each session operates independently.

- The cloud storage stores GK_J and RC_J created in the above two processes.
- The cloud storage generates RGK to distribute the refreshed group key to clients.
  - $GK_J = RGK_{adder}$;
  - $GK_I \oplus GK_J = RGK_{other}$.

In subsequent uploads, both the existing data owners from the previous session and new owners are involved. Thus, the cloud storage creates two type of refreshed group keys: the RGK_{adder} for newly added owners and RGK_{other} for existing owners. For newly added owners, RGK_{adder} includes only $GK_N + 1$, because the new owners are not aware of the previous session N. For existing owners, RGK_{other} consists of GK_N and GK_{N+1}. And, the prior group key GK_N of RGK_{other} serves to verify the ownership of previous owners.

- The cloud storage sends the generated RGK_{adder} and RGK_{other} to the CS to requests it to be sent to the data owner.

Step 4. Send refreshed group key.

- The CS sends the refreshed group key to the client based on the $h(M)$ and r_i stored in the ACL. Suppose that the clients with $h(M)$ are j (additional uploader) and i (existing owner).
  - For additional uploader j:
    1. The CS generates $CRGK_j$ by performing an XOR operation on the random value r_j of client j and the RGK_{adder}.
    2. The CS sends $CRGK_j$ to client j.
    3. The client j recovers GK_J from the value received.
       * $CRGK_j \oplus r_j = GK_J$.
  - For existing owner i:
    1. The CS generates $CRGK_i$ by performing an XOR operation on the random value r_i of client i and the RGK_{other}.
    2. The CS sends $CRGK_i$ to client i.
    3. The client i recovers GK_J from the value received.
       * $CRGK_i \oplus GK_I \oplus r_i = GK_J$.
- Both clients store the group key GK_J for session J.

5.5. Ownership Delete

Clients belonging to the owner group of the data can access the source data. If clients desire to delete the data and revoke ownership, they can initiate this process by sending a request to the CS at any time. In cases where there is a change in group information, it becomes imperative to update the group key and re-encrypted data. This is performed to prevent clients who have previously deleted their ownership from retaining access to the data, ensuring the security and integrity of data management. The process of deleting ownership is as follows:

Step 1. Request ownership revocation. A client sends an ownership release request to the CS.

- The client i submits an ownership revocation request to the CS, which includes $h(M)'$, r_i, and GK_N'. The hash value $h(M)'$ specifies which data are owned. The random value r_i informs the client of who it is. The group key GK_N' means that the client belongs to session N in progress. The small quotation mark (') on the values sent by the client visually indicates whether they match the values stored in the CS and the cloud storage.

Step 2. Check ownership. The CS checks the client's ownership,

- The CS checks whether $h(M)'$ and r_i are stored in the ACL.

If both $h(M)'$ and r_i are provided, the CS proceeds with the ownership deletion process. However, if either $h(M)'$ or r_i is missing, the CS sends an error message to the client. In cases where the client is the last owner of $h(M)'$ stored in ACL, the CS additionally sends a group-key delete request to the cloud storage, ensuring proper data management and security. If the client is the last owner of the $h(M)'$ stored in the ACL, the CS will also send a group key delete request to the cloud storage.

- The CS sends a download request to the cloud storage, which includes $h(M)'$, GK_N'. The hash value $h(M)'$ is crucial for identifying information stored in the CTL of the cloud storage. The group key GK_N' serves the purpose of decrypting the re-encrypted data in the cloud storage.

Step 3. Check group key. The cloud storage checks the client's group key.

- The cloud storage performs a check to determine whether the stored group key GK_N matches the GK'_N received from the CS. If these values match, the cloud storage sends a group key authentication success message to the CS. Otherwise, the cloud storage sends an error message to the CS.

Step 4. Revoke ownership. The CS revokes the client's ownership in ACL.

- If the message received from the cloud storage is successful, the CS removes the r_i from the ACL, then forwards the results to the client. Conversely, in case of a failure message, an error message is sent to the client.

Step 5. Re-encrypt data. The cloud storage recreates re-encrypted data. After the completion of client i's ownership revocation, two distinct scenarios emerge.

1. First, if remaining owners exist, the group key for the other owners is updated.
    - The cloud storage generates a group key, denoted as GK_{N+1}, by encrypting the results of XOR operations on $h(M)$ and session $(N+1)$ with the cloud storage's SK_C.
    - The cloud storage generates a distribution key RGK, designed for the remaining owners. The RGK created in this process is referred to as RGK_{other}.
    - The cloud storage sends RGK_{other} to the CS to request it to be sent to the data owner.
2. Second, if there are no remaining owners, all information stored in the cloud storage and the CS at $h(M)$ is deleted.
    - The cloud storage deletes all data to optimize storage efficiency.
    - The cloud storage notifies the CS that all information regarding $h(M)'$ has been erased.

Step 6. Send refreshed group key. The CS sends the group key to the client based on the ACL $(h(M), r_n)$. Suppose that a client with $h(M)$ is client j, who is an existing owner.

1. If the CS receives RGK_{other} from the cloud:
    - The CS performs an XOR operation on client j's random value r_j and RGK_{other}, and the operation result is $CRGK_j$ for client j.
    - The CS sends $CRGK_j$ to client j.
    - The client j recovers GK_{N+1} from $CRGK_j$, and the client stores GK_{N+1}.
2. If the CS receives a notification from the cloud storage that all information has been deleted:
    - The CS deletes all information related to $h(M)'$ stored in the ACL.

6. Discussion

This paper introduces a protocol enabling secure deduplication and dynamic ownership management based on secure data sharing in cloud (SeDaSC). Our proposal not only reduces reliance on the cryptographic server (CS) but also maintains high computational efficiency for clients. Additionally, it ensures safety even in scenarios involving client ownership changes. This section aims to elucidate the distinctions between our proposals and existing approaches.

6.1. Security Analysis

Certainly, the security analysis is explained with respect to the data privacy, data integrity, backward secrecy, and forward secrecy described in Section 4.2.

- **Data privacy.** In our protocol, the CS can access M, but M has blind encryption applied to plaintext m. Hash functions used in blind encryption have structural safety that cannot recover input values from hash values due to preimage resistance. Therefore, the CS cannot recover m from M. The proposed protocol can ensure safety and solve key exchange problems with a relatively simple hash operation.

The data delivered to cloud storage in the proposed protocol are a value encrypted with the message-locked encryption (MLE) key by the CS. Since these data are encrypted with the same key, if they are a request for the same plaintext, they will have the same ciphertext. Therefore, cloud storage may perform deduplication on the same encrypted data.

- **Data integrity.** In our protocol, when a client uploads data, the CS verifies if the received hash value matches the one that it computes directly. The cloud storage also checks if the hash value received from the CS matches the one it calculates independently. In essence, during the upload process, data integrity is inherently confirmed, preventing the storage of corrupted data.
- **Forward secrecy.** In our protocol, when a client deletes their ownership, they are no longer included in the ownership group for that session, and they cannot access the original data. The ownership group is updated immediately when a client's ownership changes, and the refreshed group key is also modified. Therefore, following a request for ownership deletion, whether data have been deleted or retained, the client cannot access data stored in the cloud storage.
- **Backward secrecy.** In our protocol, a client can only access data stored in the cloud if they have uploaded the data and acquired ownership. Even if a client owns the data, they do not automatically become a part of the ownership group for that session. In the proposed protocol, when a client uploads data, the ownership group is immediately updated, and the refreshed group key is changed. Therefore, even if a client uploads data, they cannot gain access to information about data previously stored by the ownership group.

Through these measures, the proposed protocol addresses the aspects of data privacy, data integrity, backward secrecy, and forward secrecy, providing a comprehensive security framework for the system.

Table 2 provides a comparison between our proposed approach and five closely related proposals from Section 2. It aims to highlight how our protocol offers enhanced security and the ability to update ownership in the context of SeDaSC. The table demonstrates the key differences and advantages of our proposal compared to existing proposals. Ref. [4] proposed the concept of convergent encryption (CE), which allows for secure data deduplication by encrypting data using the hash value of the message. However, it had the drawback of not providing a mechanism for verifying data integrity. Ref. [9] proposed a method within the framework of MLE called hash and CE with tag check (HCE2). HCE2 overcomes the limitations of CE by employing cryptographic hash functions to create tags that verify data integrity. Both of these data deduplication techniques offer privacy features but do not consider methodologies for scenarios where ownership changes. Ref. [5] proposed the SeDaSC protocol for authenticated client groups, using a CS to enhance client computational efficiency. However, it lacked data privacy as data sent to the CS were not encrypted. Moreover, it assumed the trustworthiness of the CS performing data deduplication, making it difficult to ensure data integrity since it had access to plaintext data. Ref. [7] proposed a solution to address the privacy issue in SeDaSC by using CE to provide data privacy. However, as it relies on CE, it does not guarantee data integrity. Additionally, clients had to authenticate themselves to the CS as the legitimate owners of the data to access them. And, it could lead to compliance with forward and backward secrecy. However, the purpose of this method was to prove the legitimate owner rather than manage ownership. Hence, it differs from the dynamic ownership management considered in this paper. Ref. [6] proposed a server-side deduplication protocol that considered a dynamic ownership update and was compliant with all security requirements. However, the difference lies in the fact that it does not prioritize reducing the client's computation. Referencing Table 2, our protocol exhibits unique attributes in comparison to similar protocols, ensuring data privacy, verifying data integrity, and supporting both forward and backward secrecy concurrently. Prior existing protocols have occasionally lacked in fulfilling particular aspects or critical security requirements. In contrast, our protocol excels in delivering heightened security capabilities by comprehensively addressing these aspects.

Table 2. Comparison of security requirements.

	Data Privacy	Data Integrity	Forward Secrecy	Backward Secrecy
[4]	O	X	X	X
[9]	O	O	X	X
[5]	X	X	O	O
[7]	O	X	X	X
[6]	O	O	O	O
Ours	O	O	O	O

6.2. Performance Analysis

Table 3 provides a comparative analysis of the proposed protocol concerning client computational complexity and the presence of server-aided features, particularly the server computational complexity required for the dynamic ownership update. It is important to note that our proposed protocol is a type of server-side deduplication. In Section 2.1, we compare our protocol with other server-side deduplication protocols.

The computational complexity of the client refers to the amount of computational resources required when uploading or downloading data. The server computational complexity refers to the amount of computational resources required when cloud storage updates dynamic ownership. Notably, refs. [11,12] and the data download of [15] did not provide explicit mathematical formulations in the paper.

Table 3. Comparison of computational complexity.

	Client Computational Complexity			Server-Aided	Server Computational Complexity
	Initial Upload	Subsequent Upload	Download		Dynamic Ownership Update
[4]	$1H + 1SE$	$1H + 1SE$	$1SD$	X	X
[8]	$2H + 2SE + 2M + 3E$	$2H + 2SE + 2M + 3E$	$2SD$	O	X
[10]	$2H + 4B*SE + B*DS$	$2H + 4B*SE + B*DS$	$2B*SE + B*SD$	X	X
[11]	-	-	-	O	X
[6]	$2H + 1SE + 1\oplus$	$2H + 1SE + 1\oplus$	$2H + 2SD + 1\oplus$	X	$1H + 3SE + 1\oplus$
[12]	-	-	-	X	X
[13]	$1H + 5M + (5+2B)*E + 1DDH$	$1H + 5M + (5+2B)*E + 1DDH$	$1H + 1KDF + 3M$	O	X
[14]	$3H + 1SE + 1M + 1E + 1DS$	$3H + 1SE + 1M + 1E + 1DS$	$1H + 1SD$	O	X
[7]	$1H + 1SE$	$1H + 1SE$	$1SD$	O	X
[15]	$1H + 1DS + 1PRE\text{-}Dn + 1PRE\text{-}En + 1SE$	$1H + 1DS + 1PRE\text{-}Dn + 1PRE\text{-}En$	-	X	$1PRE\text{-}ReEn$
Ours	$2H + 2\oplus$	$2H + 2\oplus$	$1\oplus$	O	$1SE + 4\oplus$

O: offer; X: not offer; SE: symmetric key encryption; SD: symmetric key decryption; H: hash function; DS: digital signature; DDH: solving the decisional Diffie–Hellman (DDH) problem; KDF: key derivation function; B: data block size; $\oplus$: XOR operation; M: multiplication; E: exponentiation, PRE-Dn: proxy re-encryption Dn function, PRE-En: proxy re-encryption En function, PRE-ReEn: proxy re-encryption ReEn function.

- Client computational complexity:
  1. **Upload.** Among the existing server-side deduplication protocols, [4,7] stand out in terms of minimal client computational requirements for data uploads, as depicted in Table 3. These protocols involve a single H and a single SE during both initial and subsequent uploads. In contrast, our protocol necessitates two operations of H and two operations of $\oplus$. SE algorithms are typically resource-intensive and computationally complex, used for encrypting data. On the other hand, operations like transforming an input into a fixed-size hash value using H and relatively simpler bit-wise operations like $\oplus$ are generally performed faster and more efficiently. However, actual performance may vary based on factors such as the algorithm used, implementation methods, and hardware configurations, among others.
  2. **Download.** Even for data download, our protocol outperforms [4,7] since they require a single SD while our protocol requires only a single $\oplus$.

  Table 3 reveals that our approach excels in minimizing computational complexity when uploading and downloading data, offering an efficient solution for clients.
- Server computational complexity, on the other hand, pertains to the computational resources required by the cloud storage server when re-encrypting data and distributing group keys during ownership changes. The inclusion of dynamic ownership update features in [6,15] and our approach is a distinct advantage. These features guarantee data confidentiality during ownership transitions and prevent departing clients from accessing data still stored in the cloud storage.
- Server-aided capabilities, a feature supported by [6–8,11,13,14] and our approach, refer to actions taken to obtain message-independent encryption keys through a key server. Our protocol generates MLE keys through independent key servers.

6.3. Analytical Synthesis

The proposed secure deduplication protocol is constructed based on Ail et al.'s SeDaSC protocol [5], aimed at improving client computational efficiency while incorporating the principles of Hur et al.'s dynamic ownership update [6]. Our proposed protocol shares similarities with the SeDaSC protocol but introduces the following key differences:

- Mitigation of CS dependency: The CS, which encrypts data on behalf of clients, allows clients to significantly reduce their computational workload. However, due to the CS's capability to access data in plaintext, it must be completely trusted. Our proposal employs blind encryption on plaintext to prevent unauthorized access to plaintext by the CS. As a result, our protocol offers a secure solution, particularly in environments where trust in CS security is low.
- Dynamic ownership update: When applying data deduplication in cloud storage environments, situations arise where ownership information changes. Two common scenarios involve either the original data owner modifying or deleting their data, resulting in the revocation of ownership, or a new client uploading data that match existing data, granting them ownership rights. Such ownership changes can occur frequently in cloud storage services and must be appropriately managed to ensure the security of the service. To solve this issue, our protocol involves the cloud storage storing data in an encrypted format using a secret key. When a change in ownership occurs, the data are re-encrypted with a new key. This newly generated key is then distributed to clients by the CS. This approach enables the prevention of revoked clients from accessing data and ensures that newly added clients cannot access previously uploaded data.
- Client computational efficiency: SeDaSC optimizes client computational efficiency by assigning encryption operations to the CS. However, to generate the same ciphertext for identical data, sending plaintext to the CS is necessary, demanding trust in the CS. To address this, we implemented blind encryption on plaintext, preventing CS access to plaintext. In our proposal, blind encryption requires one hash function

and one XOR operation. Table 3 highlights our protocol's superior computational efficiency on the client side. While our proposal involves more computations than SeDaSC, it still demonstrates greater efficiency than previously proposed server-side deduplication protocols.

This paper introduces a protocol that extends upon the SeDaSC protocol, emphasizing enhanced safety measures and diverse security aspects. Specifically, our protocol mitigates data privacy concerns by minimizing dependency on the CS, enhances storage efficiency through data deduplication techniques, and incorporates dynamic ownership management functionality. Since our protocol is based on SeDaSC, the primary point of comparison is the SeDaSC protocol. Therefore, Table 4 provides a comparison between the SeDaSC protocol and ours concerning computational and communication overhead. In this paper, the variable λ denotes the size of the data. Specifically, in Table 4, λ_P denotes the size of plaintext, λ_K represents the size of the secret key, and λ_C signifies the size of the ciphertext. These variables were utilized for the analysis of communication overhead as presented in Table 4. Firstly, our protocol marginally increases the client's computational load while reducing dependency on the CS. However, it is noteworthy that the overall communication overhead remains unchanged. Secondly, for dynamic ownership management, interaction among the client, CS, and cloud is necessary. The ownership update mentioned in Table 4 occurs when the ownership group of data changes due to another client. The majority of this interaction involves XOR operations, which minimizes the burden on each entity due to the XOR operations' computational efficiency. Consequently, our protocol addresses security concerns present in SeDaSC while maintaining similarity in computational and communication overhead aspects.

Table 4. Comparison of overheads between the SeDaSC protocol and our protocol.

		SeDaSC Protocol		Our Protocol	
		Computational Overhead	Communication Overhead	Computational Overhead	Communication Overhead
Upload	Client	0	λ_P	$2H + 2\oplus$	λ_H
	CS	$RBG + 1H + 1\oplus + 1SE$	$\lambda_K + \lambda_C$	$RBG + 1SE$	λ_C
	Cloud storage	0	0	$RBG + 1SE + 4\oplus$	$2\lambda_K$
Download	Client	0	λ_K	0	λ_H
	CS	1SD	λ_P	1SD	$\lambda_H + \lambda_C$
	Cloud storage	0	λ_C	1SD	λ_C
Ownership update	Client	-	-	$1\oplus$	0
	CS	-	-	$N_C \times \oplus$	$N_C \times \lambda_K$
	Cloud storage	-	-	$RBG + 1SE + 4\oplus$	$2\lambda_K$

H: hash function; $\oplus$: XOR operation; RBG: random bit generation; SE: symmetric key encryption; SD: symmetric key decryption; λ_P: the size of plaintext; λ_H: the output size of hash function; λ_C: the size of ciphertext; λ_K: the size of secret key; N_C: the number of clients in group.

7. Conclusions

This paper proposes an efficient and secure data deduplication protocol based on the secure data sharing in cloud (SeDaSC) protocol. Our proposal addresses three key aspects of SeDaSC. First, our approach enhances data privacy. In SeDaSC, the cryptographic server (CS) performs complex encryption operations on the behalf of clients, potentially compromising data privacy as the CS can access plaintext. Our approach mitigates this concern by having clients perform blind encryption using hash values of plaintext, thus preventing information exposure. Second, our approach enhances the efficient utilization of cloud storage space. SeDaSC introduced a data-sharing method using cloud storage. However, it lacks an effective method for storage space management. Data deduplication technology stands out as an efficient approach to managing data, involving the prevention of storing data twice in cloud storage if they are already uploaded. This technique has the potential to save storage space by up to 90% [3]. Our proposed protocol enables data deduplication based on client ownership stored in an access control list (ACL), thereby ensuring efficient use of cloud storage space. Third, our approach ensures the secure management of data, including dynamic ownership management, when the composition of a group changes. SeDaSC does not consider specific scenarios related to the addition, modification, or deletion of client ownership, which may lead to security issues. While SeDaSC only allows access to stored data by clients with legitimate ownership, it does not address scenarios involving ownership changes. For instance, security issues might arise when newly registered clients are granted access to previous data or when revoked ownership clients continue to access data stored in cloud storage. Our proposed protocol addresses these concerns by allowing for the registration or deletion of ownership and distributing refreshed group keys for the respective session to prevent both previous and new clients from accessing ciphertext.

The SeDaSC protocol requires only one hash function operation, thereby providing advantages in terms of client computation cost and time during data uploads. However, this approach may pose data privacy concerns as it exposes plaintext to the CS. Our protocol addresses this issue by conducting one hash function and one XOR operation. As indicated in Section 6.2 and Table 3, our protocol exhibits significantly less computational complexity on the client side compared to previously proposed server-side deduplication protocols. Hence, our protocol offers increased safety compared to SeDaSC and reduces computational cost and time in contrast to other protocols.

Through this research, we have presented a protocol that maintains client computational efficiency while supporting data privacy, data integrity, and ownership updates. These improvements are expected to contribute to secure and efficient data management in cloud storage environments. Cloud storage serves primary purposes: a service provider securely stores data from clients while delivering a service, or a client directly stores data in platforms such as Google Drive, AWS S3, and others. Our proposed protocol holds the advantage of guaranteeing computational efficiency for the client. As a result, our protocol has advantages in scenarios where clients directly encrypt and store their data on cloud storage. For future work, it would be interesting to incorporate efficient key revocation techniques [24] into our proposed protocol. This integration would lead to a substantial enhancement in the ownership update.

Author Contributions: Conceptualization, M.L.; methodology, M.L.; validation, M.L. and M.S.; formal analysis, M.L.; investigation, M.L.; writing—original draft preparation, M.L.; writing—review and editing, M.L. and M.S.; supervision, M.S.; project administration, M.S.; funding acquisition, M.S. All authors have read and agreed to the published version of the manuscript.

Funding: This research was supported by the Basic Research Program through the National Research Foundation of Korea (NRF) funded by the MSIT (grant number: 2021R1A4A502890711).

Data Availability Statement: The data presented in this study are openly available in IEEE Xplore at https://doi.org/10.1109/ICDCS.2002.1022312, https://doi.org/10.1109/JSYST.2014.2379646, https://doi.org/10.1109/TKDE.2016.2580139, https://doi.org/10.1109/CloudCom.2013.54, https://doi.org/10.1109/INTECH.2016.7845139, https://doi.org/10.1109/TSC.2017.2748594, https://doi.org/10.1109/IPCCC55026.2022.9894331, reference number [4–6,10,11,13,15], WILEY Online Library at https://doi.org/10.1002/cpe.6377, reference number [7], Springer at https://doi.org/10.1007/978-3-642-38348-9_18, https://doi.org/10.1007/978-3-319-42280-0_3, reference number [9,12], and Elsevier's Library at https://doi.org/10.1016/j.ins.2020.07.005, reference number [14].

Conflicts of Interest: The authors declare no conflict of interest.

References

1. Search Engine Market Share Worldwide. Available online: https://gs.statcounter.com/search-engine-market-share#monthly-202201-202212-bar (accessed on 15 October 2023).
2. Ng, W.K.; Wen, Y.; Zhu, H. Private data deduplication protocols in cloud storage. In Proceedings of the 27th Annual ACM Symposium on Applied Computing, Trento, Italy, 26–30 March 2012; pp. 441–446.

3. Dutch, M. Understanding data deduplication ratios. In Proceedings of the SNIA Data Management Forum, Orlando, FL, USA, 7 April 2008; Volume 7.
4. Douceur, J.R.; Adya, A.; Bolosky, W.J.; Simon, P.; Theimer, M. Reclaiming space from duplicate files in a serverless distributed file system. In Proceedings of the 22nd International Conference on Distributed Computing Systems, Vienna, Austria, 2–5 July 2002; pp. 617–624.
5. Ali, M.; Dhamotharan, R.; Khan, E.; Khan, S.U.; Vasilakos, A.V.; Li, K.; Zomaya, A.Y. SeDaSC: Secure data sharing in clouds. *IEEE Syst. J.* **2015**, *11*, 395–404. [CrossRef]
6. Hur, J.; Koo, D.; Shin, Y.; Kang, K. Secure data deduplication with dynamic ownership management in cloud storage. *IEEE Trans. Knowl. Data Eng.* **2016**, *28*, 3113–3125. [CrossRef]
7. Areed, M.F.; Rashed, M.M.; Fayez, N.; Abdelhay, E.H. Modified SeDaSc system for efficient data sharing in the cloud. *Concurr. Comput. Pract. Exp.* **2021**, *33*, e6377. [CrossRef]
8. Keelveedhi, S.; Bellare, M.; Ristenpart, T. DupLESS: Server-Aided encryption for deduplicated storage. In Proceedings of the 22nd USENIX Security Symposium (USENIX Security 13), Washington, DC, USA, 14–16 August 2013; pp. 179–194.
9. Bellare, M.; Keelveedhi, S.; Ristenpart, T. Message-locked encryption and secure deduplication. In *Advances in Cryptology—EUROCRYPT 2013, Proceedings of the Annual International Conference on the Theory and Applications of Cryptographic Techniques, Athens, Greece, 26–30 May 2013*; Springer: Berlin/Heidelberg, Germany, 2013; pp. 296–312.
10. Puzio, P.; Molva, R.; Önen, M.; Loureiro, S. ClouDedup: Secure deduplication with encrypted data for cloud storage. In Proceedings of the 2013 IEEE 5th International Conference on Cloud Computing Technology and Science, Bristol, UK, 2–5 December 2013; Volume 1, pp. 363–370.
11. Scanlon, M. Battling the digital forensic backlog through data deduplication. In Proceedings of the 2016 Sixth International Conference on Innovative Computing Technology (INTECH), Dublin, Ireland, 24–26 August 2016; pp. 10–14.
12. Kim, D.; Song, S.; Choi, B.Y.; Kim, D.; Song, S.; Choi, B.Y. HEDS: Hybrid Email Deduplication System. In *Data Deduplication for Data Optimization for Storage and Network Systems*; Springer: Cham, Switzerland, 2017; pp. 79–96.
13. Shin, Y.; Koo, D.; Yun, J.; Hur, J. Decentralized server-aided encryption for secure deduplication in cloud storage. *IEEE Trans. Serv. Comput.* **2017**, *13*, 1021–1033. [CrossRef]
14. Yuan, H.; Chen, X.; Wang, J.; Yuan, J.; Yan, H.; Susilo, W. Blockchain-based public auditing and secure deduplication with fair arbitration. *Inf. Sci.* **2020**, *541*, 409–425. [CrossRef]
15. Ma, X.; Yang, W.; Zhu, Y.; Bai, Z. A Secure and Efficient Data Deduplication Scheme with Dynamic Ownership Management in Cloud Computing. In Proceedings of the 2022 IEEE International Performance, Computing, and Communications Conference (IPCCC), Austin, TX, USA, 11–13 November 2022; pp. 194–201.
16. Storer, M.W.; Greenan, K.; Long, D.D.; Miller, E.L. Secure data deduplication. In Proceedings of the 4th ACM International Workshop on Storage Security and Survivability, Alexandria, VA, USA, 31 October 2008; pp. 1–10.
17. Halevi, S.; Harnik, D.; Pinkas, B.; Shulman-Peleg, A. Proofs of ownership in remote storage systems. In Proceedings of the 18th ACM Conference on Computer and Communications Security, Chicago, IL, USA, 17–21 October 2011; pp. 491–500.
18. Di Pietro, R.; Sorniotti, A. Boosting efficiency and security in proof of ownership for deduplication. In Proceedings of the 7th ACM Symposium on Information, Computer and Communications Security, Seoul, Republic of Korea, 2–4 May 2012; pp. 81–82.
19. Blasco, J.; Di Pietro, R.; Orfila, A.; Sorniotti, A. A tunable proof of ownership scheme for deduplication using bloom filters. In Proceedings of the 2014 IEEE Conference on Communications and Network Security, San Francisco, CA, USA, 29–31 October 2014; pp. 481–489.
20. Li, S.; Xu, C.; Zhang, Y. CSED: Client-side encrypted deduplication scheme based on proofs of ownership for cloud storage. *J. Inf. Secur. Appl.* **2019**, *46*, 250–258. [CrossRef]
21. Guo, C.; Jiang, X.; Choo, K.K.R.; Jie, Y. R-Dedup: Secure client-side deduplication for encrypted data without involving a third-party entity. *J. Netw. Comput. Appl.* **2020**, *162*, 102664. [CrossRef]
22. Al-Amer, A.; Ouda, O. Secure and Efficient Proof of Ownership Scheme for Client-Side Deduplication in Cloud Environments. *Int. J. Adv. Comput. Sci. Appl.* **2021**, *12*, 916–923. [CrossRef]
23. Ha, G.; Jia, C.; Chen, Y.; Chen, H.; Li, M. A secure client-side deduplication scheme based on updatable server-aided encryption. *IEEE Trans. Cloud Comput.* **2023**, *11*, 3672–3684. [CrossRef]
24. Lee, K.; Lee, D.H.; Park, J.H. Efficient Revocable Identity-Based Encryption via Subset Difference Methods. *Des. Codes Cryptogr.* **2017**, *85*, 39–76. [CrossRef]

Disclaimer/Publisher's Note: The statements, opinions and data contained in all publications are solely those of the individual author(s) and contributor(s) and not of MDPI and/or the editor(s). MDPI and/or the editor(s) disclaim responsibility for any injury to people or property resulting from any ideas, methods, instructions or products referred to in the content.

Article

Leaving the Business Security Burden to LiSEA: A Low-Intervention Security Embedding Architecture for Business APIs

Hang Li, Junhao Li, Yulong Wang, Chunru Zhou and Mingyong Yin *

Institute of Computer Application, China Academy of Engineering Physics, Mianyang 621999, China; wangyulong@caep.cn (Y.W.)
* Correspondence: yinmy@caep.cn

Abstract: In the evolving landscape of complex business ecosystems and their digital platforms, an increasing number of business Application Programming Interfaces (APIs) are encountering challenges in ensuring optimal authorization control. This challenge arises due to factors such as programming errors, improper configurations, and sub-optimal business processes. While security departments have exhibited proficiency in identifying vulnerabilities and mitigating certain viral or adversarial incursions, the safeguarding of comprehensive business processes remains an intricate task. This paper introduces a novel paradigm, denoted as the Low-Intervention Security Embedding Architecture (LiSEA), which empowers business applications to enhance the security of their processes through judicious intervention within business APIs. By strategically incorporating pre- and post-intervention checkpoints, we devise a finely grained access control model that meticulously assesses both the intent of incoming business requests and the outcomes of corresponding responses. Importantly, these advancements are seamlessly integrated into the existing business codebase. Our implementation demonstrates the effectiveness of LiSEA, as it adeptly addresses eight out of the ten critical vulnerabilities enumerated in the OWASP API Security Top 10. Notably, when the number of threads is less than 200, LiSEA brings less than 20 msec of latency to the business process, which is significantly less than the microservice security agent based on the API gateway.

Keywords: LiSEA; business security; architecture; API; access control

1. Introduction

In recent years, the business landscape has witnessed a conspicuous escalation in the magnitude of financial losses attributed to Application Programming Interface (API) security breaches. Prominent corporations, including but not limited to Facebook, LinkedIn, Shopify, and Amazon, have suffered extensive instances of user and merchant data compromise, stemming from vulnerabilities within their respective APIs [1,2]. Evidently, the proliferation of business content and the ascendancy of microservice architectures have ushered in an inexorable progression. This trajectory is characterized by the escalating complexity of business applications and software platforms, accompanied by a concomitant surge in the quantity of APIs [3]. This development trend increases the attack surface, and application security becomes harder due to the fact that security is a global property, not the sum of local security defenses. In quantifiable terms, statistical analysis reveals a discernible disparity in vulnerability density. For every 100 KLOC (Kilo Lines of Code), a monolithic application, compared to its microservice counterpart, exhibits a substantially lower average of 39 vulnerabilities. In contrast, the average number of vulnerabilities surges to 180 for a microservice-based application [4].

In contrast to conventional network security paradigms, contemporary business security challenges may not solely stem from overt and malicious attacks, but can also manifest due to inadequate oversight over the service APIs intrinsic to the business ecosystem [5,6].

This assertion finds resonance in the OWASP Security API Top 10 [7], wherein deficiencies in user authentication, object authorization, and functional access control mechanisms can potentially facilitate unauthorized user encroachments into business data, devoid of explicit attack vectors or payloads [8]. Furthermore, instances of immoderate data exposure or erroneous security configurations possess the capacity to engender inadvertent leakage of sensitive information [9]. Security departments today face a multifaceted responsibility that transcends the conventional realm of safeguarding against external network-borne viruses and external attacks. A paramount challenge in this domain resides in the imperative to meticulously oversee and substantiate the congruence of business operations with meticulously crafted architectural frameworks across an extensive spectrum of intricate scenarios. This challenge is notably pronounced in contexts featuring users endowed with legitimate authority.

LiSEA represents an innovative architectural paradigm underpinned by the ZERO TRUST framework [9], aimed at securing business processes. LiSEA provides a client Software Development Kit (SDK) tailored for integration within the business system. This SDK seamlessly incorporates the business APIs and LiSEA, thereby imbuing them with inherent security considerations. Consequently, the architecture empowers precise scrutiny and adjudication of requests and responses emanating from these business APIs. The underpinning tenet of LiSEA resides in the contextual richness of security assessments, derived from the meticulous collection and transmission of intricate business contexts via the client SDK. Importantly, this security enhancement operates harmoniously alongside the underlying business system, exerting minimal disruption.

In tandem with the architectural innovation, LiSEA introduces a bespoke business security operational framework. This framework is orchestrated through a fusion of risk modeling, business modeling, and Access Control Lists (ACLs) [10,11]. This orchestrated synergy engenders an ecosystem capable of perpetuating continuous security operations, effectively combating both known and unknown business security problems. The cohesive orchestration of LiSEA's components presents a promising trajectory for elevating the resilience and robustness of business process security.

Compared to existing business security solutions such as static analysis and unit testing [12–14], automatic detection tools [15–17], authorization and authentication [4,18–22], etc., LiSEA engenders a more encompassing suite of capabilities. By holistically embracing business semantics and ensuring seamless integration within the operational landscape, LiSEA distinctively addresses the multifaceted imperatives of contemporary business security.

We have realized the implementation of LiSEA within a representative business scenario, coupled with a thoroughgoing performance assessment. The outcomes of this evaluation robustly demonstrate the efficacy of LiSEA's instantiation. Specifically, the deployment of business systems fortified by LiSEA manifests the capability to pre-emptively mitigate the eight security vulnerabilities as articulated in the OWASP API Security Top 10. Moreover, the LiSEA augmentation effectively thwarts the occurrence of erroneous requests and responses. Impressively, this heightened security paradigm is achieved with a mere marginal increase in processing overhead, introducing a minuscule latency measured in microseconds to the intricate fabric of the business process. These empirical findings substantiate the palpable advantages inherent in the deployment of LiSEA as a potent and practical mechanism for bolstering cybersecurity within the contours of diverse business landscapes.

This paper contributes significantly to the realm of business security through the following key facets:

1. **Conceptual Clarification and Architectural Innovation:** The exposition within this paper comprehensively elucidates the foundational tenets of business security that underlie our investigation. We introduce LiSEA, an innovative architectural paradigm within the domain of business security. This framework stands as a bulwark, ensuring

the accurate operation of business processes, aligned meticulously with their intended design.
2. **Introduction of Business Security Operational Mechanism**: We delve into the intricacies of the business security operational mechanism inherent to LiSEA. This mechanism emerges as a dynamic framework capable of facilitating seamless and continuous business security operations, ensuring the ongoing fortification of organizational resilience against threats related to programming errors, improper configurations, and sub-optimal business workflows.
3. **Empirical Implementation and Validation**: Our study extends beyond theoretical constructs to concretely manifest within an implementation of LiSEA. The subsequent empirical evaluation attests to the capability of LiSEA in effectively mitigating eight distinct categories of security vulnerabilities, as classified under the OWASP API Security Top 10.

These contributions collectively attest to the substantive advancement of the field, presenting LiSEA as a potent and viable approach to elevate the security architecture of business operations.

2. Related Work

In the pursuit of comprehending the originality and substantive contributions of our endeavor, this section undertakes an exploration of established methodologies and techniques within the realm of classical business security. The distinctiveness and efficacy of our proposed work are subsequently illuminated through a comparative analysis against these extant paradigms.

The application of static analysis and unit testing represents a partial mitigation strategy against security vulnerabilities that may manifest during the runtime of a business system. Mirabella et al. [12] and Martin et al. [13] proposed automated black-box testing and deep learning-based testing to solve security issues. However, the effective and concise testing is the main challenge for this solution. The lack of a test oracle, the time taken, the level of code coverage, the lack of source code and other factors severely limit the effectiveness of testing [14].

Rahaman et al. [17], Singleton et al. [16] and Philippe et al. [15] created tools to detect programming errors. These tools match programs against known error patterns, and the quality of the error database affects the effectiveness of them. Developers will not readily accept tool reports due to their concerns on the tools' capabilities, the correctness of the suggested fixes, and the exploitability of the reported issues [23].

Authorization and authentication are the most mentioned security mechanisms [4]. Following the conceptual models of applications and applying the principle of least privilege, authorization and authentication mechanisms such as OAuth 2.0 [22], OpenID Connect [21], firewalls [20], and JWT [19] are designed to specify valid accesses. This increases the complexity of implementing security in each microservice, generating a complexity both in the development and in the increase in the attack surface, since individual attention must be given to each microservice [18]. It is crucial to underscore that these mechanisms, notwithstanding their sophistication, exhibit limitations in their capacity to utilize business semantic rules during the execution of business processes.

Business application systems are characterized by the existence of sensitive information whose violation of security leads to endangering business interests. To approach the security of electronic business in a systematic way, Segura et al. [24] and Vuli et al. [25] developed a methodology for implementing security in a distributed business environment. The authors aimed to propose a methodology to be used by persons who are not from information and communication technology backgrounds. Their concern was the security development of distributed business systems and the identification of security requirements, but they failed to propose a practical business security framework.

In order to solve issues of data leakage and unauthorized data manipulation, Hai et al. [26] designed a secure cryptography-based mechanism to protect against malicious attacks. Xu et al. [27] proffered an innovative solution in the form of a microservice security agent. By integrating this agent with API gateway technology, a secure authentication mechanism was proffered. However, it cannot use business semantics as controls and has low extensibility. Nguyen et al. [28], in an analogous vein, leveraged the Spring Security Framework and OAuth2 to fortify microservice APIs underpinned by the Spring framework. However, its protective ambit predominantly addressed CSRF, XSS, and Brute Force attacks, only underscoring a partial coverage.

A number of emerging technologies are also increasingly being applied to business security. Blockchain is primarily used as a tamper-proof, secure, and permanent record of the business [29]. Demirkan et al. [30] proposed blockchain-based technology to prevent business data tampering. Yarygina et al. [31] indicated a hardware security module, with fewer privileges, no shared memory access, secure languages, and SGX technology with enclaves to prevent data leakage. Machine learning and big data have become an imperative innovation for cybersecurity [32,33]. With its capacity to figure out a huge number of records and distinguish conceivably risky ones, machine learning and big data are progressively being utilized to reveal dangers and naturally squash them before they can unleash ruin. Nevertheless, the disadvantages of these emerging technologies are high cost and immature use.

Table 1 summarizes the business security solutions discussed above. The main issues connected with existing business security solutions is that they are basic and generic and cannot be tailored to specific business scenarios. In juxtaposition to these discernible advancements, the LiSEA framework, as propounded in this paper, engenders a more encompassing suite of capabilities. By holistically embracing business semantics and ensuring seamless integration within the operational landscape, LiSEA distinctively addresses the multifaceted imperatives of contemporary business security.

Table 1. Summary of different business security solutions and their issues.

Busienss Security Solutions	Reference	Issues
Static Analysis and Unit Testing	[12–14]	Limited effectiveness and conciseness.
Automatic Detection Tools	[15–17]	The correctness and exploitability of reports are not trusted.
Authorization and Authentication	[4,18–22]	No business semantic control capability.
Business Security Methodology	[24,25]	Low practicability.
Data leakage and tampering prevention	[26–28]	High complexity and overhead.
Emerging Technologies	[29–33]	High cost and immature application.

3. Business Security

Business security transcends the scope of mere defense against network viruses or external attacks. Instead, it pertains to the intricate realm of security challenges that might remain concealed during the stages of design and development but subsequently surface during the active business operations. This encompasses a broad spectrum of vulnerabilities, encompassing technical-level susceptibilities such as programmatic bugs, as well as managerial-level vulnerabilities stemming from misconfigurations and misauthorizations. These vulnerabilities have the potential to precipitate adverse consequences, ranging from inadvertent information leakage to financial setbacks and other unfavorable outcomes. It is imperative to recognize that the domain of business security is intricately intertwined with the very fabric of the business it safeguards, thereby exuding a pronounced resonance with specific contextual scenarios. As such, it transcends the confines of mere technicality, establishing itself as a multidimensional concern that necessitates holistic consideration [34].

3.1. Typical Business Security Scenarios

Business security challenges typically come to light within distinct contextual scenarios, often materializing as situations where authorized users adhere to appropriate operational protocols yet yield undesired outcomes [35]. The ensuing discourse outlines a selection of illustrative instances exemplifying prevalent business security scenarios.

3.1.1. Programming Errors

The realm of security risks in business settings is predominantly characterized by programming errors, which can be categorized into systemic bugs and business-related bugs. Systemic bugs typically precipitate either unavailability or conspicuous operational aberrations within the application system. In contrast, business-related bugs primarily give rise to erroneous business outcomes, without necessarily impinging upon or jeopardizing the integrity of the application system itself. Consequently, the domain of business security is primarily preoccupied with addressing and mitigating business-related bugs.

To illustrate this, consider a scenario where a business identifier comprises a 32-character hexadecimal string. Should an individual, say Alice, make a request involving a business identifier entirely composed of numerical values (e.g., 9527…1234), the program may not interpret it as a string but rather process it as scientific notation ($9.527\ldots1234 \times 10^{31}$), then save it as '9' in a database. This computational misinterpretation culminates in the system, erroneously yielding all business identifiers commencing with '9' to Alice.

3.1.2. Improper Configurations

The intricacy of business structures often correlates with an augmented intertwining of user privilege configurations, potentially engendering challenges in effectively curating subject–object binding relationships. This intricacy can precipitate dual outcomes as follows: the exploitation of user privileges for business expediency, and an inadvertent overexposure of business data to extraneous users.

To illustrate the former, consider a scenario where Bob operates as Alice's subordinate. In an endeavor to facilitate interim project processing, Bob is endowed with analogous role permissions as Alice. This renders Bob with unmitigated access to the entirety of business data associated with Alice.

Similarly, an alternative case involves distinct department managers, Alice and Cindy. To effectuate the transfer of a specific business file to Alice, the supervisor opts to directly configure the dissemination to all department managers. The eventual consequence of this approach is that both Alice and Cindy receive the transmitted data.

These illustrative instances underscore the complex terrain of user privilege management within intricate business contexts, necessitating strategic mechanisms to circumvent potential instances of abuse or unintended exposure of sensitive business data.

3.1.3. Sub-Optimal Business Processes

Business operations are intricately intertwined with processes, forming an essential foundation for its functioning [36]. These processes can be likened to interlinked trees or rings, wherein each user and data component is inherently confined within specific boundaries. Deviations from this established order can lead to disarray within the business ecosystem, potentially culminating in severe consequences, including catastrophic data leaks.

For instance, consider a scenario where Alice intends to disseminate a confidential document to all members of Bob's department. Preceding the distribution process, Bob is mandated to conduct a requisite review and approval. However, if a download hot-link is generated at the onset, Bob's approval process becomes rendered ineffectual, jeopardizing the control over this confidential document. This has the potential to culminate in a loss of control over sensitive data. In instances where the process pertains to public access, the repercussions can escalate to the point of inevitable and significant data leakage. The intricacies of process management within a business context thus assume paramount significance, underlining the criticality of meticulous control mechanisms to circumvent potential disruptions or inadvertent breaches.

3.2. Challenges

Significant interdependencies exist between business security concerns and the orchestration of business activities, underscoring the imperative for a comprehensive understanding of these activities themselves. Business processes, serving as the conduits through which organizations generate value, constitute an amalgamation of discrete business activities. These activities are indivisible atomic entities, shaped by user behaviors and data flow dynamics, with their interplay facilitated through business APIs. In this intricate landscape, the focal point of business security inquiry resides in the elemental realm of business activities, with business APIs constituting the nexus of concerted endeavor [37].

The aforementioned contextual scenarios underscore a fundamental tenet as follows: business security attainment hinges upon the precise and accurate execution of pertinent business actions. This necessitates a stringent adherence to business requirements and established design principles, not only during the invocation and fulfillment of business API calls, but also across the entire spectrum of user interactions. This intricate interplay bestows a set of challenges unto business security, precipitating a cascade of pivotal research questions that this paper endeavors to address.

1. RQ.1: How can security capabilities be accessed without imparting disruptions to the native business functioning?
2. RQ.2: What methodologies can be employed to guarantee minimal authorization and curtailment of data exposure?
3. RQ.3: How can the consistent and comprehensive integration of security capabilities be ensured across all facets of business APIs access?

3.3. Solutions

The aforementioned business security scenarios are emblematic, and their origins can be attributed to inadequacies in both the design and implementation phases of business processes. To mitigate these issues, various solutions have been devised and are currently accessible.

Web Application Firewall (WAF) stands as a prevalent network security apparatus, primarily utilized to mitigate web-based attacks [38]. Its utility has expanded to encompass business API security through feature matching, policy rules, parameter validation, and compliance assessments [39]. However, it is essential to recognize that WAF fundamentally functions as a traffic and content inspector, primarily focusing on input requests and employing rudimentary pattern matching to detect potentially malicious activities [40]. Regrettably, its protective efficacy often experiences limitations in terms of precision and fails to fully address the intricate business security scenarios elucidated above.

API Gateway, characterized as a tool aimed at orchestrating API behavior [41], has historically found application within enterprises as a foundational element of public infrastructure. However, its compatibility with contemporary lightweight, swiftly responsive architectural paradigms, such as microservices, poses challenges. Within this context, the perceived unwieldiness of API Gateway can arise. Notably, discerning the totality of APIs within an enterprise presents a challenge, compounded by complexities in seamlessly integrating the API Gateway into the developmental workflow. For Data-in APIs and Data-out APIs, which are used to handle user operations and business resources, respectively, in Figure 1, API Gateway's capabilities cannot differentiate between them, while LiSEA can set different control rules for Data-in APIs and Data-out APIs. In practical implementations, the API Gateway frequently assumes the role of a centralized intake point, potentially isolating users from the core fabric of business operations [42].

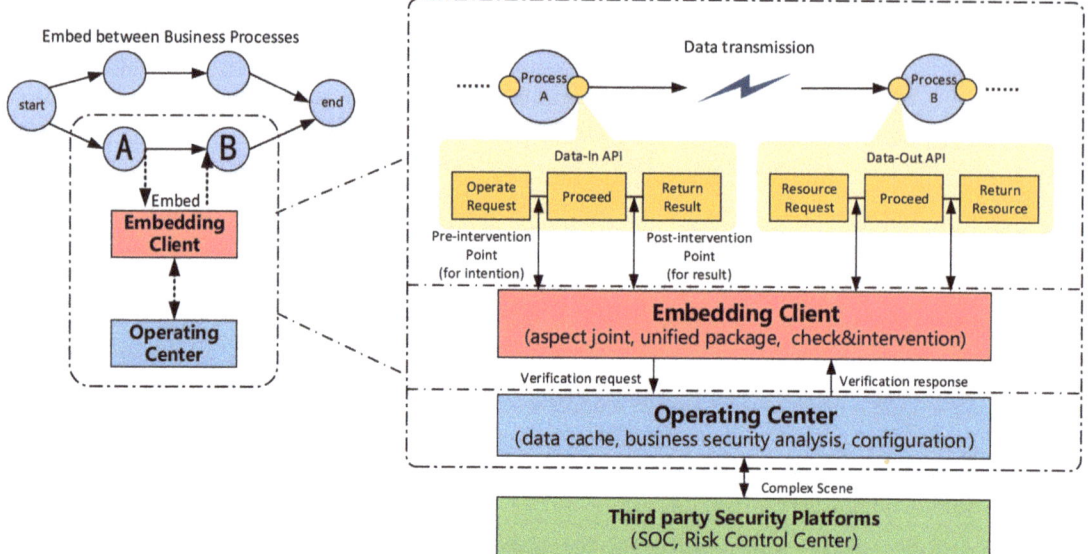

Figure 1. Overview of LiSEA.

DevSecOps, a movement that seeks to integrate contemporary security practices congruent with the DevOps methodology, underscores a paradigm shift towards proactive security implementation [7]. While the potential benefits are substantial, the practical implementation often necessitates the incorporation of developer-centric application security testing tools that seamlessly align with the accelerated practices of DevSecOps. Striking an optimal equilibrium between expeditious software delivery and robust security remains a pivotal challenge in the DevSecOps framework [43]. The pursuit of this equilibrium stands as a pivotal concern for practitioners operating within the DevSecOps realm.

4. Overview of LiSEA

LiSEA, conceived as a safeguarding framework for business processes grounded in the zero-trust paradigm, is structured upon two principal constituents—the embedding client and the operating center—as illustrated in Figure 1.

To ensure the preservation of the underlying business while demarcating business security concerns from broader application considerations, the embedding client is meticulously structured along the principles of aspect-oriented programming [44]. This design ethos enables the encapsulation of security functionalities within a coherent and cohesive package. Within the dynamics of the business process, the transmission of data between Process A and Process B transpires via API invocations. The embedding client assumes the pivotal role of infusing aspect joints into the business APIs, realizing this integration in a minimally intrusive manner. The aspect joints are dichotomized into pre- and post-intervention points, thereby harmonizing contextual insights and operational interventions during API execution. The pre-intervention point serves to validate the legitimacy of the request intention, while the post-intervention point ascertains the alignment between the response outcome and the identity of the requester.

The operating center, an indispensable facet of LiSEA, accumulates the corpus of business contextual data collated by the embedding client. This repository is judiciously harnessed to facilitate business security analysis, all of which is choreographed in consonance with configurations delineated by the security department. In essence, the operating center assumes the mantle of processing verification solicitations originating from the embedding client. Subsequent to rigorous analysis and calculated scrutiny of diverse business security scenarios, the operating center dispenses verification responses. Notably, the resultant verification records are perpetually preserved, not only serving as fodder for comprehensive business analysis and modeling but also potentially augmenting the repository of application logs.

The operational agility of the operating center is augmented through the assimilation of third-party security platform capabilities and data, including entities like security operation centers (SOC) [45] and risk control centers. By tapping into the insights of these platforms, the operating center gains a panoramic view of the security landscape, facilitating timely configuration adjustments. Additionally, it operates as an information source and a mechanism for repelling attacks discovered by these third-party security platforms.

In a holistic context, LiSEA adeptly addresses RQ.1 by ingeniously inculcating access security capabilities via the embedding client without engendering perturbations to the native business processes. This is particularly evident when the embedding client is systematically integrated with each API during the application development phase, thereby rendering all APIs discernible and amenable to operational center management. Consequently, LiSEA effectively surmounts RQ.3, ensuring comprehensive and seamless access of business APIs to security capabilities.

5. Business Security Operation Mechanism with LiSEA

In the trajectory of materializing a business architecture grounded in microservices, the business API emerges as the elemental building block of business realization. This pivotal construct is characterized as the smallest operational unit within the overarching business framework. The realm of business realization, contingent upon diverse business scales, is discernibly stratified along three distinct dimensions.

In the context of small-scale businesses, the adept orchestration of business applications driven by business APIs is deemed proficient and fitting. For medium-scale businesses, a requisite transition transpires, necessitating the creation of an encompassing business platform marked by an assemblage of distinct yet synergistic business applications. This platform serves as the linchpin for facilitating multifunctional operations. In stark contrast, large-scale enterprises assume a considerably intricate architecture, wherein the realization of a specific business domain demands concerted efforts across multiple business platforms. These platforms collectively harmonize their services to undergird the comprehensive fulfillment of the designated business sphere. This tripartite categorization delineates the strategic contours that govern the execution of business realization across various scales.

Within the context of LiSEA, the architecture's access control model is concretely instantiated through the strategic deployment of security interventions grounded in the realm of aspect-oriented programming. Depending on the requisite scope of control, distinct agents within the security joint point framework are meticulously devised, culminating in the realization of a finely calibrated and granular control mechanism, as visually elucidated in Figure 2.

Intrinsically, LiSEA recognizes that contemporary online business processes subsist within a perpetual state of vulnerability, susceptible to an array of both known and hitherto unidentified risks. To comprehensively fortify against these multifarious threats, LiSEA ingeniously amalgamates three distinct operational management mechanisms in a parallel fashion, collectively fortifying the business landscape. Risk modeling is a flexible framework with big modern data analyses based on deep learning, machine learning, and artificial intelligence to detect new, unknown risks [46]. This flexible framework leverages the prowess of modern data analysis to promptly discern novel and enigmatic risks. The proven utility of risk models, notably prevalent within diverse sectors encompassing finance, internet technologies, and power grids, underscores the ubiquity and efficacy of this approach [47]. Within LiSEA, the focus of the risk model is primarily centered on the dynamic evaluation and nuanced risk assessment of diverse business scenarios.

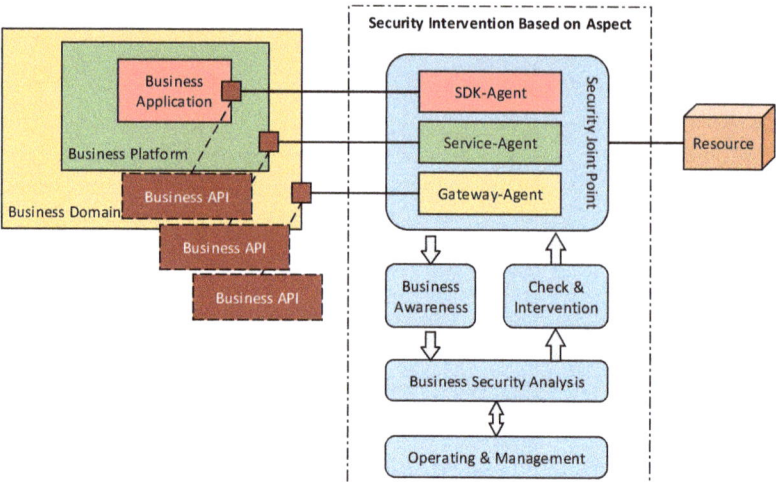

Figure 2. Multidimensional security control based on an aspect.

Business processes, serving as pivotal instruments in the value generation endeavors of organizations, are subjected to a plethora of internal and external norms and constraints [48]. The delineation of relationships and delineation of boundaries amid key business constituents such as business activities, business events, business collaborators, business resources, and data is aptly realized through meticulous business modeling. Leveraging business models, LiSEA efficaciously transmutes both the model and the stipulated security prerequisites into rigorous formal specifications, thus engendering inputs conducive for business verification.

ACLs [10,11] provide security for a private network by controlling the flow of incoming and outgoing packets. In LiSEA, the formulation of business ACLs manifest through the crafting of a sequential assemblage of rules, assiduously devised to sieve through and prohibit unauthorized access. These rules can emanate from diverse sources, ranging from threat intelligence to third-party security products, and even administrative stipulations.

LiSEA orchestrates a strategic amalgamation of three synergistic mechanisms as follows: the risk model, the business model, and ACLs. This strategic fusion acts as a robust bulwark against both familiar and novel risks, serving as a cogent response to Research Question 2 (RQ.2). In addressing unknown risks, LiSEA's API intervention points discern pertinent business contexts, subsequently underpinning a dynamic evaluation of risk by interfacing with the risk model. This process is further expedited through the constitution of a repository housing a spectrum of well-defined business scenes. This repository augments the evaluation speed of the risk assessment model. Conversely, for known risks, the efficacy of API calls is positively affirmed in congruence with the tenets stipulated within the business model. Complementing this, ACL proves instrumental in delineating forbidden API calls in line with stipulated security policies. This multidimensional assessment, premised upon risk evaluation, business validation, and rule analysis, culminates in a determination of whether an API call merits blocking, as visually explicated in Figure 3.

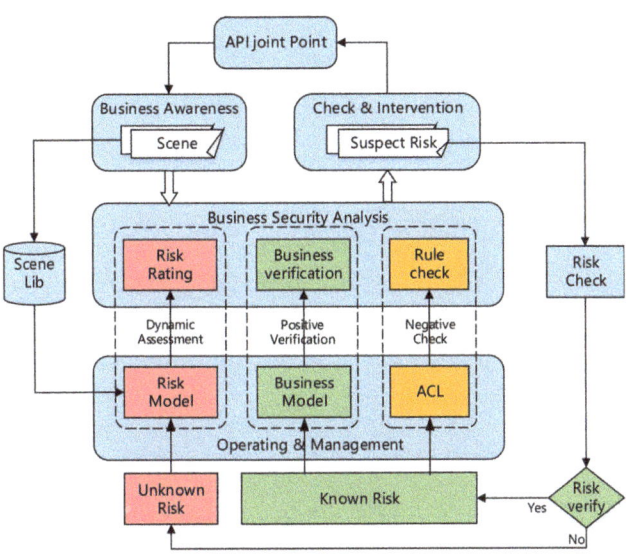

Figure 3. Business security operation mechanism with LiSEA.

Specifically, for a particular business process P, the unknown risk value $V_R(P)$ is measured by the risk model $F_R(P)$

$$V_R(P) = F_R(P) \tag{1}$$

For unknown risk warning values $W_R(P)$, calculated by setting a suitable threshold value T, the following applies:

$$W_R(P) = \begin{cases} 1, & V_R(P) \geq T \\ 0, & V_R(P) < T \end{cases} \tag{2}$$

For known risks, the business model positive determination is similar to a whitelist mechanism, and for the business policy P_B, the alert value $W_B(P)$ is calculated as follows:

$$W_B(P) = \begin{cases} 0, & P \in P_B \\ 1, & \text{otherwise} \end{cases} \tag{3}$$

For the ACL policy P_A, the alert value $W_A(P)$ is calculated as follows:

$$W_A(P) = \begin{cases} 1, & P \in P_A \\ 0, & \text{otherwise} \end{cases} \tag{4}$$

Finally, for business process P, the final security analysis result $W(P)$ was obtained by considering $W_R(P)$, $W_B(P)$, and $W_A(P)$ together.

$$W(P) = W_R(P) \bigcup W_B(P) \bigcup W_A(P) \tag{5}$$

If $W(P) = 1$, business process P is blocked. Otherwise, the execution of P is permitted.

6. Implement and Evaluation

6.1. Scene of LiSEA

LiSEA's utility manifests across three pivotal business scenarios as follows: security operations, emergency response, and business modification. Each scenario capitalizes on LiSEA's robust capabilities, engendering tangible benefits that reverberate throughout diverse operational dimensions.

6.1.1. Security Operations

In the realm of business security operations, elucidated in Figure 4, developers employ the embedding client as a conduit to establish a seamless connection between business applications and the LiSEA operating center. Leveraging the operational center's capabilities, business security experts judiciously configure protection policies congruent with prevailing security requisites, all in real-time. This adaptive configuration augments the organization's agility in safeguarding its business landscape. Simultaneously, managerial stakeholders gain real-time insights into the extent of coverage engendered by the business security fortifications. The operational center further emerges as an instrumental conduit for channeling monitoring data to third-party security platforms. This symbiotic interaction bolsters network security experts' capacity to meticulously analyze security events while also bolstering the real-time incident response capabilities of third-party security platforms.

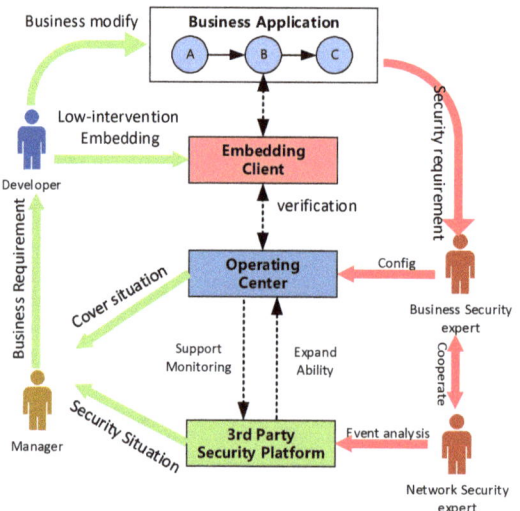

Figure 4. LiSEA used in business security operations.

6.1.2. Emergency Response

In the context of emergency response, as illustrated in Figure 5, LiSEA assumes a vanguard role in furnishing targeted security controls over discrete components, users, and data. Consider, for instance, a scenario involving a hiccup in a specific component denoted as "*a*" within a business application. In contrast to conventional approaches entailing the outright offline suspension of the entire application, LiSEA facilitates the configuration of rules within the operating center. These rules are adeptly designed to selectively block APIs associated with module "*a*", thereby circumventing any deleterious impact on the operational integrity of other application components. The versatility of LiSEA's response extends to encompass problematic individuals or data, which can be adeptly addressed through the establishment of targeted rules, obviating the need for the broad-based suspension of accounts or data deletion.

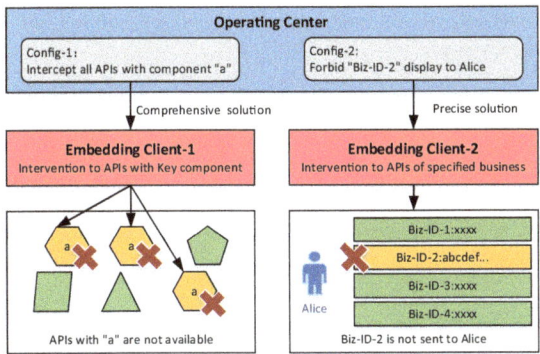

Figure 5. LiSEA used in an emergency response.

6.1.3. Business Modification

LiSEA effectively streamlines the process of business modifications. It expedites rule-based configuration via its dynamic operating center, obviating the exigency to await the cumbersome cycle of application redevelopment to facilitate live implementation. Illustrated in Figure 6, this expedient maneuver ensures that business modifications are promptly actualized without undue latency. To illustrate, envision a scenario where Cindy, entrusted with the oversight of process C, is temporarily absent on business engagements. In response, a judiciously crafted rule can be seamlessly enacted within LiSEA's operating center, effectively forestalling the assignment of process C to Cindy during her absence.

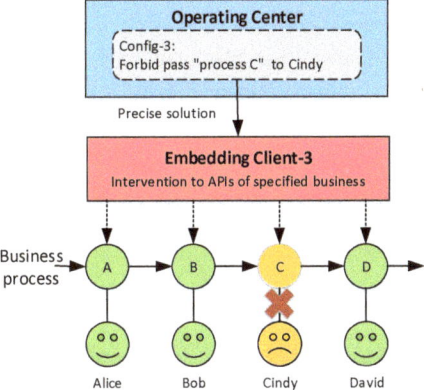

Figure 6. LiSEA used in business modifications.

6.2. LiSEA's Protective Efficacy against the OWASP API Security Top 10

6.2.1. Coverage

The OWASP API Security Top 10 2019 list of the ten most critical API security risk methodologies was used to investigate the potential threats and risks. By instituting a set of rules at both pre- and post-intervention points, LiSEA demonstrates a robust capability in mitigating eight out of the top ten risks, as delineated in Table 2.

There are business security risks with API 7 and API 9 that cannot be covered by LiSEA. For API 7, security misconfiguration is commonly a result of unsecure default configurations, incomplete or ad hoc configurations, etc. These misconfigurations may exist in the API, transport protocol, or application infrastructure. LiSEA can only control APIs and therefore cannot cover API 7. For API 9, improper Asset Management is often caused by issues such as deprecated API versions and exposed debug endpoints. These endpoints are usually overlooked by developers and obtain access to LiSEA, and thus API 9 is not covered.

Table 2. Coverage for the OWASP API Security Top 10.

API Security Top 10 2019	Prevent by LiSEA	How
API1:2019 Broken Object Level Authorization	TRUE	Introducing a post-intervention point for verifying the relationship alignment between the access subject and the designated object.
API2:2019 Broken User Authentication	TRUE	Implementing a pre-intervention point validation mechanism for corroborating attributes such as login device and network environment.
API3:2019 Excessive Data Exposure	TRUE	Instituting attribute scrutiny for returned resources via the post-intervention point.
API4:2019 Lack of Resources and Rate Limiting	TRUE	Establishing pre-intervention point limitations on access frequency and resource solicitation.
API5:2019 Broken Function Level Authorization	TRUE	Conducing a pre-intervention point scrutiny of the interplay between the access subject and the corresponding API function.
API6:2019 Mass Assignment	TRUE	Effecting a pre-intervention point validation of attributes affiliated with client-submitted objects.
API7:2019 Security Misconfiguration	FALSE	
API8:2019 Injection	TRUE	Introducing an injected feature evaluation at the pre-intervention juncture, coupled with subsequent relationship assessment between the access subject and object at the post-intervention point.
API9:2019 Improper Assets Management	FALSE	
API10:2019 Insufficient Logging and Monitoring	TRUE	Enabling comprehensive monitoring through the systematic logging of each business process and API invocation within LiSEA's framework, thus fortifying the surveillance and oversight apparatus.

6.2.2. Latency Impact on the Original Business System

When interfacing with LiSEA, business systems possess the flexibility to opt for the inclusion of protection policies solely at the pre-intervention point, exclusively at the post-intervention point, or at both the pre- and post-intervention points. To holistically gauge the quantitative impact of LiSEA on the latency dynamics inherent within the original business system, a series of three comprehensive experiments were meticulously orchestrated.

In these experiments, the testbed encapsulating the business system and LiSEA is meticulously instantiated across distinct CentOS virtual machines. Each virtual machine is configured with a 4-core CPU, 8 GB of RAM, and a capacious 200 GB disk allocation. The test business system, engineered within the Java programming paradigm, deliberately incorporates vulnerabilities culled from the OWASP API Security Top 10. The experimentation framework simulates user interactions with the system, thereby emulating thread counts ranging from 100 to 600, with a discrete step increment of 100. The orchestrated orchestration further dictates a ramp-up period of 1 s and a comprehensive iteration cycle amounting to 1000 iterations. For the benchmark, we chose the average time of round trip time for obtaining a token based on the getToken API in [27], where a microservice security agent with the API gateway technology for presenting a secure authentication mechanism was used.

In light of the insights gleaned from Figure 7a–c, it emerges unequivocally that the escalation in thread count begets a marginal increase in access latency to LiSEA. Remarkably, this augmented latency remains confined within the realm of a mere few tens of microseconds, or even diminishing to a few microseconds, when juxtaposed against the backdrop of the original business system. Importantly, the discernible trajectory of latency overhead incurred by LiSEA exhibits a consonance with that of the original business system. Crucially, this augmentation in latency fails to ascend to a threshold that could potentially jeopardize the user experience. Moreover, from the observations illustrated in Figure 7d, it becomes apparent that the latency attributed to exclusive access of either the pre-intervention control point or the post-intervention point demonstrates a remarkable similarity. However, a notable surge in latency emerges when both pre- and post-intervention points are simultaneously accessed. This discernible latency increase underscores the significant contribution of network transmission within the overall latency framework. This finding further underscores the potential for latency reduction through the strategic co-deployment of LiSEA alongside the business system.

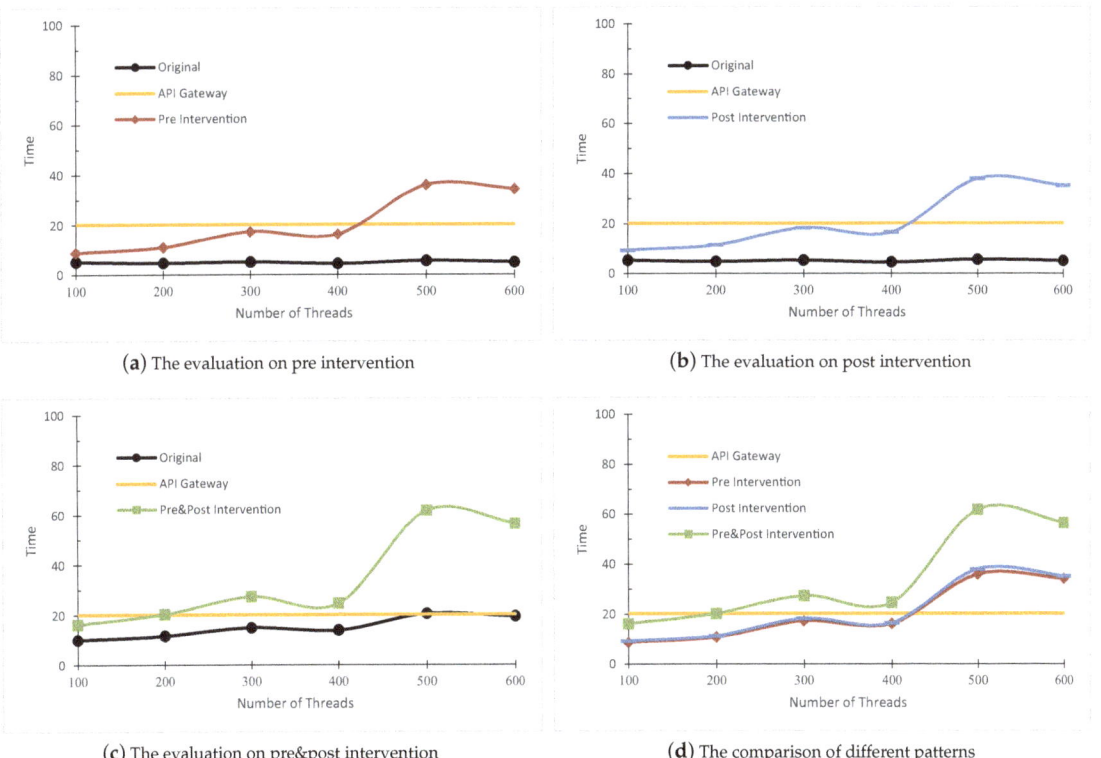

Figure 7. The evaluation on different patterns with LiSEA.

In light of benchmark comparison, a salient pattern emerges. Specifically, with a thread count of 200, the latency attributed to simultaneous access of both pre- and post-intervention points approximates the latency benchmark. It is pertinent to note that the benchmark performance is derived from a singular thread count of 1. This juxtaposition underscores the remarkable superiority of our proposed LiSEA framework in contrast to the performance exhibited by authentication mechanisms rooted in the API gateway paradigm.

7. Analysis

In the realm of business security enhancement, the LiSEA framework, as articulated within this paper, encapsulates a spectrum of notable attributes as follows:

1. Inherently Geared Towards Business-Centric Security: LiSEA is intrinsically tailored to the exigencies of business scenarios, engendering a more congruent alignment with the semantic intricacies inherent to business operations. This focus safeguards against undue semantic distortion, fostering a harmonious fusion of security and business imperatives.
2. Precision-Driven Intervention Points via APIs: The architectural underpinning of LiSEA enables the establishment of discerningly positioned intervention points through APIs, thereby furnishing an elevated degree of control granularity. This fine-tuned control mechanism augments the efficacy of security measures, ensuring a judicious allocation of security resources.
3. Multifaceted SDK for Development Streamlining: LiSEA capitalizes on a multifaceted Software Development Kit (SDK), which effectively mitigates the developmental overhead. This adaptive SDK harmoniously bridges the divide between business demands and security considerations, thereby obviating undue developmental burdens.
4. Real-Time Conduit for Proactive Illicit Access Interception: An inherent attribute of LiSEA is the real-time interception of illicit access attempts. This proactive mechanism acts as a sentinel, promptly detecting and curtailing unauthorized access endeavors, thereby precluding their escalation into potential breaches.

It is, however, imperative to underscore certain limitations inherent to this architectural paradigm. A symbiotic collaboration between application developers and security stakeholders is requisite, necessitating a cohesive alliance to optimize the synergy between LiSEA's capabilities and the broader operational landscape. Moreover, the comprehensive integration of all business interfaces with LiSEA poses a noteworthy challenge, requiring meticulous orchestration and coordination.

When harnessing the LiSEA framework to extend security capabilities, an array of strategic modalities emerges. Business models and ACLs are instrumental in affording precise control over well-acknowledged risks. Concurrently, the realm of uncharted risks is effectively addressed through dynamic risk models, which proactively evaluate and judge emerging security threats, thereby fortifying the resilience of business operations.

8. Conclusions

This paper introduces a novel paradigm termed LiSEA, which empowers applications to fortify business processes through the strategic intervention of business APIs. By strategically embedding pre- and post-intervention points, we established a granular and discriminating access control model, thereby facilitating scrutiny of both the intent of incoming requests and the outcomes of subsequent responses, all the while minimizing disruption to the existing business codebase. Our practical implementation substantiates the efficacy of LiSEA by effectively addressing eight out of the top ten OWASP-API vulnerabilities. Notably, the incremental processing latency introduced by LiSEA into the business process remains confined to the realm of microseconds, thereby further affirming its efficacy. However, LiSEA may have incompatibility problems with different development frameworks, and APIs' access to LiSEA requires the cooperation of developers. In order to overcome the above limitations, non-intervention business security frameworks will be researched in future work.

Author Contributions: Conceptualization, H.L., J.L. and M.Y.; methodology, H.L. and J.L.; writing—original draft preparation, H.L., C.Z. and Y.W.; writing—review and editing, H.L., C.Z. and Y.W.; supervision, M.Y. and J.L. All authors have read and agreed to the published version of the manuscript.

Funding: This research was funded by the National Key Research and Development Program of China grant 2021YFB3302105.

Institutional Review Board Statement: Not applicable.

Informed Consent Statement: Not applicable.

Data Availability Statement: The data presented in this study are available on request from the corresponding author.

Conflicts of Interest: The authors declare no conflicts of interest.

References

1. OWASP. OWASP API Security Top 10 2019. Available online: https://owasp.org/API-Security/editions/2019/en/0x11-t10 (accessed on 30 May 2022).
2. Idris, M.; Syarif, I.; Winarno, I. Development of vulnerable web application based on owasp api security risks. In Proceedings of the 2021 International Electronics Symposium (IES), Toronto, ON, Canada, 13–16 October 2021; pp. 190–194.
3. Hussain, F.; Hussain, R.; Noye, B.; Sharieh, S. Enterprise API security and GDPR compliance: Design and implementation perspective. *IT Prof.* **2020**, *22*, 81–89. [CrossRef]
4. Pereira-Vale, A.; Fernandez, E.B.; Monge, R.; Astudillo, H.; Márquez, G. Security in microservice-based systems: A multivocal literature review. *Comput. Secur.* **2021**, *103*, 102200. [CrossRef]
5. Mukherjee, P.; Mazumdar, C. "Security Concern" as a Metric for Enterprise Business Processes. *IEEE Syst. J.* **2019**, *13*, 4015–4026. [CrossRef]
6. Onyema, E.; Edeh, C.; Gregory, U.; Edmond, V.; Charles, A.; Richard-Nnabu, N. Cybersecurity awareness among undergraduate students in Enugu Nigeria. *Int. J. Inform. Sec. Priv. Digit. Forensic.* **2021**, *5*, 34–42.
7. Neil MacDonald, I.H. DevSecOps: How to Seamlessly Integrate Security into DevOps. Available online: https://www.gartner.com/en/documents/3463417 (accessed on 17 February 2023).
8. Díaz-Rojas, J.A.; Ocharán-Hernández, J.O.; Pérez-Arriaga, J.C.; Limón, X. Web api security vulnerabilities and mitigation mechanisms: A systematic mapping study. In Proceedings of the 2021 9th International Conference in Software Engineering Research and Innovation (CONISOFT), San Diego, CA, USA, 21–25 October 2021; pp. 207–218.
9. Gorski, P.L.; M'oller, S.; Wiefling, S.; Iacono, L.L. "I just looked for the solution!" On Integrating Security-Relevant Information in Non-Security API Documentation to Support Secure Coding Practices. *IEEE Trans. Softw. Eng.* **2021**, *48*, 3467–3484. [CrossRef]
10. Liu, A.X.; Torng, E.; Meiners, C.R. Compressing network access control lists. *IEEE Trans. Parallel Distrib. Syst.* **2011**, *22*, 1969–1977. [CrossRef]
11. Ramprasath, J.; Seethalakshmi, V. Mitigation of malicious flooding in software defined networks using dynamic access control list. *Wirel. Pers. Commun.* **2021**, *121*, 107–125. [CrossRef]
12. Mirabella, A.G.; Martin-Lopez, A.; Segura, S.; Valencia-Cabrera, L.; Ruiz-Cortés, A. Deep learning-based prediction of test input validity for restful apis. In Proceedings of the 2021 IEEE/ACM Third International Workshop on Deep Learning for Testing and Testing for Deep Learning (DeepTest), Madrid, Spain, 1 June 2021; pp. 9–16.
13. Martin-Lopez, A.; Segura, S.; Ruiz-Cortés, A. RESTest: Automated black-box testing of RESTful web APIs. In Proceedings of the 30th ACM SIGSOFT International Symposium on Software Testing and Analysis, Virtual Event, 11–17 July 2021; pp. 682–685.
14. Ehsan, A.; Abuhaliqa, M.A.M.; Catal, C.; Mishra, D. RESTful API testing methodologies: Rationale, challenges, and solution directions. *Appl. Sci.* **2022**, *12*, 4369. [CrossRef]
15. Arteau, P. Find Security Bugs. Available online: https://find-sec-bugs.github.io (accessed on 9 June 2023).
16. Singleton, L.; Zhao, R.; Song, M.; Siy, H. Cryptotutor: Teaching secure coding practices through misuse pattern detection. In Proceedings of the 21st Annual Conference on Information Technology Education, Virtual Event, 7–9 October 2020; pp. 403–408.
17. Rahaman, S.; Xiao, Y.; Afrose, S.; Shaon, F.; Tian, K.; Frantz, M.; Kantarcioglu, M.; Yao, D. Cryptoguard: High precision detection of cryptographic vulnerabilities in massive-sized java projects. In Proceedings of the 2019 ACM SIGSAC Conference on Computer and Communications Security, London, UK, 11–15 November 2019; pp. 2455–2472.
18. De Almeida, M.G.; Canedo, E.D. Authentication and authorization in microservices architecture: A systematic literature review. *Appl. Sci.* **2022**, *12*, 3023. [CrossRef]
19. Nkomo, P.; Coetzee, M. Software development activities for secure microservices. In Proceedings of the Computational Science and Its Applications–ICCSA 2019: 19th International Conference, Saint Petersburg, Russia, 1–4 July 2019; Proceedings, Part V 19; Springer: Berlin/Heidelberg, Germany, 2019; pp. 573–585.
20. Pahl, M.O.; Aubet, F.X.; Liebald, S. Graph-based IoT microservice security. In Proceedings of the NOMS 2018-2018 IEEE/IFIP Network Operations and Management Symposium, Taipei, Taiwan, 23–27 May 2018; pp. 1–3.

21. Bánáti, A.; Kail, E.; Karóczkai, K.; Kozlovszky, M. Authentication and authorization orchestrator for microservice-based software architectures. In Proceedings of the 2018 41st International Convention on Information and Communication Technology, Electronics and Microelectronics (MIPRO), Opatija, Croatia, 21–25 May 2018; pp. 1180–1184.
22. Nehme, A.; Jesus, V.; Mahbub, K.; Abdallah, A. Fine-grained access control for microservices. In Proceedings of the Foundations and Practice of Security: 11th International Symposium, FPS 2018, Montreal, QC, Canada, 13–15 November 2018; Revised Selected Papers 11; Springer: Berlin/Heidelberg, Germany, 2019; pp. 285–300.
23. Zhang, Y.; Kabir, M.M.A.; Xiao, Y.; Yao, D.; Meng, N. Automatic Detection of Java Cryptographic API Misuses: Are We There Yet? *IEEE Trans. Softw. Eng.* **2022**, *49*, 288–303. [CrossRef]
24. Segura, S.; Parejo, J.A.; Troya, J.; Ruiz-Cortés, A. Metamorphic testing of RESTful web APIs. In Proceedings of the 40th International Conference on Software Engineering, Gothenburg, Sweden, 27 May–3 June 2018; pp. 882–882.
25. Vulić, I.; Prodanović, R.; Tot, I. An Example of a Methodology for Developing the Security of a Distributed Business System. In Proceedings of the 5th IPMA SENET Project Management Conference (SENET 2019), Belgrade, Serbia, 19–21 May 2019; pp. 209–216.
26. Hai, T.; Zhou, J.; Lu, Y.; Jawawi, D.; Wang, D.; Onyema, E.M.; Biamba, C. Enhanced security using multiple paths routine scheme in cloud-MANETs. *J. Cloud Comput.* **2023**, *12*, 68. [CrossRef]
27. Xu, R.; Jin, W.; Kim, D. Microservice security agent based on API gateway in edge computing. *Sensors* **2019**, *19*, 4905. [CrossRef] [PubMed]
28. Nguyen, Q.; Baker, O.F. Applying Spring Security Framework and OAuth2 To Protect Microservice Architecture API. *J. Softw.* **2019**, *14*, 257–264. [CrossRef]
29. Li, X.; Jiang, P.; Chen, T.; Luo, X.; Wen, Q. A survey on the security of blockchain systems. *Future Gener. Comput. Syst.* **2020**, *107*, 841–853. [CrossRef]
30. Demirkan, S.; Demirkan, I.; McKee, A. Blockchain technology in the future of business cyber security and accounting. *J. Manag. Anal.* **2020**, *7*, 189–208. [CrossRef]
31. Yarygina, T.; Otterstad, C. A game of microservices: Automated intrusion response. In Proceedings of the Distributed Applications and Interoperable Systems: 18th IFIP WG 6.1 International Conference, DAIS 2018, Held as Part of the 13th International Federated Conference on Distributed Computing Techniques, DisCoTec 2018, Madrid, Spain, 18–21 June 2018; Proceedings 18; Springer: Berlin/Heidelberg, Germany, 2018; pp. 169–177.
32. Ogbuke, N.J.; Yusuf, Y.Y.; Dharma, K.; Mercangoz, B.A. Big data supply chain analytics: Ethical, privacy and security challenges posed to business, industries and society. *Prod. Plan. Control.* **2022**, *33*, 123–137. [CrossRef]
33. Gupta, A.; Gupta, R.; Kukreja, G. Cyber security using machine learning: Techniques and business applications. *Appl. Artif. Intell. Business Educ. Healthc.* **2021**, *2021*, 385–406.
34. IEEE Std 2813-2020; IEEE Standard for Big Data Business Security Risk Assessment. IEEE: Piscataway, NJ, USA, 2021.
35. Mendoza, A.; Gu, G. Mobile application web api reconnaissance: Web-to-mobile inconsistencies & vulnerabilities. In Proceedings of the 2018 IEEE Symposium on Security and Privacy (SP), San Francisco, CA, USA, 21–23 May 2018; pp. 756–769.
36. Yin, J.; Luo, Z.; Li, Y.; Wu, Z. Service pattern: An integrated business process model for modern service industry. *IEEE Trans. Serv. Comput.* **2016**, *10*, 841–853. [CrossRef]
37. Farah, A.; Saida, B.; Mourad, O.C. On the security of business processes: Classification of approaches, comparison, and research directions. In Proceedings of the 2021 International Conference on Networking and Advanced Systems (ICNAS), Annaba, Algeria, 27–28 October 2021; pp. 1–8.
38. Desmet, L.; Piessens, F.; Joosen, W.; Verbaeten, P. Bridging the gap between web application firewalls and web applications. In Proceedings of the Fourth ACM Workshop on Formal Methods in Security, Alexandria, VA, USA, 3 November 2006; pp. 67–77.
39. Appelt, D.; Nguyen, C.D.; Panichella, A.; Briand, L.C. A machine-learning-driven evolutionary approach for testing web application firewalls. *IEEE Trans. Reliab.* **2018**, *67*, 733–757. [CrossRef]
40. Seth, A. *Comparing Effectiveness and Efficiency of Interactive Application Security Testing (IAST) and Runtime Application Self-Protection (RASP) Tools*; North Carolina State University: Raleigh, NC, USA, 2022.
41. Montesi, F.; Weber, J. Circuit breakers, discovery, and API gateways in microservices. *arXiv* **2016**, arXiv:1609.05830.
42. Song, M.; Zhang, C.; Haihong, E. An auto scaling system for API gateway based on Kubernetes. In Proceedings of the 2018 IEEE 9th International Conference on Software Engineering and Service Science (ICSESS), Beijing, China, 23–25 October 2018; pp. 109–112.
43. Rajapakse, R.N.; Zahedi, M.; Babar, M.A.; Shen, H. Challenges and solutions when adopting DevSecOps: A systematic review. *Inf. Softw. Technol.* **2022**, *141*, 106700. [CrossRef]
44. Kiczales, G.; Lamping, J.; Mendhekar, A.; Maeda, C.; Lopes, C.; Loingtier, J.M.; Irwin, J. Aspect-oriented programming. In Proceedings of the ECOOP'97—Object-Oriented Programming: 11th European Conference, Jyvaskyla, Finland, 9–13 June 1997; pp. 220–242.
45. Vielberth, M.; Bohm, F.; Fichtinger, I.; Pernul, G. Security operations center: A systematic study and open challenges. *IEEE Access* **2020**, *8*, 227756–227779. [CrossRef]
46. Chehri, A.; Fofana, I.; Yang, X. Security risk modeling in smart grid critical infrastructures in the era of big data and artificial intelligence. *Sustainability* **2021**, *13*, 3196. [CrossRef]

47. Zhang, P. An interval mean–average absolute deviation model for multiperiod portfolio selection with risk control and cardinality constraints. *Soft Comput.* **2016**, *20*, 1203–1212. [CrossRef]
48. Karimi, L.; Aldairi, M.; Joshi, J.; Abdelhakim, M. An automatic attribute-based access control policy extraction from access logs. *IEEE Trans. Dependable Secur. Comput.* **2021**, *19*, 2304–2317. [CrossRef]

Disclaimer/Publisher's Note: The statements, opinions and data contained in all publications are solely those of the individual author(s) and contributor(s) and not of MDPI and/or the editor(s). MDPI and/or the editor(s) disclaim responsibility for any injury to people or property resulting from any ideas, methods, instructions or products referred to in the content.

Article

AccFlow: Defending against the Low-Rate TCP DoS Attack in Drones

Yuan Cao [1], Haotian Li [1], Lijuan Han [1], Xiaojin Zhao [2], Xiaofang Pan [3] and Enyi Yao [4],*

[1] The College of Information Science and Engineering, Hohai University, Changzhou 213022, China; caoyuan0908@gmail.com (Y.C.); 1862510127@hhu.edu.cn (H.L.); hlj20192611@gmail.com (L.H.)
[2] The College of Electronic Science and Technology, Shenzhen University, Shenzhen 518060, China; eexjzhao@szu.edu.cn
[3] The College of Information Engineering, Shenzhen University, Shenzhen 518060, China; eexpan@szu.edu.cn
[4] School of Microelectronics, South China University of Technology, Guangzhou 511442, China
* Correspondence: yaoenyi@scut.edu.cn

Abstract: As drones are widely employed in various industries and daily life, concerns regarding their safety have been gradually emerging. Denial of service (DoS) attacks have become one of the most significant threats to the stability of resource-constrained sensor nodes. Traditional brute-force and high-rate distributed denial of service (DDoS) attacks are easily detectable and mitigated. However, low-rate TCP DoS attacks can considerably impair TCP throughput and evade DoS prevention systems by inconspicuously consuming a small portion of network capacity, and whereas the literature offers effective defense mechanisms against DDoS attacks, there is a gap in defending against Low-Rate TCP DoS attacks. In this paper, we introduce AccFlow, an incrementally deployable Software-Defined Networking (SDN)-based protocol designed to counter low-rate TCP DoS attacks. The main idea of AccFlow is to make the attacking flows *accountable* for the congestion by dropping their packets according to their loss rates. AccFlow drops their packets more aggressively as the loss rates increase. Through extensive simulations, we illustrate that AccFlow can effectively safeguard against low-rate TCP DoS attacks, even when attackers employ varying strategies involving different scales and data rates. Furthermore, whereas AccFlow primarily addresses low-rate TCP DoS attacks, our research reveals its effectiveness in defending against general DoS attacks. These general attacks do not rely on the TCP retransmission timeout mechanism but rather deplete network resources, ultimately resulting in a denial of service for legitimate users. Additionally, we delve into the scalability of AccFlow and its viability for practical deployment in real-world networks. Finally, we demonstrate the effectiveness of AccFlow in safeguarding network resources.

Keywords: drones security; DoS attack; Software-Defined Networking

1. Introduction

Drones or Unmanned Aerial Systems (UAS) are unmanned aerial vehicles operated by radio remote control devices [1]. Due to their high degree of flexibility and adaptability, UAS are widely used in both military and civilian applications. However, a number of security concerns have arisen [2,3] pertaining to the confidentiality, integrity, and availability of drones. One emerging threat is the "Low-rate TCP DoS Attack". In this type of attack, assailants exploit the TCP retransmission timeout mechanism [4]. To launch such an attack, the attackers set up periodic on–off "square-wave" traffic patterns with a peak transmission rate that is significant enough to exhaust the network bandwidth. When subjected to this attack, legitimate TCP flows experience severe packet losses, resulting in retransmission timeouts. If the period of the attacking flow coincides with the retransmission timeouts, the legitimate TCP flows encounter another peak as they attempt to recover from these timeouts, leading to further packet losses and longer retransmission timeouts. This cycle continues, ultimately throttling the legitimate TCP flows to nearly zero throughput.

Citation: Cao, Y.; Li, H.; Han, L.; Zhao, X.; Pan, X.; Yao, E. AccFlow: Defending against the Low-Rate TCP DoS Attack in Drones. *Appl. Sci.* **2023**, *13*, 11749. https://doi.org/10.3390/app132111749

Academic Editors: Lip Yee Por and Abdullah Ayub Khan

Received: 14 September 2023
Revised: 24 October 2023
Accepted: 24 October 2023
Published: 27 October 2023

Copyright: © 2023 by the authors. Licensee MDPI, Basel, Switzerland. This article is an open access article distributed under the terms and conditions of the Creative Commons Attribution (CC BY) license (https://creativecommons.org/licenses/by/4.0/).

Compared to general DoS attacks in which malicious users cause a denial of service by sending continuous high-rate flows, rather than relying on the TCP retransmission timeout mechanism, the time-averaged bandwidth usage of the low-rate TCP DoS attacking flow is small. In some cases, it can even be much less than the total available bandwidth. This is why we refer to such an attack as the *low-rate* TCP DoS attack.

Another noteworthy characteristic of the low-rate TCP DoS attacking flow is its periodic traffic pattern, which bears a resemblance to legitimate TCP periodic traffic, such as video traffic adopting the DASH (Dynamic Adaptive Streaming over HTTP) [5] standard. Despite the apparent similarity in traffic patterns, a fundamental distinction exists between benign TCP periodic flows and the low-rate TCP DoS attacking flow.

The key difference lies in how they respond to the packet loss. Legitimate TCP flows follow a protocol that involves backing off and entering retransmission timeout when their packets are lost. In contrast, the low-rate TCP DoS attacking flow does not exhibit this behavior.

Although the low-rate TCP DoS attack has been proposed for nearly ten years, it has not been fully addressed. Sun et al. [6] use signal processing (autocorrelation of the traffic) to detect the periodic burst attack at the congested router. Whenever attacks have been detected, the router traces back to its upstream routers to find the attack source. Such a solution may not work if the congested router has multiple upstream routers so that the bursty traffic it detects consists of the aggregate traffic from these upstream routers. Therefore, it is possible that the upstream routers cannot detect the bursty attacking traffic, which disrupts or halts the tracing back process. The work by Chang et al. [7] addresses this problem by assigning high priorities to the packets that are destined for high loss rate TCP application ports. However, such a defense mechanism can be breached if the attackers send large volumes of traffic to a specific protected port to cause a high loss rate at this port. Consequently, the attackers' traffic will be marked as high-priority traffic. Wang et al. [8] propose a defense method based on sFlow and an improved Self-Organizing Map (SOM) model in Software-Defined Networking (SDN). This approach defines a metric to differentiate between genuine normal traffic and large-scale attack traffic, allowing for the issuance of drop or rate-limiting rules near the source of the attack. However, when two types of traffic are very similar, stricter restrictions may affect the experiences of normal users. Bhuyam et al. [9] proposed a mechanism based on correlation coefficients to detect low-rate and high-rate DDoS attacks. Partial rank correlation is used to detect low-rate attacks. However, this mechanism may not be effective when only one macro traffic attacks the network. Ruchi Vishwakarma et al. [10] present a honeypot-based approach that can be taken as a productive outset towards combatting Zero-Day DDoS Attacks to analyze ways to prevent SSH and Telnet Protocol Attacks [11]. Tang [12] proposed a detection method to identify LDOS attacks at the transport layer and used data mining technology to analyze network anomalies under LDOS attacks to complete the detection. Furthermore, because all of the aforementioned solutions target solely the ideal low-rate TCP DoS attack, one alternative strategy for attackers to circumvent the defense could be splitting their traffic into multiple attacking flows to trigger distributed DoS attacks. Additionally, they do not illustrate how their defending protocols will impact the benign periodic flows, such as the aforementioned video traffic. In this paper, we introduce an Accountable Flow (AccFlow) protocol to offer effective defense against low-rate TCP DoS attacks. AccFlow has been developed to offer effective defense against low-rate TCP DoS attacks while ensuring that there is no performance degradation for legitimate periodic flows. Additionally, AccFlow offers robust protection against general DoS or DDoS attacks.

In contrast to previous literature, our approach to designing AccFlow distinguishes itself by integrating the principles of Software-Defined Networking (SDN) [13] and emphasizing flow accountability. Within the SDN architecture, decisions concerning packet routing and forwarding are centralized, distinguishing it from conventional networking approaches. This centralized approach empowers explicit execution of distinct policies for various flows, thereby offering flexibility and innovation in network configuration.

For instance, one notable advantage of this centralized architecture is that it empowers network operators to effectively manage traffic, resulting in the creation of low-latency and congestion-free networks. This is particularly advantageous in data center environments [14,15]. Although originally not designed to address security issues in computer networking, the concept of SDN, a network architecture that centralizes control and offers innovative avenues for reevaluating and mitigating such challenges [16]. Notably, the centralized network architecture enables the controller to perform real-time traffic monitoring and analysis. When attacking flows are identified, the controller can promptly block them, preserving network resources for legitimate flows. This ability to quickly respond to threats and prioritize legitimate traffic is one of the key advantages of SDN-based defense techniques. These techniques offer immediate benefits to the deployed routers or Autonomous Systems (ASes) since they do not necessitate reconfiguration in other parts of the network. Despite these advantages, flow-based security protocols must be scalable to effectively handle a large volume of attacking flows, particularly when considering deployment in Wide Area Networks (WANs). In this paper, we propose to use flow aggregation (we use source IP address-based flow aggregation; the detailed explanation is in Sections 4.1 and 5.2) and virtual centralized controller (the concept of virtual centralized controller is that we use multiple coordinated processors to serve as the centralized controller; the details are in Section 4.2). to solve the scalability problem so that our protocol can be deployed in both Local Area Networks (LANs) and WANs.

The reason why the low-rate TCP DoS attack and other kinds of DoS attacks work well is that whenever a congestion happens, the router drops the packets from all flows regardless of who causes the congestion. In other words, *accountability* for the congestion is not considered for packets dropping [17]. As a result, even legitimate TCP flows that diligently adhere to the congestion avoidance protocol and transmit at reasonable rates are erroneously affected by congestion. This congestion is primarily caused by attacking flows that flood the network with large volumes of traffic, depleting available bandwidth. Therefore, in order to effectively combat DoS attacks, AccFlow considers congestion accountability when implementing packet drops. To be precise, the more accountable flows are to contribute to the congestion, the more assertively AccFlow drops their packets. We establish a connection between each flow's accountability for congestion and its loss rate. Essentially, the higher the loss rate, the greater the flow's accountability to cause congestion. This connection is rooted in the behavior of attacking flows, which consistently exhibit high loss rates due to their higher accountability for congestion. They do so because they must continually send an excessive number of packets to overwhelm the network. In contrast, legitimate TCP flows, with their lower accountability for congestion, rarely experience consistently high loss rates. Instead, they adapt by reducing their transmission rates and may even enter timeouts when their packets are dropped. As a result, there is a positive correlation between a flow's loss rate and its accountability for causing congestion. AccFlow safeguards the network by prioritizing the dropping of packets from flows with higher loss rates and corresponding higher probabilities. Conversely, packets from flows with lower loss rates are dropped with lower probabilities.

Through extensive simulations using ns-3 [18], we illustrate that AccFlow proves effective in defending against both the low-rate TCP DoS attack and general DoS attacks. In summary, this paper makes the following contributions.

- AccFlow is the first SDN-based security protocol that considers flow accountability when defending against DoS or DDoS attacks.
- We demonstrate that AccFlow, which does not cause any performance degradation to benign flows, can effectively defend against both the low-rate TCP DoS attack and general DoS attacks even if attackers are able to vary their strategies.
- We use flow aggregation and virtual centralized controller to solve the scalability problem of AccFlow and make it deployable in real networks.

The rest of the paper is organized as follows. In Section 2, we give a brief introduction to the low-rate TCP DoS attack. In Section 3, we elaborate on the AccFlow protocol. In

Section 4, we consider the deployment of AccFlow in real networks and its interaction with other security protocols. In Section 5, we thoroughly study the effectiveness of AccFlow in different simulation settings. Finally, we conclude in Section 6.

2. Low-Rate TCP DoS Attack

In this section, we provide a brief overview of the low-rate TCP DoS attack and its effectiveness in causing denial of service to legitimate TCP flows. The characteristics of an ideal low-rate TCP DoS attacking flow can be represented by a triple $\{R, P, D\}$, where R indicates the peak data rate, P indicates the attacking period and D indicates the burst duration within one period, as illustrated in Figure 1a. In order to overflow the network, R needs to be larger than the bottleneck link bandwidth. P should be small enough, compared to the RTTs of legitimate TCP flows, to attack most of the traversing flows. D is negatively correlated with R if the amount of traffic generated by the attackers in one period is fixed. A detailed discussion on the choice of R, P, and D can be found in [19].

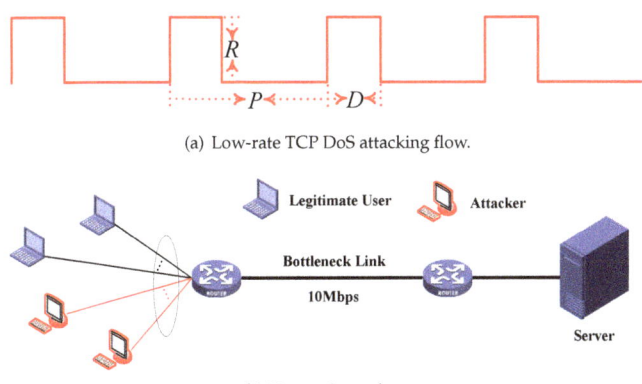

(a) Low-rate TCP DoS attacking flow.

(b) Network topology.

Figure 1. Attacking traffic and network topology.

We set up simulations on the ns-3 platform to illustrate the effectiveness of low-rate TCP DoS attacks. We create a "dumbbell" network topology whose bottleneck link bandwidth is 10 Mbps, as illustrated in Figure 1b. In this simulation setup, nine legitimate TCP flows and one attacking flow are traversing the bottleneck link. We configure the network so that each legitimate TCP flow is transmitting at 1 Mbps and the attacking flow triple $\{R, P, D\}$ is {30 Mbps, 200 ms, 67 ms}. Note that we scale down the bottleneck link bandwidth and flow rates in order to accelerate the simulation. As illustrated in Figure 2a, without being attacked, all legitimate TCP flows fairly share the bottleneck link bandwidth and achieve their desired data rates. However, they are throttled to nearly zero throughput under attack, as illustrated Figure 2b. Note that the time-averaged data rate of the attacking flow (around 3.5 Mbps) is far less than the bottleneck link bandwidth. Therefore, attackers use much less resources to achieve very effective DoS attacks.

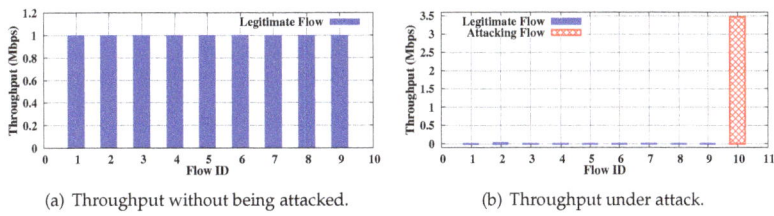

(a) Throughput without being attacked.

(b) Throughput under attack.

Figure 2. Effectiveness of the low-rate TCP DoS attack.

3. AccFlow Design

In this section, we provide an in-depth look at AccFlow. AccFlow is a transport layer protocol deployed on the SDN centralized controller. The controller's role encompasses monitoring all traversing flows, conducting flow analysis, and instructing the switches or routers to implement different routing and forwarding policies for various flows, as illustrated in Figure 3. The architecture of AccFlow is depicted in Figure 3 as well. AccFlow comprises two primary modules: Aggressive Detection and Early Drop. Aggressive Detection is responsible for blocking attacking flows that exhibit detectably aggressive behavior, whereas Early Drop is employed to safeguard the network when attackers attempt to evade detection by intelligently altering their attacking strategies. As Flow Data, computed by other layers, traverses the Transport Layer, AccFlow, equipped with these two modules, effectively safeguards the network from attacks through Flow Prioritization and Flow Analysis.

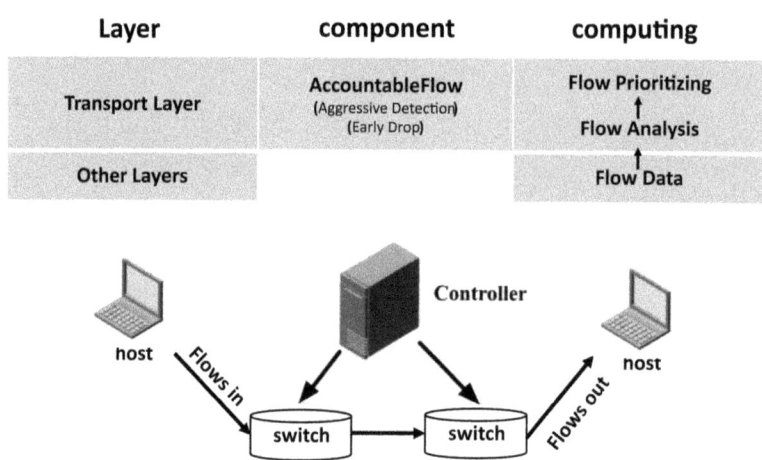

Figure 3. AccFlow architecture.

3.1. Aggressive Detection

To effectively detect attacking flows, it is essential to identify unique features that set them apart from legitimate ones. Given that attackers consistently generate high traffic volumes to overload the network, the loss rates of their flows (the ratio of lost packets to the total transmitted packets) are expected to be higher compared to legitimate flows. Consequently, a straightforward method to distinguish between legitimate flows and attacking flows is by using the loss rate as a differentiator. In order to validate the effectiveness of this intuitive approach, we conducted a study on the loss rates of each flow during the simulation, as discussed in the previous section. The centralized controller closely monitors the traffic and performs periodic statistical analysis on all traversing flows. The flow analysis period of the controller should be set to two or three times the typical Round-Trip Times (RTTs) of the traversing flows. This enables the controller to gain accurate insights into the behaviors of these flows and respond rapidly to attacks. In our simulation, we configured this period to be 0.5 s, which is approximately twice the typical RTTs of the traversing flows. In the rest of the paper, we use the term *detection period* to indicate the controller's analysis period. The results of the simulation are presented in Figure 4a.

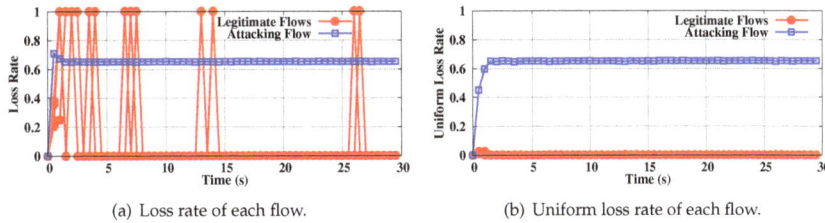

(a) Loss rate of each flow. (b) Uniform loss rate of each flow.

Figure 4. Loss rate and uniform loss rate of each flow.

It is evident that the loss rate of attacking flows remains consistently high. However, we have observed that in certain detection periods, the loss rates for some legitimate flows are even higher. Consequently, relying solely on loss rate as a detection criterion may lead to false positives.

Upon closer examination of the traffic generated by each flow, we have identified the reason behind these higher loss rates in legitimate flows during specific detection periods. This phenomenon occurs when a legitimate flow sends only one packet within a detection period, and that single packet is dropped. In such cases, the legitimate flow reacts by stepping back and waiting for one retransmission timeout before entering the TCP slow start phase. At the outset of the slow start, the flow sends out one packet to probe the available bandwidth. In cases of extreme network congestion, this newly generated packet is highly likely to be dropped. Consequently, the legitimate flow is compelled to endure an even longer retransmission timeout. This explains why the loss rate of a legitimate flow is either 1 (the only packet is dropped) or 0 (waiting in retransmission timeout). In contrast, the attacking flow adopts a different strategy. It continuously dispatches a substantial volume of packets without any form of backing off, even when a significant number of preceding packets are dropped. As a result, the attacking flow maintains a consistently high loss rate.

In our framework, we propose to use *Uniform Loss Rate (ULR)* which is defined in Equation (1). We use it to differentiate the attacking flow from legitimate flows.

$$ULR = loss\ rate \times usage\ rate \quad (1)$$

The usage rate of one flow is defined in Equation (2). In the equation, the usage rate of one flow is the ratio of the number of its transmitted packets in one detection period over the total number of arriving packets from all flows in this detection period.

$$usage\ rate = transmitted\ packets \div total\ packets \quad (2)$$

The attacking flow is featured with high ULR since it has to consistently send large numbers of packets (high usage rate) and never backs off even if its packets are dropped (high loss rate). As illustrated in Figure 4b, there is a notable gap between the ULR of the attacking flow and legitimate flows. Therefore, ULR is an effective feature to leverage to differentiate the attacking flow from legitimate ones. Whenever detecting a flow with excessively high ULR while other flows' ULRs are close to zero, the centralized controller will identify it as an attacking flow and completely block its traffic.

Although Aggressive Detection proves to be a straightforward and precise defense mechanism against the ideal low-rate TCP DoS attack, it necessitates a substantial ULR (Upstream Loss Rate) gap to effectively distinguish between the attacking flow and legitimate flows. Finding a reasonable ULR (Upstream Loss Rate) threshold can be a challenging task, particularly when attackers continuously alter their strategies to reduce the ULRs of their flows. For example, instead of launching a single attacking flow, attackers can divide their traffic into N flows and synchronize them to create periodic burst flows. The usage rate of each individual attacking flow decreases by a percentage of $\frac{N-1}{N}$, including its ULR. As the number of synchronized attacking flows increases, the ULR gaps between legitimate flows and attacking flows diminish, rendering it more challenging for the controller to detect the attacking flows. However, it is important to note that even as the ULR gaps decrease, the network still experiences the same volume of attacking traffic, allowing the DoS attack to remain effective. We present the shortcoming of Aggressive Detection in Figure 5. Note that when the attackers split their traffic into 50 synchronized flows, the ULR differences between attacking flows and legitimate flows are close to zero. To tackle such distributed attacks, we design the Early Drop module in the next subsection.

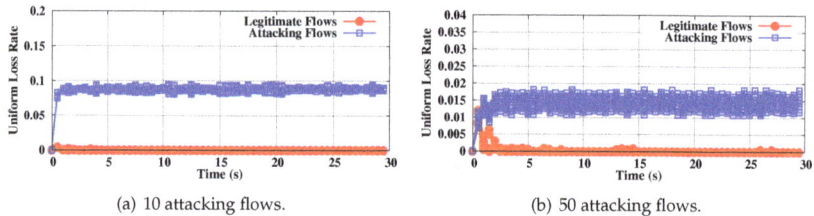

(a) 10 attacking flows.   (b) 50 attacking flows.

Figure 5. ULR of each flow under distributed DoS attack.

3.2. Early Drop

Early Drop is proposed to effectively deal with the aforementioned distributed attacks. The design of Early Drop is also based on consistent flow monitoring and periodic flow analysis by the centralized controller. However, Early Drop does not purely rely on the ULR to detect attacking flows. In fact, Early Drop is a heuristic algorithm illustrated in Algorithm 1 that conducts flow-based packet dropping according to each flow's loss rate without explicitly detecting attacking flows. Next, we elaborate on the Early Drop algorithm.

The algorithm is executed during every detection period. The first 4 lines of the code are executed only once at the beginning of each detection period, whereas the remaining lines are executed whenever a packet arrives within that detection period. The aggregate loss rate, denoted as $\mathcal{L}$ (line 2), represents the ratio of the number of dropped packets from all flows in the *previous* detection period to the total number of arriving packets in the *previous* detection period. Similarly, usage U_i of flow F_i (line 4) reflects the number of packets sent by F_i in the previous detection period. Loss rate L_i of F_i (line 4) is calculated as the ratio of the number of dropped packets from F_i in the previous detection period to U_i. It is important to note that these values, namely $\mathcal{L}$, U_i, and L_i, are computed based on statistics from the previous detection period. In the event that the current detection period is the first, the controller initializes all these values to zero. These values remain constant within the current detection period and are updated at the start of the subsequent detection period. The rest of the lines of the codes, starting from line 5 to the end, execute the packet-dropping policy based on these calculated values.

We add a condition $\mathcal{L} > Th_1$ in line 5 for packet dropping. This is because Early Drop initiates packet dropping before the network bandwidth is fully exhausted. Therefore, it is necessary to make sure that the network is being attacked before applying such an aggressive dropping policy. In other words, Early Drop is a self-protective mechanism that automatically begins dropping packets when the network shows a sign of being attacked. We use aggregate loss rate to verify whether the network is being attacked or not for the following reasons. This approach is grounded in the behavior of legitimate TCP flows, which adhere to congestion-avoidance protocols. When packets are lost due to substantial congestion, legitimate flows respond by throttling their transmission rates, aligning them with the available bandwidth. Consequently, even if these flows initially have high original transmission rates, they adjust their data rates to match the prevailing network conditions. Therefore, it is rare for the network to witness a consistently high aggregate loss rate under normal situations. However, when attackers are trying to cause denial of service to legitimate flows by exhausting the network bandwidth, they have to continuously generate traffic even though many of their packets are dropped, i.e., they never back off when meant to do so. As a result, the network will experience a very high aggregate loss rate under attack. We verify our analysis by studying the aggregate loss rate in both normal and attacked scenarios. The experimental results, illustrated in Figure 6, show that even 40 legitimate flows each with the original 1 Mbps transmission rate are traversing the 10 Mbps bottleneck link, the aggregate loss rate is well below 10% (the real network is always bandwidth over-provisioned to tolerate the traffic burst caused by legitimate flows, which makes it rare for the network to have a large aggregate loss rate under normal situation). However, when the attackers are trying to launch an attack, the aggregate loss rate is more than 65%. Thus, aggregate loss rate is an effective feature to indicate whether the network is under DoS attack or not. The network operators can have different configurations for the threshold Th_1 based on their own policies and traffic characteristics. For instance, if they want to aggressively protect their network, they need to set a relatively low threshold for Th_1 and vice versa.

Algorithm 1: Early Drop

1 **if** *the beginning of kth detection period* **then**
2   Calculate the aggregate loss rate $\mathcal{L}$;
3   **for** *each traversing flow F_i* **do**
4   Calculate its usage U_i and loss rate L_i;
            `// Loss rate L_i is the ratio of the number of dropped packets from F_i`
            `   in the previous detection period to U_i`
5 **if** $\mathcal{L} > Th_1$ **then**
        `// Th_1 is set up based on policies and traffic characteristics`
6   **for** *each arriving packet* **do**
7   Find the flow F_j it belongs to;
8   **if** $U_j > Th_2$ **then**
              `// Th_2 is set up to make sure that Early Drop will not falsely`
              `   blame the legitimate TCP flows`
9   **if** $L_j > 0.5 \times \mathcal{L}$ **then**
10   Drop the packet with probability L_j;
11   **else if** $N_{packet} > Th_3$ **then**
12   Drop the packet with probability L_j;

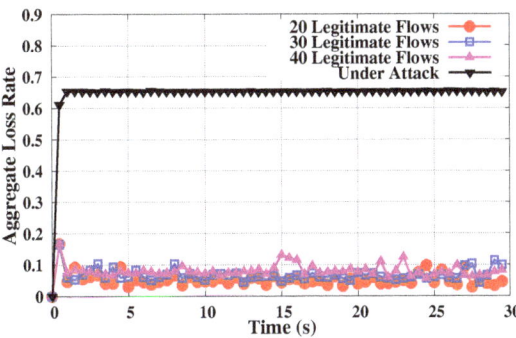

Figure 6. Aggregate loss rate for normal and attacked scenarios.

The main idea of the Early Drop algorithm is that it drops the packets from *accountable* flows with *reasonable* probabilities. By "accountable", we mean that Early Drop only blames the flows that are accountable for the congestion. By "reasonable", we mean that Early Drop drops the packets of accountable flows according to their loss rates. We achieve accountability by line 8 of the algorithm. In particular, if a flow only sends one or two packets during one detection period, it is not accountable for the congestion so that Early Drop will not drop its packets. We add the threshold Th_2 to make sure that Early Drop will not falsely blame the legitimate TCP flows who have just recovered from retransmission timeouts and send one packet in the beginning of the TCP slow start process to probe the available bandwidth. Th_2 should be small and increase with the duration of the detection period since a longer detection period may contain more TCP slow start processes. We set Th_2 as 5 in our simulations when we test the effectiveness of AccFlow in the next section. Furthermore, we accomplish reasonability by considering its loss rate while dropping packets from a particular flow (lines 9 to 12). Specifically, Early Drop divides all flows into two groups, i.e., the high loss rate group and the low loss rate group. All flows whose loss rates are above half of the aggregate loss rate $\mathcal{L}$ will be categorized into the high loss rate group and Early Drop immediately drops their packets according to their loss rates. On the contrary, flows whose loss rates are no greater than half of the $\mathcal{L}$ will be assigned to the low loss rate group and Early Drop applies packet dropping to these flows only when the number of queueing packets N_{packet} in the router is larger than Th_3. The threshold Th_3 is used to indicate that the network is slightly congested so that it is positively related to the router's buffer size. We set Th_3 to be 10% of the router's buffer size in our simulations. Again, the network operators can have different configurations for Th_3 according to their policies. To sum up, Early Drop blames the flows that are accountable for the congestion, and the higher their loss rates, the more aggressively it drops their packets. The fundamental difference between Early Drop and other Active Queue Management disciplines such as RED and WRED is that Early Drop selectively drops packets from more accountable flows (often the attacking flows) *early* before the router buffer is exhausted so that the packets from less accountable flows (often the legitimate flows) can be enqueued. However, RED and WRED simply drop all arriving packets when the buffer is full so that the legitimate flows will suffer from denial of service.

Note that we can use Aggressive Detection as a supplement to Early Drop. In particular, Early Drop is always active to protect the network whereas Aggressive Detection will be applied to completely block the attacking flows if they perform aggressively enough to be detected by the controller. In the next section, we thoroughly test the effectiveness of AccFlow through substantial amounts of simulations.

4. Deployment of AccFlow

In this section, we address the deployment of AccFlow in real networks and its interaction with other security protocols. Although AccFlow offers advantages like flexible control and real-time response to attacks, it also faces scalability challenges due to the centralized network architecture. The centralized controller must create an entry in the routing table for each distinct flow, which can strain CPU and storage resources. To overcome this scalability issue, we propose the use of flow aggregation and a virtual centralized controller. These solutions aim to optimize AccFlow's performance and ensure its practicality in large-scale networks.

Flow aggregation involves grouping similar flows together, reducing the number of distinct flows and, consequently, the load on the controller. The virtual centralized controller concept employs multiple coordinated processors to serve as the centralized controller, allowing for distributed handling of flow management. Together, these measures enhance AccFlow's scalability, making it suitable for deployment in both local area networks (LANs) and wide area networks (WANs).

By addressing scalability concerns and optimizing AccFlow's performance, we aim to make it a viable and effective solution for enhancing network security and mitigating DoS and DDoS attacks.

4.1. Flow Aggregation

Flow aggregation can prevent the attackers from amplifying their attacking scale by faking huge numbers of flows. Furthermore, with protocols like ingress filter [20] and Passport [21], ASes can limit the range of their acceptable source IP addresses. As a result, the number of distinct attacking flows that can be used to attack the bottleneck link is limited. Moreover, the existing security protocols, such as MiddlePolice [22,23], Mirage [24], Phalanx [25], Pushback [26], and DoS-limiting architecture [27], can be applied to further limit the attacking scales. For instance, Mirage adopts the concept of frequency hopping in wireless networks to "hop" the destination IP addresses among all available addresses. Each time a user wants to send traffic to this site, it has to solve a computational puzzle to obtain the new IP address, which will limit the volumes of traffic that the computationally limited attackers can send. MiddlePolice, on the other hand, allows the destination to determine which source IPs are allowed through self-defined traffic control policies. Since AccFlow does not cause disruption to the existing network infrastructure, it can effectively interact with these security protocols to defend the network against extremely large-scale DDoS attacks.

4.2. Virtual Centralized Controller

In order to deal with large numbers of flows, we can also adopt the concept of a virtual centralized SDN controller. Specifically, multiple processors can serve as the conceptual centralized controller. Each processor keeps its routing table and tackles a certain number of flows. In order to tolerate individual processor failures within the distributed virtual centralized controller system, we can adopt the Paxos protocols [28]. In fact, the B4 architecture [14], a worldwide large-scale SDN data center network built by Google, also adopts the concept of virtual centralized controller by clustering their networks to deal with millions of flows traversing Google's data centers. By embracing these techniques to solve the scalability problem, AccFlow can be deployed in real networks. We present a straightforward deployment architecture in Figure 7.

We consider deploying AccFlow on both core routers and border routers. Typically, border routers are responsible for dealing with the inter-domain flows such as BGP sessions [29] whereas core routers carry the traffic across the AS and may execute a particular traffic engineering policy such as MPLS [30]. Consider the situation where a remote legitimate client and the attacker are sending their traffic to the AS through an undeployed border router R_1. Since the attacking flow D exhausts the bandwidth of the victim border router R_1, the client's flow A is throttled to zero throughput (flow A is not able to traverse R_1 in Figure 7). Attacking flow D continues to propagate in the AS until it counters a deployed core router R_2 which drops its packets to save the network resources for the legitimate flow C (attacking flow D is not able to traverse R_2 in Figure 7). When the AS deploys AccFlow on its border router R_3, it protects the inter-domain traffic B from being attacked so that B can safely enter the AS. Apart from launching inter-domain attacks, the attacker can also compromise the nodes within the AS to generate local DoS attacking flows, such as the attacking flow E. The deployed core router R_4 can protect the network from such an attack. Furthermore, the deployed routers can stop the local attacking flows from leaving the AS to attack remote sites. To sum up, AccFlow is compatible with the existing security protocols and is incrementally deployable without disruption to the existing network infrastructure.

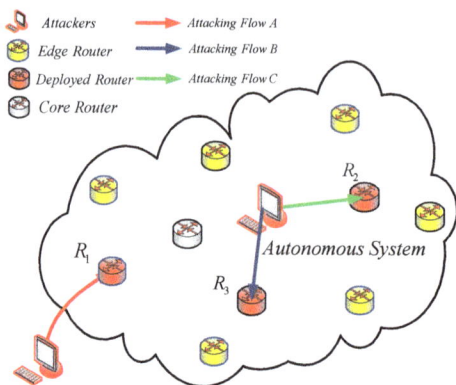

Figure 7. Deployment of AccFlow.

5. Experimental Results

In this section, we thoroughly study the effectiveness of AccFlow on the ns-3 platform in four major simulation setups. We use the network topology illustrated in Figure 1b in all simulation setups whereas the traversing flows are different under different setups (AccFlow is not limited to the simple dumbbell network topology. It is effective to protect both the inter-domain and intra-domain traffic). The first setup regards the distributed low-rate TCP DoS attack, in which we consider different types of legitimate traffic and different attacking strategies. The second setup is about another DoS attack derived from the low-rate TCP DoS attack. We call it the Short Selfish TCP Flow (SSTF) attack because the attackers selfishly consume nearly the whole network resources by generating excessive numbers of short TCP flows. The third setup is designed to verify that AccFlow does not falsely drop packets from legitimate periodic flows. Finally, we consider the general DoS attacks in the fourth setup.

5.1. Distributed Low-Rate TCP DoS Attack

In this setup, we design three different simulation settings. In setting one, we have five legitimate TCP flows each with 1 Mbps transmission rate to simulate drone activities, such as Data Transfer and Telemetry and Remote Control Signals. In a real network, the attackers are able to launch different scales of distributed attacks by splitting their traffic into different numbers of synchronized subflows which refer to the individual streams of network traffic that are coordinated or synchronized by the attacker. By dividing their traffic into multiple subflows, attackers can make the attacks more challenging to detect and mitigate, as the traffic may appear more like legitimate network activity. In our simulations, we varied the number of synchronized subflows from 1 to 50 to replicate real-world attacks. (Note that we scale down the number of flows in order to accelerate the simulation. As you can see in our experiment results, the performance of AccFlow is not impacted by the scale of DDoS attacks.) The total aggregate rate of these synchronized attacking flows reached approximately 30 Mbps, which is three times the bandwidth of the bottleneck link. This setup effectively mimics attacks that surpass the network's capacity, resulting in network congestion and potential service disruptions. The attacking period P is 200 ms and the attacking duration D in one period is 67 ms to simulate the real attacks. In setting two, we use the same attacking traffic as that of setting one but we have nine legitimate TCP flows each with a different transmission rate, ranging from 0.3 Mpbs to 1.1 Mpbs. This setup mimics diverse drone activities, including real-time adaptive data transmission and adaptive flight planning. The reason we have both setting one and setting two is that TCP uses the max–min fairness [31], where the network first satisfies the flows with smaller demands (lower transmission rates) and then evenly distributes the bandwidth to flows with larger demands if the network resources are limited. As a result, in a congested network, flows with smaller transmission rates can obtain their fair bandwidth shares more easily than flows with higher rates. Therefore, we need to consider both the two settings in our simulation. In the third setting, we test the effectiveness of AccFlow when attackers are varying their attacking rates from 20 Mbps to 60 Mbps which is more varied. Without loss of generality, we assume that attackers split their traffic into five attacking flows in this setting and we use the same legitimate TCP traffic as that of setting two. We summarize the three simulation settings in Table 1.

Table 1. Simulation settings.

Simulation Setting	Legitimate TCP Flows	Attack Scales	Aggregate Attacking Rate
Setting One	5 flows with same rate 1 Mbps	1 to 50 attacking flows	30 Mbps
Setting Two	9 flows with different rates ranging from 0.3 Mbps to 1.1 Mbps	1 to 50 attacking flows	30 Mbps
Setting Three	9 flows with different rates ranging from 0.3 Mbps to 1.1 Mbps	5 attacking flows	20 Mbps to 60 Mbps

The simulation results are illustrated in Figure 8. Figure 8a illustrates the results for setting one when five 1 Mbps legitimate TCP flows are traversing the network. Since the whole bandwidth of the bottleneck link is 10 Mbps, which is large enough to hold all the legitimate traffic, all the five flows should not experience any packet losses (in this paper, we only consider packet losses caused by network congestions). and achieve their ideal throughput when they are not attacked. As we can see in Figure 8a, AccFlow can effectively protect the legitimate flows from being attacked since the average throughput of the legitimate flows is close to the desired transmission rate. Furthermore, the performance of AccFlow does not degrade as the number of attacking flows increases. Figure 8b illustrates the simulation results for setting two. Note that we set up nine legitimate flows in this setting but we only plot the results for five of them in the figure for a concise presentation. With AccFlow, all nine legitimate flows are able to achieve their desired data rates even under large-scale attacks. In setting three, we vary the aggregate attacking rates from 20 Mbps to 60 Mbps. Again, we plot the simulation results for 5 legitimate flows in the figure. The results show that AccFlow can also effectively defend the network even if attackers are able to change their attack rates.

Here, we make a detailed explanation of the effectiveness of AccFlow. Consider one legitimate TCP flow and one attacking flow in our simulations. Assume that attackers launch DoS attacks in the detection period T_k. Due to severe packet losses in T_k, the legitimate TCP flow envisions a heavily congested network and enters a retransmission timeout. Therefore, in the next detection period T_{k+1}, either its loss rate is zero if it is still waiting in the timeout or its usage is very low if it just recovers from the timeout and sends small amounts of packets to probe the available bandwidth. Under both scenarios, AccFlow will not further blame the legitimate flow. However, the attackers have to continuously send high volumes of traffic in order to overflow the bottleneck link. Thus, the attacking flow still has a large usage in the next detection period T_{k+1} in spite of its high loss rate in T_k. Under such a situation, AccFlow will Early Drop its packets according to its loss rate. Furthermore, if the network is still congested after Early Drop, the router itself will also drop packets since it cannot deal with so much traffic. Therefore, the attacking flow will experience an even larger loss rate in the detection period T_{k+1}. This cycle repeats so that the loss rate of the attacking flow increases in each detection period until the network is not congested or its loss rate equals one. Under both scenarios, the attacking flow can no longer harm the network.

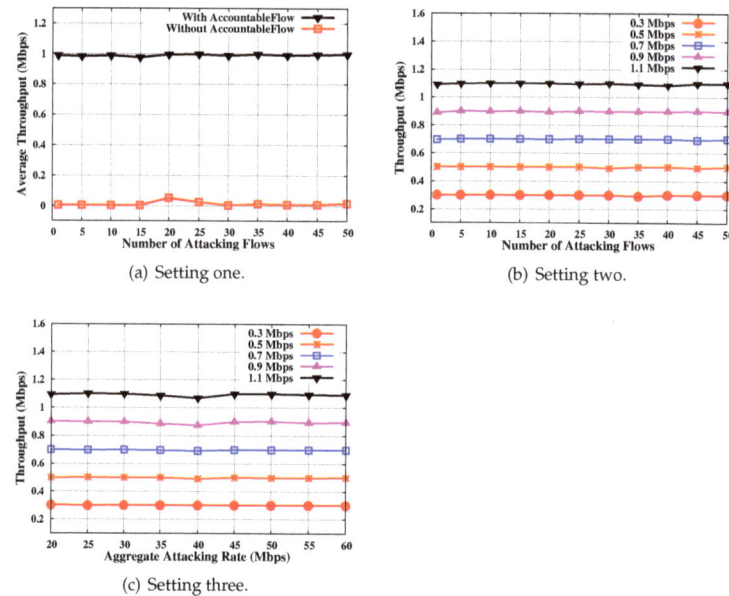

Figure 8. Under all three settings, AccFlow can effectively defend legitimate TCP flows from being attacked. The achieved throughput for each legitimate flow is almost the same as its original transmission rate.

In order to be a real-time defending technique, AccFlow needs to react to attacks very fast. Here, we study the convergence time of AccFlow, i.e., how long it takes AccFlow to clear up the attacks. We define the convergence time as the time when all legitimate flow loss rates are zero. Without loss of generality, we randomly pick up one simulation setup in each of the three settings listed in Table 1 to study its convergence time. Specifically, we test the scenarios where attackers set up 20 and 30 attacking flows in setting one and setting two, respectively. As for setting three, we use the case when attackers are generating traffic at a rate of 40 Mbps. Our simulation results are illustrated in Figure 9. Under all three scenarios, AccFlow can react to the attack quickly and the convergence time is in the order of seconds or tens of seconds.

As a flow-based defending technique, AccFlow needs to be scalable to deal with large numbers of attacking flows. Although the performance of AccFlow does not decline as the number of attacking flows increases (as illustrated in our simulation results), huge numbers of flows will exhaust the CPU and storage of the centralized controller. We discuss the scalability problem and propose our solutions in Section 4 where we consider the deployment of AccFlow in real networks.

5.2. Short Selfish TCP Flow Attack

In this section, we discuss a very effective DoS attack which is similar to but still fundamentally different from the low-rate TCP DoS attack. The attacking technique is that malicious users periodically set up many short TCP flows to gain unfair share of network resources. Specifically, the early coming short TCP flows congest the network and cause all flows (including both legitimate TCP flows and themselves) to enter retransmission timeouts. Then, the attackers selfishly start new short TCP flows to occupy the whole network bandwidth since no one apart from attackers is transmitting now. The interesting point of such DoS attacks is that it seems that the attackers never deviate from the TCP protocol since these short TCP flows will back off when their packets are lost. However, the attackers are able to cause very severe denial of service to legitimate users simply by breaking their traffic into small short flows. We name such an attack the Short Selfish TCP Flow (SSTF) attack. Note that the difference between the SSTF attack and low-rate TCP DoS attack is that the former cannot synchronize all these short TCP flows to create the regular periodic burst traffic since transmitters have to wait for the ACKs before sending new packets. We set up simulations to illustrate the effectiveness of the SSTF attack. In our simulation, we have 10 attackers and each of them sends one short TCP flow with 3 Mbps data rate every 200 ms. Furthermore, we have nine legitimate TCP flows with 1 Mbps transmission rate each. The results, illustrated in Figure 10, show that the SSTF attack is able to effectively throttle the legitimate users to almost zero throughput.

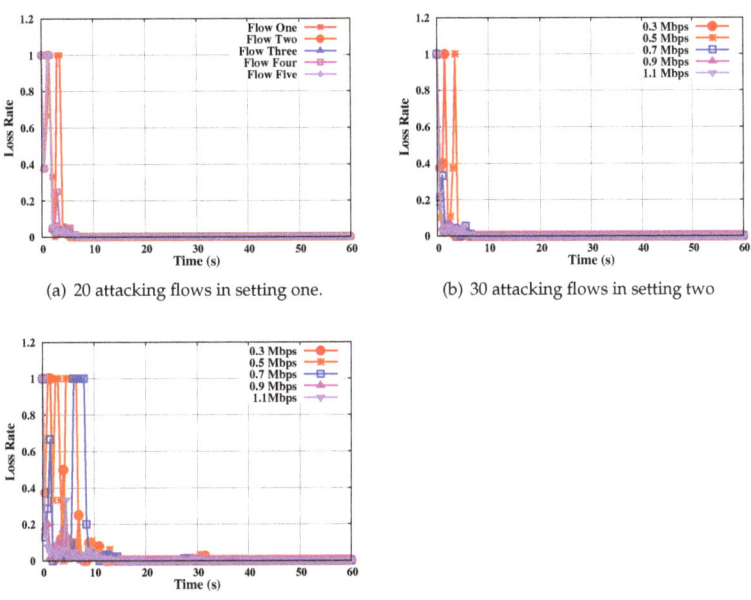

(a) 20 attacking flows in setting one.

(b) 30 attacking flows in setting two

(c) 40 Mbps aggregate attacking rate in setting three

Figure 9. Convergence time of AccFlow.

Now, we explain why the SSTF attack can cause such an effective denial of service to legitimate users even though each individual short flow itself behaves exactly the same as a legitimate TCP flow (here, we mean each short TCP flow complies with the TCP protocol and will back off when a congestion happens). First, let us reconstruct the attacking procedure. Assume that attackers first set up n short TCP flows $\mathcal{A} = \{A_1, A_2, ..., A_n\}$ to cause congestion. Then all the legitimate flows and attacking flows in $\mathcal{A}$ will suffer from severe packet losses and enter retransmission timeouts. After a short period, attackers set up another set of short TCP flows $\mathcal{B} = \{B_1, B_2, ..., B_m\}$. Since no one is transmitting now, $\mathcal{B}$ will occupy the whole network resources. When the legitimate flows try to recover from timeouts, they may face another set of short attacking flows started by the attackers after flows in $\mathcal{B}$ finish. Again, congestion happens and the legitimate flows are forced to enter even longer retransmission timeouts. The cycle repeats and the attackers are able to selfishly utilize nearly the whole network resources. In a word, by sacrificing a small fraction of their traffic, the attackers create a "clear" network environment for most of their traffic and cause severe denial of service to the legitimate users.

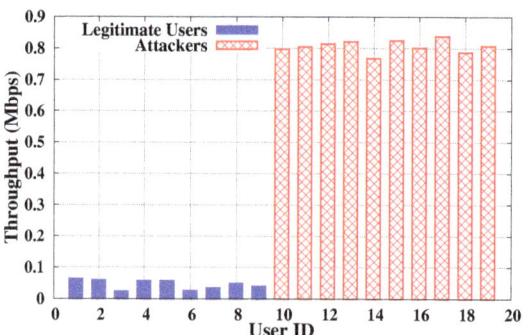

Figure 10. Effectiveness of the SSTF attack.

The trick played by the attackers is to evade accountability by continuously generating fresh short flows. In particular, it is the flows in $\mathcal{A}$ that cause the congestion so that we have no reason to blame the flows in $\mathcal{B}$. However, when flows in $\mathcal{A}$ experience severe packet losses, the source should realize that the network is congested and should not start new flows. Thus, flow set $\mathcal{B}$ should not be generated because both $\mathcal{A}$ and $\mathcal{B}$ come from the same source (attackers). Therefore, although each individual short TCP flow complies with the TCP protocol, the attackers still behave maliciously by periodically setting up new TCP flows even though the previous flows experience high loss rates.

We propose to use *flow aggregation* to defend against the SSTF attack. Specifically, all flows with the same source IP address will be aggregated as one flow. (It is possible to conduct flow aggregation based on other properties such as source IP address and application port pair. We leave the discussion of different aggregating properties in future works.) Consequently, although flow $A_i \in \mathcal{A}$ and flow $B_j \in \mathcal{B}$ are different flows, they may have the same source IP address since they are both generated by the attackers. As a result, AccFlow will aggregate them as one flow. Therefore, flow B_j will be blamed for the congestion caused by flow A_i. Similarly, the subsequent flows will be accountable for the congestion caused by their precedent flows as long as they have the same source IP address. Thus, the attackers are not able to selfishly over-utilize the network resources by creating new flows. A potential problem for conducting such flow aggregation is that attackers can spoof their source IP addresses to keep generating new flows. However, the network security community has proposed effective mechanisms such as Stackpi [32] and packet filters [33] to prevent source IP spoofing. AccFlow can embrace such security protocols to prevent attackers from faking flows. Another potential problem is that the Network Address Translation (NAT) router translates the IP addresses of the hosts within its LAN to its public IP address. Then, all the flows from different hosts will have the same source IP address after they leave the LAN. When they reach other remote sites that deploy AccFlow, they will be aggregated as one flow. Thus, a single compromised host within the LAN may cause denial of service to all the legitimate hosts within the LAN since their flows are aggregated as the same flow. To solve the problem, we can deploy AccFlow on the NAT router so that it will drop the packets from the local attacking flow and save bandwidth for legitimate flows. Therefore, the local attacking flow will not be able to leave the LAN to attack the remote sites.

We test the effectiveness of AccFlow when the network is faced with the SSTF attack under similar simulation settings in Table 1. As illustrated in Figure 11, Accountable Flow can effectively defend against the SSTF attack. Note that we set the minimum number of attacking flows to five since the SSTF attack needs to be distributed in order to be effective. The convergence time is also in the order of seconds to tens of seconds. We do not present the results for the convergence time in the paper due to space constraints. Note that the achieved data rates (throughput) for higher rate flows, i.e., ones with rates of 0.9 Mbps and 1.1 Mbps, are slightly less than their desired data rates. We attribute such slight performance degradation to the fact that TCP max–min fairness serves the low rate flows first in congested networks.

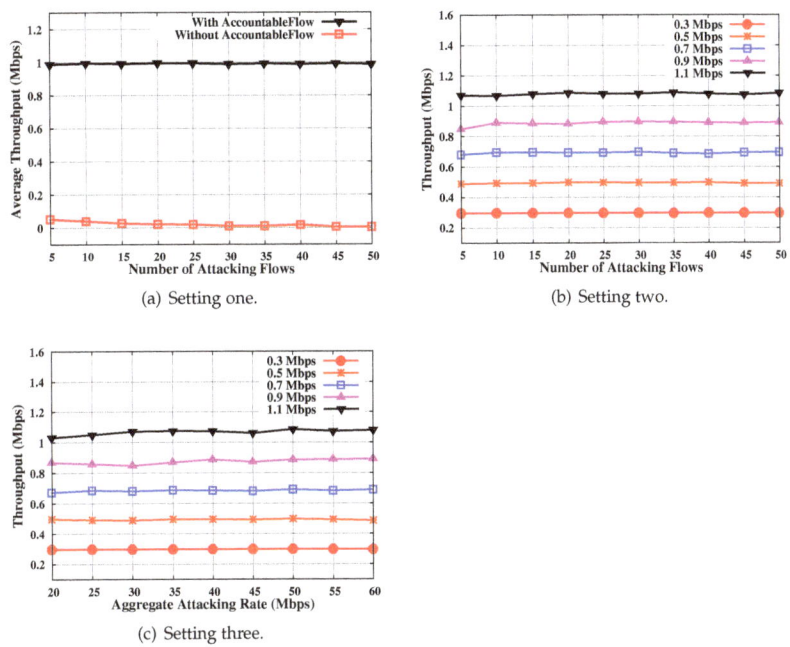

(a) Setting one.

(b) Setting two.

(c) Setting three.

Figure 11. AccFlow effectively defends against the SSTF attack.

5.3. Benign Periodic Flow

Real-life networks, such as the Internet, also carry periodic or bursty flows whose traffic patterns are similar to that of the low-rate TCP DoS attacking flows. One example is that YouTube generates periodic traffic by loading chunks of a video with pauses between each chunk [34]. In this subsection, we show that AccFlow does not falsely drop the packets from benign periodic flows through the following four experiments. In the first experimental setup, five normal TCP flows each transmitting at a rate of 1 Mbps and one benign periodic flow are sharing the network resources. The analysis in [34] reveals that the peak rate for a typical YouTube flow ranges from hundreds of kilobytes to several megabytes. The interval of each video chunk ranges from hundreds of milliseconds to seconds. We set the peak rate and period of the periodic flow in our simulation to be 3 Mbps and 200 ms so that it can represent real video traffic. Since the bottleneck link bandwidth is 10 Mbps which is large enough to hold all the traffic, the first setup is congestion free. In the second setup, we create a fairly congested network by generating nine normal TCP flows and the same periodic flow. In the third setup, the network becomes quite congested by carrying 15 normal TCP flows and the same periodic flow. Finally, in the fourth setup, the network is very congested as 20 normal TCP flows and the same periodic flow traverse the bottleneck link.

The simulation results are illustrated in Figure 12. For clear presentation, we use characters "N", "F", "Q", and "V" to represent words "Not", "Fairly", "Quite", and "Very", respectively. The character "Cg" represents the word "Congested". Thus "F Cg" means that the network is fairly congested, which corresponds to the second setup. As illustrated in Figure 12a, the benign periodic flow achieves its desired throughput in all four setups no matter whether AccFlow is applied or not. Furthermore, AccFlow also does not have any negative effect on the normal TCP flows, as illustrated in Figure 12b. The results indicate that AccFlow seamlessly coexists with benign flows, maintaining their performance without degradation. This successful coexistence can be attributed to the fundamental difference between benign periodic flows and attacking flows.

In benign periodic flows, the objective is not to overwhelm congested links, unlike attacking flows. Therefore, the network does not experience a high aggregate loss rate, and as a result, AccFlow does not implement its aggressive dropping policy. In situations where a legitimate bursty flow momentarily reaches a peak rate that might cause a high aggregate loss rate, triggering AccFlow to drop a few packets, the adverse impact does not propagate. Legitimate flows naturally adjust by entering retransmission timeouts after encountering packet losses. Consequently, the network becomes less congested, and the aggregate loss rate falls below the threshold Th_1.

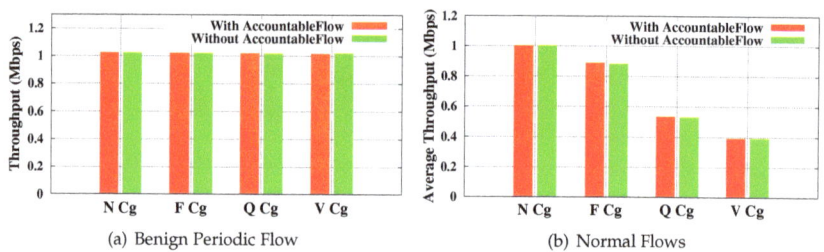

Figure 12. AccFlow harmoniously coexists with the benign periodic flow and normal flows without causing performance degradation.

5.4. General (D)DoS Attack

Although AccFlow is primarily designed to address low-rate TCP DoS attacks, it also serves as a defense mechanism against general DoS attacks. The distinction between low-rate TCP DoS attacks and general DoS attacks lies in their respective methods of operation. The former relies on the TCP retransmission timeout mechanism to launch attacks, whereas the latter disrupts legitimate users' services by inundating the network with a high volume of traffic.

As previously mentioned, the central concept behind AccFlow is to hold attacking flows accountable for network congestion by promptly dropping their packets based on their loss rates. Consequently, any attacking flows that contribute to congestion are unable to disrupt legitimate flows by excessively utilizing network resources.

In fact, the effectiveness of AccFlow against general DoS attacks stems from our deliberate decision not to rely on the periodic nature of low-rate TCP DoS attacking flows when designing the algorithm.

To test the effectiveness of AccFlow when the network is faced with general DoS attacks, we use similar simulation settings listed in Table 1 except that the attackers consistently generate traffic without pause. As illustrated in Figure 13, AccFlow can effectively defend against the general DoS attacks. Furthermore, AccFlow also has a quick convergence time under such attacks, which is in the order of tens of seconds.

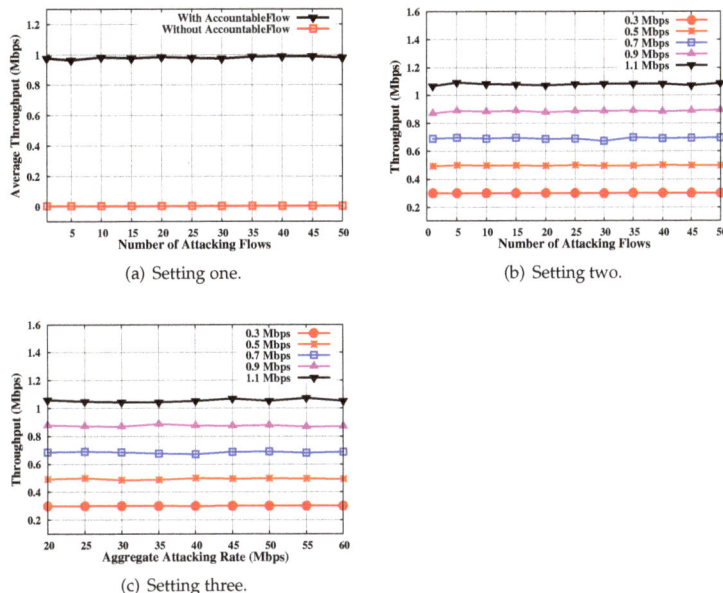

Figure 13. AccFlow provides a strong defense against the general DoS attacks.

6. Conclusions

In recent years, the defense against low-rate TCP DoS attacks in SDN has garnered significant attention from researchers. However, the application of such defenses to drones has not been a focal point of research, and there are currently no related studies. This paper introduces AccFlow, an incrementally deployable SDN-based protocol, designed to counter both low-rate TCP DoS attacks and general DoS attacks in the context of drones. Consistent with previous studies of defending DDoS attacks where they propose an SDN-assisted DDoS attack defense method [35,36] and the DDoS Attack Detection System using Apache Spark [37], we concentrate on defending low-rate TCP DoS attacks on drones and still demonstrated effectiveness for normal DDoS. We deploy AccFlow on the SDN-centralized controller and use Aggressive Detection and Early Drop to protect the network when attackers try to evade detection by varying their attacking strategies. The main idea of AccFlow is to make the attacking flows accountable. Through substantial amounts of simulations in each setup, we demonstrate that AccFlow, which does not cause any performance degradation to benign flows, can effectively defend against both the low-rate TCP DoS attacks and the general DoS attacks even if attackers are able to vary their strategies.

Author Contributions: Conceptualization, Y.C. and X.Z.; Methodology, Y.C.; Software, X.P.; Validation, L.H.; Investigation, H.L.; Supervision, E.Y.; Funding acquisition, E.Y. All authors have read and agreed to the published version of the manuscript.

Funding: This work was funded by National Natural Science Foundation of China (62274056), Guangdong Basic and Applied Basic Research Foundation (2022A1515110045 and 2023A1515011241), the Open Fund of Advanced Cryptography and System Security Key Laboratory of Sichuan Province (SKLACSS-202209), Key Research and Development Program of Jiangsu Province (BE2022098), Postdoctoral Science Foundation of Jiangsu Province (2021K605C).

Institutional Review Board Statement: Not applicable.

Informed Consent Statement: Not applicable.

Data Availability Statement: Not applicable.

Conflicts of Interest: The authors declare no conflict of interest.

References

1. Pärlin, K.; Alam, M.M.; Moullec, Y.L. Jamming of uav remote control systems using software defined radio. In Proceedings of the 2018 International Conference on Military Communications and Information Systems (ICMCIS), Warsaw, Poland, 22–23 May 2018; pp. 1–6.
2. Kardasz, P.; Doskocz, J.; Hejduk, M.; Wiejkut, P.; Zarzycki, H. Drones and possibilities of their using. *J. Civ. Environ. Eng.* **2016**, *6*, 1000233. [CrossRef]
3. Javaid, A.Y.; Sun, W.; Devabhaktuni, V.K.; Alam, M. Cyber security threat analysis and modeling of an unmanned aerial vehicle system. In Proceedings of the 2012 IEEE Conference on Technologies for Homeland Security (HST), Waltham, MA, USA, 13–15 November 2012; pp. 585–590.
4. Kuzmanovic, A.; Knightly, E.W. Low-rate tcp-targeted denial of service attacks and counter strategies. *IEEE/ACM Trans. Netw.* **2006**, *14*, 683–696. [CrossRef]
5. Stockhammer, T. Dynamic adaptive streaming over http–: Standards and design principles. In Proceedings of the Second Annual ACM Conference on Multimedia Systems, ACM, San Jose, CA, USA, 23–25 February 2011; pp. 133–144.
6. Sun, H.; Lui, J.C.S.; Yau, D.K.Y. Defending against low-rate tcp attacks: Dynamic detection and protection. In Proceedings of the 12th IEEE International Conference on Network Protocols, Berlin, Germany, 8 October 2004.
7. Chang, C.-W.; Lee, S.; Lin, B.; Wang, J. The taming of the shrew: Mitigating low-rate tcp-targeted attack. In Proceedings of the 2009 29th IEEE International Conference on Distributed Computing Systems, Montreal, QC, Canada, 22–26 June 2009.
8. Wang, M.; Lu, Y.; Qin, J. Source-based defense against ddos attacks in sdn based on sflow and som. *IEEE Access* **2021**, *10*, 2097–2116. [CrossRef]
9. Bhuyan, M.; Kalwar, A.; Goswami, A.; Bhattacharyya, D.; Kalita, J. Low-rate and high-rate distributed dos attack detection using partial rank correlation. In Proceedings of the 2015 Fifth International Conference on Communication Systems and Network Technologies, Gwalior, India, 4–6 April 2015; pp. 706–710.
10. Vishwakarma, R.; Jain, A.K. A honeypot with machine learning based detection framework for defending iot based botnet ddos attacks. In Proceedings of the 2019 3rd International Conference on Trends in Electronics and Informatics (ICOEI), Tirunelveli, India, 23–25 April 2019; pp. 1019–1024.
11. Başer, M.; Güven, E.Y.; Aydın, M.A. Ssh and telnet protocols attack analysis using honeypot technique: Analysis of ssh and telnet honeypot. In Proceedings of the 2021 6th International Conference on Computer Science and Engineering (UBMK), Ankara, Turkey, 15–17 September 2021; pp. 806–811.
12. Tang, D.; Chen, J.; Wang, X.; Zhang, S.; Yan, Y. A new detection method for ldos attacks based on data mining. *Future Gener. Comput.* **2022**, *128*, 73–87. [CrossRef]
13. McKeown, N.; Anderson, T.; Balakrishnan, H.; Parulkar, G.; Peterson, L.; Rexford, J.; Shenker, S.; Turner, J. Openflow: Enabling innovation in campus networks. *ACM SIGCOMM* **2008**, *38*, 69–74. [CrossRef]
14. Jain, S.; Kumar, A.; Mandal, S.; Ong, J.; Poutievski, L.; Singh, A.; Venkata, S.; Wanderer, J.; Zhou, J.; Zhu, M.; et al. B4: Experience with a globally-deployed software defined wan. *ACM SIGCOMM* **2013**, *43*, 3–14. [CrossRef]
15. Hong, C.-Y.; Kandula, S.; Mahajan, R.; Zhang, M.; Gill, V.; Nanduri, M.; Wattenhofer, R. Achieving high utilization with software-driven wan. In Proceedings of the SIGCOMM '13: ACM SIGCOMM 2013 Conference on SIGCOMM, Hong Kong, China, 12–16 August 2013.
16. Shin, S.; Porras, P.; Yegneswaran, V.; Fong, M.; Gu, G.; Tyson, M. Fresco: Modular composable security services for software-defined networks. In Proceedings of the Network and Distributed Security Symposium, San Diego, CA, USA, 25–27 February 2013.
17. Liu, Z. FlowPolice: Enforcing Congestion Accountability to Defend against DDoS Attacks. Ph.D. Dissertation, University of Illinois at Urbana-Champaign, Champaign, IL, USA, 2015.
18. Ns-3: A Discrete-Event Network Simulator. Available online: https://www.nsnam.org (accessed on 1 June 2021).
19. Aleksandar, K.; Edward, W.K. Low-rate TCP-targeted denial of service attacks: The shrew vs. the mice and elephants. In Proceedings of the SIGCOMM '03: 2003 Conference on Applications, Technologies, Architectures, and Protocols for Computer Communications, Karlsruhe, Germany, 25–29 August 2003.
20. Ferguson, P.; Senie, D. *Network Ingress Filtering: Defeating Denial of Service Attacks Which Employ IP Source Address Spoofing*; RFC Editor: Marina del Rey, CA, USA, 2000.
21. Liu, X.; Li, A.; Yang, X.; Wetherall, D. Passport: Secure and adoptable source authentication. In Proceedings of the 5th USENIX Symposium on Networked Systems Design & Implementation, NSDI 2008, San Francisco, CA, USA, 16–18 April 2008.
22. Liu, Z.; Jin, H.; Hu, Y.-C.; Bailey, M. MiddlePolice: Toward Enforcing Destination-Defined Policies in the Middle of the Internet. In Proceedings of the CCS '16: 2016 ACM SIGSAC Conference on Computer and Communications Security, Vienna, Austria, 24–28 October 2016.
23. Liu, Z.; Jin, H.; Hu, Y.-C.; Bailey, M. MiddlePolice: Fine-Grained Endpoint-Driven In-Network Traffic Control for Proactive DDoS Attack Mitigation. *arXiv* **2017**, arXiv:1709.05710.
24. Mittal, P.; Kim, D.; Hu, Y.-C.; Caesar, M. Mirage: Towards deployable ddos defense for web applications. *arXiv* **2011**, arXiv:1110.1060.

25. Dixon, C.; Anderson, T.; Krishnamurthy, A. Phalanx: Withstanding multimillion-node botnets. In Proceedings of the NSDI 08: 5th USENIX Symposium on Networked Systems Design USENIX Association and Implementation, San Francisco, CA, USA, 16–18 April 2008.
26. Mahajan, R.; Bellovin, S.M.; Floyd, S.; Ioannidis, J.; Paxson, V.; Shenker, S. Controlling high bandwidth aggregates in the network. *ACM SIGCOMM* **2002**, *32*, 62–73. [CrossRef]
27. Yang, X.; Wetherall, D.; Anderson, T. A dos-limiting network architecture. *ACM SIGCOMM* **2005**, *35*, 241–252. [CrossRef]
28. Chandra, T.; Griesemer, R.; Redstone, J. Paxos made live-an engineering perspective (2006 invited talk). In Proceedings of the 26th ACM Symposium on Principles of Distributed Computing-PODC, Portland, OR, USA, 12–15 August 2007; Volume 7.
29. Kent, S.; Lynn, C.; Seo, K. Secure border gateway protocol (s-bgp). *IEEE JSAC* **2000**, *18*, 582–592. [CrossRef]
30. Awduche, D.O.; Malcolm, J.; Agogbua, J.; O'Dell, M.D.; McManus. Requirements for Traffic Engineering over MPLS. *RFC 2702* **1999**, 1–29.
31. Hahne, E.L. Round-robin scheduling for max-min fairness in data networks. *IEEE J. Sel. Areas Commun.* **1991**, *9*, 1024–1039. [CrossRef]
32. Yaar, A.; Perrig, A.; Song, D. Stackpi: New packet marking and filtering mechanisms for ddos and ip spoofing defense. *IEEE J. Sel. Areas Commun.* **2006**, *24*, 1853–1863. [CrossRef]
33. Duan, Z.; Yuan, X.; Chandrashekar, J. Controlling ip spoofing through interdomain packet filters. *IEEE Trans. Dependable Secur. Comput.* **2008**, *5*, 22–36. [CrossRef]
34. Ameigeiras, P.; Ramos-Munoz, J.J.; Navarro-Ortiz, J.; Lopez-Soler, J.M. Analysis and modelling of youtube traffic. *Trans. Emerg. Telecommun. Technol.* **2012**, *23*, 360–377. [CrossRef]
35. Kiwon, H.; Youngjun, K.; Hyungoo, C.; Jinwoo, P. SDN-Assisted Slow HTTP DDoS Attack Defense Method. *IEEE Commun. Lett.* **2018**, *22*, 688–691.
36. Wisam, H.A.M. A hybrid scheme for detecting and preventing single packet Low-rate DDoS and flooding DDoS attacks in SDN. In Proceedings of the 2023 IEEE 3rd International Maghreb Meeting of the Conference on Sciences and Techniques of Automatic Control and Computer Engineering (MI-STA), Benghazi, Libya, 21–23 May 2023; pp. 707–712
37. Heena, K.; Moin, M.M.; Pooja, S.; Narayan, D.G. DDoS Attack Detection System using Apache Spark. In Proceedings of the 2021 International Conference on Computer Communication and Informatics (ICCCI), Coimbatore, India, 27–29 January 2021; pp. 1–5.

Disclaimer/Publisher's Note: The statements, opinions and data contained in all publications are solely those of the individual author(s) and contributor(s) and not of MDPI and/or the editor(s). MDPI and/or the editor(s) disclaim responsibility for any injury to people or property resulting from any ideas, methods, instructions or products referred to in the content.

Article

IoT Edge Device Security: An Efficient Lightweight Authenticated Encryption Scheme Based on LED and PHOTON

Mohammed Al-Shatari [1,*], Fawnizu Azmadi Hussin [1], Azrina Abd Aziz [1], Taiseer Abdalla Elfadil Eisa [2], Xuan-Tu Tran [3] and Mhassen Elnour Elneel Dalam [4]

[1] Department of Electrical and Electronic Engineering, Universiti Teknologi PETRONAS, Seri Iskandar 32610, Malaysia; fawnizu@utp.edu.my (F.A.H.); azrina_aaziz@utp.edu.my (A.A.A.)
[2] Department of Information Systems-Girls Section, King Khalid University, Mahayil 62529, Saudi Arabia; teisa@kku.edu.sa
[3] VNU Information Technology Institute, Vietnam National University, Hanoi 100000, Vietnam; tutx@vnu.edu.vn
[4] Department of Mathematics—Girls Section, King Khalid University, Mahayil 62529, Saudi Arabia; mdalam01@kku.edu.sa
* Correspondence: m.alshatari@gmail.com or mohammed_17005247@utp.edu.my

Abstract: IoT devices and embedded systems are deployed in critical environments, emphasizing attributes like power efficiency and computational capabilities. However, these constraints stress the paramount importance of device security, stimulating the exploration of lightweight cryptographic mechanisms. This study introduces a lightweight architecture for authenticated encryption tailored to these requirements. The architecture combines the lightweight encryption of the LED block cipher with the authentication of the PHOTON hash function. Leveraging shared internal operations, the integration of these bases optimizes area–performance tradeoffs, resulting in reduced power consumption and a reduced logic footprint. The architecture is synthesized and simulated using Verilog HDL, Quartus II, and ModelSim, and implemented on Cyclone FPGA devices. The results demonstrate a substantial 14% reduction in the logic area and up to a 46.04% decrease in power consumption in contrast to the individual designs of LED and PHOTON. This work highlights the potential for using efficient cryptographic solutions in resource-constrained environments.

Keywords: authenticated encryption; FPGA; hardware footprint; hardware security; LED block cipher; lightweight cryptography; logic resources; low power; PHOTON hash function

Citation: Al-Shatari, M.; Hussin, F.A.; Aziz, A.A.; Eisa, T.A.E.; Tran, X.-T.; Dalam, M.E.E. IoT Edge Device Security: An Efficient Lightweight Authenticated Encryption Scheme Based on LED and PHOTON. *Appl. Sci.* **2023**, *13*, 10345. https://doi.org/10.3390/app131810345

Academic Editors: Lip Yee Por and Abdullah Ayub Khan

Received: 30 August 2023
Revised: 14 September 2023
Accepted: 14 September 2023
Published: 15 September 2023

Copyright: © 2023 by the authors. Licensee MDPI, Basel, Switzerland. This article is an open access article distributed under the terms and conditions of the Creative Commons Attribution (CC BY) license (https://creativecommons.org/licenses/by/4.0/).

1. Introduction

With the ongoing advancement of embedded systems and semiconductor technology, new devices are getting smaller and faster and consuming less power. This has led to the development of the Internet of Things (IoT) [1], whereby many "things" in our real lives are connected to the internet and to each other. These current technologies are stimulating the Fourth Industrial Revolution (Industry 4.0), in which industries have started to embrace the IoT in their industrial operations, forming the so-called Industrial IoT (IIoT). These things enhance the automation of operations in the industry by utilizing hardware and mechanical components to interact with the physical world, making them vulnerable to threats and cyber-attacks. They are usually deployed in critical infrastructures where attacks may lead to damage and casualties. Attackers might steal confidential data, slow production operations, or even interrupt and stop entire operations, as happened with the Stuxnet attack [2]. Therefore, securing IIoT edge devices is a high priority and should be taken seriously, starting from the design phase. Cryptographic primitives are often used to fortify embedded system devices during transmission and communication by ensuring the confidentiality and integrity of data, as well as guaranteeing access control, authentication, and non-repudiation [3]. Researchers have developed security protocols in computer networks and other embedded systems based on proven symmetric and asymmetric cryptographic frameworks [4]. However, IIoT edge devices normally have limited resources and power and do not have the computing resources required to handle conventional cryptographic algorithms. Their limited capabilities necessitate the need for lightweight and compact cryptographic schemes [5,6].

The field of lightweight cryptography (LWC) investigates the integration of cryptographic primitives into constrained devices [7]. LWC balances the tradeoffs of cost, energy consumption, performance, and security [7,8] to provide lightweight ciphers that consume low amounts of power and achieve an acceptable level of security. Researchers have also proposed lightweight crypto engines by reducing the complexity of the conventional algorithms, but these have the drawback of reduced security [9]. For devices with limited capabilities, energy-efficient algorithms that perform well in hardware are much more appropriate [10]. A reduction in hardware chips (Gate Equivalents—GE) is imperative in LWC as it is directly proportional to the cost and the power consumption.

Cryptography can be asymmetric (public key) or symmetric (secret key). The latter guarantees data confidentiality, integrity, and authenticity by utilizing an authentication protocol. For LWC, block ciphers are the most widely used for encryption (confidentiality) as the data can be processed in blocks rather than bit streaming. For data integrity and authenticity, hash functions are commonly used by forming message authentication codes (MACs). They take a plain message as the input and produce a fixed-length tag. For more advanced functionality, ciphers and integrity mechanisms are integrated to form authenticated encryption (AE).

Lightweight edge devices such as the Internet of Things (IoT) have been widely used in recent years either for monitoring or controlling. The incremental usage of these devices raises concerns regarding the security of the data passing through these devices. Cryptographers and cryptanalysts encounter major challenges due to the rapid spread of lightweight devices, needing to safeguard their data where these devices are installed in different critical environments. These devices usually have resource constraints. Therefore, lightweight cryptographic primitives must be integrated with these devices to ensure their security and authenticity.

Lightweight block ciphers are cryptographic primitives that utilize small design spaces and Gate Equivalents (GE). The literature defines "lightweight" as ciphers utilizing less than 3000 GE [10]. Lightweight block ciphers are mainly intended for devices that have limited computation capabilities, low power, and small footprints. The ubiquitous spread of IoT and other constrained devices has increased the demand for LWC security solutions. LWC should be designed with constraints, while maintaining a certain level of security. LWC designers must balance security and the limited resources of the constrained devices. A tradeoff between security, cost, and performance should be considered when designing any lightweight cryptographic primitive [7], as illustrated in Figure 1.

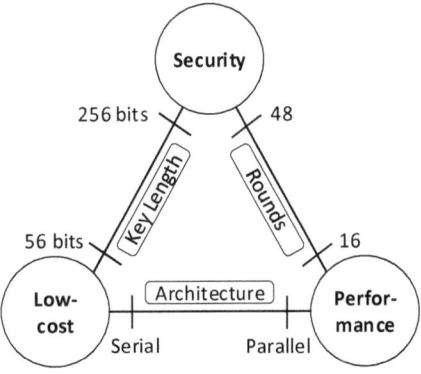

Figure 1. Tradeoffs of lightweight cryptography.

Cryptographic hardware architectures entail tradeoffs between the security level, system performance, and cost. Parallel architecture provides high performance but, in turn, increases the cost. On the other hand, serial architecture has low costs, but the system performance is degraded. The length of the secret key in the cryptographic algorithms reflects the tradeoff of security versus cost. A longer key increases the security of the system but also raises the cost because more resources are utilized. Meanwhile, reducing the key length helps to reduce the cost but lowers the level of security too. In addition, rounds in cryptographic algorithms affect the system's performance and security. A higher number of rounds guarantees a higher level of security but reduces the throughput of the system. In contrast, reducing the number of rounds increases the system performance but reduces the security level.

Confidentiality can be guaranteed using block and stream ciphers where only authorized entities can access the message. However, encryption ciphers do not guarantee the tampering of the encrypted message will not occur [11]. Authenticated encryption (AE) schemes can overcome this problem and provide authenticity and integrity to the message on top of the confidentiality provided by the encryption cipher.

The AE can be extended to encompass some additional non-encrypted data, as in a network packet header, where both the payload and the header are authenticated but encryption is applied only to the payload.

In IPsec and transport layer security (TLS), AE techniques are commonly employed. As of August 2018, the current version of TLS no longer supports non-AE algorithms like AES in cipher block chaining (CBC) mode, although end-to-end encryption is provided by such techniques in popular messaging applications.

Three separate common methods referred to as generic composition are used to create authenticated encryption schemes [12]. The order of the encryption and authentication activities varies between these methods. The first composition, encrypt-then-MAC (EtM), is a sequential encryption and authentication. It begins with the encryption of the message followed by the authentication of the encrypted version of the message. The second composition, encrypt-and-MAC (E&M), is a concurrent encryption and authentication method whereby encryption and authentication are carried out independently for the original input messages. The third composition, MAC-then-encrypt (MtE), refers to the use of authentication then encryption. Initially, it computes a MAC for the message, then encrypts both the resulting MAC tag and the original message in combination.

When examined from numerous security perspectives, most of the current AE techniques are weak. Generic composition approaches have been subjected to a number of security attacks, and EtM proved to be the most secure [12,13].

In industries and other critical environments, the deployed devices encounter resource limitations, lacking the necessary computation and communication capabilities. Despite these conditions, and the insufficiency of the conventional cryptographic algorithms, it is important to guarantee security for these devices. Several surveys, as referenced in [11,14–18], have been conducted to address the importance of information protection within lightweight devices. There are several works related to the single-architecture design related to LED block ciphers [19–25] and the PHOTON hash function [19,23,26–30]. These designs were synthesized on different hardware platforms and targeting different optimization goals. Several authenticated encryption architectures based on different composition methods were presented, including the latest designs in [10,21,31–35]. However, some of them were synthesized and simulated on different platforms and others consume large amounts of logic resources when composing the encryption with the authentication.

The work in [10] integrated the PRESENT block cipher [36] and the SPONGENT hash function [37] to construct an authenticated encryption. Both PRESENT and SPONGENT were designed by the same group with similar permutation functions. Therefore, the authors of [10] achieved a good reduction rate of logic resources by sharing the common functions within both primitives. However, they implemented their design in ASIC and reported their results in Gate Equivalent. Additionally, their design resulted in a very low operating frequency and throughput.

The authors of [21,31] presented an authenticated encryption composed of an LED block cipher [38] and a PHOTON hash function [39], with the objective of reusing the common datapath functions and reducing the footprints. They achieved a considerable operating frequency and throughput; however, they could share only small parts of the datapath and achieved a low reduction rate of the footprints. Additionally, they implemented their design on Xilinx FPGA and reported their results in Slices.

The work reported in [33] utilized the AES block cipher with an Offset Tow Round (OTR) to create an authenticated encryption. They implemented their design on Altera Startix FPGA from the Virtex family. They achieved high speeds and reduced the logic resource utilization to almost half of the original architecture design. However, their reduced architecture design is still considered high when compared to other proposals.

The authors of [34,35] introduced an authentication framework for smart homes and industrial environments. They utilized Ascon authenticated encryption with a hash function to construct their architecture, as referenced in [34], and an AEAD encryption algorithm with a hash function, as referenced in [35]. However, their design was implemented on software and their results were reported based on the computational, communication, and storage costs.

The work reported in [40] introduced a new proposal of authenticated encryption submitted to the NIST. The work was implemented on Xilinx FPGA Sparta 6. They achieved higher speeds but at the cost of larger footprints, even compared to their competitors' proposals.

In this study, an authenticated encryption (AE) architecture is proposed that aims to reduce its footprint compared to other existing AE architectures. This is accomplished by employing the most minimal versions of the LED block cipher (LED-64) and the PHOTON hash function (PHOTON-80/20/16) and sharing similar resources between the two. The round-dependent constants generated by the linear feedback shift register (LFSR) serve a dual purpose: they control the permutation rounds and the multiplexer selectors. Furthermore, employing look-up tables (LUTs) in place of Galois multiplications decreases the computational intensity of the *MixColumns* matrices, leading to the reduced utilization of logical resources. These shared resources, combined with the use of LFSR and LUTs, make a substantial impact in terms of minimizing the logic resources needed for the architecture of the AE (authenticated encryption).

Paper Organization

The first section of this paper introduces the background of lightweight cryptography and authenticated encryption, followed by an analysis of the related work in the same section. In Section 2, we provide a detailed explanation of the algorithm of the LED block cipher and PHOTON hash function, as well as their individual implementation. The design procedure of the proposed authenticated encryption is provided in Section 3, as well as the implementation of hardware architecture for the authenticated encryption, and a summary of the hardware resource utilization. Section 4 contains the results and a discussion of the proposed authenticated encryption. It discusses the outcomes of the simulation and resource utilization and benchmarking with the available related work. Finally, the summary and conclusions and the paper's key findings are provided in Section 5.

2. Algorithm and Implementation

A design for a composite authenticated encryption system is proposed. It combines encryption by an LED block cipher with authentication by the PHOTON hash function. The primary objective of the design is to reduce the logic area utilization; thus, the variants with the smallest sizes of the LED and PHOTON were selected. We present a lightweight authenticated encryption (AE) architecture based on the primitives in Sections 2.1 and 2.2 with generic EtM composition.

The design utilizes the shared logic resources for reusability. The internal permutation functions are designed using Verilog HDL and synthesized on several families of Altera FPGAs. The design tools of Altera Quartus II and ModelSim are used for the synthesis and simulation.

2.1. LED-64 Block Cipher

An LED-64 block cipher [38] is a lightweight symmetric security primitive, the structure and mathematical operations of which are based on the substitution permutation network (SPN). It has a 64-bit input block, 32 permutation rounds, a 64-bit encryption key, and a 64-bit output ciphertext. The arrangement of the input in the state is organized in a 4×4 row-based matrix. Each cell of the matrix has a 4-bit nibble within the Galois Field (GF) (2^4) with the irreducible polynomial function of $X^4 + X + 1$ (10011). The round permutation function of the LED is an AES-like function, where there are four operations in every round; these are processed sequentially, as shown in Figure 2.

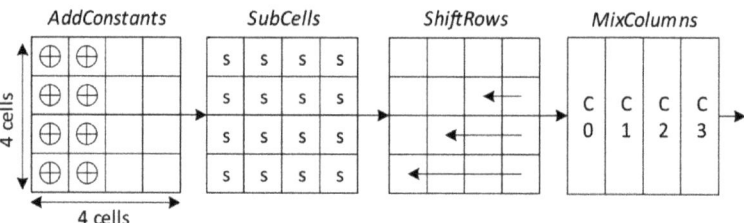

Figure 2. LED permutation blocks.

The architecture of the LED is designed in a round-based mode. Figure 3 shows the architecture of LED-64 block cipher. P refers to the original input message—plaintext. K is the encryption key, STR is the state register, AC is the AddConstant block, SC is the SubCells block, SR is the ShiftRows block, MC is the MixColumns block, RC is the round constants block, and C is the output ciphertext. The input message is XORed with the encryption key after every 3 rounds for 32 rounds. Figure 4 illustrates the control flow of the encryption operation. In the first round, the input is XORed with the encryption key, and, in rounds 1, 5, 9, 13, 17, 21, 25 and 29, the output of the MC block is XORed with the key. Meanwhile, in the other rounds, the output of the MC is loaded directly to the STR register. The *STR* register is updated every round to hold the updated state matrix. The round constants are generated by the RC block where the RC feeds the AC and controls the inputs to STR.

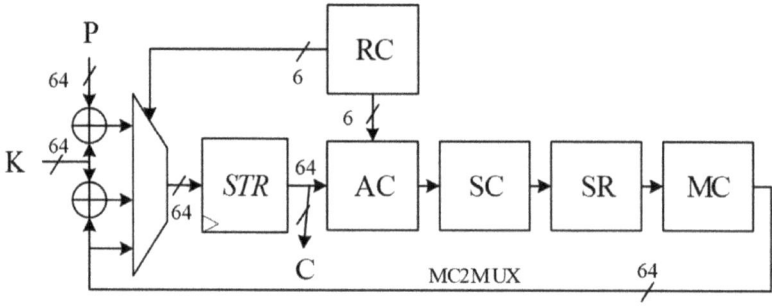

Figure 3. Architecture of the LED-64 block cipher.

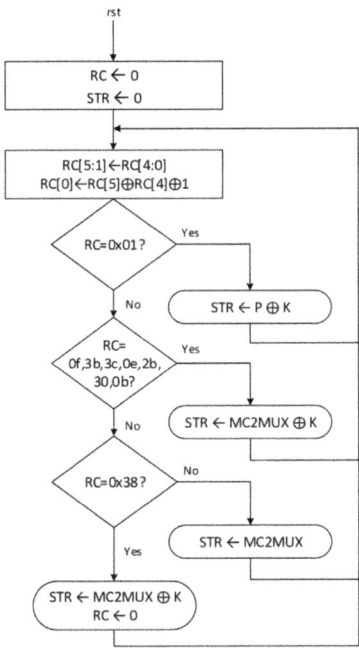

Figure 4. ASM of the LED-64 cipher.

2.1.1. AddConstants (*AC*)

AC modifies the first two columns of the state matrix. These columns are XORed with pre-defined constants. The first column is XORed with an 8-bit integer that represents the encryption key size and is denoted by (ks_7–ks_0). A 6-bit round-dependent constant (RC5 to RC0) is produced by LFSR and XORed with the second column of the state matrix. It is initialized with zeros at the beginning and updated every round, where RC0 is the result of (RC5$\oplus$RC4$\oplus$1). The matrix below shows the variables to be XORed with the first two columns of the state, whereas the other columns are kept unchanged. The values of the key size bits are represented by inverting the corresponding bits instead of using XOR operations.

$$\begin{pmatrix} ks_7 \| ks_6 \| ks_5 \| ks_4 & 0 \| RC_5 \| RC_4 \| RC_3 & 0000 & 0000 \\ ks_7 \| ks_6 \| ks_5 \| ks_4 \oplus 1 & 0 \| RC_2 \| RC_1 \| RC_0 & 0000 & 0000 \\ ks_3 \| ks_2 \| ks_1 \oplus 1 \| ks_0 & 0 \| RC_5 \| RC_4 \| RC_3 & 0000 & 0000 \\ ks_3 \| ks_2 \| ks_1 \oplus 1 \| ks_0 \oplus 1 & 0 \| RC_2 \| RC_1 \| RC_0 & 0000 & 0000 \end{pmatrix}$$

2.1.2. SubCells (*SC*)

SC obscures the relationship between the utilized encryption key and the resulting ciphertext. LED reutilize the substitution box presented in PRESENT block cipher [36]. The SC process is a non-linear operation represented by look-up tables (LUTs). All the cells of the internal state matrix are matched and swapped with the corresponding values from the substitution box, as shown in Table 1.

Table 1. Substitution box of the PRESENT cipher.

X	0	1	2	3	4	5	6	7	8	9	A	B	C	D	E	F
S[x]	C	5	6	B	9	0	A	D	3	E	F	8	4	7	1	2

2.1.3. ShiftRows (SR)

SR shifts all the matrix rows (R0, R1, R2, R3) to the left by the value of the respective indices. The first row R0, indexed with 0, is unmodified. Row R1 is shifted one cell to the left, row R2 is shifted two cells to the left, and the last row, R3, is shifted three cells to the left. SR is a wire shift, whereby it does not consume logic resources.

2.1.4. MixColumns (MC)

MC, in addition to SR, provides data diffusion. Every column in the state matrix undergoes an individual multiplication with a specified matrix shown in Equation (1):

$$M = \begin{pmatrix} 4 & 1 & 2 & 2 \\ 8 & 6 & 5 & 6 \\ B & E & A & 9 \\ 2 & 2 & F & B \end{pmatrix} \quad (1)$$

The MC operation requires a significant amount of logic resources due to the multiplication involved in the matrix calculation. However, the intensive computation of the column multiplication is replaced by functions of LUTs.

2.2. PHOTON Hash Function

The PHOTON hash function [39] is a lightweight security primitive designed for low-resource devices. It has a sponge-based construction, as shown in Figure 5, and its permutation function is an AES-like function, following the SP network shown in Figure 6. Sponge construction has two phases: the absorbing phase and the squeezing phase. The original input message is fully absorbed by the absorbing phase whereas the output hash is produced by the squeezing phase.

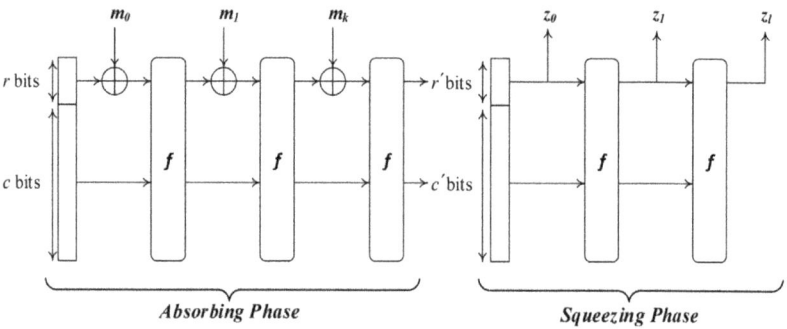

Figure 5. PHOTON sponge construction.

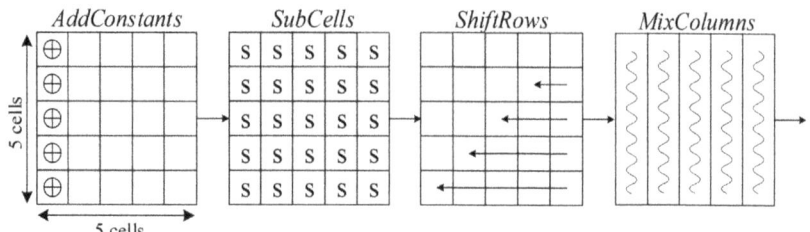

Figure 6. PHOTON permutation.

PHOTON-80/20/16 has an output hash size (n) of 80 bits, an input rate (r) of 20 bits, an output rate (r') of 16 bits, and a (5 × 5) state matrix size (t) of 100 bits with a 4-bit cell size (s). Figure 7 shows the architecture of this variant of the PHOTON hash function. M is the input message, IV is the initialization vector, and h is the output *hash*. It takes 12 rounds for the absorbing phase for each 20-bit absorbed message, and another 12 rounds for the squeezing phase for each 16-bit squeezed output, as shown in the sponge construction in Figure 5 and the PHOTON control flow in Figure 8. Each cell within the matrix corresponds to an element from the Galois field GF (2^4) with the irreducible polynomial $X^4 + X + 1$.

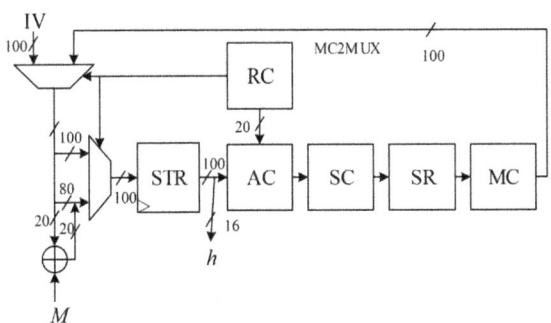

Figure 7. Architecture of PHOTON-80/20/16.

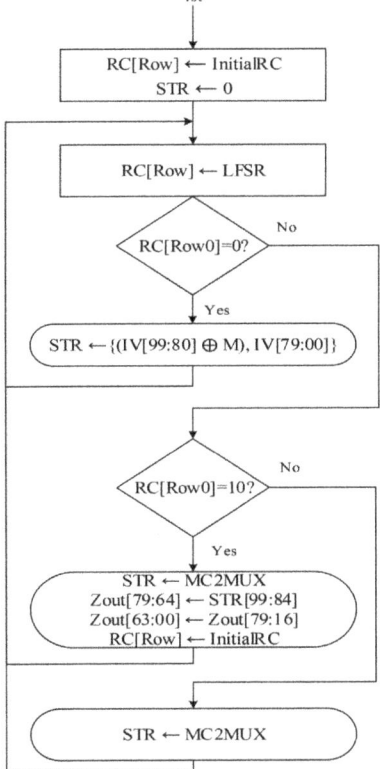

Figure 8. ASM chart of PHOTON-80/20/16.

2.2.1. AddConstants (AC)

The AC operation only affects the first column of the state matrix. There are two constants with values that depend on the permutation round and the matrix dimensions. The round constant (RC) changes with the round sequences. It is a four-bit constant generated from an initialized LFSR, as shown in Table 2. The other constant is the internal constant (IC_d), which depends on the size of the matrix dimensions. For PHOTON-80/20/16, the internal constant is $IC_d = [0, 1, 3, 6, 4]$. These two constants are XORed only with the cells of the first column of the state matrix.

Table 2. Round dependents for PHOTON-80/20/16.

Row \ N_R	1	2	3	4	5	6	7	8	9	10	11	12
1	1	3	7	E	D	B	6	C	9	2	5	A
2	0	2	6	F	C	A	7	D	8	3	4	B
3	2	0	4	D	E	8	5	F	A	1	6	9
4	7	5	1	8	B	D	0	A	15	4	3	12
5	5	7	3	A	9	F	2	8	D	6	1	E

2.2.2. SubCells (SC)

The SC obscures the correlation of the encryption key and the output ciphertext nonlinearly. The substitution box of the PRESENT block cipher [36] is reused by the LED. Each cell of the internal state matrix is matched and replaced by its corresponding value from the substitution box, as illustrated in Table 1.

2.2.3. ShiftRows (SR)

SR shifts all the matrix rows (R1, R2, R3, R4, and R5) to the left by respective defined indices. The first row (R0, indexed with 0) remains unchanged, R1 is shifted one position, R2 is shifted two positions, R3 is shifted three positions, and R4 is shifted four positions. SR is a wire shift, whereby it does not consume many logic resources.

2.2.4. MixColumns (MC)

MC enhances the property of diffusion in addition to SC. MC is designed in parallel instead of using the serialized pre-defined matrix. All the columns of the state matrix are multiplied separately with the defined 5×5 matrix shown in Equation (2):

$$A_{100} = \begin{Bmatrix} 1 & 2 & 9 & 9 & 2 \\ 2 & 5 & 3 & 8 & D \\ D & B & A & C & 1 \\ 1 & F & 2 & 3 & E \\ E & E & 8 & 5 & C \end{Bmatrix} \quad (2)$$

MC requires significant logic resources due to the finite multiplications performed on the matrices. The intensive computation of the column multiplication is replaced by functions of LUTs.

3. LED–PHOTON AE Implementation

The proposed authenticated encryption scheme makes use of shared resources between the block cipher (LED) and the hash function (PHOTON). The encryption process is followed by a MAC process using the generic method of encrypt-then-MAC. The processing begins by resetting the registers of the state (STR) and the selector (LP), and initializing the round constants register (RC) by using a suitable value from the LFSR. RC is utilized to count the round indices of the permutation in both primitives (LED and PHOTON). STR holds the input values to the state matrix. LP is the selector used for performing LED encryption followed by PHOTON authentication. The encryption process begins when LP is set to one; it carries out all four permutation blocks and generates the output ciphertext while also taking advantage of shared resources with the permutation operations of PHOTON. Once the plaintext encryption is completed and the ciphertext is generated, LP is set and the authentication of the ciphertext begins. PHOTON applies authentication to the ciphertext generated by the LED. The permutation operation of PHOTON is processed while sharing the possible resources with the LED. The round count of the permutation operation is controlled by the LFSR. Figure 9 illustrates the block diagrams for the top-level design, and Figure 10 illustrates the arithmetic state machine, of the proposed authenticated encryption architecture.

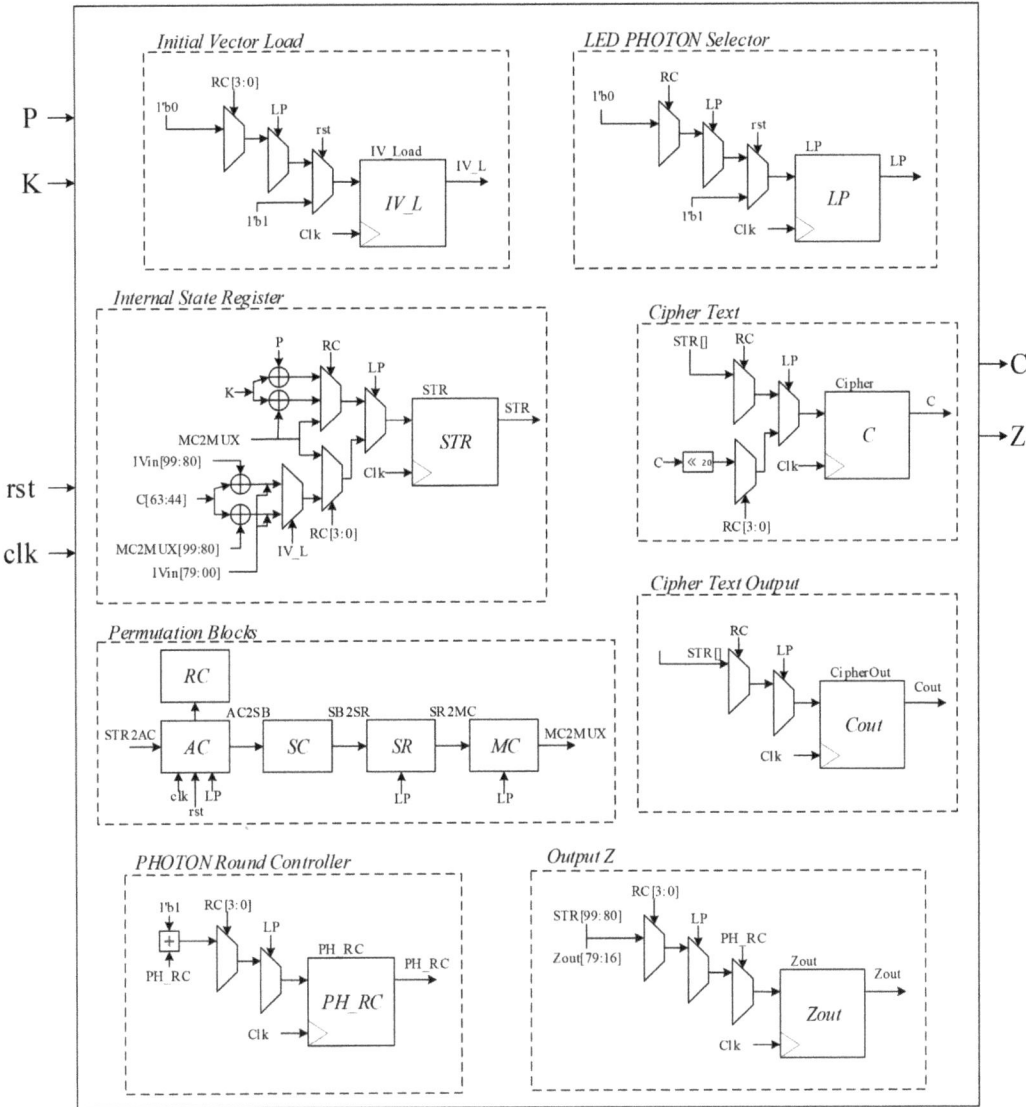

Figure 9. Top-level design of the LED–PHOTON authenticated encryption.

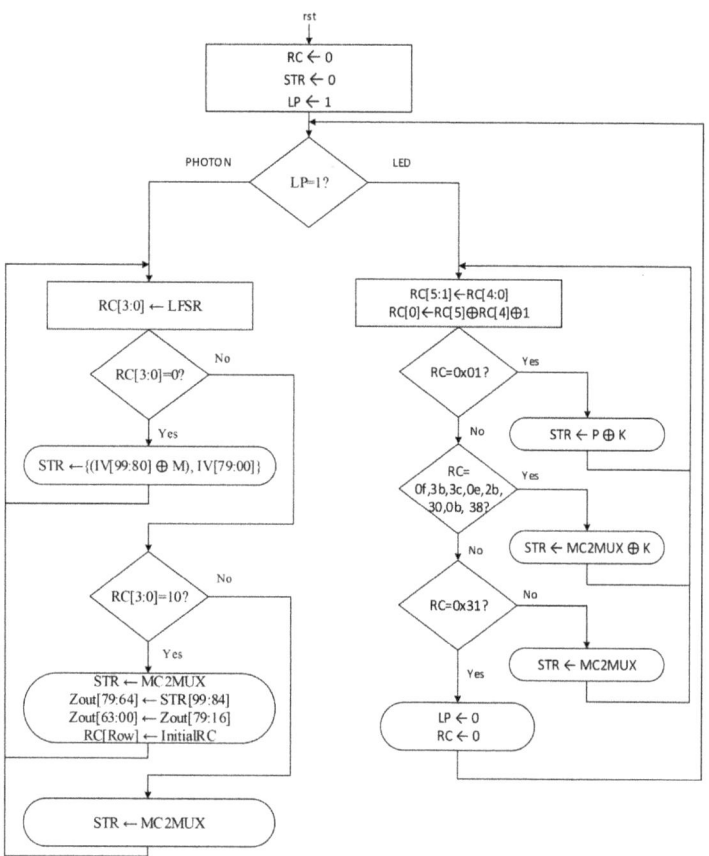

Figure 10. ASM chart of authenticated encryption.

The design of the LED block cipher architecture is inherited from the PHOTON hash function, as they are produced by the same group. The internal permutation structure for both LED and PHOTON is an AES-like structure following the substitution permutation network (SPN). Therefore, the LED–PHOTON authenticated encryption (AE) process has some similarities within the permutation modules. The similarity between LED and PHOTON permutation functions is exploited to reduce the logic area utilization.

The LED block cipher applies the encryption to the input message. The architecture of the individual design of LED-64 is shown in Figure 3. The processing of the LED begins by XORing the input plaintext (P) with the encryption key (K), and the output is loaded to the state register (STR) to be processed in the permutation blocks. This XOR operation of K and P is repeated every four rounds. The round constants (RCs) are fed every round to control the XOR and permutation operations, whereas the STR register is updated every round to hold the current state values. Once the STR is loaded, the state is passed through the permutation blocks for the main encryption operations. The output ciphertext is generated after 32 rounds of permutation functions.

The PHOTON hash function performs the authentication process on the ciphertext encrypted by the LED. The architecture of the individual design of PHOTON-80/20/16 is shown in Figure 7. Four 20-bit input messages are considered, because the input to PHOTON is the 64-bit ciphertext from LED. The 64-bit input is padded with zeros to form a multiple of 20 to be absorbed by the sponge construction. The operation of PHOTON begins by XORing the 20 most significant bits of the initialization vector (IV) with the input message (*M*) and concatenating the result with the 80 least significant bits of *IV* and loading it to the *STR* register. The state matrix is passed through the permutation blocks for the main authentication operations. The *RC* controls the selections of the multiplexers and permutation rounds. The output hash function is generated after 48 rounds for the absorbing phase and 60 rounds for the squeezing phase to absorb the 64-bit input message and squeeze the 80-bit hash output.

For the proposed AE scheme of LED–PHOTON, the design of the internal state follows PHOTON because it has a larger state size than LED. Thus, the state size is 100 bits organized in a 5×5 matrix. As in a substitution permutation network, the permutation function consists of four operations: AddConstants (AC), SubstitutionBox (SB) or SubCells (SC), ShiftRows (SR), and MixColumns (MC).

3.1. AddConstants (AC)

The Add Constants (AC) operation in the authenticated encryption architecture partially modifies the internal state matrix according to the specific algorithm of the cryptographic primitive. In LED, the AC permutation involves XOR operations for the first two columns, while the other two columns remain unchanged. The first column is XORed with an eight-bit key-size representation constant, whereas the second column is XORed with a six-bit round constant generated from LFSR. Meanwhile, the AC operation in PHOTON applies modification only to the first column by XORing a four-bit LFSR-generated round constant and a predefined internal constant. The Add Constants modules of LED and PHOTON partially share the logic resources and reuse several XOR operations. To minimize the number of XOR gates, the high bit of the key size representation in LED is inverted instead of using an XOR operation, and the XOR operation in the LFSR of PHOTON is converted to XNOR. The bits of various rows in PHOTON are flipped to reduce the number of XOR gates in the Add Constants module. The first row, Row 0, is produced by flipping specific bits of rows 1–4, namely, the least significant bit (b_0) of row 1, the two least significant bits of row 2 ($b_1\ b_0$), the two mid-bits of row 3 ($b_2\ b_1$), and the third bit of the last row (b_2). The round constants in each row are equal to the round constants in the first row after being XORed with their respective internal constants.

3.2. SubCells (SC)

SCs modify the internal state in a nonlinear manner. The same substitution box (PRESENT) [36] is employed by both LED and PHOTON. The non-linear values of the substitution box replace the equivalent cells of the state matrix, as shown in Table 1. Since the same confusion technique is utilized by both LED and PHOTON with the same substitution box, the SubCells modules are fully shared.

3.3. ShiftRows (SR)

SR is the third permutation operation in the SPN (substitution–permutation network) structure. LED and PHOTON apply similar operations, whereby all the rows in the matrix are rotated to the left based on their index values. The first row, indexed with 0, remains unchanged, while all the other rows are rotated according to the respective positions. The SR modules of LED and PHOTON are partially shared, but they do not take up a significant amount of the logic area as they are just a simple wire shift. There are some mismatched matrix cells for two modules when shifting the rows. Therefore, separate multiplexers were used to match these matrix cells.

3.4. MixColumns (MC)

MC is the final permutation operation in the SPN structure. This operation works in conjunction with the ShiftRows function to ensure data diffusion. For both LED and PHOTON, an algorithm-specific pre-defined matrix is multiplied with each row of the state matrix. Although the structure of the LED's MC operation is inherited from PHOTON, the size of the internal matrix state and the pre-defined matrices are different. The columns of the state in LED are multiplied by a 4 × 4 matrix, shown in Equation (1), while the columns in PHOTON are multiplied by a 5 × 5 matrix, shown in Equation (2).

The MixColumns operations in LED and PHOTON share some of the logic resources. The output of the MC is generated by feeding the input into a 100-bit LUT to obtain the relevant multiplication values for the particular cipher.

3.5. Summary of Resource Reusability

The authenticated encryption architecture being proposed leverages the common logic resources shared by both the LED block cipher and the PHOTON hash function. The state matrices of both primitives are merged into a unified 100-bit register in the authenticated encryption shared architecture.

In the AddConstants module, part of the internal state is directly modified using XOR operations. The sharing ability reduces the number of XOR gates used in this module by half. The four-bit LFSR of PHOTON is considered a part of the six-bit LFSR of LED, as it takes its four LSB bits. Therefore, these two LFSRs are combined into one. For the SubCells module, since it is generated from the same substitution box for both LED and PHOTON, it may be used by both, with the exception that LED's state is now 100 bits long rather than 64 bits long, to match PHOTON. The ShiftRows module is applied to both LED and PHOTON but, since the number of cells in the state is not the same for LED and PHOTON, there are some mismatched cells, and they are treated individually. Therefore, the ShiftRows module is partially shared. MixColumns, on the other hand, consumes more logic resources than the other modules, even though look-up tables are used to replace the finite intensive multiplications. Since the sizes of the state matrices and pre-defined matrices are not the same for LED and PHOTON, the two modules are not fully merged. However, some similar cells of the pre-defined matrices were exploited to reuse the mask for the LUTs. Generally, the similarity of the operations and the network structure between the LED block cipher and the PHOTON hash function allows for the reusability of the logic resources.

4. Results and Discussion

Modules related to cryptography are among the highest in terms of logic resources consumption compared to other modules in IoT edge devices [41]. Therefore, plenty of attention is paid to the cryptographic modules in resource-constrained devices to satisfy their limitations.

We have presented detailed discussions of the proposed AE, and further parameters were considered in addition to synthesis and simulation on different platforms. The block cipher (LED) and hash function (PHOTON) were combined to create an authenticated encryption with the aim of utilizing and reusing the common operations between the two cryptographic primitives. Therefore, a lightweight authenticated encryption primitive is implemented on the register transfer level (RTL) using Verilog Hardware Description Language (HDL). The most lightweight variants, the LED-64 block cipher and the PHOTON-80/20/16 hash function, are merged to compose the proposed authenticated encryption. The generic composition method used in this architecture design is the encrypt-then-MAC method, which is the most provably secure. The architecture is synthesized and simulated on several Altera FPGA devices with the help of their provided software. Figure 11 and Table 3 demonstrate the results of the proposed authenticated encryption. The results of the single architectures of the LED block cipher and the PHOTON hash function, as well as the composite authenticated encryption, are generated by Altera Quartus II. The results of the resource utilization and maximum operating frequency are taken directly from the analysis generated by Quartus II. Power consumption was measured using the power analyser tools (PowerPlay) provided by Quartus II. The percentages of the reduction rates of the resource utilization and power consumption are found by comparing the composite architecture to the single architectures. The efficiency is obtained from the input data, maximum allowable frequency, latency, and logic utilization.

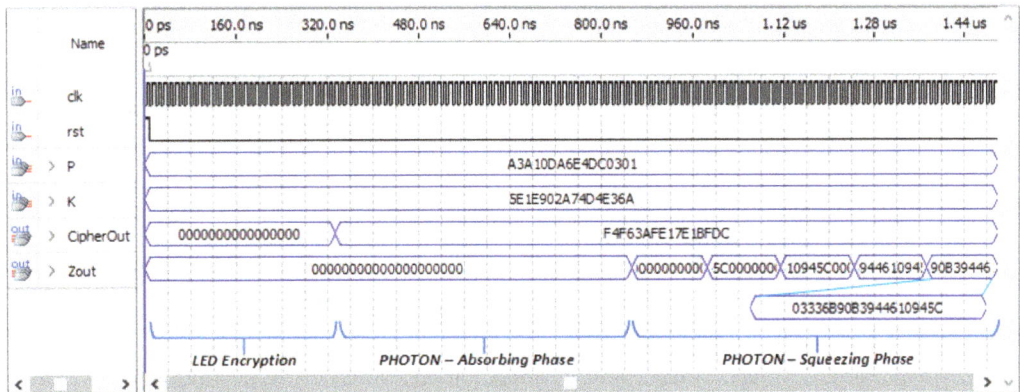

Figure 11. Simulation waveform of LED–PHOTON authenticated encryption.

Table 3. Synthesis and simulation results of authenticated encryption, LED, and PHOTON.

Design	Datapath (Bits)	No. of LEs	No. of Clock Cycles	Max. Freq. (MHz)	Power (mW)	LE Reduction Rate (%)	Power Consumption Reduction Rate (%)	FPGA Device
AE	100	1030	140	140.39	99.30	13.52	24.19	
LED	64	365	32	208.72	89.38			Cyclone II
PHOTON	100	826	108	321.44	41.60			
AE	100	1017	140	184.77	89.73	13.67	39.03	
LED	64	357	32	271.96	82.19			Cyclone III
PHOTON	100	821	108	338.75/250.0	64.99			
AE	100	1018	140	150.51	157.97	13.73	46.04	
LED	64	357	32	231.21	150.45			Cyclone III LS
PHOTON	100	823	108	336.36/250.0	142.21			
AE	100	1024	140	176.87	147.38	13.58	33.06	
LED	64	357	32	254.19	120.52			Cyclone IV E
PHOTON	100	828	108	361.53/250.00	99.65			
AE	100	1020	140	164.31	217.51	13.56	19.65	
LED	64	357	32	265.46	173.61			Cyclone IV GX
PHOTON	100	823	108	368.32/250.0	97.10			

The authenticated encryption is processed in 140 permutation rounds. LED-64 encrypts the 64-bit input block in 32 rounds. PHOTON-80/20/16 processes the input data in two phases, the absorbing phase and the squeezing phase. The absorbing phase processes a single 20-bit message in 12 rounds, resulting in 48 rounds for all four input messages. The squeezing phase also takes 12 rounds for each 16-bit output, resulting in 60 rounds for the whole concatenated hash digest of 80 bits. Therefore, the ciphertext takes 32 rounds to be generated, whereas the hash digest is produced in another 108 rounds, as illustrated in the simulation waveform in Figure 11.

The performance of the proposed AE scheme is proportional to the performance of our architectures for the single LED cipher and the PHOTON hash function. The performance metric is based on the maximum operating frequency of the single architectures and the composite architecture of the proposed AE. PHOTON runs at a high frequency, whereas LED runs at a slightly lower frequency. If the encryption of the LED block cipher is authenticated by the PHOTON hash function, it will run within the frequency of the lower primitive, regardless of the generic composition method used. Therefore, the proposed

AE runs at a frequency within the range of the single design of the LED. Table 3 illustrates the operating frequency of the single architecture, as well as the composite architecture. The operating frequency of the proposed AE is slightly lower than the frequency of both LED and PHOTON. This is because this design completes a full permutation round in a single cycle, as well as sharing more than a single operation in one cycle. Therefore, the cycle count is the same as the total number of permutation rounds of LED and PHOTON.

The proposed AE scheme is efficient in terms of power consumption and area reduction. For the same number of permutation rounds, the utilization of logic resources is proportional to the power consumption. Sharing the common resources between LED and PHOTON and reducing the utilization of logic resources will result in a reduction in the power consumption. This includes the tradeoffs of security, cost, and architecture design. In this work, we aimed to optimize the architecture to reduce the logic resources, thus reducing the cost and power consumption.

The available previous work related to targeted cryptographic primitives aims for a single-architecture design. Moreover, these architecture designs are mostly synthesized on Xilinx FPGA devices. Therefore, a proposed authenticated encryption architecture synthesized on Altera FPGA devices is compared with our single LED and PHOTON architecture designs.

The LED and PHOTON architectures were individually designed and synthesized on several FPGA platforms. The cyclone family was used for synthesis and simulation. The results show similar resource utilization levels for all cyclone devices, as shown in Table 3. For the LED block cipher, the resource utilization was approximately 365 LE, whereas the PHOTON hash function utilizes 826 LE. The total logic utilization for both LED and PHOTON, when synthesized individually, is 1191 LE. However, the proposed architecture of LED–PHOTON authenticated encryption utilizes about 1030 LE for Altera Cyclone devices. This results in a reduction in the utilization of logic resources by approximately 14% in comparison with individual architectures.

The datapath width and the number of cycles for LED, PHOTON, and the AE are the same for all FPGA devices. However, the performance of the individual implementation of LED, PHOTON, and AE varies from one FPGA device to another. The individual design of LED achieves 208.72 MHz to 265.46 MHz, and PHOTON achieves 321.44 MHz to 368.32 MHz, depending on the type of FPGA device. When LED and PHOTON are merged without sharing the logic resources, the maximum frequency of PHOTON is cut off at the lower frequency of the LED. On the other hand, the proposed authenticated encryption achieves 140.39 MHz to 176.87 MHz for the same FPGA devices as the single designs. The proposed AE has a slightly lower maximum allowable frequency in comparison to the individual designs of LED and PHOTON. However, the degradation in performance is quite reasonable compared to the reduction in logic resource usage that is accomplished.

As the logic area utilization is mostly proportional to the power consumption, the reduction in the logic resources also improves the power consumption. For the individual designs of LED and PHOTON, the total power consumption for both ranges from 130.98 mW to 292.66 mW, whereas the power consumption of the proposed architecture ranges from 89.73 mW to 217.51 mW, depending on the FPGA device of the Cyclone family. Therefore, the power consumption was reduced by a minimum of 19.65% and a maximum of 46.04% based on the FPGA device, as shown in Table 3.

A comparison of the related work with the proposed work is provided in Table 4. The work detailed in [33] implemented an authenticated encryption on Stratix 4 FPGA and other devices from the Virtex family with the goal of reducing the logic area and achieving high speeds. They used an AES block cipher with an offset two-round (OTR) method, comprising an authenticated encryption. The authors were able to reduce the logic area by almost half compared to the original design. However, since they had to keep the speed in gigabits, the architecture still utilizes a large area compared to the proposed lightweight authenticated encryption. Z'aba et al. [40] introduced CiliPadi lightweight authenticated encryption, and the first design was submitted to the first round of the

US NIST project. Their design was implemented on the Virtex 6 Xilinx FPGA device. They achieved higher frequencies compared to our work and the benchmarked work, but their most lightweight design (CiliPadi-Mild) still consumes more logic resources, even in comparison to their benchmarked proposals [42,43]. The authors of [21] aimed to design an authenticated encryption architecture and reuse the datapath functions by integrating an LED block cipher with the PHOTON hash function. They performed design space exploration for the LED and PHOTON resources and reported their results in logic slices. They were able to achieve an 8.6% reduction in logic resource utilization. The authors of [10] constructed an authenticated encryption by composing a PRESENT block cipher and a SPONGENT hash function with the goal of reusing the common datapath blocks. The design of the SPONGENT architecture was inherited from the sponge construction with the permutation function instantiated from the PRESENT block cipher. The authors of [10] reported their results in Gate Equivalent (GE) and were able to reduce the logic resources by 27% compared to the individual architectures of both primitives. However, the performance of their composite authenticated encryption was degraded.

Table 4. Comparison of related work with the proposed work.

Ref.	Generic Composition	Logic Utilization	Clock Cycles	Max. Freq. (MHz)	Power (mW)	Logic Reduction Rate (%)	Platform
[10]	PRESENT and SPONGENT	2508 GE	-	-	3.9	27	ASIC
[21]	LED and PHOTON	415 Slices	44	587	469	8.6	Xilinx Vertix-5
[21]	LED and PHOTON	825 Slices	140	332	60	8.6	Xilinx Spartan-3
[33]	AES-OTR	11 k ALMs	-	-	-	50	Altera Stratix 4
[40]	LED and MonkeyDuplex	303 Slices	72	640	-	-	Xilinx Virtex-6
Proposed	LED and PHOTON	1030 LE	140	140.39	99.30	13.52	Altera Cyclone II
Proposed	LED and PHOTON	1017 LE	140	184.77	89.73	13.67	Altera Cyclone III
Proposed	LED and PHOTON	1018 LE	140	150.51	157.97	13.73	Altera Cyclone III LS
Proposed	LED and PHOTON	1024 LE	140	176.87	147.38	13.58	Altera Cyclone IV E
Proposed	LED and PHOTON	1020 LE	140	164.31	217.51	13.56	Altera Cyclone IV GX

There are always tradeoffs between security, cost, and architecture design, where improving one of them can result in compromising one or both of the others. The architecture design in this paper was optimized to reduce the utilization of logic resources. Nevertheless, the performance results are still quite acceptable. For example, for the Cyclone II FPGA device, the utilization of logic elements was reduced to 1030 LEs, and the power consumption was reduced to about 99 mW, but the operating frequency was still high (around 140 MHz) and the throughput was around 100 Mbps. Therefore, the proposed architecture can be used for many potential applications ranging from video surveillance to IoT.

Security Aspects

The security feature of authenticated encryption (AE) is an important aspect of the design. AE provides both confidentiality (encryption) and data integrity (authentication) in a single operation. It ensures not only that the data are kept secret from unauthorized parties (confidentiality), but also that the data have not been tampered with during transmission or storage (integrity). The proposed AE scheme focuses mainly on reducing the logic resources within FPGA devices to construct a compact AE suitable for resource-efficient applications. The generic composition method used to integrate encryption and authentication primitives in this design has the primary purpose of improving the footprints. The security of the proposed AE scheme is directly tied to the encryption and authentication mechanisms that were utilized to construct this AE. Therefore, the security level for encryption is based on the cryptanalysis of the original LED block cipher, whereas the security level for the authentication is based on the cryptanalysis of the PHOTON hash functions.

The LED block cipher has proven confidentiality and was designed to be resistant to the following attacks: brute-force attacks, differential cryptanalysis, linear cryptanalysis, and slide attacks. On the other hand, the PHOTON hash function has proven authenticity and was designed to be resistant to the following attacks: preimage attacks, collision attacks, second preimage attacks, differential cryptanalysis, linear cryptanalysis, and slide attacks. No cryptanalysis of post-quantum attacks is reported in the original paper of the utilized primitives. Moreover, the cost of quantum attacks is very high [29]. There are some analyses of the attacks applied to the single architectures of the LED block cipher and the PHOTON hash function. However, the main objective of this paper is to reduce the footprints without compromising the security level of the original utilized cryptographic primitives. Table 5 shows the security provability of some related AE schemes compared to the security of the proposed scheme based on the original primitives.

Table 5. Comparison of security features and related attacks.

AE Scheme	Ref.	Provable Confidentiality	Provable Authenticity	Nonce Misuse Resistance	Attacks
AES-CLOC	[44]	√	√	×	Fault attack [45]
PRIMATEs	[46]	√	√	√	Cube attack [47]
AES-JAMBU	[48]	×	×	√	Nonce-misuse attack [49]
Tiaoxin	[50]	×	×	×	Fault attack [51]
Ketje_v2	[52]	√	√	×	Key-recovery attack [53] Fault attack [54] Cube-like attack [55,56] State-recovery attack [57]
MORUS_v2	[58]	×	×	×	Cube attack [59] State-recovery attack [60] Fault attack [60]
JOLTIK	[61]	√	√	√	Key-recovery attack [62] Differential attack [63]
SILC-AES	[64]	√	√	×	Fault attack [65,66]
SILC-LED	[64]	√	√	×	Fault attack [65,66]
Keyak	[67]	√	√	×	Fault attack [54]
ACORN_v3	[68]	√	√	×	Fault attack [69]
ASCON_v1.2	[70]	√	√	×	Preimage attack [71] Template attack [72] Side-channel attack [73] Cube attack [74]
LED-PHOTON	Proposed	√	√	×	Fault attack on LED [75] S-Box attack on LED [76]

5. Conclusions

The proposed design of the LED–PHOTON lightweight authenticated encryption uses a repetitive architecture implemented on multiple FPGA devices from Altera. This architecture is based on rounds, whereby the permutation operations are performed in a single iteration. The LED-64 block cipher takes 32 permutation rounds to complete the encryption of one 64-bit input block. The PHOTON-80/20/16 sponge structure's absorbing phase requires 48 rounds to handle four 20-bit messages, and the squeezing phase generates the 80-bit hash output in 60 rounds. The proposed design is more efficient in terms of area–performance tradeoffs compared to existing designs because it employs common components from both types of architecture. The proposed encrypt-then-MAC design consumes fewer logic resources while maintaining the performance of the single architectures. The proposed design of LED–PHOTON authenticated encryption consumes about 1017–1030 logic elements, achieving approximately a 14% reduction rate in logic utilization depending on the targeted FPGA device. Since there is an area–performance tradeoff, the proposed AE exhibits a slight degradation in performance, whereby the maximum allowable frequency was slightly reduced. However, the performance is considerable compared to the achieved area reduction. As a future recommendation, we suggest implementing the design on actual hardware to obtain more accurate timing data and investigating potential design alternatives, including serialized architectures with smaller areas and pipelined architectures with higher throughput.

Author Contributions: Conceptualization, M.A.-S. and F.A.H.; methodology, M.A.-S.; software, M.A.-S.; validation, M.A.-S., F.A.H. and A.A.A.; formal analysis, X.-T.T.; investigation, M.A.-S. and F.A.H.; resources, T.A.E.E. and M.E.E.D.; data curation, M.A.-S.; writing—original draft preparation, M.A.-S.; writing—review and editing, F.A.H., A.A.A. and X.-T.T.; visualization, T.A.E.E. and M.E.E.D.; supervision, F.A.H., A.A.A. and X.-T.T.; project administration, F.A.H.; funding acquisition, T.A.E.E. and M.E.E.D. All authors have read and agreed to the published version of the manuscript.

Funding: The Deanship of Scientific Research at King Khalid University funded this work through a large-group research project under grant number (RGP2/52/44).

Institutional Review Board Statement: Not applicable.

Informed Consent Statement: Not applicable.

Data Availability Statement: Not applicable.

Acknowledgments: The authors express their appreciation to the Deanship of Scientific Research at King Khalid University for funding this work.

Conflicts of Interest: The authors declare no conflict of interest.

References

1. Ashton, K. That 'internet of things' thing. *RFID J.* **2009**, *22*, 97–114.
2. Langner, R. Stuxnet: Dissecting a cyberwarfare weapon. *IEEE Secur. Priv.* **2011**, *9*, 49–51. [CrossRef]
3. Mushtaq, M.F.; Jamel, S.; Disina, A.H.; Pindar, Z.A.; Ahmad, N.S.; Shakir, M.M.D. A Survey on the Cryptographic Encryption Algorithms. *Int. J. Adv. Comput. Sci. Appl.* **2017**, *8*, 333–344.
4. Maurer, U. Modelling a public-key infrastructure. In *European Symposium on Research in Computer Security*; Springer: Berlin/Heidelberg, Germany, 1996; pp. 325–350.
5. San, I.; At, N. Compact Keccak hardware architecture for data integrity and authentication on FPGAs. *Inf. Secur. J. A Glob. Perspect.* **2012**, *21*, 231–242. [CrossRef]
6. Tsantikidou, K.; Sklavos, N. Hardware Limitations of Lightweight Cryptographic Designs for IoT in Healthcare. *Cryptography* **2022**, *6*, 45. [CrossRef]
7. Poschmann, A.Y. Lightweight Cryptography: Cryptographic Engineering for a Pervasive World. Ph.D. Thesis, Ruhr-University Bochum, Bochum, Germany, 2009.
8. Sklavos, N. On the hardware implementation cost of crypto-processors architectures. *Inf. Secur. J. A Glob. Perspect.* **2010**, *19*, 53–60. [CrossRef]
9. Leander, G.; Paar, C.; Poschmann, A.; Schramm, K. New lightweight DES variants. In *International Workshop on Fast Software Encryption*; Springer: Berlin/Heidelberg, Germany, 2007; pp. 196–210.
10. Hatzivasilis, G.; Floros, G.; Papaefstathiou, I.; Manifavas, C. Lightweight authenticated encryption for embedded on-chip systems. *Inf. Secur. J. A Glob. Perspect.* **2016**, *25*, 151–161. [CrossRef]
11. Jimale, M.A.; Z'aba, M.R.; Kiah, M.L.M.; Idris, M.Y.I.; Jamil, N.; Mohamad, M.S.; Rohmad, M.S. Authenticated encryption schemes: A systematic review. *IEEE Access* **2022**, *10*, 14739–14766. [CrossRef]

12. Bellare, M.; Namprempre, C. Authenticated encryption: Relations among notions and analysis of the generic composition paradigm. *J. Cryptol.* **2008**, *21*, 469–491. [CrossRef]
13. Degabriele, J.P.; Paterson, K.G. On the (in) security of IPsec in MAC-then-encrypt configurations. In Proceedings of the 17th ACM Conference on Computer and Communications Security, Chicago, IL, USA, 4–8 October 2010; pp. 493–504.
14. Zakaria, A.A.; Azni, A.; Ridzuan, F.; Zakaria, N.H.; Daud, M. Systematic Literature Review: Trend Analysis on the Design of Lightweight Block Cipher. *J. King Saud Univ.-Comput. Inf. Sci.* **2023**, *35*, 101550. [CrossRef]
15. Rajalakshmi, S.; Duraisamy, P. A Review on Lightweight Cryptographic algorithms in Internet of Things. In Proceedings of the 2023 5th International Conference on Inventive Research in Computing Applications (ICIRCA), Coimbatore, India, 3–5 August 2023; pp. 1448–1451.
16. Sami, T.M.G.; Zeebaree, S.R.; Ahmed, S.H. A Comprehensive Review of Hashing Algorithm Optimization for IoT Devices. *Int. J. Intell. Syst. Appl. Eng.* **2023**, *11*, 205–231.
17. Seok, B.; Park, J.; Park, J.H. A lightweight hash-based blockchain architecture for industrial IoT. *Appl. Sci.* **2019**, *9*, 3740. [CrossRef]
18. Madushan, H.; Salam, I.; Alawatugoda, J. A review of the nist lightweight cryptography finalists and their fault analyses. *Electronics* **2022**, *11*, 4199. [CrossRef]
19. Nalla Anandakumar, N.; Peyrin, T.; Poschmann, A. A very compact FPGA implementation of LED and PHOTON. In *International Conference on Cryptology in India*; Springer: Berlin/Heidelberg, Germany, 2014; pp. 304–321.
20. Subramanian, S.; Mozaffari-Kermani, M.; Azarderakhsh, R.; Nojoumian, M. Reliable hardware architectures for cryptographic block ciphers LED and HIGHT. *IEEE Trans. Comput.-Aided Des. Integr. Circuits Syst.* **2017**, *36*, 1750–1758. [CrossRef]
21. Abbas, Y.A.; Jidin, R.; Jamil, N.; Zaba, M.R. Reusable data-path architecture for encryption-then-authentication on FPGA. *Int. Rev. Comput. Softw.* **2016**, *11*, 56–63. [CrossRef]
22. Abbas, Y.A.; Jidin, R.; Jamil, N.; Z'aba, M.R. Reusable Data-Path Architectures for EtM and MtE on FPGA. *J. Comput. Theor. Nanosci.* **2018**, *24*, 757–761. [CrossRef]
23. Hammad, B.T.; Abbas, Y.A.; Jamil, N.; Rusli, M.E.; Zaba, M.R. FPGA Implementation of DLP-PHOTON Hash Function. *Int. J. Future Gener. Commun. Netw.* **2017**, *10*, 71–78. [CrossRef]
24. Al-Shatari, M.; Hussin, F.A.; Abd Aziz, A.; Witjaksono, G.; Rohmad, M.S.; Tran, X.-T. An efficient implementation of LED block cipher on FPGA. In Proceedings of the 2019 First International Conference of Intelligent Computing and Engineering (ICOICE), Hadhramout, Yemen, 15–16 December 2019; pp. 1–5.
25. Nafl, S.M.; Noaman, S.A.; Fadel, A.H.; Khalaf, B.A.; Hameed, R.S. Fast lightweight encryption device based on LFSR technique for increasing the speed of LED performance. *AIP Conf. Proc.* **2023**, *2593*, 030003.
26. Nalla Anandakumar, N. SCA Resistance Analysis on FPGA Implementations of Sponge Based MAC-PHOTON. In Proceedings of the International Conference for Information Technology and Communications, Bucharest, Romania, 11–12 June 2015; Springer: Berlin/Heidelberg, Germany, 2015; pp. 69–86.
27. Al-Shatari, M.O.A.; Hussin, F.A.; Abd Aziz, A.; Witjaksono, G.; Tran, X.-T. FPGA-based lightweight hardware architecture of the PHOTON hash function for IoT edge devices. *IEEE Access* **2020**, *8*, 207610–207618. [CrossRef]
28. Windarta, S.; Suryadi, S.; Ramli, K.; Pranggono, B.; Gunawan, T.S. Lightweight Cryptographic Hash Functions: Design Trends, Comparative Study, and Future Directions. *IEEE Access* **2022**, *10*, 82272–82294. [CrossRef]
29. Lee, W.-K.; Jang, K.; Song, G.; Kim, H.; Hwang, S.O.; Seo, H. Efficient implementation of lightweight hash functions on gpu and quantum computers for iot applications. *IEEE Access* **2022**, *10*, 59661–59674. [CrossRef]
30. Heera, W.; Bhagyashree, K.; Patil, R.; Iyer, N.; Hiremath, S. Implementation of Photon Hash Function on FPGA. In *Advances in Signal Processing, Embedded Systems and IoT, Proceedings of the Seventh ICMEET-2022, Andhra Pradesh, India, 22–23 July 2022*; Springer: Berlin/Heidelberg, Germany, 2023; pp. 407–418.
31. Al-Shatari, M.; Hussin, F.A.; Abd Aziz, A.; Rohmad, M.S.; Tran, X.-T. Composite Lightweight Authenticated Encryption Based on LED Block Cipher and PHOTON Hash Function for IoT Devices. In Proceedings of the IEEE 15th International Symposium on Embedded Multicore/Many-Core Systems-on-Chip (MCSoC), Penang, Malaysia, 19–22 December 2022; pp. 134–139.
32. Bellare, M.; Hoang, V.T. Efficient schemes for committing authenticated encryption. In Proceedings of the Advances in Cryptology–EUROCRYPT 2022: 41st Annual International Conference on the Theory and Applications of Cryptographic Techniques, Trondheim, Norway, 30 May–3 June 2022; pp. 845–875.
33. Mancillas-López, C.; Ovilla-Martínez, B. An Ultra-Fast Authenticated Encryption Scheme with Associated Data Using AES-OTR. *J. Circuits Syst. Comput.* **2022**, *31*, 2250167. [CrossRef]
34. Alasmary, H.; Tanveer, M. ESCI-AKA: Enabling Secure Communication in an IoT-Enabled Smart Home Environment Using Authenticated Key Agreement Framework. *Mathematics* **2023**, *11*, 3450. [CrossRef]
35. Tanveer, M.; Badshah, A.; Alasmary, H.; Chaudhry, S.A. CMAF-IIoT: Chaotic map-based authentication framework for Industrial Internet of Things. *Internet Things* **2023**, *23*, 100902. [CrossRef]
36. Bogdanov, A.; Knudsen, L.R.; Leander, G.; Paar, C.; Poschmann, A.; Robshaw, M.J.; Seurin, Y.; Vikkelsoe, C. PRESENT: An ultra-lightweight block cipher. In *International Workshop on Cryptographic Hardware and Embedded Systems*; Springer: Berlin/Heidelberg, Germany, 2007; pp. 450–466.
37. Bogdanov, A.; Knežević, M.; Leander, G.; Toz, D.; Varıcı, K.; Verbauwhede, I. SPONGENT: A lightweight hash function. In *International Workshop on Cryptographic Hardware and Embedded Systems*; Springer: Berlin/Heidelberg, Germany, 2011; pp. 312–325.

38. Guo, J.; Peyrin, T.; Poschmann, A.; Robshaw, M. The LED block cipher. In Proceedings of the 13th International Conference on Cryptographic Hardware and Embedded Systems, Nara, Japan, 28 September–1 October 2011; pp. 326–341.
39. Guo, J.; Peyrin, T.; Poschmann, A. The PHOTON family of lightweight hash functions. In *Annual Cryptology Conference*; Springer: Berlin/Heidelberg, Germany, 2011; pp. 222–239.
40. Z'aba, M.R.; Jamil, N.; Rohmad, M.S.; Rani, H.A.; Shamsuddin, S.; Maisara, C. The CiliPadi family of lightweight authenticated encryption, v1. 2. *Malays. J. Math. Sci.* **2021**, *15*, 1–23.
41. Singh, A.; Chawla, N.; Ko, J.H.; Kar, M.; Mukhopadhyay, S. Energy efficient and side-channel secure cryptographic hardware for IoT-edge nodes. *IEEE Internet Things J.* **2018**, *6*, 421–434. [CrossRef]
42. Chakraborti, A.; Datta, N.; Nandi, M.; Yasuda, K. Beetle family of lightweight and secure authenticated encryption ciphers. *Cryptol. Eprint Arch.* **2018**. [CrossRef]
43. Dobraunig, C.; Eichlseder, M.; Mendel, F.; Schläffer, M. Ascon v1. 2. Submission to the CAESAR Competition. Available online: https://competitions.cr.yp.to/round3/asconv12.pdf (accessed on 30 August 2023).
44. Iwata, T.; Minematsu, K.; Guo, J.; Morioka, S. CLOC: Authenticated encryption for short input. In *International Workshop on Fast Software Encryption*; Springer: Berlin/Heidelberg, Germany, 2014; pp. 149–167.
45. *Proceedings of Security, Privacy, and Applied Cryptography Engineering*; Carlet, C., Anwar Hasan, M., Saraswat, V., Eds.; Springer: Cham, Switzerland, 2016; ISBN 978-3-319-49444-9.
46. Andreeva, E.; Bilgin, B.; Bogdanov, A.; Luykx, A.; Mendel, F.; Mennink, B.; Mouha, N.; Wang, Q.; Yasuda, K. PRIMATEs v1. Submission to the CAESAR Competition. 2014. Available online: https://competitions.cr.yp.to/round2/primatesv102.pdf (accessed on 30 August 2023).
47. Lukas, K.; Daemen, J. Cube Attack on Primates. 2017. Available online: https://acad.ro/sectii2002/proceedings/doc2017-4s/01artSupl.pdf (accessed on 30 August 2023).
48. Wu, H.; Huang, T. JAMBU lightweight authenticated encryption mode and AES-JAMBU. *CAESAR Compet. Propos.* **2014**.
49. Peyrin, T.; Sim, S.M.; Wang, L.; Zhang, G. Cryptanalysis of JAMBU. In Proceedings of the Fast Software Encryption: 22nd International Workshop, FSE 2015, Istanbul, Turkey, 8–11 March 2015; pp. 264–281.
50. Nikolic, I. Tiaoxin-346. Submission to the CAESAR Competition. 2014. Available online: https://competitions.cr.yp.to/round2/tiaoxinv2.pdf (accessed on 30 August 2023).
51. Salam, I.; Mahri, H.Q.A.; Simpson, L.; Bartlett, H.; Dawson, E.; Wong, K.K.-H. Fault attacks on Tiaoxin-346. In Proceedings of the Australasian Computer Science Week Multiconference, Brisbane, QLD, Australia, 29 January–2 February 2018; pp. 1–9.
52. Bertoni, G.; Daemen, J.; Peeters, M.; Van Assche, G.; Van Keer, R. CAESAR Submission: Ketje v2. Candidate CAESAR Compet. 2016. Available online: https://competitions.cr.yp.to/round3/ketjev2.pdf (accessed on 30 August 2023).
53. Zhou, H.; Li, Z.; Dong, X.; Jia, K.; Meier, W. Practical key-recovery attacks on round-reduced Ketje Jr, Xoodoo-AE and Xoodyak. *Comput. J.* **2020**, *63*, 1231–1246. [CrossRef]
54. Dobraunig, C.; Mangard, S.; Mendel, F.; Primas, R. Fault attacks on nonce-based authenticated encryption: Application to keyak and ketje. In Proceedings of the Selected Areas in Cryptography–SAC 2018: 25th International Conference, Calgary, AB, Canada, 15–17 August 2018; pp. 257–277.
55. Dong, X.; Li, Z.; Wang, X.; Qin, L. Cube-like attack on round-reduced initialization of Ketje Sr. *IACR Trans. Symmetric Cryptol.* **2017**, *2017*, 259–280. [CrossRef]
56. Song, L.; Guo, J. Cube-attack-like cryptanalysis of round-reduced Keccak using MILP. *IACR Trans. Symmetric Cryptol.* **2018**, *2018*, 182–214. [CrossRef]
57. Fuhr, T.; Naya-Plasencia, M. State-recovery attacks on modified Ketje Jr. *IACR Trans. Symmetric Cryptol.* **2018**, *2018*, 29–56. [CrossRef]
58. Wu, H.; Huang, T. The authenticated cipher MORUS (v2). CAESAR Submission. 2014. Available online: https://competitions.cr.yp.to/round3/morusv2.pdf (accessed on 30 August 2023).
59. Ye, T.; Wei, Y.; Meier, W. A new cube attack on MORUS by using division property. *IEEE Trans. Comput.* **2019**, *68*, 1731–1740. [CrossRef]
60. Shi, T.; Guan, J. Real-time state recovery attack against MORUS in nonce-misuse setting. *Sci. China Inf. Sci.* **2019**, *62*, 39109. [CrossRef]
61. Jean, J.; Nikolić, I.; Peyrin, T. Joltik v1. 3. *CAESAR Round* **2015**, *2*. Available online: https://competitions.cr.yp.to/round2/joltikv13.pdf (accessed on 30 August 2023).
62. Li, R.; Jin, C.; Pan, H. Key recovery attacks on reduced-round Joltik-BC in the single-key setting. *Inf. Process. Lett.* **2019**, *151*, 105834. [CrossRef]
63. Zong, R.; Dong, X. Milp-aided related-tweak/key impossible differential attack and its applications to qarma, joltik-bc. *IEEE Access* **2019**, *7*, 153683–153693. [CrossRef]
64. Minematsu, K.; Guo, J.; Kobayashi, E. SILC: SImple Lightweight CFB. 2015. Available online: https://competitions.cr.yp.to/round2/silcv2.pdf (accessed on 30 August 2023).
65. Roy, D.B.; Chakraborti, A.; Chang, D.; Kumar, S.D.; Mukhopadhyay, D.; Nandi, M. Two efficient fault-based attacks on CLOC and SILC. *J. Hardw. Syst. Secur.* **2017**, *1*, 252–268. [CrossRef]

66. Roy, D.B.; Chakraborti, A.; Chang, D.; Kumar, S.V.D.; Mukhopadhyay, D.; Nandi, M. Fault Based Almost Universal Forgeries on CLOC and SILC. In Proceedings of the Security, Privacy, and Applied Cryptography Engineering: 6th International Conference, SPACE 2016, Hyderabad, India, 14–18 December 2016; Springer: Cham, Switzerland, 2016.
67. Bertoni, G.; Daemen, J.; Peeters, M.; Van Assche, G.; Van Keer, R. Keyak v2. CAESAR Submission. 2015. Available online: https://competitions.cr.yp.to/round3/keyakv22.pdf (accessed on 30 August 2023).
68. Wu, H. Acorn v3. Submission to CAESAR Competition. 2016. Available online: https://www3.ntu.edu.sg/home/wuhj/research/caesar/caesar.html (accessed on 30 August 2023).
69. Zhang, X.; Feng, X.; Lin, D. Fault attack on ACORN v3. *Comput. J.* **2018**, *61*, 1166–1179. [CrossRef]
70. Dobraunig, C.; Eichlseder, M.; Mendel, F.; Schläffer, M. Ascon v1. 2: Lightweight authenticated encryption and hashing. *J. Cryptol.* **2021**, *34*, 1–42. [CrossRef]
71. Li, H.; He, L.; Chen, S.; Guo, J.; Qiu, W. Automatic Preimage Attack Framework on\ascon Using a Linearize-and-Guess Approach. *Cryptol. Eprint Arch.* **2023**.
72. You, S.-C.; Kuhn, M.G.; Sarkar, S.; Hao, F. Low Trace-Count Template Attacks on 32-bit Implementations of ASCON AEAD. *IACR Trans. Cryptogr. Hardw. Embed. Syst.* **2023**, *2023*, 344–366. [CrossRef]
73. Luo, S.; Wu, W.; Li, Y.; Zhang, R.; Liu, Z. An Efficient Soft Analytical Side-Channel Attack on Ascon. In Proceedings of the International Conference on Wireless Algorithms, Systems, and Applications, Dalian, China, 24–26 November 2022; Springer: Berlin/Heidelberg, Germany, 2022; pp. 389–400.
74. Baudrin, J.; Canteaut, A.; Perrin, L. Practical cube attack against nonce-misused Ascon. *IACR Trans. Symmetric Cryptol.* **2022**, *2022*, 120–144. [CrossRef]
75. Zhang, F.; Huang, R.; Feng, T.; Gong, X.; Tao, Y.; Ren, K.; Zhao, X.; Guo, S. Efficient Persistent Fault Analysis with Small Number of Chosen Plaintexts. *IACR Trans. Cryptogr. Hardw. Embed. Syst.* **2023**, *2023*, 519–542. [CrossRef]
76. Im, N.; Choi, S.; Yoo, H. S-Box Attack Using FPGA Reverse Engineering for Lightweight Cryptography. *IEEE Internet Things J.* **2022**, *9*, 25165–25180. [CrossRef]

Disclaimer/Publisher's Note: The statements, opinions and data contained in all publications are solely those of the individual author(s) and contributor(s) and not of MDPI and/or the editor(s). MDPI and/or the editor(s) disclaim responsibility for any injury to people or property resulting from any ideas, methods, instructions or products referred to in the content.

Article

Effects on Long-Range Dependence and Multifractality in Temporal Resolution Recovery of High Frame Rate HEVC Compressed Content

Ana Gavrovska

School of Electrical Engineering, University of Belgrade, Bulevar kralja Aleksandra 73, 11120 Belgrade, Serbia; anaga777@gmail.com or anaga777@etf.bg.ac.rs; Tel.: +381-3218350

Citation: Gavrovska, A. Effects on Long-Range Dependence and Multifractality in Temporal Resolution Recovery of High Frame Rate HEVC Compressed Content. *Appl. Sci.* **2023**, *13*, 9851. https://doi.org/10.3390/app13179851

Academic Editors: Lip Yee Por and Abdullah Ayub Khan

Received: 13 August 2023
Revised: 28 August 2023
Accepted: 29 August 2023
Published: 31 August 2023

Copyright: © 2023 by the author. Licensee MDPI, Basel, Switzerland. This article is an open access article distributed under the terms and conditions of the Creative Commons Attribution (CC BY) license (https:// creativecommons.org/licenses/by/ 4.0/).

Abstract: In recent years, video research has dealt with high-frame-rate (HFR) content. Even though low or standard frame rates (SFR) that correspond to values less than 60 frames per second (fps) are still covered. Temporal conversions are applied accompanied with video compression and, thus, it is of importance to observe and detect possible effects of typical compressed video manipulations over HFR (60 fps+) content. This paper addresses ultra-high-definition HFR content via Hurst index as a measure of long-range dependency (LRD), as well as using Legendre multifractal spectrum, having in mind standard high-efficiency video coding (HEVC) format and temporal resolution recovery (TRR), meaning frame upconversion after temporal filtering of compressed content. LRD and multifractals-based studies using video traces have been performed for characterization of compressed video, and they are mostly presented for advanced video coding (AVC). Moreover, recent studies have shown that it is possible to perform TRR detection for SFR data compressed with standards developed before HEVC. In order to address HEVC HFR data, video traces are analyzed using LRD and multifractals, and a novel TRR detection model is proposed based on a weighted k-nearest neighbors (WkNN) classifier and multifractals. Firstly, HFR video traces are gathered using six constant rate factors (crfs), where Hurst indices and multifractal spectra are calculated. According to TRR and original spectra comparison, a novel detection model is proposed based on new multifractal features. Also, five-fold cross-validation using the proposed TRR detection model gave high-accuracy results of around 98%. The obtained results show the effects on LRD and multifractality and their significance in understanding changes in typical video manipulation. The proposed model can be valuable in video credibility and quality assessments of HFR HEVC compressed content.

Keywords: video; high frame rate (HFR); temporal resolution recovery; change detection; constant rate factor; multifractals

1. Introduction

Video content evolves to more complex forms of media, with a variety of different combinations of spatial resolution, dynamic range, color range, codecs, containers and frame rates. Among others, it is well known that high-frame-rate (HFR) video content is important for high-quality consummation and especially further relevant video investigation, since transmission bandwidth and storage is affected by new frame rate formats [1]. Generating new video and immersive media comes with a lot of challenges for traditional infrastructures and sharing possibilities, particularly for higher resolutions, like temporal. HFR contributes to the increase in perceived quality, but in most practical applications, video still rarely exceeds 60 frames per second (fps) [1,2].

Low frame rates (LFR) or standard frame rates (SFR) have become an obvious limitation, especially when it comes to sport, fast action genres (as in cinema and gaming) and immersive virtual reality (VR) and augmented reality (AR) content [2]. This is also recognized in BT.2020 or the ultra-high-definition (UHD) television standard, where up to 100- and 120-frame frequencies are adopted for further exploitation [3]. Moreover, in the Advanced Television Systems Committee (ATSC) 3.0 ecosystem, high or very high frame rates are expected, as well as video services developed by interconnecting 5G communication networks and ATSC 3.0 broadcasting. Currently, in these cases, high-efficiency video coding (HEVC or H.265) is adopted to deal with novel video technology formats like HFR [4–6]. Progressive formats are accompanied by picture rates with possible dealing with SFR and HFR (like 120 fps) recovery and temporal filtering [5,6]. Media over Internet Protocol (IP) provides a high level of flexibility, and new broadcast systems are already using IP infrastructures [7]. The infrastructures enable HFR distribution, but dealing with video in such manner also leads to significant changes in bandwidth requirements. Besides future formats and services, compression technologies are of crucial interest [6]. The perceptual quality improvement resulting from HFR is recognized in industrial and academic communities [8]. HFR is preferable for applications in order to enhance the smooth end-user experience and to produce different effects [9,10]. It is not easy to select and adopt frame rates, since frame frequency changes produce distortions. In typical workflows, the frame rate is decided before any acquisition. This leads to general suggestions that production needs to be as high as possible during the production phase, where end-user deliverables are adopted/modified to final needed frame rates [10]. An increasing number of modern content creator captures show their activities using HFR on social networks and sharing IP platforms [11–13]. Working with fast-forward video and similar content that is not the result of temporal consecutive frames is especially challenging, since the quality is jointly dependant on frame rate and compression [14]. Video reproductions in HFR have been reported and analyzed in [13–23]. Video conversion, on the other hand, usually means frame rate upscaling or upconversion, often referred to as frame interpolation [24,25]. One should have in mind that it also comes with compression format [26–32].

There has been extensive analysis of video tracing by long-range dependency (LRD) and multifractals [33–38]. One of the most popular tracing tools is the Fast Forward Moving Picture Experts Group (Fast Forward MPEG or ffmpeg) solution [33], while self-similarity is considered as one of the most powerful properties [34], where LRD and multifractals have been used in many applications related to different types of sequences [35], statistical modeling and analysis of video traffic [36,37] and queuing performance [38]. Video traces after frame parsing have been examined for two main purposes: the purpose of traffic modeling [39–55] or towards characterization of compressed video by focusing on specific standard [56–59]. For traffic modeling, studies are related to specific protocols [39], queuing [40], variable bitrates [41], specific prediction models [41–51], buffering [52], dynamic bandwidth allocation [53], attacks [54] and various content [55]. On the other hand, characterizations of compressed video using specific standard and video traces are considered using MPEG-4 Advanced Simple Profile (ASP) [56], MPEG-4 version 2 and H.263 in [57] and advanced video coding (AVC or H.264) [58] and its extensions in [59]. So far, to the author's knowledge, LRD- and multifractals-based studies oriented towards characterization of compressed video by focusing on specific standard and different compression factors have only been examined up to MPEG-4/AVC content [56–59], while HEVC should deal with modern HFR video content. Since each standard affects tracing differently, it is crucial to understand the LRD and multifractal behavior of HEVC HFR compressed content while having in mind different compression quality. Moreover, studies related to detection of frame rate upconversions, i.e., temporal resolution recovery (TRR), are presented in [60–63]. In recent works, MPEG-4 traces have been investigated [60]. They are mostly investigated for original LFR content: frame rates of 24 fps upconverted to 30 fps [61], frame rates of 15 fps [62] and frame rates of 15 to 30 fps [63]. Recent previous studies have shown that it is possible to perform TRR detection [60–63] using MPEG-4/AVC SFR video content/traces.

The purpose of this work is to analyze video traces corresponding to HFR HEVC compressed content using LRD and multifractals and to tackle issue of TRR detection by examining effects found in TRR. Namely, this paper addresses HEVC (or H.265) frame size traces extracted from HFR video content that are considered from an LRD and multifractal point of view. As a consequence of the above, the analysis of HFR should go hand in hand with compression observed using constant rate factors. Here, the focus is on UHD HEVC video traces collected from data corresponding to HFR and frequency up to 120 fps, where tests have been performed using publicly available reference HFR video content. Temporal resolution recovery (TRR) has also been examined. The contributions of this paper are as follows:

- HFR HEVC frame size traces show specific behavior in LRD- and multifractal-based analysis, where difference before and after temporal resolution recovery (TRR) exist.
- The experimental results are obtained for HEVC compressed HFR video frame size traces for the first time in multifractal domain, which may contribute to recognition of possible changes like TRR.
- Having in mind the obtained results and spectra behavior, a novel detection method is proposed for TRR detection regardless of compression level expressed through constant rate factors.
- The proposed TRR detection model based on weighted k-nearest neighbors (weighted kNN or WkNN) classifier shows high accuracy detection percentage in the performed experimental analysis using a relatively low number of features.

This paper is organized as follows. After the introduction, in Section 2, a brief description of HFR, video quality and coding is given. In Section 3, additional details on works related to multifractal analysis of compressed video content are presented. Video frame size traces and data gathering are explained in Section 4. Applied methods for LRD and multifractal spectrum calculation are described in Section 5. HFR content is characterized using LRD and multifractal properties before and after TRR. Moreover, novel model for TRR detection is proposed based on HFR video multifractal analysis, WkNN classifier and a relatively low number of multifractal features. The experimental results on 4k 120 fps HFR content are shown in Section 6, where a high accuracy percentage is obtained for different content and compression rate factors. Finally, conclusions are given in Section 7.

2. HFR Processing and Challenges

It is well known that frame rate impacts quality of experience related to how realistic content being consumed is or which style one desires to obtain, like motion blur, slow motion or fast forward. HFR video is expected to approach realism when there are a lot of actions happening, as in sports, busy scenes in movies and gaming but also in live and realistic experience with crisp information. One of the benefits is increased realism, where video seems more immersive by making the viewer's experience more lifelike.

Frame rate is generally described as number of frames per second (fps), which is illustrated in Figure 1, where HFR means that temporal resolution is increased and more images are captured in a given amount of time. HFR can be described as video content captured or displayed at a frame rate of 60 fps or higher. This is in contrast to the SFR/LFR that is typically used for television [5,6]. Besides the realistic experience which is tied to the perception of motion, HFR reduces motion blur when an object is moving and enables its clearer representation, described as smooth motion given in more detail. Even so, differences in frame rates in acquisition and reproduction may produce uneven pacing and sometimes longer frames. Inconsistent frame times, known as judder, and decreasing low frame rate producing so-called stutter effects are only some of the issues [12]. Video quality estimation may produce different results due to varying video behavior when transforms are made in frame rates according to specific quality mode selections. Wearable and lightweight cameras like action cameras are popular in the consumer industry, meaning that both professional and nonprofessional content has a variety of distortions [13].

Temporal resolution changes through objective measurements are still mainly analyzed using standard full-reference approaches [17]. Quality assessments are usually made by mean squared error, peak signal-to-noise ratio, structural similarity index, video multimethod assessment fusion and similar metrics [18–20]. In [12], frame rate differences have been considered by using video multimethod assessment fusion (VMAF) and entropy differences. Video collections like Youtube-UGC [21] or Konstanz KoNViD-1k [22] are made for research using different quality scores, compression results and distortion diversity, which can be used for purposes like constructing general no-reference models. Still, a few studies have been specifically considering HFR with publicly video sets that are acquired with frame rates equal to or above 60 fps for research reasons, like Waterloo HFR [16], LIVE-YT-HFR [12] and BVI-HVR [1]. Primarily, for HFR experimental analysis, the video tracing and compression analysis Ultra Video Group (UVG) dataset can be used, since it consisted of 120 fps sequences of even higher spatial resolution, meaning containing RAW video content up to 4k 120 fps [23]. This is the reason why this dataset is chosen here. The general suggestion in production is to keep the frame rate high as much as possible, where the choice of video frame rate may be intentionally HFR [10].

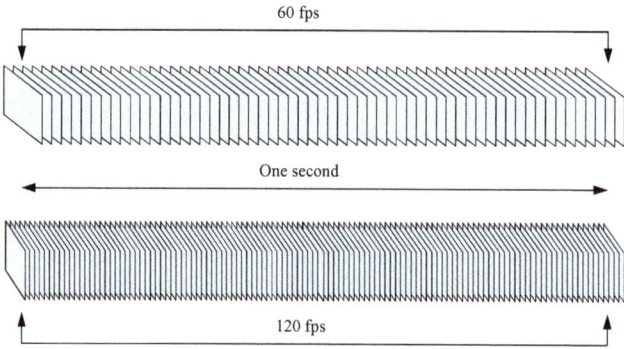

Figure 1. High frame rate (HFR) as high number of frames per second.

One should have in mind that even if an acquired video is HFR, this can be a significant barrier for many systems and devices. Devices with limited processing power may require downsampling, like frame dropping. HFR may be experienced even as unnatural and not easy to follow by the human visual system, leading to frame rates being decreased. Moreover, interoperability between components of a system may cause lower frame rates for HFR processing tasks. Frame rate can be downscaled, leading to significant decrease in cost in storage or streaming. On the other hand, it is well known that decreasing the frame rate can also result in choppy video experience. This means that video conversion can also be followed by frame rate upscaling, usually referred as frame interpolation, where temporal resolution is increased by adding the frames between the known frames [24,25]. This represents temporal resolution recovery or TRR.

Any conversion is difficult and comes with a lot of challenges, especially in the temporal domain. HFR leads to higher video file size and bandwidth challenges. Since frame rate affects storage and the capacity of telecommunication channel, HFR quality is accompanied with compression. This inevitably introduces possible unwanted artifacts and undesirable components in motion picture result, where coding and compression solutions enable to decrease the video size by keeping the video quality high. Giving appropriate insight into such content is needed.

HFR assessment goes with video compression. In a nutshell, the design of variety of coding standards and codecs is needed to achieve specific tasks. MPEG is dedicated to efficient coding and compression algorithms, where MPEGx and H26x standards have been popular over the years [26–31]. Algorithms are becoming more complex, and advancements are being made to deal with new video technologies. In general, coding steps include block-oriented making intra- and interpredictions, transformation and quantization, filtering and entropy coding. MPEG-2 has become popular over the years in practical applications like broadcasting, where MPEG-4 continues to be the leading choice for streaming implementations. H.264, or AVC standard (MPEG-4 Part 10), was introduced in 2003 by International Telecommunication Union—Telecommunication (ITU-T) Standardization Sector and Organization for Standardization/International Electrotechnical Commission (ISO/IEC) [26–28].

It is a video compression standard based on block-oriented and motion-compensated coding supported by a wide range of devices and systems and is still one of the most widely accepted standards known for high compression efficiency and high-definition television implementation.

AVC was followed by HEVC, introduced in 2013, also known as H.265 or MPEG-H Part 2 [29,30]. HEVC, briefly speaking, enables compression of approximately half the size of AVC as a next-generation standard. It supports streaming and broadcasting with higher resolution, where HEVC is mostly used in action cameras and smart phones for HFR purposes. Also, there are many other available solutions for IP delivery, like VP9 and its successor AV1 [31–33]. Nevertheless, it should not be neglected that AVC is still in force for various implementations, but when it comes to HFR, it is expected to transfer to standards like HEVC [26]. HFR HEVC compressed video content effects have not been considered to a large extent, and this is relevant to practical implementations. For example, recently, in [32], HFR was analyzed from a perceptual quality point of view in the case of HEVC and VP9 by authors for full high-definition (HD) video sequences and five constant quality factor values, showing the better performance of HEVC for higher rates using standard metrics.

Frame size trace sequences for AVC HD and 4k/UHD HEVC video can be seen in Figure 2 for a sequence taken from the publicly available UVG dataset described in [23]. Comparison after frame frequency alignment in Figure 2 shows different trace sequence behavior. Still, self-similarity-based analysis related to HFR HEVC has not been performed so far to the best of the author's knowledge.

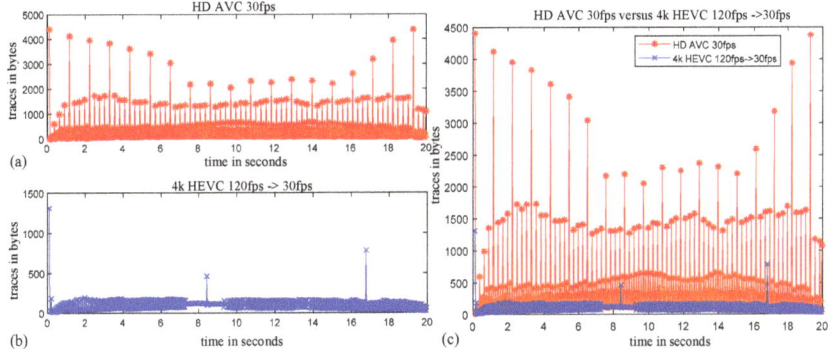

Figure 2. Frame size trace sequence for (**a**) high-definition (HD) low frame rate (LFR) content in advanced video coding (AVC) format and (**b**) 4k or ultra-high-definition (UHD) HFR content in high-efficiency video coding (HEVC) format, as well as (**c**) their comparison after frame frequency alignment presented in a twenty seconds interval.

There are a lot of challenges related to HFR processing that need to be further investigated, such as effects due to compression and codec settings, effects due to differences in frame rates, no-reference HFR content characterization, HFR reproduction, editing and hardware utilization. Here, only some of these issues are tackled. Effects due to compression are considered in this paper for HEVC standard and TRR, but other standards like VP9 and content modifications can also be taken into account. No-reference characterization and quality estimation is of general interest for HFR processing. A relatively large amount of different raw HFR video content is needed in the research community. Also, HFR reproduction, decoding and editing require additional resource utilization compared with SFR due to the high number of frames per second, where possible effects of available acceleration approaches need to be researched further.

3. Self-Similarity and Multifractal Analysis of Compressed Video Content

Video can be manipulated in many ways, affecting and controlling the overall quality. The most frequent choices are setting constant quality factor or buffer size or using constant, constrained or variable bit rates [33–46]. A large number of physical systems and nonstationary signals tend to show similar behavior at different scales, known as having self-similarity properties [34–36]. These properties have been analyzed using fractal and multifractal theory for compressed video content and video tracing.

In order to ensure a desirable quality of service, self-similarity is investigated for constant and variable bit rates in [37]. Self-similar patterns are explored for high-speed network traffic in [38]. In early works, long-range dependency or LRD in video traffic represented by traces has been mostly quantified by a single-parameter Hurst exponent [37,38]. LRD means that traces exhibit correlation over a range of time scales, where among standard statistical video traffic metrics, like mean and variation in video traces, additional self-similarity properties have been investigated under different conditions, where LRD is only one feature of fractal-like behavior. In [39], Transport Control Protocol (TCP) traffic collected through a number of bytes arriving per time is multifractal and is analyzed using spectra, enabling valuable statistical estimation. Multifractals are applied for behavior of a queuing system in [40]. Tail distributions in a multifractal sense while measuring variable bit rate are compared in [41].

Generally, there are two main directions in analysis of video traces. The first one is traffic modeling. Self-similarity has been widely recognized, and multifractal-based traffic modeling has been found suitable for video tracing [39–45]. Different self-similarity models are tested for network traffic analysis and prediction: using fractional traffic Brownian motion model [41], wavelets [42,43], multiplicative approaches [44,45], autoregressive models [46–49] and Markov chains [50,51]. Experimental multifractal analysis is applied for dimensioning, buffer capacity interpretation and statistical multiplexing of video streams [52], as well as for dynamic bandwidth allocation [53]. Multifractal spectra have been compared during the normal work and force attacks in a communication network [54], while differentiation between spectra is used to show the consistency of LRD [55].

The second direction in investigating self-similarity properties of video traces is oriented towards the characterization of compressed video, having in mind specific standards. Most of the research uses MPEG-4 traces for testing, being one of the most valuable practical standards, like in [56,57]. MPEG-4 Advanced Simple Profile (ASP)-based encoded traffic is tested for estimating queuing performance [56]. In [57], MPEG-4 version 2 and H.263 video traces are compared using accompanied parsers in order to extract ten sequences, so-called frame size traces, which are found statistically valuable for testing performance. This work has been continued on new encoders like H.264/MPEG-4 AVC [58,59]. H.264 video compressed traces are analyzed using multifractal and fractal approaches [58]. Trace analysis with extended encoding standards is performed in [59]. The whole encoding or transcoding process takes time and, due to settings, it is hard to compare the former generated traces with the new traces [56,58]. Frame size trace sequence according to each standard is different.

4. HFR HEVC Video Traces and Temporal Recovery Data

Temporal recovery or frame upconversion detection has been examined in [60–63] using MPEG-4/AVC traces. In [62], motion-compensated frame rate upconversion is proposed with the possibility of its detection via optical flow algorithm, where original frame rates were of 15 fps. A frame rate conversion detection is also analyzed in [63], having in mind interpolation schemes like common nearest neighbor interpolation. An automatic approach using machine learning is proposed for four original frame rates of 15 to 30 fps and conversions up to 30 fps. Multifractality may be useful in recovery detection, having in mind video tracing and multifractal analysis [56–59,64–66]. For example, machine learning and multifractal features are applied for an intrusion detection system in an unmanned aerial system [65]. Moreover, Legendre multifractal spectrum is applied in [66] for animation frame analysis and its differentiation from real and partially animated ones, especially due to self-similarity properties found also in video traffic analysis.

In this paper multifractal analysis of HFR frame size traces of HEVC compressed video sequences is the focus. LRD and self-similarity effects are considered for compressed video characterization, with special attention to their application in video change/modification detection. Here, HFR video traces are collected similarly to as is explained in the previous section, where frame size sequences are extracted using an accompanied parser [57]. HEVC compressed video represents input for the parser, which is applied for obtaining the xml trace file needed for statistical analysis, as shown in Figure 3.

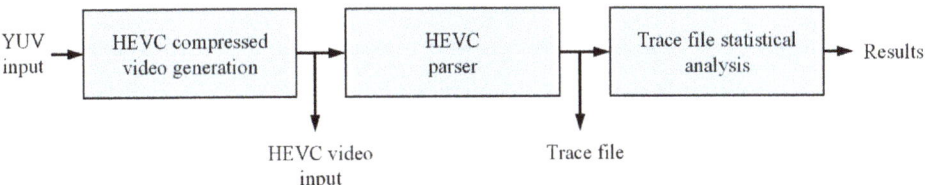

Figure 3. Statistical analysis of HEVC traces.

Video trace sequences are generated using ffmpeg v5.1.2 for different content. If audio exists within a file, it is removed. Constant rate factor, denoted as crf, i.e., two-pass crf, is selected as a model for controlling the output. The crf option is available for popular codecs and keeps the output quality level by rate control method, which is applied in practical implementations. Lower crf values in compressed data correspond to higher video quality. Six crf values are used, ranging here from 20 to 40. The supported preset option focused on speed and codec complexity is set to default, meaning medium, for the video trace collection, and no additional tuning is applied. The trace/data collection and the experimental analysis are carried out on Intel(R) Core(TM) i7-10750H Central Processing Unit (CPU), 2.60 GHz with 16 GB Random-Access Memory (RAM) on Windows 10 Pro 64 bit operating system without including specific graphical acceleration possibilities.

Since it is of interest to investigate the behavior of video traces, the testing circumstances are selected to be as simple as possible. In order to perform the analysis, the experimental procedure employs LRD and multifractal methods for estimation of HFR. The most common HFR video change is temporal resolution recovery, named here as TRR. The scenario of typical TRR found in practice includes temporal filtering, followed by temporal resolution matching. Significant savings in memory and channel capacity can be probably temporarily made in the temporal domain by decreasing frame frequency, and this is called temporal filtering [5,6]. Frame frequency alignment leads to HFR TRR. It is generated by the increase in frame number after a loss of original data, where specific temporal upsampling is ignored, as in [67], to avoid the choice of different methods and adding undesirable artifacts. Here, it is assumed that self-similarity properties of video traces may be observed in TRR scenario. TRR is valuable, since the practical implementations often need savings and further comparisons in the HFR domain.

This HFR TRR after temporal filtering can be considered common in practices where it is needed to have a matching frame rate, as in the original HFR video case. In this paper, the focus in on differentiating these TRR and original sequences. Additionally, it is possible to decrease frame rate to match original one expecting similar traces to the original ones, but it is evident that in the HFR 120 fps case, this is not still common in practice. The losses in HFR video recovery may produce specific tracing behavior that may contribute to possible detection of such changes. Besides temporal resolution changes, selected compression quality is expressed here through crf. For the experimental analysis, reference and publicly available HFR video sequences are selected. Additional tests are made using an action camera.

The basis of the experiments represents video trace collection that is made according to UVG dataset [23]. Recently, the benchmark was widened in 2020 for additional sequences, where of particular interest here are the 120 fps source files, available in YUV format in

4k/UHD or 2160 p spatial resolution. Source files representing HFR YUV 8-bit video sequences used for the analysis are listed in Table 1.

Table 1. Test source video files.

No.	Source (YUV)	Spatial Resolution	Frame Rate	Frame Number	Bit Depth
1	Beauty	3180 × 2160 (2160 p)	120 fps	600	8
2	Bosphorus	3180 × 2160 (2160 p)	120 fps	600	8
3	HoneyBee	3180 × 2160 (2160 p)	120 fps	600	8
4	Jockey	3180 × 2160 (2160 p)	120 fps	600	8
5	ReadySetGo	3180 × 2160 (2160 p)	120 fps	600	8
6	YachtRide	3180 × 2160 (2160 p)	120 fps	600	8

Each source video file contributes to original and TRR video trace sequences corresponding to different crf values. Applied methods are related to LRD, or to be more precise, Hurst index evaluation, as well as multifractal spectra calculation for further comparison and testing.

5. Methods for Estimation of HFR Video Characteristics

5.1. Hurst Index

In time series analysis, specific behavior is analyzed using common statistical measures, as shown in Figure 3. LRD is especially of interest in order to understand behavior of a structure/sequence, especially in the cases of video traffic analysis. Particularly, Hurst index or exponent, H, is evaluated as a statistical measure to better determine the characteristics of traffic, cardiac dynamics or finance [38,57,58,68,69]. Hurst exponent H can be estimated for LRD tests in different ways via: R/S statistics, periodogram, aggregated variance method, absolute moments method, detrended fluctuation analysis, etc. [68–72]. The Hurst index is found in the range 0.5–1, where H equals 0.5 in the case of pure random process like Brownian motion, with no correlation between incremental signal changes. An index is applied for measuring dependence in a structure/sequence, and it can be considered as a fractal-related feature. In the case when the index is less than 0.5, $0 < H < 0.5$, the process is negatively correlated. Likewise, when the Hurst index is higher than 0.5, $0.5 < H < 1$, it indicates a persistent behavior with long-term positive autocorrelation, meaning that higher values are probably followed by another high value. This self-similarity expressed by H values higher than 0.5 means that LRD occurs. LRD can be described having a relatively high degree of correlation between distant data points.

In a nutshell, the complexity can be evaluated using a correlation sum $C(r)$ calculated for a range of distances, or points within a radius r, where the correlation sum scales with radius as $C(r) \sim r^D$, giving the exponent D as a correlation dimension [68,72]. It is possible to estimate the dimension as the local slope of $\log(C(r))$ versus $\log(r)$ for a sufficiently large range of small r values. Since the variance of local slope can be relatively high, different approaches may be used for as a function of distances between considered points in a structure. In a generalized case and fractal geometry [68,71,72], Hurst index H, as a measure of LRD, which is directly related to fractal dimension, can be described as a function of parameter denoted as q for a time series $x(t)$, using the scaling properties given as:

$$\frac{<|x(t+r) - x(t)|^q>}{<|x(t)|_q>} \sim r^{qH(q)}, \qquad (1)$$

where radius or lag averaging over the considered time window is denoted by $<.>$. Another common algorithm is Detrended Fluctuation Analysis (DFA) [71–73]. Firstly, integrated sequence y_k is obtained based on x, and then the local trend denoted by the y_m

of boxes or subseries of length m is found. This is followed by the calculation of the root mean square fluctuation:

$$F(m) = \sqrt{\frac{1}{N}\sum_{k=1}^{N}[y_k - y_m(k)]^2}. \qquad (2)$$

The index is finally calculated as the slope of linear regression, which compares $\log(F(m))$ and $\log(m)$.

The alternative for Hurst index calculation can be periodogram method [70,71,74]. Specifically, the method relies on calculating the periodogram:

$$I_L(\omega_k) = \frac{1}{L}\left|\sum_{t=1}^{L} x(t)e^{-2\pi i(t-1)\omega_k}\right|^2, \qquad (3)$$

and it is based on the discrete Fourier transform applied for a set of samples $\{x_t: t = 1, \ldots L\}$, where $\omega_k = k/L$, $k = 1, \ldots, [L/2]$ are corresponding frequencies. When plotting the periodogram in a log–log domain, the index H can be found according to the slope of regression line as $H = (1 - slope)/2$.

One of the best-known procedures for calculating the LRD is the R/S statistics or the R/S method [70,73,74]. Firstly, a times series can be divided into d subseries or blocks of length n, where each subseries $m = 1, \ldots, d$ is normalized in order to generate cumulative time series $y_{i,m}$ for $I = 1, \ldots, n$. The range is calculated for each block as $R_m = \max\{y_{i,m}: I = 1, \ldots n\} - \min\{y_{i,m}: I = 1, \ldots n\}$ and rescaled. The mean value of all subseries of length n can be found as

$$(R/S)_n = \frac{1}{d}\sum_{m=1}^{d} R_m/S_m, \qquad (4)$$

where the ratio R/S follows the rule $(R/S)_n \sim n^H$, enabling estimation of the H index as the slope of linear regression line in a $\log(R/S)$ versus $\log(n)$ plot.

One should have in mind that each of the abovementioned methods for Hurst index estimation may give different H values. Here, they are used for LRD estimation of HFR data. Hurst indices for self-similar series are in the range of 0.5–1, where it can be considered that for higher H value that is closer to 1, the degree of self-similarity increases. The difference between the Hurst indices of a recovered/modified and original sequence is calculated as

$$H_{diff} = \frac{H_{rec} - H_{original}}{H_{original}}, \qquad (5)$$

where H_{rec} denotes index of a recovered sequence, and H_{orig} is the index of a corresponding sequence where no frame rate change is made.

5.2. Multifractal Spectrum

The Hurst index is suitable to describe the behavior of self-similar processes using a single value. Nevertheless, the asymptotical consideration of a regression slope in a log–log domain may not always be sufficient to fully understand the video traces. Thus, multifractal concept represents a generalization of a fractal one, where instead of one dimension or exponent, a spectrum of exponents is defined to describe dynamics of time series. There are different multifractal approaches for spectrum calculation [74–78].

In general, multifractal formalism is based on dimensions defined for a set of exponents within a small range, where dimensions can be given as

$$D_h = \inf_q(qh(q) - \tau(q) + k), \qquad (6)$$

where q describes singularity, $\tau(q)$ is a nonlinear function and k is a constant. For $q = 1$, information dimension is obtained, while for $q > 1$, strong singular, and for $q < 1$ less singular, structures are described. The Legendre transformation for α enables obtaining the multifractal spectrum $f(\alpha)$ as

$$\alpha = \frac{d\tau(q)}{dq}, f(\alpha) = q\alpha - \tau(q) \qquad (7)$$

Multifractal or singularity spectrum denoted as $f(\alpha)$ can be described as a distribution of the quantity or Hölder exponent α. In practice, Legendre spectrum gives a smooth concave function of the exponent useful in understanding the behavior of different structures [39–41,58]. Here, for the spectrum calculation, Fraclab software version 2.2 is used [78]. An example of multifractal spectrum is presented in Figure 4 as function $f(\alpha)$.

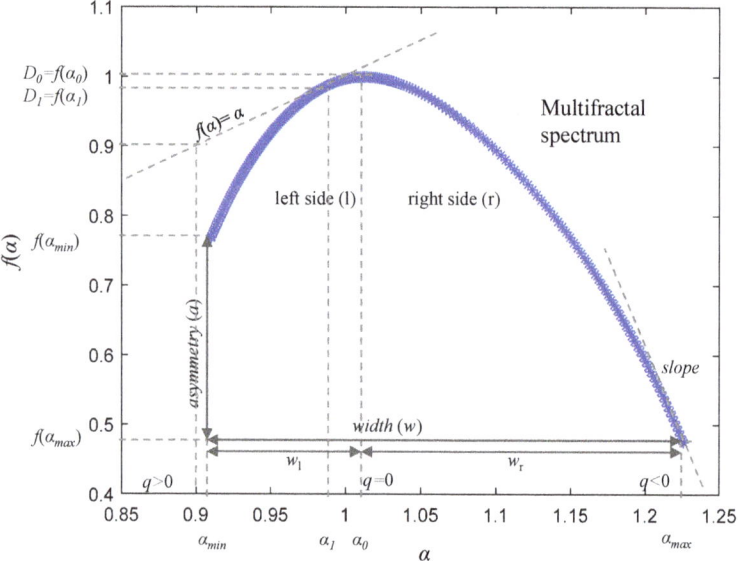

Figure 4. An example of multifractal spectrum and corresponding characteristics.

The main characteristics are shown in the same figure and are used as features in discrimination and classification models in different fields [75–77]. The structure of a spectrum is usually considered through its left and right sides or tails by dividing singularity of components into two parts. The features represent width w, asymmetry a, tail slopes and similar. Also, there are characteristic points of a spectrum that are foundation of these features, like minimum α value (α_{min}), maximum α value (α_{max}) and α corresponding to the curve maximum (α_0). Moreover, information dimension can be found asymptotically using $f(\alpha) = \alpha$ dimension. This is applied here as well to make a difference between video traces using multifractals in a statistical manner. Besides the Hurst exponent, these multifractal properties are also considered.

5.3. Detection Model and Evaluation

In the analysis of multifractal properties, different features were examined, like the left endpoint of a spectrum or the endpoint of a right tail [41]. Feature values directly rely on the content being analyzed. Thus, it is expected that properly selected features would enable a differentiation between temporally recovered sequences from corresponding original sequences. So, it is convenient to have a reference or a pseudoreference which will enable such differentiation. However, this is not an easy task in practice, where different motion or entropy is related to various signals/sequences. Thus, multifractal features are performed on cumulative sums of trace sequences. Feature extraction is performed on the corresponding spectra in order to make differentiation between no frame rate change and the temporal recovery case [78].

In this paper, a TRR detection model is proposed. The focus is on differentiation between 120 fps original video and corresponding TRR video recovered from 60 fps compressed with HEVC and characterized by six crf values. The bases of the proposed approach are new multifractal features, representing primarly the relative width and height of multifractal spectra, calculated as

$$w_{rel} = \frac{w_r}{w} = \frac{\alpha_{\max} - \alpha_0}{\alpha_{\max} - \alpha_{\min}},\qquad(8)$$

$$h_{rel} = \frac{a}{f(\alpha_{\max})} = \frac{f(\alpha_{\min}) - f(\alpha_{\max})}{f(\alpha_{\max})}.\qquad(9)$$

The different quality of signals represented through crf values may show similar trends in the case of relative trends. Besides the slope corresponding to right side of a spectrum [79], the left side was examined utilizing information dimension. That is, a distance between two characteristic points is applied to describe the curve shape:

$$d_{\inf} = \left((\alpha_1 - \alpha_0)^2 + (f(\alpha_1) - f(\alpha_0))^2\right)^{1/2}.\qquad(10)$$

It is thought that it is possible to identify differences between the two groups, meaning original and TRR, i.e., to detect whether temporal recovery is performed or not in practice. Four multifractal features are selected in experimental analysis in order to develop a detection model without a reference using machine learning. Extracted features are utilized for machine-learning-based temporal recovery detection. Several classifiers are tested, like Support Vector Machine (SVM), decision tree and k-nearest neighbors (kNN) [80–82]. SVM is often applied for classification, with the ability to generate a hyperplane to perform differentiation between original and nonmodified data. The decision tree (DT) also represents one of the common choices when it comes to classification, where results are obtained according to a learned tree based on selected features. Also, one of the most popular picked solutions is the kNN algorithm. During the training/learning process, the algorithm tries to find k samples that are the closest to the targets. According to the selected metric, the distances between the specific point and the target point in the known category/group are calculated in a nonparametric approach. The smallest distances from the specific point (x_q, y_q) are found, where the label of a point is found using majority voting:

$$\hat{y}_q = \underset{j}{\mathrm{argmax}} \sum_{x_i \in kNN(x_q)} I(y_i = j),\qquad(11)$$

where *kNN* in (11) denotes the neighborhood, and *I* is the indicator function. The main concept of kNN classification is illustrated in Figure 5a. Here, a modified kNN or weighted kNN (WkNN)-based model is proposed for TRR detection, and it is presented in Figure 5b. After generating trace sequences, where each video from the database contributes to each group (TRR and non-TRR meaning original), feature extraction is applied using the multifractal features explained in the previous paragraph. The WkNN classification model includes the so-called Mahalanobis distance calculations in the feature domain, their sorting, taking k-nearest neighbors, assigning weights and voting. For the WkNN model, training and testing are performed in order to obtain results, where 1 (Yes/True) denotes that TRR exists and 0 (No/False) denotes that the tested video is original.

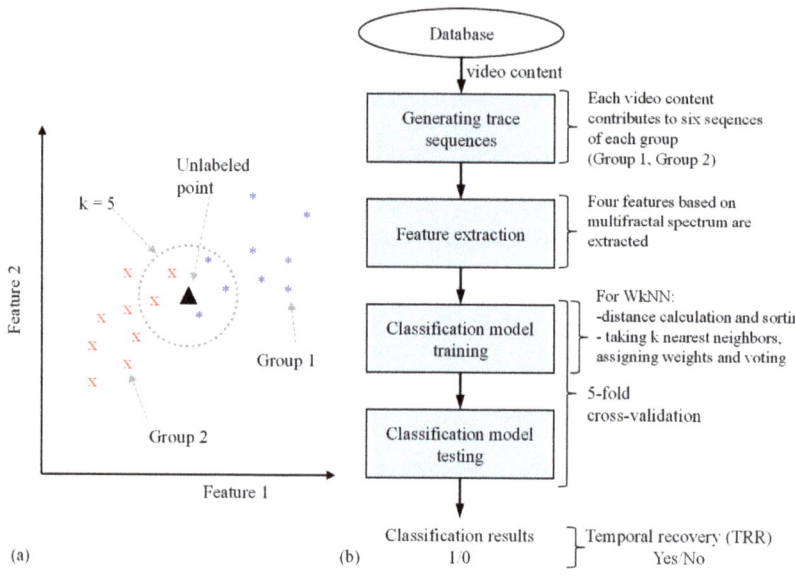

Figure 5. (**a**) The concept of k-nearest neighbors (kNN) binary classification and (**b**) the proposed model for temporal resolution recovery (TRR) detection.

An improved version of kNN is the WkNN [81,82], where feature space is corrected. Namely, features are assigned according to position between the points. If weights W_i are calculated using squared inverse method based on the distances d, the voting can be written as

$$\hat{y}_q = \text{argmax}_j \sum_i W_i I(y_i = j) = \frac{\sum_i W_i y_i}{\sum_i W_i}, \quad W_i = \frac{1}{d(x_q, x_i)^2}. \quad (12)$$

There are various metrics [83] that can be applied for finding distance between two feature vectors $x = (x_1, x_2, \ldots, x_m)$ and $y = (y_1, y_2, \ldots, y_m)$ for classifying the point into one of the groups. For example, Euclidean, Cityblock and Mahalanobis are common choices, expressed by

$$d^2_{Euclid} = \sum_{i=1}^{m}(x_i - y_i)^2, \quad (13)$$

$$d_{Cityblock} = \sum_{i=1}^{m}|x_i - y_i|, \quad (14)$$

$$d^2_{Mahalan} = (x-y)^T C^{-1}(x-y), \quad (15)$$

respectively, where C is the corresponding covariance matrix. Euclidean distance assumes that features are somewhat independent with a spherical distribution, where Mahalonobis is similar to Euclidean but seems to be a good alternative in such cases by taking into account the distance between a point and a distribution [82].

The temporal recovery detection model through trace sequences is presented in Figure 5b. The binary classification between the temporal recovered and original data are performed similarly to [82,84] with 5-fold cross-validation. Video content that was included in the training process for each crf was not part of the testing. The classification performance is measured using accuracy (Acc):

$$Acc = (TP + TN)/(TP + TN + FP + FN), \quad (16)$$

And true positive rate (*TPR*) or recall, as well as positive predictive value (*PPV*) or precision, are calculated as

$$TPR = TP/(TP + FN), \ PPV = TP/(TP + FP), \quad (17)$$

Using true positives (*TP*), true negatives (*TN*), false positives (*FP*) and false negatives (*FN*) in TRR detection.

6. Experimental Results and Discussion

6.1. Hurst Index Differences between Original and Temporal Recovery Data in LRD Estimation

HFR traces are collected for different video content of 120 fps of the same duration, where the original content has been compressed according to HEVC standard. Hurst exponent is calculated for LRD estimation, where it varies depending on the coarse approach applied in the calculation. After examination, it is evidenced that in most cases it has values in the expected range, i.e., $0.5 < H < 1$. This is presented for four Hurst index methods and ReadySetGo sequence in Table 2. LRD behavior is evident for the different index calculation methods applied: generalized method, DFA method, Hurst exponent calculated using periodogram and R/S statistics [68–74]. For example, the periodogram method applied in the case of crf36 is illustrated in Figure 6 for the ReadySetGo and YachtRide sequence. Lower Hurst values are obtained for TRR compared with the original, where in Figure 6, the TRR trend is presented with a solid line compared with original, which is presented with a dashed line. Still, these lower Hurst values are above 0.5, showing LRD. The dashed lines are found for data where no frame rate change is made. In the case of R/S statistics, it is also evident that the temporal resolution recovery case shows a decrease in Hurst index. This is illustrated in Figure 7. Such difference between indices may be useful for better understanding the changes found in recovered video data. The differences in Hurst evaluation using R/S statistics for UHD 120 fps compressed ReadySetGo sequence are shown in Table 3 for different crf values (H_{diff}). The method was used repeatedly for the other five original videos from Table 1. The averaged difference values $H_{diff,average}$ for each tested crf are also shown in the table. The relative difference varies from −11.51 to 1.30 percent. The highest absolute relative difference is obtained for crf24. Higher crfs show less variations in Hurst indices than the original sequences. This means that a higher difference in temporal recovered from nonrecovered data are expected in lower crfs, meaning higher video quality. Similar calculations are made in the case which is not common in practice for 120 fps HFR, where frame rate primarily increases and then decreases to 120 fps. In the additional case, such modifications show behavior more similar to the original data, as shown Figure 8. Nevertheless, temporal recovery data are still different from the original case. This additional case and its similarity to original traces are also illustrated in Figure 8.

Table 2. Long-range dependency (LRD) estimation via Hurst index calculation for ultra-high-definition (UHD) 120 fps compressed ReadySetGo sequence.

No.	Hurst Method	crf20	crf24	crf28	crf32	crf36	crf40
1	Hurst (Generalized)	0.6928	0.7058	0.7164	0.7138	0.7126	0.7089
2	Hurst (DFA)	0.7527	0.7962	0.8132	0.8024	0.7975	0.7832
3	Periodogram	0.7554	0.6036	0.5154	0.5512	0.5901	0.6113
4	R/S statistics	0.8652	0.8943	0.8848	0.8721	0.8678	0.8585

The obtained Hurst index differences between original and temporal recovery data in LRD estimation show that TRR case generally decreases index values. If the original and corresponding TRR sequences are available, such differences may be useful in recognizing the TRR change. Moreover, each content shows different behavior, where maximum absolute difference in Hurst index may vary depending on the content.

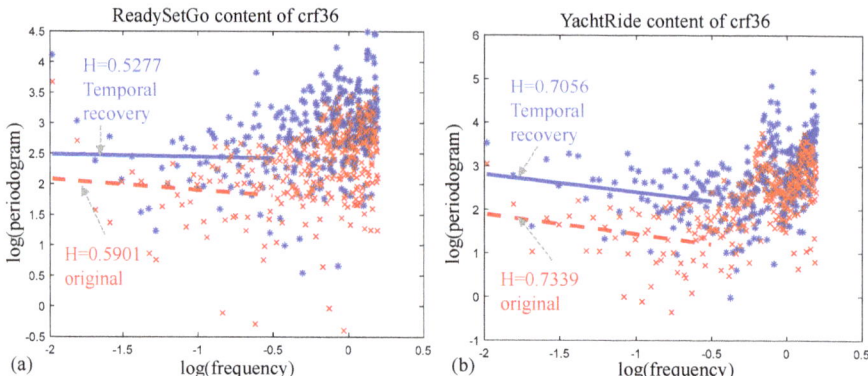

Figure 6. Periodogram method applied for constant rate factor (crf) 36 (crf36) of the (**a**) ReadySetGo and (**b**) YachtRide sequence, where the TRR trend is presented with a solid line and the corresponding original is presented with a dashed line.

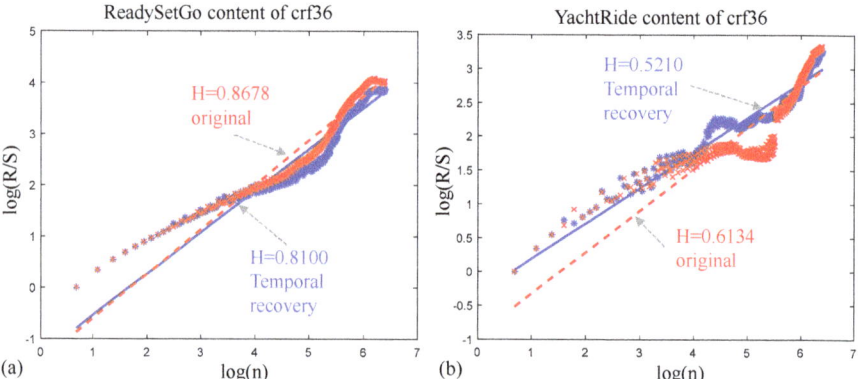

Figure 7. R/S statistics method applied for crf36 of the (**a**) ReadySetGo and (**b**) YachtRide sequence, where the TRR trend is presented with a solid line and the corresponding original is presented with a dashed line.

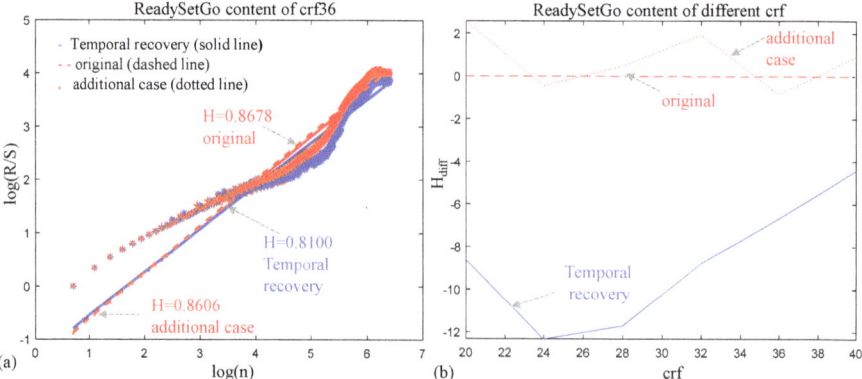

Figure 8. (**a**) R/S statistics method applied for ReadySetGo with crf36; (**b**) R/S statistics method applied for different crf values, where the TRR trend is presented with a solid line and the corresponding original is presented with a dashed line.

Table 3. Differences in Hurst evaluation using R/S statistics for UHD 120 fps compressed ReadySetGo sequence.

No.	Description	crf20	crf24	crf28	crf32	crf36	crf40
1	Temporal recovery	0.7910	0.7840	0.7807	0.7957	0.8100	0.8212
2	Original	0.8652	0.8943	0.8848	0.8721	0.8678	0.8585
3	H_{diff}	−8.58%	−12.33%	−11.77%	−8.76%	−6.67%	−4.34%
4	$H_{diff,average}$	−8.74%	−11.51%	−7.65%	−7.94%	−3.29%	+1.30%

6.2. Differences between Original and Temporal Recovery Data in Multifractal Spectrum Estimation

Different crf values from 20 to 40 are applied to demonstrate the effect of compression levels in practice. The standard effect of crf selection can be seen in Figure 9. If the crf increases, frame sizes are smaller, and the decreasing trend of trace sum is obvious in Figure 9a. In Figure 9b, the change in crf value selection is shown in the multifractal domain. This is demonstrated via multifractal spectra and six crf values for compressed UHD ReadySetGo sequence of 120 fps. Six spectra are found for sequences that are named as original here, since no TRR is applied in Figure 9b. The lowest crf values show narrower spectra, meaning the spectrum width is relatively small and vice versa.

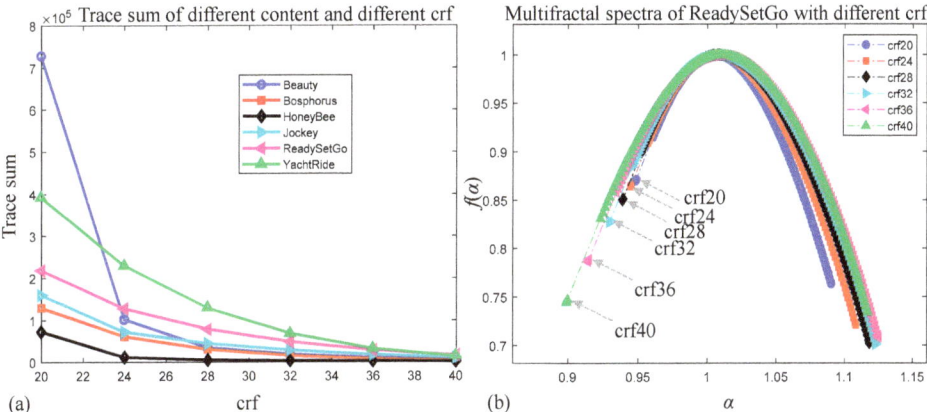

Figure 9. (**a**) Decreasing trend of trace sum; (**b**) multifractal spectra for ReadySetGo with different crf values.

Multifractal spectra for ReadySetGo with crf24 are presented in Figure 10a, where TRR is compared with the original. Similarly, TRR spectrum is shown for crf36, where it can be noticed that the relation is quite different, especially in terms of asymmetry (*a*), as opposed to the higher quality in crf24, as shown in Figure 10b. The calculation of multifractal characteristics enables going a step further with the analysis and the comparison between the two scenarios/cases: TRR and original. It is believed that significant data loss in TRR can be manifested through specific features compared with original UHD 120 fps sequences. Each spectrum is characterized by several points: minimum α value (α_{min}), maximum α value (α_{max}), α corresponding to curve maximum (α_0), and α corresponding to information dimension (α_1). These traditional characteristics, along with spectrum width, are presented in Table 4 for TRR and six crf values. Similarly, these characteristics are shown for original sequences and six crf values in Table 5.

Wider widths are generally found in the TRR case, and this can be a suitable feature if a reference/original exists. Unfortunately, this is not the case in practical implementations. Similar results can be obtained for the right slope and other characteristics since, for the ReadySetGo details and motion, spectra are quite different in TRR compared with the original, regardless of crf selection. When a compressed video has a lot of details, particularly recovered video, the right side, for example, expressed through w_r, contributes to the wider width. This is illustrated in Figure 11a. An additional case is also represented, and it is evident that similar results compared to the original data are obtained. Six TRR and six original sequences are presented in Figure 11a in multifractal domain. This is repeated for other UHD 120 fps video content as well. The spectra for HoneyBee and YachtRide are also presented in Figure 11, precisely Figure 11b and Figure 11c, respectively. By examining the cases and corresponding characteristics for other spectra, it can be seen that the abovementioned features are not suitable for possible recovery detection, regardless of crf and video content. For example, in Figure 11, the width feature values of all spectra for HoneyBee spectra are quite different from the widths of all spectra found in Figure 11a,c. The right side is not pointed in Figure 11b due to the video content itself, where little motion is present. Thus, cumulative sums of trace sequences are presented in multifractal domain in order to have a novel consideration of content from the standpoint of the multifractal concept.

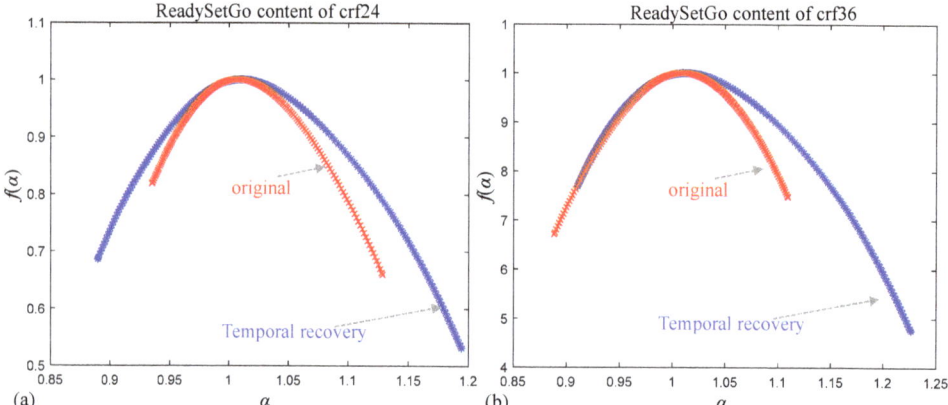

Figure 10. Multifractal spectra for ReadySetGo with (**a**) crf24 and (**b**) crf36 for temporal recovery compared with the original.

Table 4. Traditional multifractal characteristics of temporally recovered UHD ReadySetGo sequence.

No.	Parameter	crf20	crf24	crf28	crf32	crf36	crf40
1	α_{min}	0.8901	0.8891	0.8820	0.8899	0.9100	0.9129
2	α_1	0.9888	0.9894	0.9889	0.9882	0.9876	0.9856
3	α_0	1.10112	1.0106	1.0112	1.0120	1.0129	1.0154
4	α_{max}	1.2182	1.1941	1.2052	1.2126	1.2262	1.2314
5	w	0.3282	0.3050	0.3231	0.3227	0.3162	0.3185

Table 5. Traditional multifractal characteristics of original UHD ReadySetGo sequence.

No.	Parameter	crf20	crf24	crf28	crf32	crf36	crf40
1	α_{min}	0.9376	0.9350	0.9178	0.8949	0.8882	0.8698
2	α_1	0.9921	0.9929	0.9924	0.9913	0.9906	0.9901
3	α_0	1.0083	1.0073	1.0076	1.0086	1.0092	1.0095
4	α_{max}	1.1602	1.1285	1.1115	1.1084	1.1093	1.1010
5	w	0.2225	0.1934	0.1937	0.2135	0.2212	0.2312

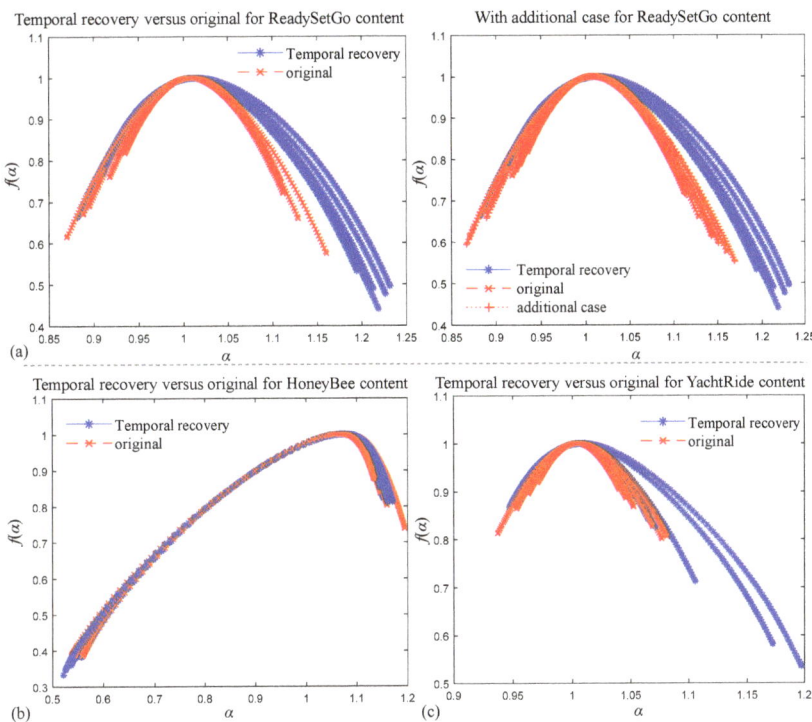

Figure 11. Legendre multifractal spectra presented for different HFR signals with different crf values: (**a**) ReadySetGo, (**b**) HoneyBee and (**c**) YachtRide.

Spectra curves obtain similar concave shapes due to a cumulative trend, as presented in Figure 12. The multifractal spectra of a cumulative sum of traces are presented for the sequences of ReadySetGo and HoneyBee in Figure 12. The structures seem more suitable to observe the behavior of data. Feature extraction is performed on the corresponding spectra in order to mark the differentiation between temporal recovery and the original case. Still, the width is not a proper selection as a feature for TRR detection. Thus, features are selected in a manner not to deal with the width but with the relative width, as in (8). Moreover, the right side of the spectra is zoomed for ReadySetGo and HoneyBee sequence in Figure 12 in order to observe additional features. Besides the slope, features (8)–(10) are applied in TRR detection.

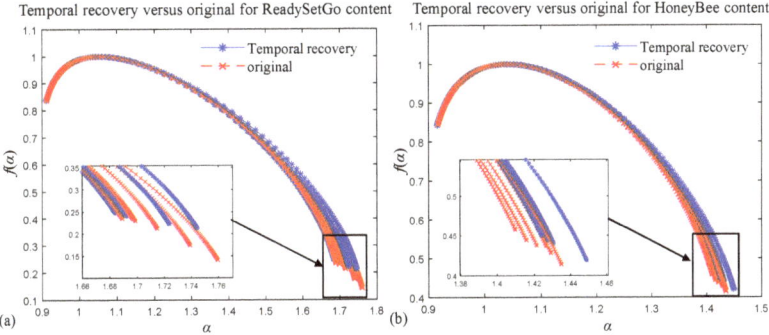

Figure 12. Legendre spectra structure and its right side for different crf values and different UHD 120 fps video content: (**a**) ReadySetGo and (**b**) HoneyBee.

Differences between original and temporal recovery data in multifractal spectrum estimation, as in the case of the Hurst index differences, show the possibility to recognize TRR content. Common features such as spectrum width can be applied in most cases when original data of the same compression quality are available. Nevertheless, if different compression quality and content are taken into account, this is not an easy task, due to spectra overlapping. Thus, in practice, common features may not be useful, and TRR detection should be based on specific features.

6.3. Temporal Recovery Detection Results Using the Proposed Model based on Multifractal Features

It is of practical importance to distinguish TRR from original HFR video data. Simply reducing and recovering HFR can be considered as one of the typical procedures in order to compensate found losses and to match original frequency. Nevertheless, it should not be neglected that distortions exist and need not be replaced with original data in cases where media integrity and authentication are involved. This should be available for any quality of level expressed here through compression. The selected crf mode enables a practical and sophisticated approach compared with setting constant quantization or output quality level. So, such settings are beneficial in practice, since they lead to results that are dependable on video content itself. The functional TRR detection approach presented in Figure 5b should serve a wide purpose as a tool. Here, UHD 120 fps data are analyzed.

After preparing video data and generating video trace sequence, feature extraction is performed according to four multifractal features that can be noted as feature1 to feature4, respectively, they are relative width, relative height, right side slope of multifractal spectra and left side distance based on two characteristic points of a spectrum. This is followed by a classifier which employs features that do not apply any reference. The performance of different classifiers in multifractal TRR detection is calculated using five randomly selected video source files from Table 1. These files give two groups of samples by using six crf values. In five-fold cross-validation, totally, sixty samples are used, presented in Figure 13a, where videos numerated from 1 to 5 are included. In Figure 13a, samples are presented as points in two feature domains. There is a linear trend of slope 1.07, and the norm of residuals calculated as the square root of the sum of the squares is 0.037. By examining cases, linear fits can be made for each group here. Namely, each group has similar norm of residuals close to 0.021 but with similar regression slopes close to 1.07, implying that appropriate fitting lines can be considered as parallel. The proposed model for temporal recovery detection is based on WkNN using Mahalanobis metric. In Figure 13b, a cross-validation result is presented, where one point is misdetected as temporally recovered. In this case, this is a point corresponding to the Beauty sequence of crf20. The trends of samples for each of the group are noticeable, even though different content is included in the tests. The experiment is performed on data recovered from 60 fps. Additional tests in practice were conduced in order to recover HFR HEVC data from 30 fps, showing satisfying results, as shown in Figure 14.

This is confirmed for YachtRide numerated as the sixth source video from [23] and TRR from 30 fps, which was not included in the cross-validation. Multifractal spectra of TRR data from different frame rates, like 24 fps, 30 fps, 60 fps and 96 fps, are presented in Figure 14f. Even though all YachtRide recovered data are correctly detected, one should be aware that cross-validation is performed only on TRR from 60 fps and original data of 120 fps, and that such cases with different downsampling should probably be included in the training. Future experiments need to include various combinations in the spatial–temporal domain, which was not the focus of this paper. Here, it was of interest to show that the multifractal domain and the proposed TRR detection can show high accuracy detection percentage in the set experiment using a relatively low number of features.

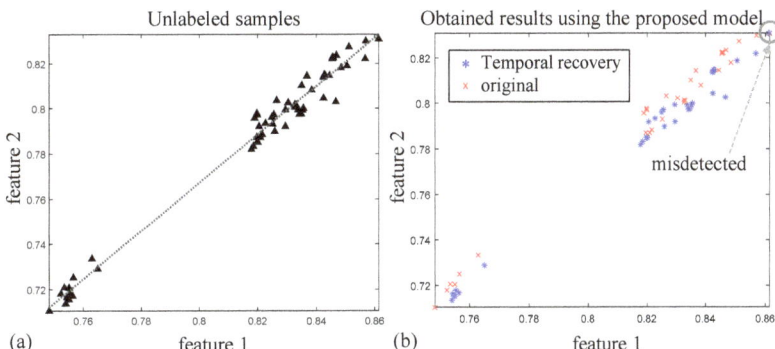

Figure 13. Points included in cross-validation: (**a**) unlabeled samples and (**b**) weighted k-nearest neighbors (WkNN)-based, distinguishing between TRR and original samples.

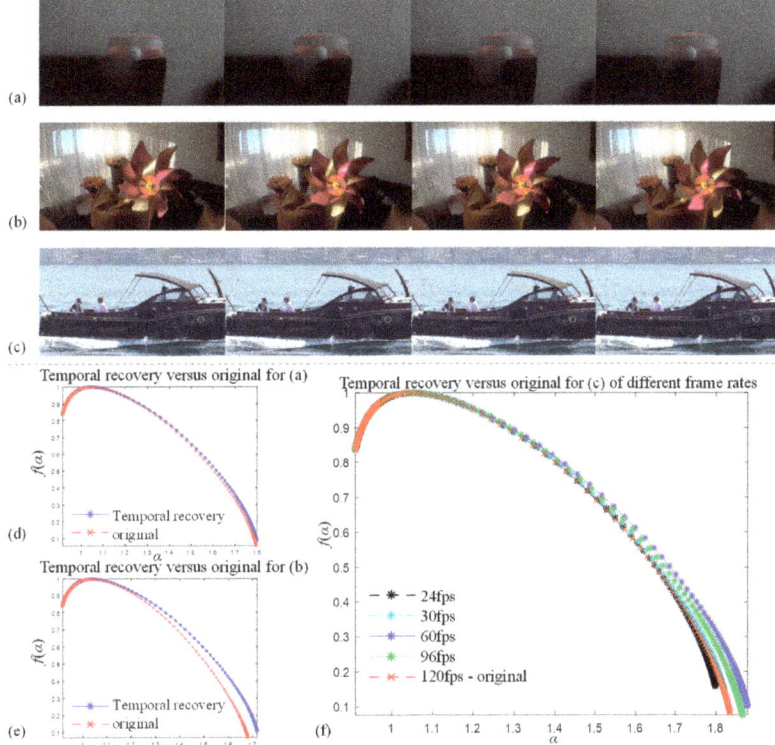

Figure 14. (**a**–**c**) Recovered sequences from 30 fps and corresponding (**d**–**f**) spectra presented with original data, where, in (**f**), temporal recovery is performed using different frequency rates.

In Figure 15a, recovered ReadySetGo is presented using several successive frames, obtaining recovered 120 fps suitable for comparing with 120 fps original data, where the difference between these two 120 fps is not easy to observe by a standard viewer. This is shown in order to point out that even though video content is very similar, a difference exists between HFR data depending on whether TRR is applied or not. Moreover, the analysis shows that such TRR detection based on multifractal features can be developed.

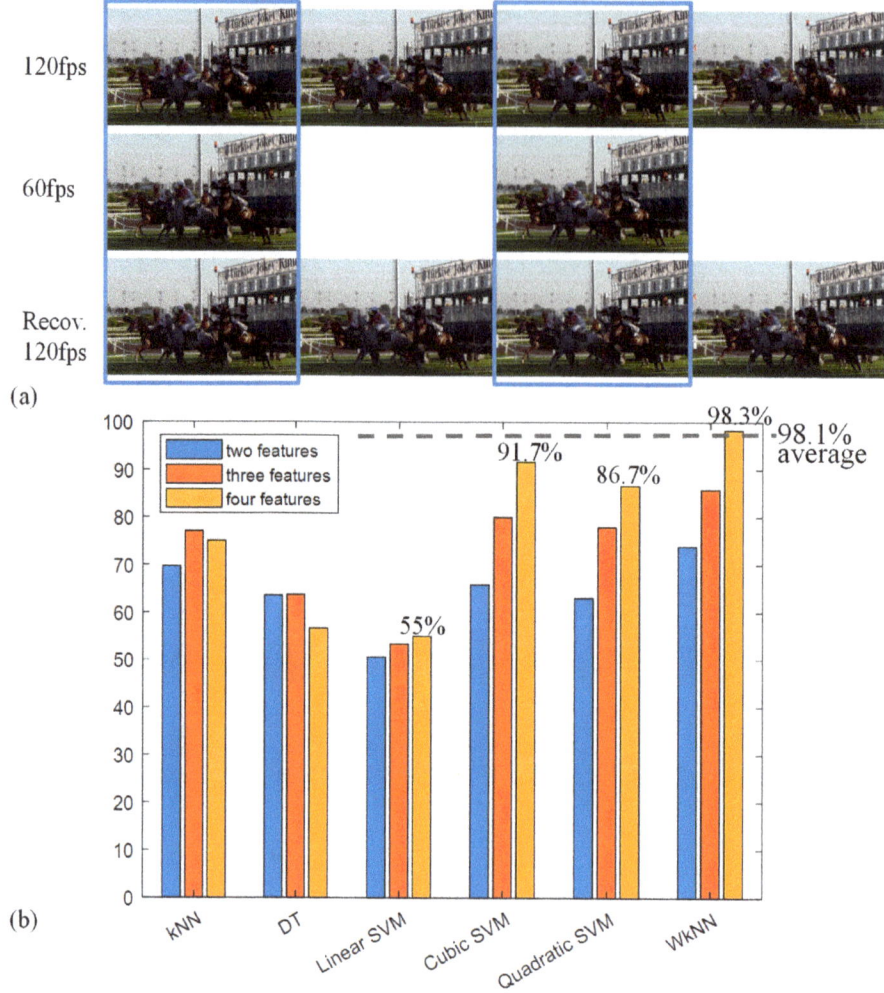

Figure 15. (**a**) Recovered ReadySetGo and (**b**) different number of features included in the cross-validation, taking into account tested classifiers with average performance.

The comparison between different distance measures showed significant advantage of the Mahalanobis metric (15) compared with other choices. In Table 6, the area under the curve is above 0.86 for different metrics for WkNN. The outcomes of the suggested approachbased on four features for (13)–(15) are given in Table 6, where the significant advantage of Mahalanobis is obtained compared with other distances [83]. Moreover, the performance is examined in the feature domain based on different classifiers, like kNN, decision tree and SVM, based on polynomial kernel functions such as linear, cubic and quadratic, as well as WkNN using the Mahalanobics metric, where a cross-validation procedure is applied. This is presented in Table 7, where recall, precision and accuracy are calculated, showing the highest value of accuracy for the proposed WkNN approach. Similar results are obtained for different 120 fps video data from the reference UVG dataset.

For different video content included in the cross-validation, high accuracy is confirmed. Namely, the average for six iterations for the proposed model still gives a high accuracy of 98.1%, as shown in Figure 15b. The obtained experimental results for TRR detection in the performed analysis seem promising, giving an accuracy above 98%. All four features are selected in the proposed model, where the performance based on fewer features is shown in Figure 15. The proper choice of classifier and selecting the right distance metric are necessary to obtain high accuracy results. Video sequences of different complexities and crf values are tested in the experiment which originated in 2160 p resolution, where only temporal conversion was applied with TRR HEVC detection, mainly focused on 120 fps. Compared with this, in [63], where recovery detection is tested, about 96% accuracy for AVC 60 fps video is reported. Future work should be oriented towards spatial conversions and other combinations. Here, HEVC compressed video content which originated in 2160 p resolution and 120 fps is trained and tested, which is usually carried out for much lower resolution formats and AVC [60–63]. It is expected that for proper training applied to different content and crf values, the model could be applicable for lower frame rates and lower spatial resolutions.

Table 6. Performance of WkNN classifier with different metrics.

No.	Classifier Type	True Positive Rate (TPR)	Positive Predictive Value (PPV)	Accuracy (Acc)
1	WkNN with Euclidean metric (13)	66.7	80	75
2	WkNN with Cityblock metric (14)	70	80.8	76.7
3	WkNN with Mahalanobis metric (15) (proposed approach)	96.7	100	98.3

Table 7. Performance of different classifiers in temporal resolution detection.

No.	Classifier Type	True Positive Rate (TPR)	Positive Predictive Value (PPV)	Accuracy (Acc)
1	kNN	70	77.8	75
2	Decision tree	60	56.3	56.7
3	Linear SVM	46.7	56	55
4	Cubic SVM	93.3	90.3	91.7
5	Quadratic SVM	89.3	83.3	86.7
6	WkNN with Mahalanobis metric (proposed approach)	96.7	100	98.3

All the experimental analyses were performed on the same platform, and ffmpeg was applied for the decoding tasks. This paper's emphasis is on the effects on LRD and multifractality and not the hardware or power consumption. Generally, playing 4k HFR HEVC may produce freezing. Nevertheless, the method does not require reproduction, and the parsing enables collecting traces in the offline mode with minimal graphic utilization. Even though tools for video reproduction can be used, specific graphical processing acceleration possibilities were not applied, such as Nvidia-GeForce-based ones, and the settings were kept as simple as possible. Here, CPU utilization is about twenty percent without visualization. Also, the abovementioned information does not affect the model. Any visualization increases both CPU and graphics unit utilization. In general, in decoding processes, there may be slight differences in trace sequences due to testing environment. Here, by repeating the process and testing different types of content, the model can be considered as robust. For content creation, action cameras like GoPro can be used. Also, for editing like audio removal, ffmpeg can be applied. Moreover, precision editing can be one of the possible challenges which need to be further analyzed. For content creation, it is possible to set prior acquisition time. Nevertheless, nonadequate editing such as trimming for modern standards like HEVC may produce corrupted video as an unwanted effect, which is well known in the forensic field. The proposed model was not developed for any broadcasting. So far, parsing was performed for sequences of particular length in offline mode, meaning that a significant amount of data are available for obtaining the trace sequences and applying the model. However, the tested duration can be treated as a minimal requirement for the method compared with the commonly used long movie trace sequences [58].

One of the advantages of the proposed approach is found in the selection of a small number of features that do not rely on a reference. In opposition to this, it is expected that including reference or pseudoreference calculations may additionally improve results, which is conducted in recent HFR works for HEVC content of different crf values for perceptual and objective quality assessment [32,67]. Also, multifractal and fractal approaches have been applied on previous compression standards like LFR/SFR MPEG-4 content using frame size video traces [56–59]. TRR detection related to HEVC HFR has not been performed so far to the author's knowledge. The effects have not yet been thoroughly investigated in the research community due to difficulties found when dealing with HFR and possible corresponding distortions [10]. HFR changes in temporal resolution affect video content, which is presented here from the LRD and multifractal standpoint. Temporal recovery detection results using the proposed model based on WkNN and specific multifractal features show satisfying performance. The TRR detection approach can be considered useful for HEVC HFR compressed data of different compression quality.

7. Conclusions

This paper presents experimental results obtained for HEVC compressed HFR video frame size traces for the first time in a multifractal domain. In the analysis, it is presented that HFR trace sequences manifest long-range dependence and multifractal behavior. In comparison between temporally recovered UHD 120 fps HFR and corresponding nonrecovered or original HFR data, lower Hurst indices are obtained, as well as often wider multifractal spectra. By analyzing spectra for different crf compressed sequences, it is assumed that it is possible to differentiate TRR signals from the original ones. The proposed WkNN approach was able to detect recovered video data, where the Mahalanobis measure was applied. Also, the feature vector is of low length, and features are extracted as nonreference. Input can be a TRR sample, which can be detected without prior assumption related to constant rate factors and without direct comparison between modified and original sequence. The proposed detection approach gave above 98% in accuracy during the cross-validation.

Overall, the differences between TRR and original HFR video are not easy to notice, even though Hurst indices like the ones calculated using R/S statistics show these differences. Multifractal spectra and their characteristics are also indicative in differentiating between the two groups consisting of various content and motion. By examination of the reference UVG dataset included in the video trace analysis, this research shows that multifractal descriptors and the trained model may be adequate for detection. The model enabled high-accuracy results regardless of compression rate or content. However, further development of the proposed model should be oriented towards other distortion possibilities in HFR domain.

Integrity and authentification issues may arise, and the approach may be useful in TRR or frame rate upconversion detection. Namely, there are a lot of challenges associated with HFR, and HFR needs to be properly addressed in order to truly realize its potential. The obtained results in this work can be considered valuable for future research. It can be concluded that HFR represents a significant advancement in the field of video technologies, and tracing analysis is important for dealing with specific behavior that HFR brings.

Funding: This work was partially supported by the Ministry of Science, Technological Development and Innovation of the Republic of Serbia, no.: 451-03-47/2023-01/200103.

Institutional Review Board Statement: Not applicable.

Informed Consent Statement: Not applicable.

Data Availability Statement: Data analyzed are available in a publicly accessible repository at https://ultravideo.fi/ (accessed on 1 May 2023) [23]. Additional data are available from the corresponding author upon reasonable request.

Conflicts of Interest: The author declares no conflict of interest. The funders had no role in the design of the study; in the collection, analyses, or interpretation of data; in the writing of the manuscript; or in the decision to publish the results.

References

1. Mackin, A.; Zhang, F.; Bull, D.R. A study of high frame rate video formats. *IEEE Trans. Multimed.* **2018**, *21*, 1499–1512. [CrossRef]
2. Armstrong, M.G.; Flynn, D.J.; Hammond, M.E.; Jolly, S.J.E.; Salmon, R.A. High frame-rate television. *SMPTE Motion Imaging J.* **2009**, *118*, 54–59. [CrossRef]
3. Sugawara, M.; Choi, S.Y.; Wood, D. Ultra-high-definition television (Rec. ITU-R BT. 2020): A generational leap in the evolution of television [standards in a nutshell]. *IEEE Signal Process. Mag.* **2014**, *31*, 170–174. [CrossRef]
4. Noland, M.; Whitaker, J.; Claudy, L. ATSC: Beyond Standards and a Look at the Future. *SMPTE Motion Imaging J.* **2021**, *130*, 29–38. [CrossRef]
5. Advanced Television Systems Committee (ATSC). ATSC 3.0 Standards. [Online]. Available online: https://www.atsc.org/standards/atsc-3-0-standards/;https://prdatsc.wpenginepowered.com/wp-content/uploads/2021/04/A341-2019-Video-HEVC.pdf (accessed on 20 May 2023).
6. You, D.; Kim, S.H.; Kim, D.H. ATSC 3.0 ROUTE/DASH Signaling for Immersive Media: New Perspectives and Examples. *IEEE Access* **2021**, *9*, 164503–164509. [CrossRef]
7. Weber, K.; van Geel, R. History and Future of Connecting Broadcast Television Cameras: From Multicore to Native IP. *SMPTE Motion Imaging J.* **2021**, *130*, 46–52. [CrossRef]
8. Wu, J.; Yuen, C.; Cheung, N.M.; Chen, J.; Chen, C.W. Enabling adaptive high-frame-rate video streaming in mobile cloud gaming applications. *IEEE Trans. Circuits Syst. Video Technol.* **2015**, *25*, 1988–2001. [CrossRef]
9. Berton, J.A.; Chuang, K.L. Effects of very high frame rate display in narrative CGI animation. In Proceedings of the 2016 20th International Conference Information Visualisation (IV), Lisbon, Portugal, 19–22 July 2016; pp. 395–398. [CrossRef]
10. Davis, T. Rethinking Frame Rate and Temporal Fidelity in a Cinema Workflow. *SMPTE Motion Imaging J.* **2017**, *126*, 62–71. [CrossRef]
11. Gomez-Barquero, D.; Li, W.; Fuentes, M.; Xiong, J.; Araniti, G.; Akamine, C.; Wang, J. IEEE transactions on broadcasting special issue on: 5G for broadband multimedia systems and broadcasting. *IEEE Trans. Broadcast.* **2019**, *65*, 351–355. [CrossRef]
12. Madhusudana, P.C.; Yu, X.; Birkbeck, N.; Wang, Y.; Adsumilli, B.; Bovik, A.C. Subjective and objective quality assessment of high frame rate videos. *IEEE Access* **2021**, *9*, 108069–108082. [CrossRef]
13. Wen, S.; Wang, J. A strong baseline for image and video quality assessment. *arXiv* **2021**, arXiv:2111.07104.
14. Silva, M.M.; Ramos, W.L.S.; Ferreira, J.P.K.; Campos, M.F.M.; Nascimento, E.R. Towards semantic fast-forward and stabilized egocentric videos. In Proceedings of the European Conference on Computer Vision, Amsterdam, The Netherlands, 11–14 October 2016; Springer: Cham, Switzerland, 2016; pp. 557–571. [CrossRef]
15. European Broadcasting Union (EBU) TR 050. *Subjective Evaluation of 100Hz High Frame Rate*; European Broadcasting Union: Geneva, Switzerland, 2019.
16. Nasiri, R.M.; Wang, J.; Rehman, A.; Wang, S.; Wang, Z. Perceptual quality assessment of high frame rate video. In Proceedings of the 2015 IEEE 17th International Workshop on Multimedia Signal Processing (MMSP), Xiamen, China, 19–21 October 2015; pp. 1–6. [CrossRef]
17. Lee, D.Y.; Ko, H.; Kim, J.; Bovik, A.C. Space-time video regularity and visual fidelity: Compression, resolution and frame rate adaptation. *arXiv* **2021**, arXiv:2103.16771. [CrossRef]
18. Rahim, T.; Shin, S.Y. Subjective Evaluation of Ultra-high Definition (UHD) Videos. *KSII Trans. Internet Inf. Syst. (TIIS)* **2020**, *14*, 2464–2479. [CrossRef]
19. Sara, U.; Akter, M.; Uddin, M.S. Image quality assessment through FSIM, SSIM, MSE and PSNR—A comparative study. *J. Comput. Commun.* **2019**, *7*, 8–18. [CrossRef]
20. Li, Z.; Bampis, C.; Novak, J.; Aaron, A.; Swanson, K.; Moorthy, A.; Cock, J.D. VMAF: The journey continues. *Netflix Technol. Blog* **2018**, *25*, 1.
21. Wang, Y.; Inguva, S.; Adsumilli, B. YouTube UGC dataset for video compression research. In Proceedings of the 2019 IEEE 21st International Workshop on Multimedia Signal Processing (MMSP), Kuala Lumpur, Malaysia, 27–29 September 2019; pp. 1–5. [CrossRef]
22. Hosu, V.; Hahn, F.; Jenadeleh, M.; Lin, H.; Men, H.; Sziranyi, T.; Li, S.; Saupe, D. The Konstanz natural video database (KoNViD-1k). In Proceedings of the 2017 Ninth International Conference on Quality of Multimedia Experience (QoMEX), Erfurt, Germany, 31 May–2 June 2017; pp. 1–6. [CrossRef]
23. Mercat, A.; Viitanen, M.; Vanne, J. UVG dataset: 50/120fps 4K sequences for video codec analysis and development. In Proceedings of the 11th ACM Multimedia Systems Conference, Istanbul, Turkey, 8–11 June 2020; pp. 297–302. [CrossRef]
24. Danier, D.; Zhang, F.; Bull, D. A Subjective Quality Study for Video Frame Interpolation. *arXiv* **2022**, arXiv:2202.07727. [CrossRef]
25. Vanam, R.; Reznik, Y.A. Frame rate up-conversion using bi-directional optical flows with dual regularization. In Proceedings of the 2020 IEEE International Conference on Image Processing (ICIP), Abu Dhabi, United Arab Emirates, 25–28 October 2020; pp. 558–562. [CrossRef]

26. MPEG. Available online: https://www.mpeg.org/ (accessed on 28 May 2023).
27. ITU-T, H. 264: Advanced Video Coding for Generic Audiovisual Services. Available online: https://www.itu.int/rec/T-REC-H.264-202108-I/en (accessed on 22 May 2023).
28. Wiegand, T.; Sullivan, G.J.; Bjontegaard, G.; Luthra, A. Overview of the H. 264/AVC video coding standard. *IEEE Trans. Circuits Syst. Video Technol.* **2003**, *13*, 560–576. [CrossRef]
29. ITU-T, H. 265: High Efficiency Video Coding. Available online: https://www.itu.int/rec/T-REC-H.265 (accessed on 22 May 2023).
30. Bordes, P.; Clare, G.; Henry, F.; Raulet, M.; Viéron, J. An overview of the emerging HEVC standard. In Proceedings of the International Symposium on Signal, Image, Video and Communications, ISIVC, Valenciennes, France, 4–6 July 2012.
31. Belton, J. Introduction: BEYOND HEVC. *SMPTE Motion Imaging J.* **2019**, *128*, 12–13. [CrossRef]
32. Rahim, T.; Usman, M.A.; Shin, S.Y. Comparing H. 265/HEVC and VP9: Impact of high frame rates on the perceptual quality of compressed videos. *arXiv* **2020**, arXiv:2006.02671. [CrossRef]
33. FFmpeg. Available online: https://ffmpeg.org/ (accessed on 28 May 2023).
34. Mandelbrot, B.B. *The Fractal Geometry of Nature*; WH Freeman: New York, NY, USA, 1982; Volume 1. [CrossRef]
35. Durán-Meza, G.; López-García, J.; del Río-Correa, J.L. The self-similarity properties and multifractal analysis of DNA sequences. *Appl. Math. Nonlinear Sci.* **2019**, *4*, 267–278. [CrossRef]
36. Garrett, M.W.; Willinger, W. Analysis, modeling and generation of self-similar VBR video traffic. *ACM SIGCOMM Comput. Commun. Rev.* **1994**, *24*, 269–280. [CrossRef]
37. Willinger, W.; Taqqu, M.S.; Sherman, R.; Wilson, D.V. Self-similarity through high-variability: Statistical analysis of Ethernet LAN traffic at the source level. *IEEE/ACM Trans. Netw.* **1997**, *5*, 71–86. [CrossRef]
38. Ritke, R.; Hong, X.; Gerla, M. Contradictory relationship between Hurst parameter and queueing performance (extended version). *Telecommun. Syst.* **2001**, *16*, 159–175. [CrossRef]
39. Riedi, R.; Véhel, J.L. Multifractal Properties of TCP Traffic: A Numerical Study. Rapport de recherché, L'Institut national de recherche en informatique et en automatique (INRIA), Le Chesnay-Rocquencourt, France. 1997. Available online: https://hal.inria.fr/file/index/docid/73560/filename/RR-3129.pdf (accessed on 20 May 2023).
40. Gao, J.; Rubin, I. Multifractal analysis and modelling of VBR video traffic. *Electron. Lett.* **2000**, *36*, 1. [CrossRef]
41. Vieira, F.H.T.; Bianchi, G.R.; Lee, L.L. A network traffic prediction approach based on multifractal modeling. *J. High Speed Netw.* **2010**, *17*, 83–96. [CrossRef]
42. Ribeiro, V.J.; Riedi, R.H.; Baraniuk, R.G. Wavelets and multifractals for network traffic modeling and inference. In Proceedings of the 2001 IEEE International Conference on Acoustics, Speech, and Signal Processing. Proceedings (Cat. No. 01CH37221), Salt Lake City, UT, USA, 7–11 May 2001; Volume 6, pp. 3429–3432. [CrossRef]
43. Jiang, J.; Xiong, Z. Wavelet-based modeling and smoothing for call admission control of VBR video traffic. In Proceedings of the Thrity-Seventh Asilomar Conference on Signals, Systems & Computers, Pacific Grove, CA, USA, 9–12 November 2003; Volume 2, pp. 1510–1513. [CrossRef]
44. Krishna, M.; Gadre, V.; Desai, U. Multiplicative multifractal process based modeling of broadband traffic processes: Variable bit rate video traffic. In Proceedings of the 2002 International Zurich Seminar on Broadband Communications Access-Transmission-Networking (Cat. No. 02TH8599), Zurich, Switzerland, 19–21 February 2002; p. 18. [CrossRef]
45. Huang, X.D.; Zhou, Y.H.; Zhang, R.F. A multiscale model for MPEG-4 varied bit rate video traffic. *IEEE Trans. Broadcast.* **2004**, *50*, 323–334. [CrossRef]
46. Rocha, F.G.C.; Vieira, F.H.T. Modeling of MPEG-4 video traffic using a multifractal cascade with autoregressive multipliers. *IEEE Lat. Am. Trans.* **2011**, *9*, 860–867. [CrossRef]
47. Yu, Y.; Song, M.; Fu, Y.; Song, J. Traffic prediction in 3G mobile networks based on multifractal exploration. *Tsinghua Sci. Technol.* **2013**, *18*, 398–405. [CrossRef]
48. Ergenç, D.; Onur, E. On network traffic forecasting using autoregressive models. *arXiv* **2019**, arXiv:1912.12220. [CrossRef]
49. Lazaris, A.; Koutsakis, P. Modeling multiplexed traffic from H.264/AVC videoconference streams. *Comput. Commun.* **2010**, *33*, 1235–1242. [CrossRef]
50. Lucantoni, D.M.; Neuts, M.F.; Reibman, A.R. Methods for performance evaluation of VBR video traffic models. *IEEE/ACM Trans. Netw.* **1994**, *2*, 176–180. [CrossRef]
51. Nogueira, A.; Salvador, P.; Valadas, R.; Pacheco, A. Modeling network traffic with multifractal behavior. *Telecommun. Syst.* **2003**, *24*, 339–362. [CrossRef]
52. Haßlinger, G.; Takes, P. Real time video traffic characteristics and dimensioning regarding QoS demands. In *Teletraffic Science and Engineering*; Elsevier: Amsterdam, The Netherlands, 2003; Volume 5, pp. 1211–1220. [CrossRef]
53. De Godoy Stênico, J.W.; Ling, L.L. A multifractal based dynamic bandwidth allocation approach for network traffic flows. In Proceedings of the 2010 IEEE International Conference on Communications, Cape Town, South Africa, 23–27 May 2010; pp. 1–6. [CrossRef]
54. Dymora, P.; Mazurek, M. An innovative approach to anomaly detection in communication networks using multifractal analysis. *Appl. Sci.* **2020**, *10*, 3277. [CrossRef]

55. Park, C.; Hernández-Campos, F.; Le, L.; Marron, J.S.; Park, J.; Pipiras, V.; Smith, F.D.; Smith, R.L.; Trovero, M.; Zhu, Z. Long-range dependence analysis of Internet traffic. *J. Appl. Stat.* **2011**, *38*, 1407–1433. [CrossRef]
56. Liew, C.H.; Kodikara, C.K.; Kondoz, A.M. MPEG-encoded variable bit-rate video traffic modelling. *IEE Proc.-Commun.* **2005**, *152*, 749–756. [CrossRef]
57. Fitzek, F.H.; Reisslein, M. MPEG-4 and H. 263 video traces for network performance evaluation. *IEEE Netw.* **2001**, *15*, 40–54. [CrossRef]
58. Reljin, I.; Samčović, A.; Reljin, B.H. 264/AVC video compressed traces: Multifractal and fractal analysis. *EURASIP J. Adv. Signal Process.* **2006**, *2006*, 75317. [CrossRef]
59. Seeling, P.; Reisslein, M. Video transport evaluation with H. 264 video traces. *IEEE Commun. Surv. Tutor.* **2011**, *14*, 1142–1165. [CrossRef]
60. Bestagini, P.; Battaglia, S.; Milani, S.; Tagliasacchi, M.; Tubaro, S. Detection of temporal interpolation in video sequences. In Proceedings of the 2013 IEEE International Conference on Acoustics, Speech and Signal Processing, Vancouver, BC, Canada, 26–31 May 2013; pp. 3033–3037. [CrossRef]
61. Bian, S.; Luo, W.; Huang, J. Detecting video frame-rate up-conversion based on periodic properties of inter-frame similarity. *Multimed. Tools Appl.* **2014**, *72*, 437–451. [CrossRef]
62. Ding, X.; Zhang, D. Detection of motion-compensated frame-rate up-conversion via optical flow-based prediction residue. *Optik* **2020**, *207*, 163766. [CrossRef]
63. Yoon, M.; Nam, S.H.; Yu, I.J.; Ahn, W.; Kwon, M.J.; Lee, H.K. Frame-rate up-conversion detection based on convolutional neural network for learning spatiotemporal features. *Forensic Sci. Int.* **2022**, *340*, 111442. [CrossRef]
64. Wang, S.H.; Qiu, Z.D. A novel multifractal model of MPEG-4 video traffic. In Proceedings of the IEEE International Symposium on Communications and Information Technology, 2005. ISCIT 2005, Beijing, China, 12–14 October 2005; Volume 1, pp. 101–104. [CrossRef]
65. Zhang, R.; Condomines, J.P.; Lochin, E. A Multifractal Analysis and Machine Learning Based Intrusion Detection System with an Application in a UAS/RADAR System. *Drones* **2022**, *6*, 21. [CrossRef]
66. Zajić, G.J.; Vesić, M.D.; Gavrovska, A.M.; Reljin, I.S. Animation frame analysis. In Proceedings of the 2015 23rd Telecommunications Forum Telfor (TELFOR), Belgrade, Serbia, 24–26 November 2015; pp. 732–735. [CrossRef]
67. Madhusudana, P.C.; Birkbeck, N.; Wang, Y.; Adsumilli, B.; Bovik, A.C. ST-GREED: Space-time generalized entropic differences for frame rate dependent video quality prediction. *IEEE Trans. Image Process.* **2021**, *30*, 7446–7457. [CrossRef] [PubMed]
68. Mandelbrot, B. Statistical methodology for nonperiodic cycles: From the covariance to R/S analysis. In *Annals of Economic and Social Measurement*; NBER: Cambridge, MA, USA, 1972; Volume 1, pp. 259–290.
69. Menkens, O. Value at risk and self-similarity. *Numer. Methods Financ.* **2007**, 1–23.
70. Weron, R. Estimating long-range dependence: Finite sample properties and confidence intervals. *Phys. A Stat. Mech. Its Appl.* **2002**, *312*, 285–299. [CrossRef]
71. Bărbulescu, A.; Serban, C.; Maftei, C. Evaluation of Hurst exponent for precipitation time series. In Proceedings of the 14th WSEAS International Conference on Computers, Corfu Island, Greece, 23–25 July 2010; Volume 2, pp. 590–595.
72. Kugiumtzis, D.; Tsimpiris, A. Measures of analysis of time series (MATS): A MATLAB toolkit for computation of multiple measures on time series data bases. *arXiv* **2010**, arXiv:1002.1940. [CrossRef]
73. García, M.D.L.N.L.; Requena, J.P.R. Different methodologies and uses of the Hurst exponent in econophysics. *Stud. Appl. Econ.* **2019**, *37*, 96–108. [CrossRef]
74. Montanari, A.; Taqqu, M.S.; Teverovsky, V. Estimating long-range dependence in the presence of periodicity: An empirical study. *Math. Comput. Model.* **1999**, *29*, 217–228. [CrossRef]
75. Véhel, J.L.; Tricot, C. On various multifractal spectra. In *Fractal Geometry and Stochastics III*; Birkhäuser: Basel, Switzerland, 2004; pp. 23–42. [CrossRef]
76. Ihlen, E.A.; Vereijken, B. Multifractal formalisms of human behavior. *Hum. Mov. Sci.* **2013**, *32*, 633–651. [CrossRef]
77. Krzyszczak, J.; Baranowski, P.; Zubik, M.; Kazandjiev, V.; Georgieva, V.; Sławiński, C.; Siwek, K.; Kozyra, J.; Nieróbca, A. Multifractal characterization and comparison of meteorological time series from two climatic zones. *Theor. Appl. Climatol.* **2019**, *137*, 1811–1824. [CrossRef]
78. Fraclab. Available online: https://project.inria.fr/fraclab/ (accessed on 20 June 2023).
79. Gavrovska, A.; Zajić, G.; Reljin, I.; Reljin, B. Classification of prolapsed mitral valve versus healthy heart from phonocardiograms by multifractal analysis. *Comput. Math. Methods Med.* **2013**, *2013*, 376152. [CrossRef] [PubMed]
80. Gajan, S. Modeling of seismic energy dissipation of rocking foundations using nonparametric machine learning algorithms. *Geotechnics* **2021**, *1*, 534–557. [CrossRef]
81. Fan, G.F.; Guo, Y.H.; Zheng, J.M.; Hong, W.C. Application of the weighted k-nearest neighbor algorithm for short-term load forecasting. *Energies* **2019**, *12*, 916. [CrossRef]
82. Sharma, A.; Jigyasu, R.; Mathew, L.; Chatterji, S. Bearing fault diagnosis using weighted K-nearest neighbor. In Proceedings of the 2018 2nd International Conference on Trends in Electronics and Informatics (ICOEI), Tirunelveli, India, 11–12 May 2018; pp. 1132–1137. [CrossRef]

83. Chomboon, K.; Chujai, P.; Teerarassamee, P.; Kerdprasop, K.; Kerdprasop, N. An empirical study of distance metrics for k-nearest neighbor algorithm. In Proceedings of the 3rd International Conference on Industrial Application Engineering, Kitakyushu, Japan, 28–31 March 2015; Volume 2. [CrossRef]
84. Jusman, Y.; Anam, M.K.; Puspita, S.; Saleh, E.; Kanafiah, S.N.A.M.; Tamarena, R.I. Comparison of dental caries level images classification performance using knn and svm methods. In Proceedings of the 2021 IEEE International Conference on Signal and Image Processing Applications (ICSIPA), Kuala Terengganu, Malaysia, 13–15 September 2021; pp. 167–172.

Disclaimer/Publisher's Note: The statements, opinions and data contained in all publications are solely those of the individual author(s) and contributor(s) and not of MDPI and/or the editor(s). MDPI and/or the editor(s) disclaim responsibility for any injury to people or property resulting from any ideas, methods, instructions or products referred to in the content.

Article

APIASO: A Novel API Call Obfuscation Technique Based on Address Space Obscurity

Yang Li, Fei Kang *, Hui Shu, Xiaobing Xiong, Yuntian Zhao and Rongbo Sun

State Key Laboratory of Mathematical Engineering and Advanced Computing, Zhengzhou 450001, China; grit1232021@163.com (Y.L.); shuhui123@126.com (H.S.); bingxiaoxiong@163.com (X.X.); www.manyer@yeah.net (Y.Z.); satoshi626@163.com (R.S.)
* Correspondence: kfminnie@163.com

Abstract: API calls are programming interfaces used by applications. When it is difficult for an analyst to perform a direct reverse analysis of a program, the API provides an important basis for analyzing the behavior and functionality of the program. API address spaces are essential for analysts to identify API call information, and therefore API call obfuscation is used as a protection strategy to prevent analysts from obtaining call information from API address spaces. API call obfuscation avoids direct API calls and aims to create a more complex API calling process. Unfortunately, current API call obfuscation methods are not effective in preventing analysts from obtaining usable information from the API address space. To solve this issue, in this paper, we propose an API call obfuscation model based on address space obscurity. The key functions within the API are encrypted and moved to the user code space for execution. This breaks the relationship between the API and its address space, making it impossible for analysts to obtain address information about a known API from the API address space. In our experiments, we developed an archetypical compiler-level API call obfuscation system to automate the obfuscation of input source code into an obfuscated file. The results show that our approach can thwart existing API deobfuscation techniques and is highly resistant to various open-source dynamic analysis platforms. Compared to other obfuscation techniques, our scheme improves API address space obscurity by more than two times, the detection rate of deobfuscation techniques such as Scylla, etc. is zero, and the increase in obfuscation overhead is not more than 20%. The above results show that APIASO has better obfuscation effect and practicability.

Keywords: API address space obscurity; API call obfuscation; anti-reverse analysis; hash function generators

1. Introduction

Windows applications rely on APIs to interact with the system and perform various functions, including network communication, file access, and message interaction. Understanding these APIs is crucial for comprehending program behavior. When direct reverse analysis is challenging, APIs serve as an indispensable reference for analysts to identify program behavior and intent [1].

To protect the API calling process, program developers often employ various obfuscation techniques to prevent detection. The basic premise of API call obfuscation is to use a more complex approach than the Windows API call process to make it difficult for analysts to identify which API has been called. However, over the past two decades, analysts have proposed a range of techniques to overcome API obfuscation. The key step in API deobfuscation is to associate the virtual memory address accessed by the program during runtime with the API name. Analysts typically employ program analysis methods such as symbolic execution or taint analysis to track program execution. This involves collecting call instructions and function addresses, and then correlating them with the loaded APIs in memory to identify any obfuscated APIs.

The ability to collect address information related to known APIs during API calls is a critical factor in the ongoing game between obfuscation and deobfuscation techniques. Sections 2.1 and 2.2 of this paper systematically summarize existing API call obfuscation and deobfuscation techniques. The findings reveal that even the most advanced deobfuscation methods are still capable of collecting addresses associated with known APIs. As a result, none of the currently available API call obfuscation methods can effectively prevent analysts from conducting API deobfuscation. Therefore, the development of a more secure API call obfuscation scheme is a pressing concern.

In this paper, we propose a new approach to API call obfuscation called API address space obscurity (APIASO), which aims to prevent analysts from accessing address information associated with known APIs during the API call process. APIASO protects the entire API call process by moving the API's critical internal functions into the user code space. When a program calls the API, it first executes the functions that have been moved into the user code space and then proceeds to execute the non-critical functions within the API. This prevents analysts from obtaining information directly related to the known API from the API call. Additionally, for the API code extraction process, our approach provides a wide range of alternative API name hash schemes by designing a hash function generator to achieve more secure API address resolution. The API name hash serves as a cryptographic key to move the key functions of the API to the user code space, making it impossible for analysts to access usable information from the process of API address resolution and function movement.

We conducted extensive experiments to evaluate the effectiveness and obfuscation overhead of APIASO. To quantitatively assess the impact of APIASO on the API address space, we measured the obscurity degree of the API address space. We also tested the resistance of APIASO against four representative deobfuscation techniques. In addition, we demonstrated the availability and correctness of APIASO by developing an automated API call obfuscation system.

The main contributions of this paper are:

- We provide a comprehensive overview of existing API call obfuscation and deobfuscation techniques. We also discuss the limitations of current API obfuscation techniques and their inability to effectively counter advanced deobfuscation techniques.
- We present API address space obscurity (APIASO), an API call obfuscation technique specifically designed for Windows applications. APIASO provides stronger protection than existing API call obfuscation techniques by protecting the entire API call process and preventing analysts from accessing address information associated with known APIs during the API call process.
- We compare APIASO with several other existing API call obfuscation techniques. Our experiments show that APIASO is highly effective in thwarting existing deobfuscation techniques, and it provides a significant increase in the protection strength of program API information.
- We implement an automatic API call obfuscation system based on LLVM [2], which can automatically obfuscate the input program source code. The source code is available on GitHub (https://github.com/Rookiellvm/APIASO, accessed on 13 August 2022).

2. Background

In this section, we systematically provide a review of current API call obfuscation and deobfuscation techniques. While API call obfuscation techniques are commonly utilized for API call protection, analysts have developed numerous deobfuscation techniques to improve analysis efficiency. These techniques employ program analysis techniques such as monitoring program execution for jump instructions and function addresses to expose hidden traces of API calls.

We provide a comprehensive summary of existing mainstream API call obfuscation and deobfuscation techniques to highlight the shortcomings of current API call obfuscation techniques when it comes to effectively countering deobfuscation techniques. Finally, we introduce the design goals of APIASO as a means of addressing these limitations.

2.1. API Call Obfuscation Techniques

Kawakoya [3] et al. provided a formal definition of the concept of API call obfuscation and introduced various specific patterns of API call obfuscation. In a recent study by API-Xray [4], it was revealed that the primary aim of API call obfuscation is to evade the standard API resolution and calling process provided by Windows. Table 1 shows three API call obfuscation methods, each of which is described below.

Table 1. Classification of API call obfuscation techniques.

Classification	Pathways
IAT redirection [4]	Anti-debugging, exception triggering, ROP
Position obfuscation [5]	Instruction stolen, function stolen, DLL stolen
Call site tampering [6]	GetModuleHandle/LoadLibrary and GetProcAddress

IAT redirection: IAT redirection is achieved by tampering with the IAT table; Figure 1b shows the process of an API call after IAT redirection obfuscation. The API address stored in the IAT table entry is replaced with an "induction area" address so that the address obtained in the IAT does not point directly to the API. Figure 1b shows the redirection method of triggering an exception in the "induction area" by a divide-by-zero operation. In addition, it is possible to redirect API calls by adding anti-debugging functions or ROP techniques to the "induction area".

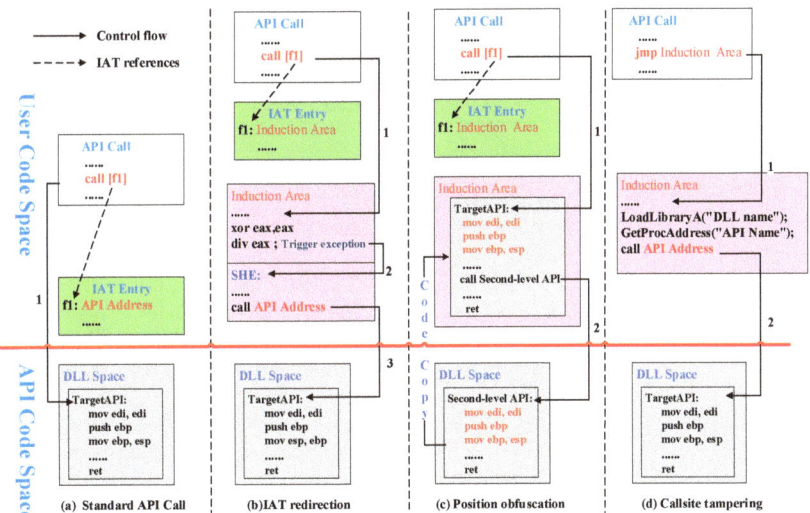

Figure 1. Overview of API call obfuscation techniques.

API position obfuscation: Position obfuscation makes the API call address fail to point to the API entry point by moving the API code to execute in user space. Depending on the scope of the moved code, position obfuscation is divided into three cases: (1) Instruction stolen, which moves part of the API instruction to the user code space for execution, and then jumps to the target API code. (2) Function stolen, which moves the entire API to the user code space for execution. Figure 1c describes the process of calling the API after the function is stolen, replacing the API address stored in the IAT table entry with the "induction area" address, which stores the API code copied from the system load DLL space. When the program calls the API, it executes the API in the "induction area". (3) Dynamic

Link Library (DLL) stolen, which loads the entire DLL into user code space and calls the API through the self-loaded DLL.

API call site tampering: API call site tampering eliminates the dependence of API calls on IAT and resolves the API address at program runtime. Figure 1d shows the API call process of the program after call site tampering. The program encrypted stores the called API name. When the program calls the API, it decrypts the API name and obtains the address of the API through the combination of the functions GetModuleHandle/LoadLibrary and CreateProcAddress. Additionally, to further complicate the analysis, the API name resolution process does not use the aforementioned function calls to obtain the API address. Instead, the program uses the PEB to obtain the DLL address and retrieves the required API address from the export table of the DLL.

2.2. API Deobfuscation Techniques

To improve the efficiency of an analysis, analysts perform API monitoring to obtain API call information for programs that implement API call obfuscation. Table 2 provides an overview of current API deobfuscation techniques. These techniques can be categorized into the following three groups based on their starting point: call site monitoring, position monitoring, and hybrid monitoring.

Table 2. Classification of API deobfuscation techniques.

Classification	Citations
Call site monitoring	BinUnpack [7], SOK [8], Scylla [9], Eureka [10], RePEc [11], PinDemonium [12], Arancino [13], Arg Prediction [14]
Position monitoring	API Chaser [15], QuietRIATT [16], Secure unpack [17], Taint-assisted [18]
Hybrid monitoring	API-Xray [4], RePEconstruct [19]

Call site monitoring: Figure 2 depicts that the deobfuscation techniques for API call site monitoring follow two steps: (1) Instruction scanning (I in Figure 2), which runs PE files to find possible API call sites in memory, including indirect calls, direct calls, or indirect jumps. (2) Address association (II in Figure 2), which correlates the destination address of a possible call site with the exported API address of the loaded dynamic link library. The basic principle of call site monitoring is that the destination address of a jump instruction in memory is always found to be the address of the system-loaded API. As illustrated in Figure 1b,d, there are instructions in the memory space "induction area" in which the target address is the system load API address.

Position monitoring: Position monitoring is the monitoring of system load DLL pages. The basic principle is that regardless of the API call obfuscation technique used, the program eventually executes the system load DLL area code. Position monitoring includes API hook monitoring and taint analysis association. API hook monitoring (III in Figure 2) monitors the execution of API code in the DLL. QuietRIATT and secure unpack use the API hook approach to set hooks in the loaded API code area, which is logged when the program calls the API where the hooks are set; alternatively, the taint analysis association [17,18] (IV in Figure 2) method involves attaching taint tags to the API code, and when the program executes the code in the DLL space, the API executed is determined by the attached taint tags.

Hybrid monitoring: The call site monitoring technique can monitor the call site of the whole program, but the call site address of the program applying API position obfuscation is a non-API-related address, which makes the call site monitoring invalid. The position monitoring approach can effectively prevent API position obfuscation, but it can only address a single path at a time and has low coverage. API-Xray and RePEconstruct have taken the benefits of both call site monitoring and position monitoring methods into account. They propose a hybrid monitoring approach that combines both techniques to enhance the efficiency of deobfuscation.

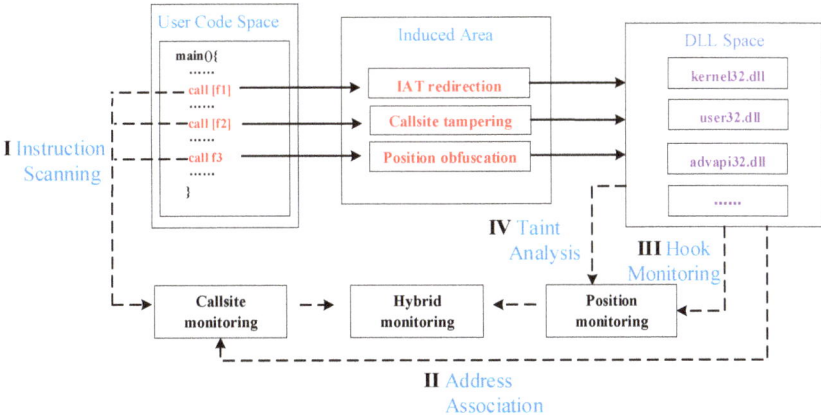

Figure 2. Overview of API deobfuscation techniques.

2.3. Motivation

Existing API call obfuscation and deobfuscation techniques are summarized above. As shown in Figure 2, API deobfuscation monitors all stages of existing obfuscation techniques, rendering them ineffective. IAT redirection and call site tampering introduce control flow jump to increase the execution distance between the call site and the system-loaded API, but there are still instructions to call the API in the "induction area" of the method (in Figure 1a,c). The API can be associated with the jump address obtained through call site monitoring (I and II in Figure 2). Position obfuscation, as shown in Figure 1b, increases the execution distance within the API by moving the code. However, current methods only move the first level of functions inside the API. This means that internal calls still provide enough information for deobfuscation to detect the API. As a result, deobfuscation can be successfully implemented by analyzing the functions called inside the API through the methods of hook monitoring and taint analysis, as shown in (III) and (IV) in Figure 2. The obfuscation scheme of DLL stolen is not practical because of its high overhead on program execution and vulnerability to monitoring.

In summary, existing API call obfuscation methods are ineffective against deobfuscation attacks. The main objective of these methods is to hide the address information during API calls to make it difficult to correlate virtual memory addresses with API names. However, this goal has not been achieved effectively so far.

The API address space is the basis for identifying API calls, so the goal of APIASO is to obfuscate the API address space information so that the analyst cannot establish a relationship between the virtual memory address of the function from the API call process and the API address space, and therefore cannot identify it as an API call.

Table 3 shows the differences between APIASO and other obfuscation techniques in terms of the means of obfuscation and the resistance to deobfuscation monitoring. APIASO obfuscates the entire process of the API call, while being able to withstand all types of existing deobfuscation techniques.

Table 3. Differences between APIASO and other obfuscation techniques.

Obfuscation Type	Resolution Process	Calling Process	Anti-Call Site Monitoring	Anti-Position Monitoring	Anti-Hybrid Monitoring
IAT redirection	×	√	×	×	×
Position obfuscation	×	√	√	×	×
Call site tampering	×	√	×	×	×
APIASO	√	√	√	√	√

3. API Address Space Obscurity Model

In this section, we introduce an obfuscation model for API address space obscurity, which focuses on two key processes in the API call process.

(1) API call space obfuscation: This process involves the movement of API internal functions to user space for execution. The movement of the function requires a deeper analysis of the API's internal functions. A function selection strategy is constructed by considering the call relationship, the function's properties, the cost of the move, and the analyst's experience.

(2) API name clue obfuscation: This process involves building hash function generators and using more secure API address resolution methods and function movement schemes to obscure API name clues.

3.1. Overview of the APIASO

Figure 3 illustrates the APIASO based on the guidance of the address space obscurity idea. When the program calls the API, it first executes the part of the API moved to the user code space, and then jumps to the system DLL space to execute the unmoved function inside the API. The function selection strategy involves making the function executed in the DLL space so it cannot be directly associated with the valid API. The collision-free hash function generator provides a separate hash scheme for each API name. The generated hash value is used as an encryption key to ensure the security of the function move, which makes the mapping relationship before and after the function move more complicated.

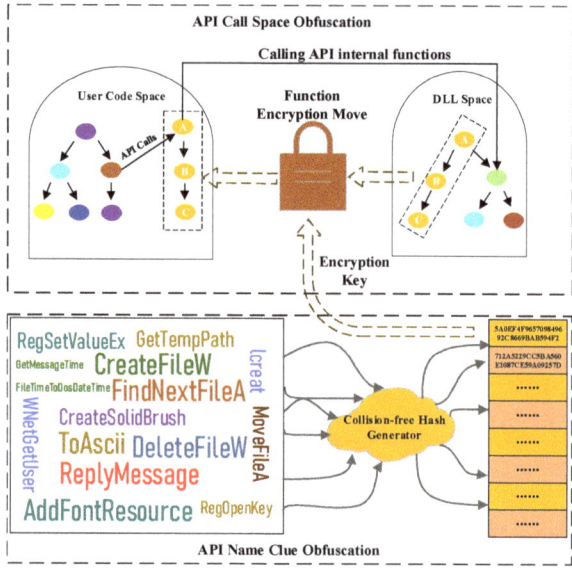

Figure 3. Diagram of API address space obscurity.

The obfuscation model discussed in this section protects various stages of API calls, and different technical points are discussed in subsequent sections. Specifically, the API function selection strategy is described in Section 3.2, while Section 3.3 discusses the API address extraction method and function movement scheme. Table 4 shows the symbolic description of API address space obscurity.

Table 4. Explanation of notations.

Notation	Description
$DASpace$	DLL address space
$APl_{Entry} = \{f_{e_1}, f_{e_2}, \cdots, f_{e_m}\}$	API entry functions
$APl_{Internal} = \{f_{m+1}, f_{m+2}, \cdots, f_n\}$	API internal functions
G	Function call graph
$AASpace_{APl_i}$	API address space
A	Adjacency matrix
P	Reachable matrix
$Level(f_q)$	Level of functions in the DLL address space

3.2. API Call Space Obfuscation

The goal of API call space obfuscation is to obscure the boundary between API and user functions so that the analyst fails to obtain information associated with known APIs. APIs typically have complex internal call relationships. As a result, obfuscation of key functions can effectively protect API calls, while obfuscation of non-key functions can result in higher overhead. The following chapter provides an analysis of the API's internal call relationships and discusses the API call space obfuscation strategy.

Definition 1. *Define the DLL address space as* $DASpace = \{APl_{Entry}, APl_{Internal}, G_{DLL}\}$, *which comprises three parts:* $APl_{Entry} = \{f_{e_1}, f_{e_2}, \cdots, f_{e_m}\}$, *includes the set of API entry functions called directly by the user;* $APl_{Internal} = \{f_{m+1}, f_{m+2}, \cdots, f_n\}$, *includes the set of API internal functions called indirectly by the user; and m, which refers to the number of functions inside the DLL space that can be called directly by the user. n denotes the total number of functions inside the DLL space.* G_{DLL} *represents the function call graph within the DLL address space, and is denoted as* $G_{DLL} = \{F_{DLL}, E_{DLL}\}$. F_{DLL} *in* G_{DLL} *refers to the set of functions inside the DLL address space, i.e.,* $F_{DLL} = APl_{Entry} + APl_{Internal}$.

Definition 2. *Define each API address space as* $AASpace_{APl_i} = \{\{f_{e_i}\}, \{f_{i_1}, \cdots, f_{i_x}, \cdots f_{i_k}\}, G_{APl_i}\}, (1 \leq i \leq m, m+1 \leq i_x \leq n)$. $f_{e_i} \in APl_{Entry}$ *indicates the functions that can be called directly by the user inside the API address space,* $\{f_{i_1}, f_{i_2}, \cdots, f_{i_k}\} \subset APl_{Internal}$ *indicates the set of internal call functions, and there is a direct or indirect call relationship between* f_{e_i} *and* f_{i_x}. G_{APl_i} *denotes the* APl_i *internal function call graph, denoted as* $G_{APl_i} = \{F_{APl_i}, E_{APl_i}\}, (1 \leq i \leq m)$, *where* F_{APl_i} *denotes the set of functions, i.e.,* $F_{APl_i} = \{\{f_{e_i}\}, \{f_{i_1}, \cdots, f_{i_x}, \cdots f_{i_k}\}\}$.

According to each API function call graph, $G_{APl_i}, (1 \leq i \leq m)$ can calculate G_{DLL}, the calculation process is as follows:

$$G_{DLL} = G_{APl_1} \cup G_{APl_2} \cup \cdots G_{APl_n} \quad (1)$$

The adjacency matrix can be used to describe the relationship between function calls. Based on the function call graph G_{DLL} inside the DLL address space generates the adjacency matrix as A. If there exists a function f_p calling a function $f_q (1 \leq p \neq q \leq n)$ inside the DLL address space, then $A_{pq} = 1$, otherwise $A_{pq} = 0$. Obviously, the matrix A is a square matrix and the number of matrix ranks is equal to the number of DLL space functions n. The reachable matrix P and the adjacency matrix A are both Boolean matrices. $P_{pq} = 1$ means that there is a call path from function f_p to f_q. The reachable matrix P can be obtained from the adjacency matrix A, which is calculated as follows:

$$P = A^1 \vee A^2 \vee A^3 \vee \ldots \vee A^n, n = r(A) = c(A) \quad (2)$$

Definition 3. *Define the level of functions in the DLL address space. For a function $f_q \in AASpace_{API_i} (1 \leq i \leq m, m+1 \leq q \leq n)$, if there exists another function $f_p \in AASpace_{API_j}$ $(1 \leq j, p \leq m, j \neq i)$ and there is a call path from f_p to f_q, then the level of the function f_q is added by 1. Specifically, the API entry function called directly by the user is conventional of level 0, so for function $f_q \in API_{Internal} \in AASpace_{API_i}$ level is expressed as:*

$$Level(f_q) \begin{cases} 1 & \forall f_p \notin ASpace_{API_i} \text{ and } A_{pq} = 0 \\ > 1 & \exists f_p \notin ASpace_{API_i} \text{ and } A_{pq} = 1 \end{cases} (m+1 < q < n) \quad (3)$$

Functions with a higher level are more difficult for analysts to associate with known APIs because they are called by more upper-level functions. Conversely, functions with a lower level are associated with fewer APIs, thereby enabling effective identification of the APIs called by the program. Therefore, the function level is an important criterion for moving the function to the user space.

When a function in the API address space $AASpace_{API_i} = \{\{f_{e_i}\}, \{f_{i_1}, \cdots, f_{i_x}, \cdots f_{i_k}\}, G_{API_i}\}$ is moved to the user space, the API entry function is moved directly to the user space because it is not called inside the address space. When a function f_{i_x} called from within the API is moved, moving it directly requires modifying the address of the f_{i_x} call instruction in the API address space. Modification of the instruction in the API address space will affect the correctness of other functions using the function. Therefore, it is necessary to move all the functions that dominate the function in the address space together to ensure the integrity of the call relationship.

The function f_{i_p} dominates the function $f_{i_q} (i_1 \leq i_p, i_q \leq i_k, p \neq q)$, which means that the API entry function f_{e_i} to f_{i_q} must pass through f_{i_p}, which is denoted as f_{i_p} dom f_{i_q}. if there exists i_p such that $P_{i_p i_q} = 1$ and for any $i_l (i_1 \leq i_p, i_q, i_l \leq i_k, p \neq q \neq l)$, if it satisfies $P_{i_l i_q} = 1$ and $P_{i_p i_l} = 1$ or $P_{i_l i_q} = 0$, then it is denoted f_{i_p} dom f_{i_q}.

A necessary condition for API internal function movement: For the API address space $AASpace_{API_i} = \{\{f_{e_i}\}, \{f_{i_1}, \cdots, f_{i_x}, \cdots f_{i_k}\}, G_{API_i}\}$, if the function is the entry function f_{e_i}, it will be moved directly; if the function is internal $f_{i_q} (1 < q < k)$, then all functions that satisfy f_{i_p} dom f_{i_q} are moved to user space together.

Based on the above definition, for a given API address space $AASpace_{API_i} = \{\{f_{e_i}\}, \{f_{i_1}, \cdots, f_{i_x}, \cdots f_{i_k}\}, G_{API_i}\}$, the function nodes that do not satisfy the address space obfuscation condition are pruned from the call graph G_{API_i}.

(1) Pruning high-level function nodes: As can be seen from Definition 3, there are low-level and high-level functions in the API address space $AASpace_{API_i}$. Low-level functions are strongly associated with the upper API, and functions of Level 0 and 1 in the low-level functions are directly associated with the API itself, so such functions must be moved completely, while low-level functions of Level greater than 1 can be moved selectively according to the need for protection strength. Higher-level functions are called by many different APIs in the upper layers, and their calls are not sufficient to provide directly usable information for reconstructing the APIs. Moving them causes large memory and runtime overhead, so the higher-level function nodes are pruned on the call graph.

(2) Adding special function nodes: In addition to low-level functions in the API address space $AASpace_{API_i}$, there are also functions with certain special call relationships. Although these functions are not low-level functions, they still provide key information for accessing the API. For example, the *CreateFileA* function call eventually translates into a call to *CreateFileW*, and address space obfuscation is required for API calls with dependencies on *xxxA* and *xxxW*. In addition, some APIs call functions with names beginning with *Nt* exported from Ntdll.dll, using the system call number to enter the kernel. This class of API names provides information that can be used for deobfuscation. These functions may not be lower-level functions in that address space, so it is significant to recover this part of the pruned special function node.

(3) Adding bogus function node: low-level functions have a strong association with the API, and the movement of low-level functions in the address space of the protected API can hide the association, while the introduction of low-level functions in the address space of other APIs can increase the association with other APIs, thus misleading the analysts. Therefore, the low-level functions in other address spaces are chosen to be moved to the user space together as bogus function nodes.

According to the above conditions, the function call graph G_{API_i} in the obfuscated API address space $AASpace_{API_i}$ is first pruned of its internal low-level function nodes; then, the special function nodes are restored, and bogus low-level function nodes are introduced on the pruned call graph, and the dominant function nodes and corresponding call edges are added to obtain the final call graph. It is worth noting that the API address space obscurity strategy provided in this paper is a controlled scheme, for example, the criteria for identifying low-level functions can be set to any level such as Levels 1, 2, and 3. The higher the set criteria, the more functions are moved, and with them the greater the obfuscation strength, and therefore the greater the overhead, which will be evaluated in Section 5.1.1 for the set value of the level.

3.3. API Name Clue Obfuscation

API address space obscurity gets the API code at runtime, and the position of the API code in memory can be obtained by API name resolution. The current API call obfuscation uses a name resolution method where the API name is mapped to a fixed length hash by a hash function, and the program executes to resolve the required API address by hashing the hash operation, and then matching the hash value. The main problem with this method is that the hash function is fixed and does not guarantee a diverse range of hash functions for more secure API address resolution.

To address the above problem, APIASO uses the more secure API name resolution method. To address the problem of using a single hash function, a hash function generator is designed to generate many fast and collision-free hash functions, and different API names are encrypted using different hash functions to ensure that a variety of hash functions are available. The details of this solution are described below.

The hash function generator is used to generate many lightweight collision-free hash functions, providing a variety of options for the API name resolution. API names are represented as sets $W = \{w_1, w_2, \ldots, w_k\}$ and the total number of API names is k. The 64-bit hash generation space S takes values in the range $[0, 2^{64} - 1]$. We use a fast perfect hash function generation algorithm based on random graphs [20] to generate a hash function that satisfies the mapping of the set W to the hash value space S with no collisions, and the generic expression of the generated hash function is as follows:

$$h(w) = g(f_i(w)) + g(f_j(w)) \quad (4)$$

where f_i and f_j are the operator functions that map the API names to the interval $[0, N - 1]$, and N is the smallest integer that satisfies the collision-free hash function generation. G is the mapping function that maps the results of the operations of functions f_i and f_j to the hash value space S. Given the set of operator functions $F = \{f_1, f_2, \ldots, f_l\}$, the execution of the algorithm can find the mapping function g. The specific algorithm execution process is as follows:

1. An integer N greater than k is selected randomly, and two hash functions f_i and f_j from the set F are selected randomly afterward.
2. For each element w_q in the set W, find $f_i(w_q)$ and $f_j(w_q)$.
3. An undirected graph G is created, of which the vertices are defined by $f_i(w_q)$ and $f_j(w_q)$. Then, each pair of vertices $f_i(w_q)$ and $f_j(w_q)$ are linked up to obtain graph edges, in which each edge corresponds to each element w_q of the set W.
4. G is checked to see if it is acyclic, and if not, returns to Step 1.

5. N values are randomly selected in the hash generation space S and randomly assigned to the N edges of the graph G as the value of each element w_q.
6. A randomly selected vertex is assigned a value of 0, and then a depth-first search is performed to traverse the graph G vertices. Correspondingly, the value of two vertices that share the same edge is assigned according to the hash value of this edge, such that the sum of the values of these two adjacent vertices equals to the hash value of the edge.
7. The sequence of vertices of the graph G and their assigned hash values form a mapping function g. Thereby f_i and g constitute a collision-free hash function.

The time complexity of this algorithm is $O(N)$ and the space required to store the generated functions is $O(N \log N)$ bits, which is optimal for generating perfect collision-free hash functions [21]. It is almost impossible to involve all the APIs in the program's API call process, so the size of the algorithm input k can be further optimized by adjusting k to the number of all API names in the DLL export table on which the program calls the APIs. Since only the API name hashes in the specified DLL import table need to be satisfied without collisions, this process greatly reduces the search space of the algorithm. The implementation of the above algorithm assigns a unique hash function to each API name, increasing the resistance of the API name resolution process to reverse analysis.

The API address space obscurity algorithm is shown in Algorithm 1. The inputs to the algorithm are the program P, the DLL address space $DASpace$, and the obfuscation threshold ε, where ε represents the set criteria for the moved low-level function.

Algorithm 1: Address Space Obscurity Algorithm

Input: Program P, $DASpace$, Obfuscation threshold: ε
Output: $o(P)$ denotes the obfuscated program

1. Define the obfuscated API call graph: $OG_{API_i} = \{OF_{API_i}, OE_{API_i}\}$
2. **procedure CallSpaceObf** ($AASpace_{API_i}, \varepsilon$):
3. $OG_{API_i} = G_{API_i} - G_{API_i} \cap G_{DLL}$ // Prune all common function nodes
4.   **foreach** f_q **in** F_{API_i}:
5.   **if** level $(f_q) \leq \varepsilon$ **and** $f_q \notin OF_{API_i}$:
6. $OF_{API_i} = OF_{API_i} + f_q$
7.   **if** $f_q \in SpecialFunc$ **and** $f_q \notin OF_{API_i}$:
8. $OF_{API_i} = OF_{API_i} + f_q$
9. $k = 0$
10.   **do**
11.   **foreach** f_q **in** F_{DLL}:
12.   **if** level $(f_q) \leq \varepsilon$ **and** $f_q \notin F_{API_i}$:
13. $OF_{API_i} = OF_{API_i} + f_q$
14. k++
15.   **while** ($k \leq \varepsilon$)
16.   **foreach** f_q **in** OF_{API_i}:
17.   **if** $\exists\, p\ P_{qp} = 1$ **and** $f_p \in API_{Internal}$:
18. $OF_{API_i} = OF_{API_i} + f_p$
19.   **Return** OG_{API_i}
20. **end procedure**
21. // Algorithm Entry
22. Get the API collection for program P: $APISet = \{API_1, \ldots, API_k\}$
23. $HashSet = \{hash_1, \ldots, hash_n\} \longleftarrow$ **NameClueObf** ($APISet$) // API name clue obfuscation
24. **foreach** API_1 **in** $APISet$:
25.   Get the address space corresponding to API_i: $AASpace_{API_i}$
26. $OG_{API_i} = \{OF_{API_i}, OE_{API_i}\} \longleftarrow$ **CallSpaceObf** ($AASpace_{API_i}, \varepsilon$)
27.   Choose a random hash function $hash_i$ for API_i
28.   Calculate the corresponding hash value: $hash_i(API_i)$
29.   Record Triads: $<OG_{API_i}, hash_i, hash_i(API_i)>$
30. **Return** $o(P)$

The API collection of the program is first extracted, and API name trail obfuscation is performed to generate a collection of hash functions (22–23). Then, the API collection is traversed, and API call space obfuscation is performed for each API (24–26).

First, the call space obfuscation process prunes low-level function nodes and restores special function nodes (2–8); second, it adds bogus low-level function nodes (9–13); then adds function nodes on the call path according to the API internal function move requisites (14–18); and finally returns the obfuscated API internal call graph.

After performing call space obfuscation, a unique hash function is assigned to each API, and the obfuscated call graph, hash function, and name hash triads (27–29) are kept in the program, thus completing the obfuscation process.

After obfuscation, when the program executes the API call, it parses the API according to the triads and uses the saved hash to encrypt the mobile function to the user space for a more secure API call process.

4. System Implementation

The framework of LLVM [2] is an extensible program optimization platform that provides APIs for analyzing and modifying intermediate language code. In this section, we implement an obfuscation system on top of LLVM for automated API call obfuscation. Figure 4 demonstrates the system composition of the obfuscation system, which takes a C/C++ source program as input and outputs a binary file that has been obfuscated by the API calls. The obfuscation process is divided into the following four phases: (1) the front-end code compilation phase, (2) the obfuscated function addition phase, (3) the API call substitution phase, and (4) the code generation phase.

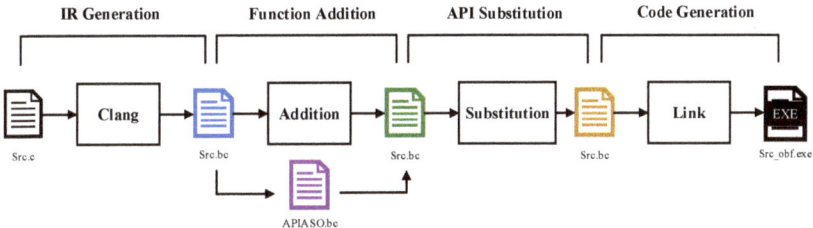

Figure 4. Obfuscation system components.

In the first stage, the Clang pre-section compiler converts the C/C++ source program into an intermediate representation of LLVM.

In the second stage, the obfuscated function is added to the intermediate language file of the program, and the obfuscated function completes the run-time API name and address space obfuscation.

In the third phase, the intermediate language is analyzed and the API calls that need to be protected are replaced.

In the fourth stage, the obfuscated "bc" file is linked by the compiler to produce the final executable.

5. Experimental Evaluation

In this section, we perform an experimental verification of APIASO on a Windows 10 system with an Intel Core i7-9700 CPU @ 3.00 GHz and 32 G RAM. The APIASO automatically obfuscates API calls for programs. We evaluate it from the following two aspects:

(1) Model protection strength evaluation: We compare the advantages of APIASO with other API call obfuscation techniques in resisting API deobfuscation techniques, and compare the dynamic analysis resistance of programs before and after APIASO protection using online antivirus and sandbox platforms.

(2) Model protection efficiency evaluation: We test large-scale code to evaluate the availability and accuracy of APIASO and the program time execution overhead, before and after obfuscation.

5.1. Model Protection Strength Evaluation

5.1.1. The Obscurity Degree of API Address Space

The obscurity degree of API address space is a key indicator of the effectiveness of API call obfuscation. To describe the ability of the obfuscation model to obfuscate the address space, we propose the concept of the obscurity degree of the API address space to quantitatively describe the degree of the obscurity of the API address space before and after obfuscation. Assuming that the program to be obfuscated is P, the obfuscated program is represented as $O(P)$. The obscurity degree of P is expressed as follows:

$$APIASODegree(P) = \sum_{i}^{4} (-1)^{i-1} \frac{X_i - min(X_i)}{max(X_i) - min(X_i)} \quad (5)$$

X_1–X_4 correspond to $LevelPer(P)$, $Cost(P)$, $ComplexIncreaseR(P)$, and $R(P)$, respectively.

$LevelPer(P)$ indicates the proportion of high-level functions in DLL space executed when the program calls the API. The higher the percentage of high-level functions, the more low-level functions are moved to the user code space and the higher the degree of address space obscurity. $HighLevel(P)$ indicates the accessed high-level functions. $Level(P)$ indicates the total number of levels of the program. The $LevelPer(P)$ calculation process is expressed as follows:

$$LevelPer(P) = \frac{HighLevel(P)}{Level(P)} \quad (6)$$

$Cost(P)$ denotes the cost of obfuscation of APIASO, which is expressed as the ratio of the number of functions moved to the total number of functions. $MoveFun(P)$ denotes the number of functions moved. $Fun(P)$ denotes the total number of APIs and their internal functions in the program. The $Cost(P)$ calculation procedure is expressed as:

$$Cost(P) = \frac{MoveFun(P)}{Fun(P)} \quad (7)$$

$ComplexIncreaseR(P)$ represents the rate of increase in the complexity of the API call process after obfuscation. The complexity of the API call process is measured by the complexity of the API call relationship graph. $APICallComplex(P)$ represents the complexity of the program API call process, then the $ComplexIncreaseR(P)$ calculation procedure is expressed as:

$$ComplexIncreaseR(P) = \frac{APICallComplex(O(P))}{APICallComplex(P)} \quad (8)$$

The program remains semantically equivalent before and after API call obfuscation, but it becomes more difficult for the analyst to understand it. Ideally, any means of API call obfuscation can be cracked given enough time. In practice, however, program reverse analysis does not always result in the same level of difficulty as understanding the original program. $R(P)$ is expressed as the experience of the reverse analyst. The higher the experience of the analyst, the closer the result of the reverse analysis is to the original program, and the easier it is to understand the program. The similarity between the reverse analysis result and the original program in the API call space in terms of data flow and control flow is used as the evaluation basis. The higher the similarity, the closer the reverse analysis result is to the original program, and the higher the reverse analyst's experience

$R(P)$. P^{-1} denotes the result of reverse analysis; $AC(P)$ and $AD(P)$ denote the control flow and data flow of API call space, respectively; and $R(P)$ denotes as follows:

$$R(P) = Similarity\left[AC(P), AC(P^{-1})\right] + Similarity\left[AD(P), AD(P^{-1})\right]. \tag{9}$$

As described in Section 3.2, APIASO is a method to control the strength of obfuscation. The threshold set by the lower level function determines the number of functions to move when obfuscating. To verify the effect of obfuscation under different thresholds, the $APIASODegree(P)$ is chosen as the judging basis for the obfuscation of six magnitudes of programs under Windows.

In Figure 5, the magnitude I is represented as a program containing 20 APIs, and the magnitude I to VI programs are incremented by 10 APIs. Figure 5 represents the results of $APIASODegree(P)$ versus execution time overhead for function levels set to 1, 2, 3, and 4. The horizontal coordinate represents the obscurity degree of the API address space at different level setting criteria, and the vertical coordinate represents the ratio of program execution time before and after program obfuscation. The results show that the best address space obfuscation is achieved at a low runtime overhead with a threshold of 2. Therefore, all subsequent experiments will be conducted with a threshold of 2.

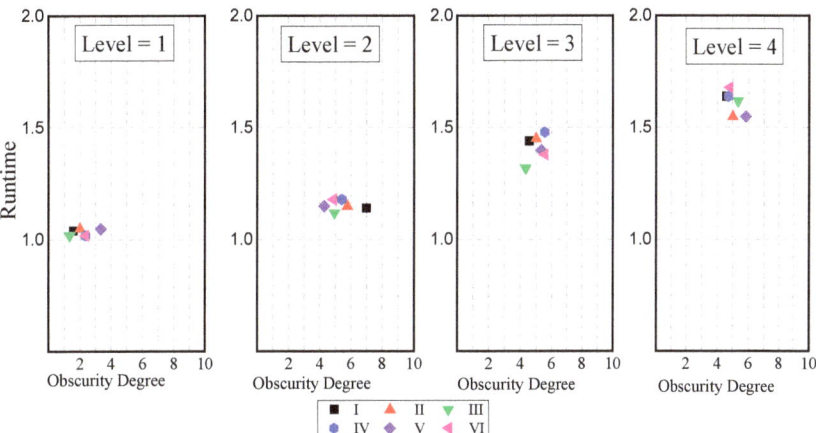

Figure 5. Address space obscurity at different levels.

According to the previous section, the API call obfuscation methods include IAT tampering, basic block-level position obfuscation, function-level position obfuscation, DLL-level position obfuscation, and API call site tampering. We applied the above obfuscation means and APIASO to six magnitudes of programs under Windows. The DLL space functions called by the program are recorded and the $APIASODegree(P)$, which is shown in Figure 6. The horizontal coordinate represents the obfuscated program, and the vertical coordinate represents the $APIASODegree(P)$ after obfuscation. The results show that the APIASO is significantly higher than other obfuscation methods.

To visually describe the distribution of functions in memory during API calls, we track the execution of all functions specifically associated with *CreatefileA* calls. We count these functions and record their offset address and virtual memory address.

As shown in Figure 7, the Windows standard call procedure is compared with the calling procedure under the obfuscation of the other four types of API calls, with the vertical coordinate indicating the address offset of the function and the horizontal coordinate indicating the virtual memory address of the function. During a standard API call, only one call instruction exists in the user code space, so there is only one function associated with the API call. However, during API calls with call site tamper and IAT redirection, functions related to the obfuscation also exist in the user space in addition to the function containing the call instruction. No changes occur within the API code space. When it comes to API calls under position obfuscation, the code related to the entry function of *CreatefileA* exists in the user code space, while the entry function of *CreatefileA* in the API code space is hidden. Lastly, for API calls under APIASO, low-level, bogus, and special functions exist in the user code space along with the other obfuscation-related functions mentioned above. Only high-level functions remain in the API code space, while other key functions are hidden within the user code space.

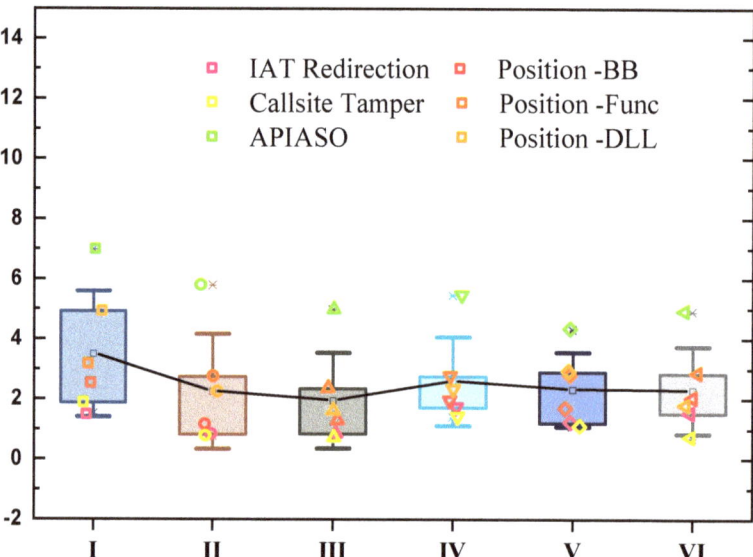

Figure 6. Degree of address space obscurity.

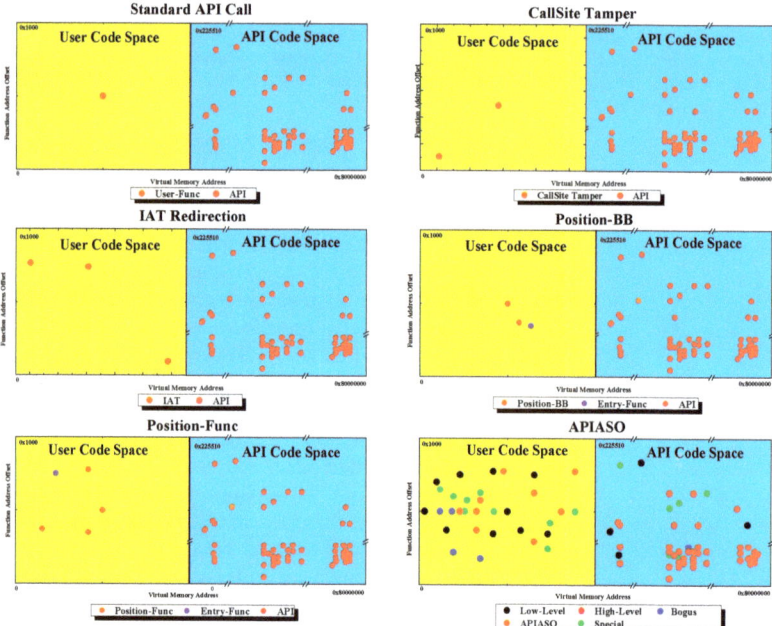

Figure 7. Function execution trajectory during API calls.

Therefore, APIASO significantly obscures the boundary between user code space and API code space compared to other obfuscation techniques, which significantly increases the difficulty of API call analysis.

5.1.2. Anti API Deobfuscation Techniques

Table 5 shows the different API call obfuscation techniques used in ten popular packers' software. To compare the advantages of APIASO with other API call obfuscation techniques in terms of resistance to deobfuscation detection, an application with the volume IV (containing 120 APIs) in the previous section is obfuscated using 10 packers and APIASO.

Table 5. Packer software corresponds to API obfuscation technology.

No.	Tools	Types
1	Yoda's Crypter	1
2	Yoda's Protector	1
3	TELock	1
4	ZProtect	1
5	Enigma	1
6	Armadillo	1
7	Obsidium	1
8	PESpin	1, 2
9	PELock	1, 2
10	PEP	1, 3

Section 2.2 provides a summary of the various deobfuscation techniques currently used with APIs in Table 2. For our experimental evaluation, we selected four representative techniques: Scylla, PinDemonium, QuietRIATT, and RePEconstruct. Scylla and PinDemonium employ call site monitoring, while QuietRIATT utilizes a position monitoring approach and RePEconstruct uses a hybrid monitoring approach.

In Figure 8, a radar chart is presented to show the deobfuscation capabilities of four different techniques when faced with various API call obfuscation methods. The results of our experiments were that none of these techniques were able to successfully deobfuscation the program when APIASO was used. Furthermore, the recovered API information contained errors, including bogus APIs that had been introduced, leading to an increase in the overhead associated with analysis for the analyst.

The experimental results are predictable from the principles of the four deobfuscation techniques. Scylla and PinDemonium collect the target addresses of calls and jump instructions from the program memory under APIASO obfuscation, but since these cannot be associated with the API addresses exported by the DLL, they cannot identify the obfuscated APIs. QuietRIATT sets hooks at API entry points that may be called by programs. Programs under APIASO obfuscation do not execute API entry functions, and therefore cannot be logged by QuietRIATT. RePEconstruct uses a binary instrumentation tool to record instructions that jump into DLL space, while the destination addresses of calls and jump instructions in memory are collected. The destination addresses of instructions that do not exist in the memory of programs under APIASO obfuscation are API addresses, and the addresses monitored in DLL space cannot be associated with valid APIs. Therefore, RePEconstruct cannot implement deobfuscation.

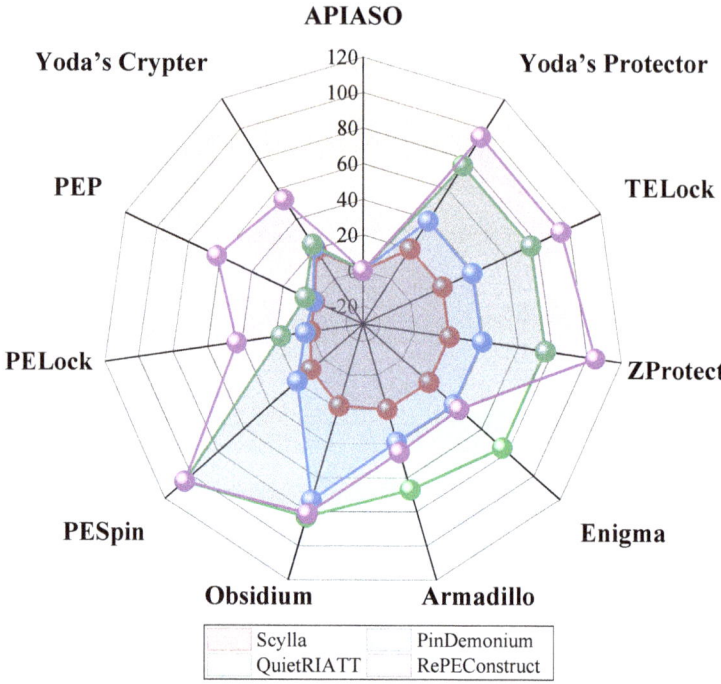

Figure 8. API deobfuscation Capability Radar Chart.

5.1.3. Sandbox and Antivirus Platform Detection

Analysts often use the results of online sandbox detection as basics for further reverse analysis, while API calls are an essential metric in detection. In this section, programs protected by APIASO are analyzed using VirusTotal (https://www.virustotal.com/gui/home/upload, accessed on 13 August 2022), Cuckoo (https://cuckoosandbox.org/, accessed on 13 August 2022), and Sandboxie (https://sandboxie-plus.com/, accessed on 13 August 2022) to compare the differences in output results between platforms before and after obfuscation. We collect 100 publicly available malicious programs with source code from GitHub, then submit the obfuscated malicious programs to VirusTotal and Cuckoo to compare the difference in output results between platforms before and after obfuscation.

VirusTotal uses a total of 78 different antivirus detection tools to mark submitted malicious programs as malicious or benign based on each security vendor's judgment; the more security vendors mark them as malicious, the less resistant the program is to analysis. The analysis results are shown in Figure 9. VirusTotal detects significantly fewer security vendors for obfuscated malicious programs due to APIASO obfuscating the API call information of malicious programs, with nearly half of the security vendors marking them as benign compared to before obfuscation.

Cuckoo is a dynamic malicious program analysis sandbox that calculates a malicious rating for each submitted program based on the hit signature: less than 1.0 is benign, 1.0–2.0 is a warning, 2.0–5.0 is malicious, and above 5.0 is dangerous. Figure 10 Indicates the results of Cuckoo's detection. APIASO successfully reduced Cuckoo's score, with the obfuscation-protected programs all having malicious scores below 5.0 and significantly lower malicious behavior levels, all dropping below the malicious level.

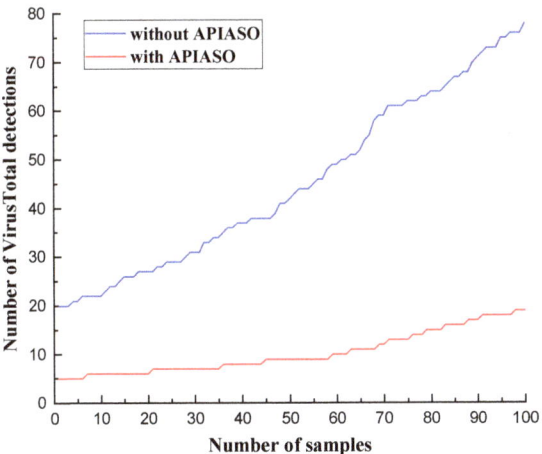

Figure 9. VirusTotal analysis results.

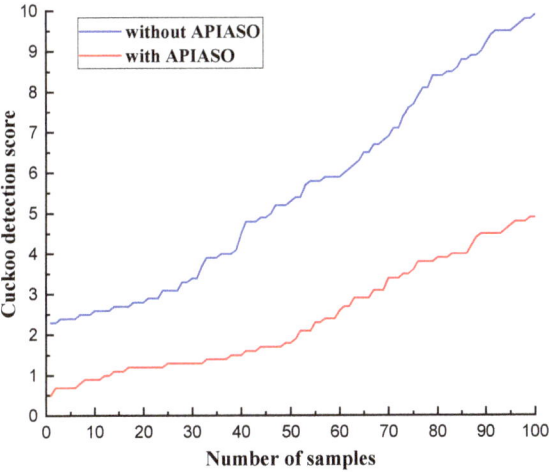

Figure 10. Cuckoo analysis results.

We build Sandboxie in an experimental environment to run six API-weight programs after APIASO obfuscation. Sandboxie is a sandbox-based isolation program for Windows NT-based 32-bit and 64-bit operating systems. It was developed by David Xanatos since it was open sourced, and before that, it was developed by Sophos. It creates a sandbox-like isolated operating environment in which applications can be run or installed without permanent modification of local or mapped drives. Unobfuscatedly, the four programs are run in Sandboxie's isolated sandbox, and upon execution, an event log of that program's execution is generated, recording events such as file and registry operations. As a comparison, the API calls obfuscation techniques are applied to protect the above programs. The principle of the Sandboxie detecting API is to hook in the API area loaded by the system; when the program is executed, the API called will be recorded, so the method of position obfuscation cannot achieve the effect of API monitoring by hook monitoring. The results in Table 6 show that the program behavior under the protection of APIASO and position obfuscation cannot be captured, while several other obfuscation methods can be effectively observed in the event log.

Table 6. Sandboxie behavior monitoring results.

Program Type	Sandboxie					
	I	II	III	IV	V	VI
IAT redirection	√	√	√	√	√	√
Position obfuscation	×	×	×	×	×	×
Call site tampering	√	√	√	√	√	√
APIASO	×	×	×	×	×	×

5.2. Model Protection Effect Evaluation

The API address space is obscured using API code extracted from the system DLL, while the accuracy of this process still needs to be verified. The Windows API includes thousands of functions that can be called, and Microsoft officially classifies these functions into the following broad categories: basic services, component services, user interface services, graphics multimedia services, messaging and collaboration, networking, and web services. To cover the above types of services, the following 12 types of programs are implemented by using over 1000 Windows APIs: file handlers, network programs, message handlers, printers, text and font functions, menu handlers, bitmap, and raster arithmetic programs, drawing programs, device scenario programs, hardware and system programs, process and thread programs, and control and messaging programs.

Figure 11 describes this verification process. The test process is based on LLVM and is divided into the following stages: (I) converting the source program containing the API calls into the corresponding intermediate language file Src.bc; (II) extracting the API code from the system DLL file using a decompiling tool; (III) completing the API replacement at the intermediate language level with LLVM, link the intermediate file; (IV) outputting the unobfuscated binary; (V) running the binary before and after the obfuscation to compare the two functions and verify the correctness of the API execution. In the end, the experimental results confirm the availability of APIASO.

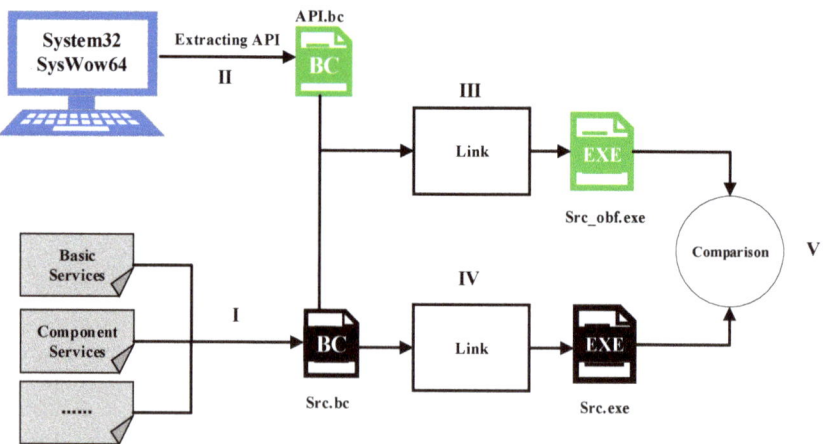

Figure 11. APIASO availability testing.

The APIASO is compared with the above three API call obfuscation methods to evaluate the program execution efficiency, and the obfuscated program is selected for six API magnitudes.

For each test program, to accurately measure the running time of the program, each program was looped 100 times, and the average running time before and after the obfuscation was calculated.

Figure 12 shows the time overhead before and after obfuscation for APIASO versus the other three API call obfuscation methods. The x-axis represents each test program, and the y-axis represents the ratio of post-obfuscation to pre-obfuscation time overhead. The results show that APIASO is close to the other obfuscation methods in terms of time overhead, and the overall obfuscation time overhead is no more than 20%.

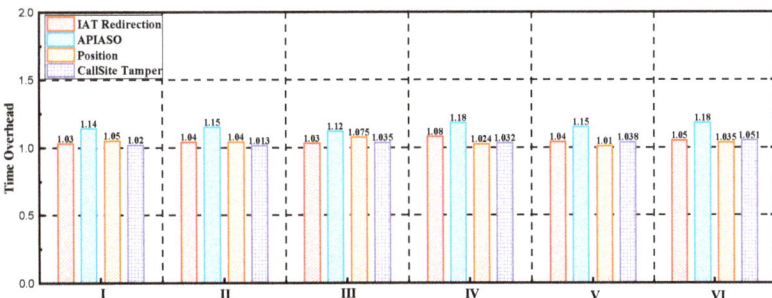

Figure 12. Time overhead comparison.

6. Discussion

A perfect solution for obfuscating API calls is far-fetched, and there is a constant cat-and-mouse game between program protectors and attackers. In this section, we discuss the following possible attack methods against APIASO and the corresponding countermeasures:

Kernel-level hook: APIs are divided into user-level and kernel-level parts, and an attacker may use a kernel-level API hook for API monitoring purposes, but a kernel-level hook is not sufficient for API monitoring. This is because there is no bijective mapping [22] between the user-level API and the kernel-level API. On the one hand, some user-level APIs such as path-related APIs and DLL management APIs (e.g., GetProcAddress) provide user-level services exclusively, which means that they do not call any kernel-level APIs at all; on the other hand, the kernel part of the API (e.g., NTCreateFile) serves multiple APIs at the upper level, and it is difficult to fully recover upper-level API calls through kernel-level API Hooks alone. The hook is difficult to fully recover upper-level API call information.

Instruction sequence similarity matching: APIASO copies the API to the user code space for execution, still retaining the original control flow structure of the API. With the help of API identification techniques (BinShape [23], IDA FLIRT [24], etc.), the runtime memory is compared with known APIs for similarity, and the called APIs can be found. For the above problem, control flow obfuscation techniques at the binary level can be introduced to perform control flow transformations and instruction transformations on the internal functions of the moved APIs to achieve resistance to similarity analysis purposes.

Monitoring NX bits: Seokwoo [25] et al. proposed monitoring the NX bit to detect the copying process of API code and monitor the DLL page memory access rights during program runtime. Since all API position obfuscation methods must move the API code through read and write operations, the API can be associated with the copied API memory address through read and write operations. However, read and write operations are frequent during program runtime, and restoring the API through read and write operations alone is difficult. Alternatively, the DLL can be read as a file during runtime, making the acquisition of API code independent of the DLL in the system load space.

7. Conclusions

In this paper, we systematically analyze existing API call obfuscation and deobfuscation techniques. It is shown that none of the existing API call obfuscation models can effectively resist the attacks of API deobfuscation techniques. The reason for the poor obfuscation effect of the existing API call obfuscation models is the insufficient obscure of the API address space. Therefore, we propose and construct the API address space obfuscation model. Compared with existing API call obfuscation schemes, APIASO obfuscates the API resolution and calling process with higher security. The experiments show that, after obfuscation, the API address space obscurity increases by more than two times, the detection rate of VirusTotal, etc. decreases by more than four times, the detection rate of deobfuscation techniques such as Scylla, etc. is zero, and the increase in obfuscation overhead is not more than 20%. The above results show that APIASO has better obfuscation effect and practicability.

In future work, the generalization of the obfuscation system still needs to be refined. The prototype code obfuscation system implemented in this paper was carried out when the program was available in source code, and future work will be carried out by applying the obfuscation system to the binary level. The conversion technology from binary code to LLVM intermediate language is already available, which provides technical support for code obfuscation at the binary level. In addition, the obfuscated prototype system currently only accepts C/C++ source code as input, but the LLVM platform supports a wide range of high-level programming languages, which can be converted into a unified intermediate language form. Therefore, future work will need to test code in many different programming languages to improve the generalizability of the obfuscation system.

Author Contributions: Conceptualization, Y.L. and F.K.; Methodology, Y.L. and H.S.; Investigation, Y.L. and X.X.; Writing—original draft preparation, Y.L.; writing—review and editing, Y.L., Y.Z. and R.S.; Supervision, F.K.; Funding acquisition, H.S. All authors have read and agreed to the published version of the manuscript.

Funding: This paper is supported by the National Key R&D Program of China, grant number 2019QY1305. The authors would like to acknowledge them.

Institutional Review Board Statement: Not applicable.

Informed Consent Statement: Informed consent was obtained from all subjects involved in the study.

Data Availability Statement: The data of this study are included within the article.

Conflicts of Interest: The authors declare no conflict of interest.

References

1. Choi, J.; Kim, K.; Lee, D.; Cha, S.K. NTFuzz: Enabling type-aware kernel fuzzing on windows with static binary analysis. In Proceedings of the 2021 IEEE Symposium on Security and Privacy (SP), San Francisco, CA, USA, 24–27 May 2021; pp. 677–693.
2. Lattner, C.; Adve, V. LLVM: A compilation framework for lifelong program analysis & transformation. In Proceedings of the International Symposium on Code Generation and Optimization, CGO 2004, San Jose, CA, USA, 20–24 March 2004; pp. 75–86.
3. Kawakoya, Y.; Shioji, E.; Otsuki, Y.; Iwamura, M.; Yada, T. Stealth loader: Trace-free program loading for API obfuscation. In Proceedings of the International Symposium on Research in Attacks, Intrusions, and Defenses, Atlanta, GA, USA, 18–20 September 2017; pp. 217–237.
4. Cheng, B.; Ming, J.; Leal, E.A.; Zhang, H.; Fu, J.; Peng, G. Obfuscation-Resilient Executable Payload Extraction From Packed Malware. In Proceedings of the 30th USENIX Security Symposium (USENIX Security 21), Virtual, 11–13 August 2021; pp. 3451–3468.
5. Suenaga, M. *A Museum of Api Obfuscation on Win32*; Symantec Security Response; Symantec Corp: Tempe, AZ, USA, 2009.
6. Roundy, K.A.; Miller, B.P. Binary-code obfuscations in prevalent packer tools. *ACM Comput. Surv. (CSUR)* **2013**, *46*, 1–32. [CrossRef]
7. Cheng, B.; Ming, J.; Fu, J.; Peng, G.; Chen, T.; Zhang, X.; Marion, J. Towards paving the way for large-scale windows malware analysis: Generic binary unpacking with orders-of-magnitude performance boost. In Proceedings of the 2018 ACM SIGSAC Conference on Computer and Communications Security, Toronto, ON, Canada, 15–19 October 2018; pp. 395–411.
8. Ugarte-Pedrero, X.; Balzarotti, D.; Santos, I.; Bringas, B.G. SoK: Deep packer inspection: A longitudinal study of the complexity of run-time packers. In Proceedings of the 2015 IEEE Symposium on Security and Privacy, San Jose, CA, USA, 17–21 May 2015; pp. 659–673.
9. Aguila. Scylla—x64/x86 Imports Reconstruction. 2016. Available online: https://github.com/NtQuery/Scylla (accessed on 28 May 2022).
10. Sharif, M.; Yegneswaran, V.; Saidi, H.; Porras, P.; Lee, W. Eureka: A framework for enabling static malware analysis. In Proceedings of the European Symposium on Research in Computer Security, Málaga, Spain, 6–8 October 2008; pp. 481–500.

11. Wei, T.E.; Chen, Z.W.; Tien, C.W.; Wu, J.S.; Lee, H.M.; Jeng, A.B. RePEF—A system for restoring packed executable file for malware analysis. In Proceedings of the 2011 International Conference on Machine Learning and Cybernetics, Guilin, China, 10–13 July 2011; Volume 2, pp. 519–527.
12. D'alessio, S.; Mariani, S. PinDemonium: A DBI-based generic unpacker for Windows executables. In Proceedings of the Black Hat USA 2016, Las Vegas, NV, USA, 30 July–4 August 2016.
13. Polino, M.; Continella, A.; Mariani, S.; D'Alessio, S.; Fontana, L.; Gritti, F.; Zanero, S. Measuring and defeating anti-instrumentation-equipped malware. In Proceedings of the International Conference on Detection of Intrusions and Malware, and Vulnerability Assessment, Bonn, Germany, 6–7 July 2017; p. 7396.
14. Kotov, V.; Wojnowicz, M. Towards generic deobfuscation of windows API calls. *arXiv* **2018**, arXiv:1802.04466.
15. Kawakoya, Y.; Iwamura, M.; Shioji, E.; Hariu, T. Api chaser: Anti-analysis resistant malware analyzer. In Proceedings of the International Workshop on Recent Advances in Intrusion Detection, Rodney Bay, St. Lucia, 23–25 October 2013; pp. 123–143.
16. Raber, J.; Krumheuer, B. QuietRIATT: Rebuilding the import address table using hooked DLL calls. In Proceedings of the Black Hat Technical Security Conference, Washington, DC, USA, 29–30 July 2009.
17. Josse, S. Secure and advanced unpacking using computer emulation. *J. Comput. Virol.* **2007**, *3*, 221–236. [CrossRef]
18. Kawakoya, Y.; Iwamura, M.; Miyoshi, J. Taint-assisted IAT Reconstruction against Position Obfuscation. *J. Inf. Process.* **2018**, *26*, 813–824. [CrossRef]
19. Korczynski, D. Repeconstruct: Reconstructing binaries with self-modifying code and import address table destruction. In Proceedings of the 2016 11th International Conference on Malicious and Unwanted Software (MALWARE), Fajardo, PR, USA, 18–21 October 2016; pp. 1–8.
20. Czech, Z.J.; Havas, G.; Majewski, B.S. An optimal algorithm for generating minimal perfect hash functions. *Inf. Process. Lett.* **1992**, *43*, 257–264. [CrossRef]
21. Havas, G.; Majewski, B.S. *Optimal Algorithms for Minimal Perfect Hashing*; Key Centre for Software Technology, Department of Computer Science, University of Queensland: Brisbane, Australia, 1992.
22. Bayer, U.; Comparetti, P.M.; Hlauschek, C.; Krügel, C. Scalable, behavior-based malware clustering. In Proceedings of the Network and Distributed System Security Symposium, NDSS 2009, San Diego, CA, USA, 8–11 February 2009; Volume 9, pp. 8–11.
23. Shirani, P.; Wang, L.; Debbabi, M. Binshape: Scalable and robust binary library function identification using function shape. In Proceedings of the International Conference on Detection of Intrusions and Malware, and Vulnerability Assessment, Bonn, Germany, 6–7 July 2017; pp. 301–324.
24. Hex-Ray Corporation. Fast Library Identification and Recognition Technology [EB/OL]. Available online: https://hex-rays.com/products/ida/tech/flirt/ (accessed on 30 July 2021).
25. Choi, S. API Deobfuscator: Identifying Runtime-obfuscated API calls via Memory Access Analysis. In Proceedings of the Black Hat Asia, Singapore, 24–27 March 2015.

Disclaimer/Publisher's Note: The statements, opinions and data contained in all publications are solely those of the individual author(s) and contributor(s) and not of MDPI and/or the editor(s). MDPI and/or the editor(s) disclaim responsibility for any injury to people or property resulting from any ideas, methods, instructions or products referred to in the content.

Article

Secure Application of MIoT: Privacy-Preserving Solution for Online English Education Platforms

Jiming Yin [1,†] and Jie Cui [2,*,†]

1 School of Foreign Studies, Anhui Jianzhu University, Hefei 230601, China; 080058@ahjzu.edu.cn
2 School of Computer Science and Technology, Anhui University, Hefei 230039, China
* Correspondence: cuijie@mail.ustc.edu.cn; Tel.: +86-055163861263
† These authors contributed equally to this work.

Abstract: With the increasing demand for higher-quality services, online English education platforms have gained significant attention. However, practical application of the Mobile Internet of Things (MIoT) still faces various challenges, including communication security, availability, scalability, etc. These challenges directly impact the utilization of online English education platforms. The dynamic and evolving nature of the topology characteristics in Mobile Internet of Things networks adds complexity to addressing these issues. To overcome these challenges, we propose a software-defined MIoT model that effectively handles the dynamic and evolving network topology features, thereby enhancing the system's flexibility and adaptability. Additionally, our model can provide communication security and privacy protection, particularly in emergency situations. In our scheme, the control plane is responsible for computing routes for online learning devices (OLDs) and forward entries for switches. By utilizing the information collected from OLDs and facilities, the controller is able to effectively coordinate the overall system. To ensure the authenticity and reliability of messages sent by OLDs, we have proposed a new signature and authentication mechanism based on traditional encryption algorithms. Moreover, we introduce an emergency-handling system that integrates multicast technology into software-defined MIoT, generating a Steiner Tree among impacted nodes to promptly notify OLDs when there is an emergency. The security analysis proves that our scheme is able to ensure communication security in software-defined MIoT. A performance evaluation indicates that our scheme outperforms other existing schemes.

Keywords: MIoT; software-defined MIoT; security; signature; authentication; multicast; online English education

Citation: Yin, J.; Cui, J. Secure Application of MIoT: Privacy-Preserving Solution for Online English Education Platforms. *Appl. Sci.* **2023**, *13*, 8293. https://doi.org/10.3390/app13148293

Academic Editors: Lip Yee Por and Abdullah Ayub Khan

Received: 13 June 2023
Revised: 14 July 2023
Accepted: 14 July 2023
Published: 18 July 2023

Copyright: © 2023 by the authors. Licensee MDPI, Basel, Switzerland. This article is an open access article distributed under the terms and conditions of the Creative Commons Attribution (CC BY) license (https://creativecommons.org/licenses/by/4.0/).

1. Introduction

The Internet of Things (IoT) has drawn attention from both industry and academic fields for years due to its advantages, such as efficiency and providing more secure communication environments. Among the various applications of IoT, online education has emerged as a significant application of Mobile IoT (MIoT). IoT provides the necessary technological support and infrastructure for online education to be conducted on mobile devices and over the Internet. English, being a globally universal language, is widely learned and considered a core subject in schools across most countries. Consequently, the application of MIoT in online English education has rapidly become an important method and primary tool for individual learning and communication. This is a novel education model that puts students at the center and relies on software platforms to deliver personalized learning experiences [1,2]. Compared to traditional offline classroom education, online English education offers advantages such as higher efficiency [3,4] and freedom from geographical constraints [5]. Here, online learning devices (OLDs) have the capability to communicate with other devices and infrastructure, such as roadside units in certain models, enabling access to the MIoT [6]. Thus, OLDs are allowed to report information and emergencies, which will be used to improve the quality of services [7,8]. However, if OLDs are allowed to broadcast messages without any verification or limitation, the communication mechanism will become vulnerable and easy to compromise [9–11]. For example, if messages sent in MIoT are not signed with an online learning device's unique identities, then a malicious user can broadcast fraud messages or sign them with fabricated identities to bypass a weak system. To solve problems in secure communication, some studies have been dedicated to designing privacy-preserving authentication schemes [12–14]. However, due to the feature of changing topology, it is hard to balance efficiency and security in conventional MIoT. Then, a brand-new technology came into researchers' sights.

Software-defined network (SDN) is an innovative technology that embodies a network structure distinct from traditional networks [15,16]. In SDN, controlling and forwarding are separated and work in different layers [17,18]. The control plane represents the centralized point as the brain of the whole architecture [19]. The data plane communicates with the control plane via southbound interfaces. It is mainly responsible for querying controllers for forwarding tables and forward packets. Using the programmability and scalability, the combination of VANETs and SDN offers a new approach to solve inherent problems in VANETs.

Software-defined MIoT has been proposed for years and there have been many research efforts demonstrating the advantages of this new combination [20,21]. Meanwhile, some schemes are proposed to cope with problems in quality of services (QoS) [22], heterogeneous network accessing [23], factory managing [24,25] and so many others in different fields by combining with SDN [26]. Inspired by [27], we design a scheme that uses multicast technology to solve the driving direction and secure communication problems in software-defined MIoT.

In traditional MIoT, OLDs mainly rely on broadcasting each other to receive network condition information, which lacks timeliness and overall planning [28–30]. By introducing multicast, the controller is allowed to manage OLDs and balance network throughputs more efficiently. In addition, some technology used not to be suitable for MIoT, like Steiner Tree, which is computation intense and scale sensitive [27]. But with SDN introduced, those algorithms can provide new methods for the development of MIoT [31,32].

Thus, we propose a new secure communicating and device movement path scheme in this paper. By using multicast [33] and privacy-preserving authentication technologies, we aim to design a secure and efficient model in software-defined MIoT. Concretely, the primary contributions of this paper can be outlined as follows.

Our Contribution

This work provides the following key contributions.

(1) We propose a novel software-defined MIoT-based model that provides security communication in the underlying data plane. The outstanding computing power of the control plane greatly relieves the overhead of the upper layer, which offers users higher-quality services.

(2) We design an authentication system to ensure the authenticity and reliability of messages, so that OLDs are encouraged to spread real information. Otherwise, they will be punished. In addition, an emergency-dealing scheme is offered to provide in-time services based on multicast, which not only takes current network situations into consideration, but also predictions of instantaneous changing.

(3) A security analysis demonstrates that the proposed scheme is capable of achieving the security objectives of software-defined MIoT. In addition, adopting elliptic curve cryptography avoids heavy overhead brought by bilinear pairing operations, which is demonstrated by the comparison results.

The structure of the remaining sections in this paper is as follows. Section 2 provides an overview of related works. Section 3 presents the system models and outlines our design objectives. In Section 4, we provide a comprehensive and elaborate explanation of the proposed scheme. The security analysis is presented in Section 5, followed by a comparison of computation overhead in Section 6. Finally, Section 7 concludes the paper.

2. Related Works

Online education has a significant impact on the learning process by leveraging the IoT, cloud computing and big data. The key to integrating online educational resources lies in the storage of massive teaching data. Wei et al. [34] applied cloud storage technologies and methods to the construction of integrated online educational resources, which effectively saves educational resources for schools, enhances the utilization of online educational resources and thereby improves the teaching quality of subjects. Hui Tao [35] proposed an online English teaching system approach based on IoT technology. The author studied the English SPOC (Small Private Online Course) teaching mode, constructed a multimedia teaching system based on IoT technology, improved the teaching system and enhanced and learned the teaching mode, resulting in an improvement in the quality of English teaching.

Chen et al. [36] developed an IoT-oriented online English education platform with the aim of providing a conducive learning environment and enhancing students' overall English proficiency. To improve the ability to find optimal solutions, they incorporated a reverse learning (RL) mechanism into the grey wolf optimization (GWO) algorithm, resulting in the development of the RLGWO algorithm. They further constructed the RLGWO-BP model, which was utilized to assess the impact of the IoT-oriented online education platform on English language instruction. Gao et al. [37] utilized preliminary results obtained through the use of IoT to establish an interactive educational paradigm. They deployed numerous sensors with the aim of improving learners' English language correction by comparing learners' wording and speech with the software's standard wording and speech.

In the security in MIoT and the software-defined MIoT research field, a threshold anonymous authentication protocol using group signature technology was proposed by Shao et al. [9]. In this scheme, the decentralized group model is integrated. It achieved threshold authentication, anonymity, unforgeability, traceability and revocation of MIoT communication. However, the huge computation cost of bilinear pairing may create obstacles to implementation. Azees et al. [38] proposed a scheme that enabled roadside units to authenticate vehicles anonymously before providing certain messages to them. It also allowed vehicles to communicate with roadside units anonymously. The scheme reduced costs of certificate and signature verification and achieved privacy preserving and traceability in vehicular ad hoc networks. However, there were no timestamps attached to messages, which could be used by malicious parities to start replay attacks.

To solve the problems of insecurity of master keys, invalidity of PIDs in [12], and to cope with inherent problems in MIoT, Li et al. [39] proposed a certificate-less protocol and demonstrated the security of it. Xiang et al. [40] proposed a novel CLS (certificate-less signcryption) scheme to address critical issues such as data integrity and identity authentication in the IoT environment. The scheme eliminates the cumbersome certificate management in certificate-based signature systems and the key escrow problem in identity-based cryptography. Furthermore, it is designed to securely resist various attacks, such as public key-replacement attacks or malicious but passive key-generation center attacks. Garg et al. [31] proposed secure communication models by introducing SDN architecture. They enabled both mutual authentication among communicating entities and intrusion-detecting systems to detect potential attacks from the underling networks.

Hong et al. [41] proposed a time-limited secure attribute-based online/offline signature scheme (TS-ABOS-CMS) with a constant message length. The scheme achieves high efficiency by introducing online/offline signature methods while maintaining communication overhead at a constant level. Additionally, a key update mechanism is adopted to provide time-limited security protection for IoT terminals. Khashan et al. [42] proposed a blockchain-based hybrid centralized IoT system authentication architecture. Edge servers are deployed to provide centralized authentication for associated IoT devices. Subsequently, a blockchain network is established for the centralized edge servers to ensure decentralized authentication and verification of IoT devices belonging to different and heterogeneous IoT systems. Wang et al. [43] adopted the low-energy distributed ledger technology IOTA to design a lightweight and scalable mechanism for managing the identity of IoT devices and access control of large-scale IoT data. This mechanism ensures the reliability of the source of IoT data and the security of data sharing.

In the multicast in the SDN research field, Zhou et al. [27] proposed the cost-efficient Degree-dependent Branch-node Weighted Steiner Tree (DBWST) problem in the SDN architecture. It solved the scalability problem of multicast by introducing Steiner Tree to span nodes. The scheme reduced the total cost and the number of branch nodes when generating the multicast tree T. Do et al. [26] proposed an architecture that allowed both multicast and broadcast services in the SDN-based mobile packet core. It had the advantages of programmability and flexibility of SDN and reduced the signaling cost compared with traditional network paradigms. However, the system may suffer certain security problems in terms of communication.

Lai et al. [44] proposed an integrated network architecture for secure group communication in SDN-based 5G vehicular ad hoc networks. The scheme was a group-oriented vehicular environment, in which vehicles are divided into groups based on their geographic positions. This also inspired us to manage vehicles by dividing them in a transaction-oriented way. Kim et al. [24] proposed a multicast scheme with Group Shared Tree (GST) switching in large-scale IIoT networks. To overcome inherent problems, such as transmitting multicast packets under congestions and configuring optimal paths dynamically, it adopted SDN-based architecture. They proved that the new architecture outperformed other models.

3. Models and Design Goals

3.1. System Model and Assumptions

According to [13], the layered control plane is thought to be more realistic in practical applications. Based on that, our system is composed of the following: the Global Controller (GC), many Local Controllers (LCs), many OpenFlow Switches (OF-Switches), Base Stations (BSs), Access Points (APs) and online learning devices (OLDs). GC and LCs are responsible for dealing with collected information and making optimal decisions. The others make up the data plane, which is mainly for transport packages and collecting road information. Figure 1 depicts the system model.

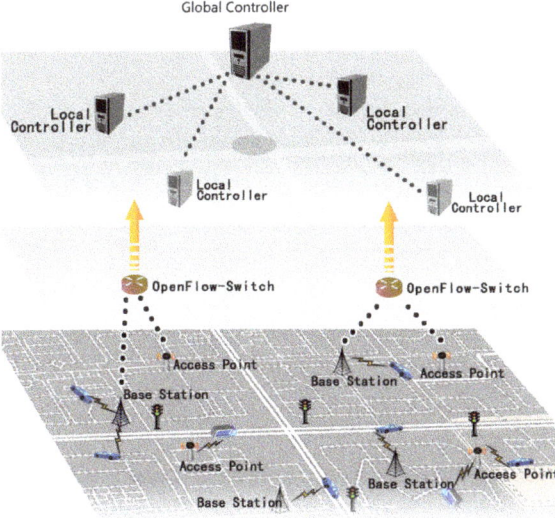

Figure 1. The system model.

(1) **GC:** This is the main controller of the control plane. In traditional SDN systems, the controller is a logically centralized point that has extremely outstanding storage and computing capabilities. Typically, it directs switches to deliver and forward packages by building routing rules. In our system, the GC assumes the primary responsibility of generating system parameters, calculating the device's movement path and constructing route tables for OF-Switches. When there are accidents or emergencies happening, it also selects impacted devices and forms a temporary multicast group. It generates a multicast tree for this group to inform them of conditions in time.

(2) **LCs:** These are distributed geographically and manage a specific small area. In our system, the LCs primarily serve the purpose of distributing the computation and storage loads of the GC. They can reduce realistic deployment costs as well. LCs set system parameters and communicate with OLDs. They can verify messages in their local areas and compute fine-grained navigation for OLDs. When there are road situations, they are also composed of multicast nodes to inform and direct OLDs in their areas.

(3) **OF-Switches:** Different from conventional switches, OF-Switches are OpenFlow-enabled data switches that communicate with external controllers over the OpenFlow channel. The OpenFlow protocol offers separation of programming network devices and underlying hardware [44]. In our system, OF-Switches perform package lookup and forwarding according to flow tables installed on them.

(4) **OLDs:** OLDs offer network access services via wireless communication capabilities, which have limited computing power and storage [45]. Also, tamper-proof equipment is embedded in each OLD that is robust and responsible for generating key cryptographical parameters and performing many encryption and decryption operations [46].

(5) **BSs and APs:** OLDs obtain access to the Internet via various ways. Cellular networks like 5G network via BSs and city WiFi via APs are both supported by our system. For software-defined MIoT, to balance heterogeneous networks and allow OLDs in different networks to communicate is much easier compared with conventional networks.

* The GC is absolutely trusted and will not suffer any compromise. It has ample computing power and storage space.
* LCs are trustworthy, but in cases in which they are compromised, we do not provide them capabilities of trace OLDs' real identities. LCs have sufficient computing and storage space.
* The parameters and data stored in OLDs are not available for others.

3.2. Multicast Subsystem

When an emergency occurs, impacted OLDs may request new movement paths rather than remaining stuck. Commonly, the conventional systems only replan new paths based on the present road conditions but do not take dynamically instantaneous changing into consideration. We design a multicast mechanism-based emergency system, which uses Stein Tree to compute a multicast tree between those nodes to inform affected OLDs in time.

3.2.1. Steiner Tree

In general, to connect n nodes, the Minimum Spanning Tree (MST) is the most commonly selected algorithm. But in networks, there are lots of factors that need to be taken into consideration, such as bandwidth, transport delay of networks and so on. Hence, Steiner Tree, a spanning tree algorithm with weights, is more suitable. The generation of Steiner Tree is thought to be computation intensive, so there are few applications in conventional multicast schemes. But as for SDN controller, it becomes feasible since the forwarding information is preloaded in network switches. In addition, the global visibility and programmability can also help to construct a better multicast tree more efficiently [21].

3.2.2. Multicast Tree

In our scheme, we take the Degree-dependent Branch-node Weighted Steiner Tree (DBWST) proposed in [21] to construct our multicast tree. Algorithm 1 describes the specific procedure. Based on the DBWST, consider an undirected graph $G_v = \{V, L\}$, in which V denotes OLDs and other entities taking part in communication in software-defined MIoT, and L represents a collection of links. For example, the link $l = (v, w) \in L$ denotes the link from $v \in V$ and $w \in V$. Then the cost of link l is $Cst(l) : L \mapsto R^+$, where R^+ is nonnegative. Let s be the source of a multicast and $U \subset V - \{s\}$ be the set of destination nodes, which in our system is the affected OLDs. The size of this group corresponds to the quantity of $|R|$. Let $T = (s, U)$ denote the multicast tree whose source is s and spanning all nodes $OLD_i \in U, 1 < i < |U|$. According to the definition of branch node in Steiner Tree, if the degree of node OLD_i is no less than three, then OLD_i would be one. Let π_u represent that u is a branch node in T. Based on the above description, finally the cost of the tree T can be denoted as:

$$Cst(T) = \sum_{l \in T} Cst(e) + \sum_{u \in T} \pi_u \cdot Cst(u) \qquad (1)$$

Based on the DBWST, it is computationally uncomplicated to find a tree $T = (s, U)$ which makes the $Cst(T)$ lowest. The constructed multicast tree can not only help to distribute messages more efficiently, but can also be applied to other fields, such as video conferences and streaming media subscribing.

Algorithm 1 Directing Process

Input: input departure, Dp; destination, Ds
Output: reach $Ds = 1$
1: OLD_i request path
2: control plane return path $C = \{LC_k\}^*, 0 < k < n$
3: $LC_k : ST = ST + \{OLD_i\}$
4: **while** $C != \emptyset$ **do**
5:      OLD_i leaves LC_k
6:      // OLD_i does:
7:      $C = C - \{LC_k\}, 1 < k \leq n$
8:      // LC_k does
9:      $ST = ST - OLD_i, 0 \leq |ST| \leq n$
10:     **if** LC_k unreachable = true **then**
11:         $T = DBWST(d, n)$
12:         // d represents the total number of affected OLDs
13:         // $0 < d \leq m$
14:         jump tp line 1
15: **end while**

3.2.3. Application Process

With the multicast tree having been constructed, the process can be described as follows. When an OLD starts driving, firstly it will request a path to the controller. Commonly, it tends to store all the forwarding entries in the control plane to program the routing process. However, given m OLDs and n LCs, the worst condition is that the spatial complexity will reach $O(n^m)$. Even the lowest will reach $O(n^2)$. So, we propose to only maintain a subscriber table in each LC. For example, an OLD_i gained a path passing through x consecutive LCs. Let C denote the set of x LCs, $|C| = x$. Then each LC will add OLD_i into its subscriber table ST. Every time OLD_i leaves an area, it will send a leaving packet to the control plane. After that, OLD_i and LCs will perform $C = C - \{LC_k\}, 1 < k \leq n$ and $ST = ST - \{OLD_i\}, 0 \leq |ST| \leq m$, respectively. This step is designed to prevent OLDs that have passed through the area from being rearranged. By only maintaining subscriber tables, the spatial complexity can be decreased to $O(m^n)$, where $n \ll m$. The process of subscribing is shown in Figure 2.

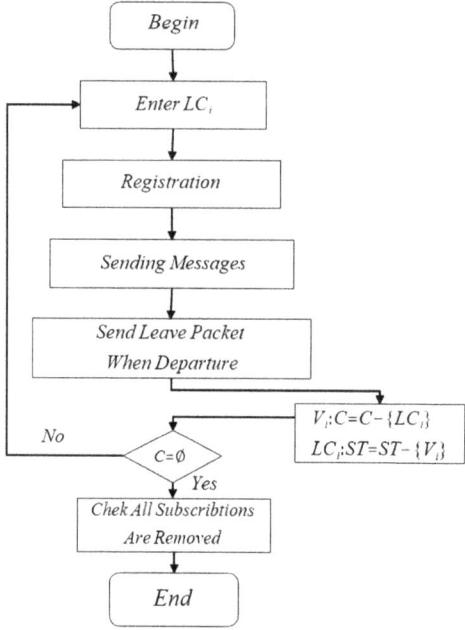

Figure 2. The process of subscribing.

3.3. Design Goals

Our objective is to create an efficient system to offer OLDs a secure environment to communicate and services such as avoiding risks. It will satisfy the following desirable properties. *Routing Plan*: Making use of the global ability, the control plane will generate the most suitable using plan for OLDs. *Emergency Handling*: When an emergency occurs, to avoid a second occurrence, the control system informs the impacted OLDs promptly via its multicast mechanism. Then it replans new routes for OLDs by balancing all network situations. *Secure Communication*: The most important factor is that all the messages sent by OLDs need to be trustworthy and factual. Considering that, the system should have the following security properties.

(1) Anonymity: OLDs in our system will not communicate with other entities with real identities. Based solely on the messages sent by OLDs and some public information, malicious users cannot ascertain the real identity of the sender. This way, OLDs are allowed to send messages without exposing sensitive privacy information.

(2) Authentication and Privacy: Each interactive party in our system can authenticate the others to ensure reliability and legitimacy. In particular, in different areas, messages sent by OLDs should reflect the present LC's information without exposing them to adversaries, which ensures location privacy would not be compromised.

(3) Traceability: We will not exclude the possibility of the existence of malicious entities. They aim to interrupt or interfere normal communications or spread false and deceptive messages to gain convenience and benefits for themselves. When misbehavior occurs, the controller plane should be able to trace the real identities and punish them by cutting services or submitting their information to related authorities.

(4) Unlinkability: The proposed scheme would not enable third parties to link scattered messages to the same OLDs. That is to say, no third party could know one specific OLD's activities by analysing those intercepted messages.

(5) Resistance to common attacks: The scheme must have the ability to effectively counter prevalent attacks that occur in conventional networks, including replay attacks, impersonation attacks, modification attacks and others.

4. Proposed Scheme

Here, we propose our secure communication scheme in software-defined MIoT. In our scheme, firstly messages should be signed and then distributed to ensure non-repudiation. Then, to prevent the privacy information of vehicles from being exposed, OLDs should communicate via pseudo identities, which include a rough location of their current LC area. All above information can only be derived via GC but not other third parties. When emergencies occur, GC will extract OLDs' locations from messages they sent. When malicious messages are found, GC will extract OLDs' real identities from those messages and take actions to punish them.

4.1. Control Plane Initialization

The scheme utilizes F_p as the finite field over a large prime number p, with p denoting the field's size. The parameters $(a, b) \in F_p$ define the elliptic curve $E : y^2 = x^3 + ax + b \bmod p$. A group G is generated from E in the system, where P serves as the generator and q represents the prime order of E. Table 1 presents additional notations and definitions employed in the scheme.

Table 1. Notations and definitions.

Notations	Definitions
GC	The Global Controller
LC_i	Local Controller i
OLD_i	The i-th online learning device
G	An additive cyclic group
P, q	The generator and order of G
p	The size of a field
P_{pub}, s	A public and private key of GC
NLC_i	The number of NLC_i
ID_i	The identity of OLD_i
PID_i	The pseudo identity of OLD_i
PK_i, sk_i	A public and private key of OLD_i
M	A message
msg	An encapsulated message
σ	The signature of a message
T_t	The time stamp

(1) **GC Initialization:** By randomly selecting the master key s from Z_q, the GC derives its public key as $P_{pub} = s \cdot P$ and computes $\alpha = s \cdot h(P_{pub})$. Subsequently, the GC chooses the hash function $h : G \to Z_q^*$, $H0 : G \times \{0,1\}^* \to Z_q^*$, $H1 : \{0,1\}^* \to Z_q^*$, $H2 : \{0,1\}^* \times \{0,1\}^* \times \{0,1\}^* \times G \times G \to Z_q^*$. The value of α is transmitted to LCs, while $\{P_{pub}, p, q, a, b, P, H0, H1, H2\}$ is published as the system parameters. In order to ensure the overall security of the system, the GC must keep the hash function h confidential.

(2) **LC Initialization:** After receiving α via a secure channel in the control plane, LC_i computes $l_i = \alpha \cdot NLC_i$ as its secret key, where NLC_i is a unique number of each LC and a list of them is only stored in the GC. Since s is unknown to any third party and each NLC_i also stays secret, it is also difficult to compute l_i based on public parameters. Next, it calculates $L_i = l_i \cdot P$ to generate its public key, and adds L_i into the GC's system parameters. Finally, $\{P_{pub}, p, q, a, b, P, H0, H1, H2, L_i\}$ is the local system parameters of this specific area.

4.2. Online Learning Device Initialization

When an online learning device OLD_i enters into the area of LC_i and it is necessary to publish messages in the current environment, it loads parameters and randomly selects $sk_i \in Z_q$ as its private key and calculates $PK_i = sk_i \cdot P$ as the public key. Then $PID_{i,1} = ID_i \oplus H0(sk_i \cdot L_i \| T_t)$, $PID_{i,2} = (sk_i \cdot L_i) \oplus H1(T_t)$. It uses $PID_i = \{PID_{i,1}, PID_{i,2}\}$ as its pseudo name.

4.3. One-Time Key Generation and Message Signature

A message M_i could include status, emergency information or other related requests. When OLD_i tends to send message M_i, it will firstly select a number r_i randomly and compute $R_i = r \cdot P$. Let $w_i = H2(M_i \| PID_i \| T_t \| R_i \| PK_i)$, where T_t is the current timestamp. Then it signs M_i with $\sigma = sk_i + w_i \cdot r_i \mod q$. Then, OLD_i will send encapsulated msg: $\{M_i, T_t, PK_i, R_i, PID_i\}$ to nearby communication-related entities.

4.4. Emergency Location Extraction

To ensure the basic location privacy of OLDs, the specific LC where it is located cannot be exposed in msg. Otherwise, by connecting and analysing several messages it has sent, it is feasible for malicious parties to draw rough activity areas of one OLD. But when an emergency occurs, the control plane needs to roughly locate affected OLDs. By fully balancing affected and unaffected areas' densities of OLDs, the control plane is able to construct a most efficient multicast tree with average lowest source consumption $Cst(T)$.

When there are abnormal conditions, OLDs around will broadcast a message msg to report. After receiving those msgs, the GC will perform the following computation to decide a rough location of LC.

$$\begin{aligned}
PID_{i,2} &= (sk_i \cdot L_i) \oplus H1(T_t) \\
&= (sk_i \cdot \alpha \cdot NLC_i \cdot P) \oplus H1(T_t) \\
&= (PK_i \cdot \alpha \cdot NLC_i) \oplus H1(T_t) \\
&\Downarrow \\
NLC_i &= (PID_{i,2} \oplus H1(T_t)) \cdot (PK_i \cdot \alpha)^{-1}
\end{aligned} \quad (2)$$

By locating the LC, the GC will handle this area's packets preferentially to deal with emergencies.

4.5. Message Authentication

To verify whether OLDs have sent false messages or packets have been modified, other entities can verify signatures of received messages. To enhance verification efficiency, the proposed scheme also provides the capability to simultaneously verify messages in a batch. The processes for verifying a single message and verifying messages in a batch are described below, respectively.

(1) **Single Verification**

After receiving a message $\{M_i, T_t, PK_i, R_i, PID_i\}$, to verify its validation, a receiver will perform the following steps in order with the system parameters $\{P_{pub}, p, q, a, b, P, H0, H1, H2, L_i\}$.

* Check if the timestamp T_t is fresh. If it is not, the received message is abandoned. If it is fresh, keep performing the operation.
* The receiver performs $\sigma \cdot P$ and $PK_i + w_i \cdot R_i$ and calculates whether they are equal. If they are not, the receiver chooses to abandon them. If they are equal, it admit the validation of this message.
Since $P_{pub} = s \cdot P$, $w_i = H2(M_i \| PID_i \| T_t \| R_i \| PK_i)$, $R_i = r \cdot P$, $PK_i = sk_i \cdot P$ and $PID_i = \{PID_{i,1}, PID_{i,2}\}$, where $PID_{i,1} = ID_i \oplus H0(sk_i \cdot L_i \| T_t)$, $PID_{i,2} = (sk_i \cdot L_i) \oplus H1(T_t)$ and $\sigma = sk_i + w_i \cdot r_i \mod q$, the following equations can be derived.

$$\begin{aligned}
\sigma \cdot P &= (sk_i + w_i \cdot r_i) \cdot P \\
&= sk_i \cdot P + w_i \cdot r_i \cdot P \\
&= PK_i + w_i \cdot R_i
\end{aligned} \quad (3)$$

(2) **Batch Verification**

Verifying each of the n messages individually consumes a significant amount of time and computing resources when a receiver receives a batch of messages within a short time interval. Therefore, our scheme incorporates batch verification to efficiently utilize resources. Firstly, to guarantee the non-repudiation of signatures using batch verification, we choose a vector comprising small random integers. Let the vector $\zeta = \{\zeta_1, \zeta_2, \zeta_3, ..., \zeta_n\}$, where $\zeta_i \in [1, 2^\zeta]$ and ζ is a secure parameter. After receiving a message $\{M_1, T_{t,1}, PK_1, R_1, PID_1\}, \{M_2, T_{t,2}, PK_2, R_2, PID_2\}, ..., \{M_n, T_{t,n}, PK_n, R_n, PID_n\}$, to verify its validation, a receiver will perform the following steps in order with the system parameters $\{P_{pub}, p, q, a, b, P, H0, H1, H2, L_i\}$.

* Check if the timestamp $T_{t,1}, T_{t,2}, ..., T_{t,i}, ..., T_{t,n} (1 < i \leq n)$ are fresh. If they are not, the received message is abandoned. If they are fresh, keep performing the operation.
* The receiver performs (4) and calculates whether they are equal. If they are not equal, the receiver will find the malicious message via the invalid signature search algorithm and choose to abandon it. If they are equal, it admits the validation of this series of messages.

$$\begin{aligned}
\sum_{i=1}^{n}(\zeta_i \cdot \sigma_i) \cdot P &= (\sum_{i=1}^{n} \zeta_i \cdot (sk_i + w_i \cdot r_i)) \cdot P \\
&= \sum_{i=1}^{n}(\zeta_i \cdot (sk_i \cdot P + w_i \cdot r_i \cdot P)) \\
&= \sum_{i=1}^{n}(\zeta_i \cdot PK_i + \zeta_i \cdot w_i \cdot R_i) \\
&= \sum_{i=1}^{n}(\zeta \cdot PK_i) + \sum_{i=1}^{n}(\zeta_i \cdot w_i \cdot R_i)
\end{aligned} \quad (4)$$

By this, the validation of the batch verification of a series of message is proved. The interactions of the above parties are shown in Figure 3.

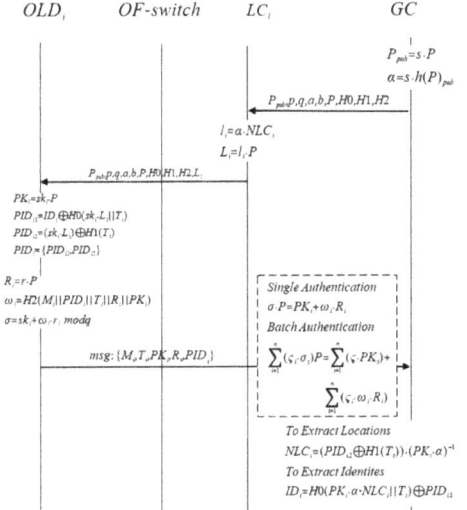

Figure 3. The interactions of parties.

5. Security Proof and Analysis

The communication security of the proposed scheme will be analyzed in this part. In Section 2, we presented some of our security goals and the threats that may be met. Here, firstly, we introduce the definition of the elliptic curve discrete logarithm problem (ECDLP) upon which the entire analysis is based.

Definition 1 (ECDLP). *Let P be the generator of group G, with $n \in Z_q$ and $N = nP \in G$. The ECDLP states that it is computationally infeasible to determine the value of n given $N = nP$.* To establish the security model for the proposed scheme, a game is defined involving adversary $\mathcal{A}$ and challenger $\mathcal{C}$, leveraging the aforementioned network.

5.1. Security Proof

In this game, the adversary $\mathcal{A}$ is allowed to execute the queries listed below.

- *Setup Oracle*: When $\mathcal{A}$ revokes the query, $\mathcal{C}$ sends the generated private key and the corresponding system parameters to $\mathcal{A}$.
- *H0 Oracle*: $\mathcal{C}$ randomly selects a point $d \in Z_q$ and includes $\{m, d\}$ in its list L_{H0}. Then it returns d to $\mathcal{A}$ when $\mathcal{A}$ revokes the query.
- *H1 Oracle*: $\mathcal{C}$ randomly selects a number $d \in Z_q$ and includes $\{m, d\}$ in its list L_{H1}. Then it returns d to $\mathcal{A}$ when $\mathcal{A}$ revokes the query.
- *H2 Oracle*: $\mathcal{C}$ randomly selects a point $d \in Z_q$ and includes $\{m, d\}$ in its list L_{H2}. Then it returns d to $\mathcal{A}$ when $\mathcal{A}$ revokes the query.
- *Sign Oracle*: Based on the M_i sent by $\mathcal{A}$, $\mathcal{C}$ computes a $msg : \{M_i, T_t, PK_i, R_i, PID_i\}$. Then $\mathcal{C}$ returns $\{M_i, T_t, PK_i, R_i, PID_i\}$ to $\mathcal{A}$ when $\mathcal{A}$ revokes the query.

If the adversary $\mathcal{A}$ has the ability to fabricate a legitimate login request message, it indicates a violation of the proposed secure communication scheme by $\mathcal{A}$. We define $\Phi(\mathcal{A})$ as the probability of $\mathcal{A}$ violating the scheme.

Definition 2. *For any polynomial adversary $\mathcal{A}$, our scheme is considered secure if the probability $\Phi(\mathcal{A})$ is negligible.*

By conducting a security evaluation of our scheme under the random oracle model, we establish the following theorem.

Theorem 1. *The proposed scheme exhibits security within the random oracle model.*

Proof. Suppose there is an adversary $\mathcal{A}$ who has the ability to forge a $msg : \{M_i, T_t, PK_i, R_i, PID_i\}$. Our signature scheme is executed by a challenger $\mathcal{C}$ that we construct. By performing the following queries revoked by $\mathcal{A}$, challenger $\mathcal{C}$ can leverage $\mathcal{A}$ as a subroutine to solve the ECDLP problem with a probability that is not negligible. □

Setup Oracle: First, a key parameter k is provided as input. Subsequently, $\mathcal{C}$ selects a random number s as its private key and calculates $P_{pub} = s \cdot P$. $\mathcal{C}$ then transmits $\{P_{pub}, p, q, a, b, P, H0, H1, H2\}$ to $\mathcal{A}$.

H0 Oracle: $\mathcal{C}$ maintains an initially empty list $L_{H0} : (sk_i, L_i, T_t, h_{0,i})$. When $\mathcal{A}$ makes a query with (sk_i, L_i, T_t), $\mathcal{C}$ verifies if $L_{H0} : (sk_i, L_i, T_t, h_{0,i})$ already exists in L_{H0}. If the entry exists, $\mathcal{C}$ provides the corresponding $h_{0,i}$. Otherwise, $\mathcal{C}$ generates a random $h_{0,i} = H0(sk_i \cdot L_i \| T_t)$, inserts $L_{H0} : (sk_i, L_i, T_t, h_{0,i})$ into the list and yields $h_{0,i}$ to $\mathcal{A}$.

H1 Oracle: $\mathcal{C}$ maintains an initially empty list $L_{H1} : (T_t, h_{1,i})$. When $\mathcal{A}$ makes a query with (T_t), $\mathcal{C}$ verifies if $L_{H1} : (T_t, h_{1,i})$ already exists in L_{H1}. If the entry exists, $\mathcal{C}$ provides the corresponding $h_{1,i}$. Otherwise, $\mathcal{C}$ generates a random $h_{1,i} = H1(T_t)$, inserts $L_{H1} : (T_t, h_{1,i})$ into the list and yields $h_{1,i}$ to $\mathcal{A}$.

H2 Oracle: $\mathcal{C}$ maintains an initially empty list $L_{H2} : (PID_i, L_i, T_t, R_i.PK_i, M_i, h_{2,i})$. When $\mathcal{A}$ makes a query with $(PID_i, L_i, T_t, R_i.PK_i, M_i)$, $\mathcal{C}$ verifies if $L_{H2} : (PID_i, L_i, T_t, R_i.PK_i, M_i)$ already exists in L_{H2}. If the entry exists, $\mathcal{C}$ provides the corresponding $h_{2,i}$. Otherwise, $\mathcal{C}$ generates a random $h_{2,i} = H2(PID_i\|L_i\| \ T_t\|R_i\|PK_i\|M_i)$, inserts $L_{H2} : (PID_i, L_i, T_t, R_i.PK_i, M_i, h_{2,i})$ into the list and yields $h_{2,i}$ to $\mathcal{A}$.

Sign Oracle: When $\mathcal{A}$'s query with message M_i and pseudo identity PID_i is received, $\mathcal{C}$ checks if $(sk_i, L_i, T_t, h_{0,i})$ and $(T_t, h_{1,i})$ already exist in L_{H0} and L_{H1}, respectively. $\mathcal{C}$ gains $h_{0,i}$ from $(sk_i, L_i, T_t, h_{0,i})$ and $h_{1,i}$ from $(T_t, h_{1,i})$. Otherwise, $\mathcal{C}$ selects three random numbers $\sigma, w_i, PID_i \in Z_q$, where $PID_i = f1(h_{0,i}, h_{1,i})$, $\sigma = f2(w_i, PID_i)$. Then $\mathcal{C}$ sends $\{M_i, T_t, PK_i, R_i, PID_i\}$ to $\mathcal{A}$. It is feasible to verify that $\sigma \cdot P = PK_i + w_i \cdot R_i$ holds.

According to the Forking Lemma, assuming that $\mathcal{A}$ has produced two valid signatures, we have $\sigma \cdot P = PK_i + w_i \cdot R_i$ and $\widetilde{\sigma} \cdot P = PK_i + \widetilde{w}_i \cdot R_i$. To violate σ, $\mathcal{A}$ will perform the following steps.

$$\begin{aligned}(\sigma - \widetilde{\sigma}) \cdot P &= \sigma \cdot P - \widetilde{\sigma} \cdot P \\ &= (PK_i + w_i \cdot R_i) \cdot P - (PK_i + \widetilde{w}_i \cdot R_i) \cdot P \\ &= w_i \cdot Ri \cdot P - \widetilde{w}_i \cdot Ri \cdot P \\ &= (w_i - \widetilde{w}_i) \cdot r_i \cdot P^2\end{aligned} \quad (5)$$

By calculating $(\sigma - \widetilde{\sigma})((w_i - \widetilde{w}_i) \cdot P^2)^{-1}$, $\mathcal{C}$ demonstrates that $\mathcal{A}$ has effectively resolved the ECDLP problem within a polynomial time, thereby contradicting the principles defined in Definition 1. As a consequence, we reach the conclusion that the communication within our scheme remains impervious to adaptive chosen message attacks when operating within the random oracle model.

5.2. Security Analysis

We set several security goals in Section 2. Next, we delve into a detailed analysis of the security properties associated with the proposed scheme.

(1) Anonymity: OLDs in our system will not communicate with other entities with pseudo identities PID_i, where $PID_i = \{PID_{i,1}, PID_{i,2}\}$, $PID_{i,1} = ID_i \oplus H0(sk_i \cdot L_i\|T_t)$, $PID_{i,2} = (sk_i \cdot L_i) \oplus H1(T_t)$. Malicious users are not able to obtain the sender's privacy only via public parameters and messages sent. This way, vehicles are allowed to send messages without exposing their real identities.

(2) Authentication and Privacy: All messages sent by communicating parties should sign these messages before sending. They compute $\sigma = sk_i + w_i \cdot r_i \mod q$, where $w_i = H2(M_i\|PID_i\|T_t\|R_i\|PK_i)$. Then encapsulated messages $msg = \{M_i, T_t, PK_i, R_i, PID_i\}$ are broadcasted. Thus, all interactive parties in our system can authenticate each other to ensure reliability and legitimacy. In addition, an encapsulated message msg includes no LC NLC_i explicitly, which will keep the basic location privacy of OLDs. But when needed, the GC can derive the rough location of v_i by computing $(PID_{i,2} \oplus H1(T_t)) \cdot (PK_i \cdot \alpha)^{-1}$ from the msg.

(3) Traceability: When malicious messages are detected, the GC will extract vehicles' real identities by computing $ID_i = H0(PK_i \cdot \alpha \cdot NLC_i\|T_t) \oplus PID_{i,1}$, since $sk_i \cdot L_i = sk_i \cdot \alpha \cdot NLC_i \cdot P = PK_i \cdot \alpha \cdot NLC_i$ and $NLC_i = (PID_{i,2} \oplus H1(T_t)) \cdot (PK_i \cdot \alpha)^{-1}$ can be easily derived via messages.

(4) Unlinkability: Every time, to generate a message $msg : \{M_i, T_t, PK_i, R_i, PID_i\}$, a random number $r_i \in Z_q$ will be reselected and a new $w_i = H2(M_i\|PID_i\|T_t\|R_i\|PK_i)$ will be recomputed. Due to the randomness of r_i and the variability of w_i, a malicious party is unable to link messages sent by one OLD to itself. Therefore, the proposed scheme offers unlinkability in interactive communications.

(5) Resistance to common attacks: Our scheme is capable of countering common attacks present in traditional networks, such as the following:

 * *Replay Attack*: By encapsulating the timestamp T_t within the message, it prevents the message from being forwarded again in the future. Upon receiving the message, receivers first check the timestamp to verify its freshness. If it is still

* *Impersonation Attack*: An adversary needs to generate a signature for the message msg that satisfies $\sigma \cdot P = PK_i + w_i \cdot R_i$ in order to impersonate a legitimate vehicle. However, based on Theorem 1, no adversary can forge such a signature in polynomial time, which proves that our scheme is capable of resisting impersonation attacks.
* *Modification Attack*: A signature $\sigma = sk_i + w_i \cdot r_i \bmod q$ is a digital signature related to M_i since $w_i = H2(M_i \| PID_i \| T_t \| R_i \| PK_i)$. If M_i is modified by a malicious party, then w_i will change consequently, which makes σ change as well. Hence, the modification can be easily detected if the message itself is modified. This way, our scheme is able to resist modification attacks.
* *Sybil Attack*: To start a sybil attack, the adversary must generate multiple identities to play multiple roles. However, the pseudo identities are computed by a tamper-proof device. An adversary must violate the device first to generate those identities, which is infeasible via current technologies. Hence, our scheme successfully defends against sybil attacks.

6. Performance Analysis

In this analysis, we evaluate the performance of our scheme in comparison to the schemes proposed by Pournaghi et al. [47], Li et al. [6] and Tzeng et al. [48]. The evaluation is conducted on a system equipped with an Intel Core CPU i7-6700 operating at 3.40 GHz and 8 GB RAM, running the Windows 7 operating system. Firstly, we adopt a bilinear pairing denoted $E : G_1 \times G_1 \to G_T$, which ensures a security level equivalent to 80 bits, where P' serves as the generator of G_1. And G_1 is defined as a super singular elliptic curve $E' : y^2 = x^3 + x \bmod p'$, where p' is a 512-bit prime number and q' represents its order, which is a prime number of 160 bits. Let q denote the order of the group G on the super elliptic curve $E : y^2 = x^3 + ax + b \bmod p, (a, b \in Z_p^*)$; in this context, both q and p are 160-bit prime numbers. The symbols used throughout this section are as follows:

- T_{bp}: The duration of executing a bilinear pairing operation $e(Q', R')$, $Q', R' \in G_1$.
- T_{bm}: The duration of the scale multiplication operation $x' \cdot P'$ of bilinear pairing, where $x' \in Z_{q'}, P' \in G_1$.
- T_{ba}: The duration of the point addition operation $Q' + R'$ of bilinear pairing, where $Q', R' \in G_1$.
- T_{mtp}: The duration of a MapToPoint hash operation of bilinear pairing.
- T_{em}: The duration of the scale multiplication operation $x \cdot P$, where $x \in Z_q, P \in G$.
- T_{ea}: The duration of a point addition operation $Q + R$, where $Q, R \in G$.
- T_h: The duration of an one-way hash function operation.

The time taken for each operation is presented in Table 2.

Table 2. Running time of operations.

Operations	Running Time (ms)
T_{bp}	5.086
T_{bm}	0.694
T_{ba}	0.0018
T_{mtp}	0.0992
T_{em}	0.3218
T_{ea}	0.0024
T_h	0.001

6.1. Computation Cost Analysis

In the scheme proposed by Pournaghi et al. [47], when signing a single message, the bilinear pairing scale multiplication operation is performed four times, the bilinear pairing addition operation is performed once, the bilinear pairing MapToPoint function is performed once and the hash function is performed twice. The total time required for these operations is approximately 2.8790 ms, calculated as $4T_{bm} + T_{ba} + T_{mtp} + 2T_h$. And when the batch verification is implemented, the bilinear pairing addition operation is performed $3(n-1)$ times, the bilinear pairing scalar multiplication operation is performed n times, the bilinear pairing operation is performed three times, the MapToPoint operation is performed n times and the one-way hash function is performed n times. The total approximate time for these operations can be expressed as $3(n-1)T_{ba} + nT_{bm} + 3T_{bp} + nT_{mtp} + nT_h \approx 0.7996n + 15.2598$ ms.

In the scheme proposed by Tzeng et al. [48], when signing a single message, the bilinear pairing scale multiplication operation is performed three times and the hash function operation is performed twice, resulting in approximately 2.0840 ms, calculated as $3T_{bm} + 2T_h$. During batch verification, the bilinear pairing addition operation and the bilinear pairing scalar multiplication operation are both performed $(2n+1)$ times, the bilinear pairing operation is performed twice and the one-way hash function is performed n times, resulting in approximately $1.3926n + 10.8678$ ms, calculated as $(2n+1)T_{ba} + (2n+1)T_{bm} + 2T_{bp} + nT_h$.

In the scheme proposed by Li et al. [6], when signing a single message, the scale multiplication operation is performed once and the one-way hash function is performed twice, resulting in approximately 0.3238 ms, calculated as $T_{em} + 2T_h$. During batch verification, the scale multiplication operation is performed $(2n+2)$ times, the point addition operation is performed n times and the one-way hash function is performed $(2n)$ times, resulting in approximately $0.648n + 0.6436$ ms, calculated as $(2n+2)T_{em} + nT_{ea} + (2n)T_h$.

In our scheme, when signing a single message, the scale multiplication operation is performed once and the one-way hash function is executed twice, resulting in approximately 0.3228 ms, calculated as $T_{em} + T_h$. During batch verification, the scale multiplication operation is performed $2n$ times, the point addition operation is performed n times and the one-way hash function is performed n times, resulting in approximately $0.647n$ ms, calculated as $2nT_{em} + nT_{ea} + nT_h$.

As Figure 4 shows, to sign a message, our scheme costs lower computation power than the other three schemes. In Figure 5, we conducted a comparison of the execution time for batch verifications and the result indicates that our scheme demonstrates superior performance.

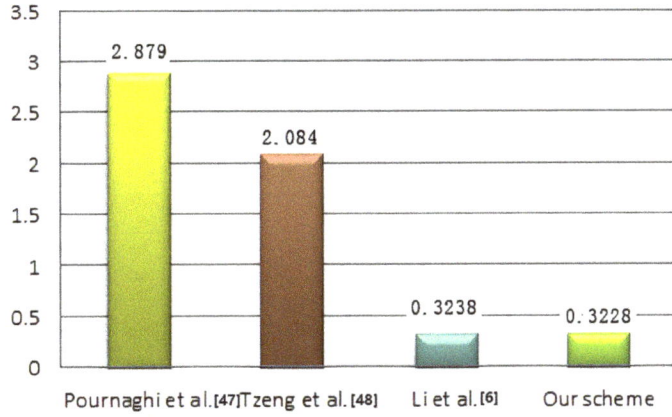

Figure 4. The time consumed for signing.

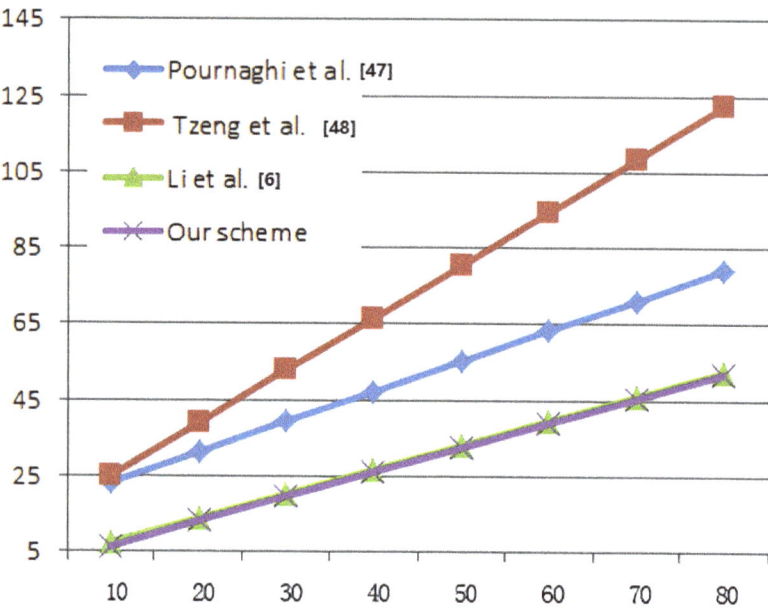

Figure 5. The time consumed for batch verifications.

6.2. Communication Cost Analysis

We only analyze our scheme in detail since the analyzing process is the same. In our scheme, the online learning devices will send the anonymous identity and signature $\{M_i, T_t, PK_i, R_i, PID_i\}$, in which $PID_i = \{PID_{i,1}, PID_{i,2}\} \in G, \sigma \in Z_q$ and T_t is the timestamp. Therefore, in our scheme, the communication cost is $40 \times 4 + 20 + 4 = 184$ bytes, while the scheme proposed by Pournaghi et al. [47] requires 296 bytes, the scheme by Tzeng et al. [48] requires 388 bytes and the scheme by Li et al. [6] requires 144 bytes.

Table 3 provides a summary of the comparison among the different schemes in terms of computation costs and communication costs.

Table 3. Comparison of computational and communication costs.

	Signature	Batch Authentication	Communication Cost
[47]	$4T_{bm} + T_{ba}$ $+T_{mtp} + 2T_h$	$(n+2)T_m + (3n-1)T_a + 2nT_h$	296 bytes
[48]	$3T_{bm} + 2T_h$	$(2n+1)T_{ba} + (2n+1)T_{bm}$ $+2T_{bp} + (n)T_h$	388 bytes
[6]	$1T_{em} + 2T_h$	$(2n+2)T_{em} + (n)T_{ea} + (2n)T_h$	144 bytes
Our	$1T_{em} + T_h$	$2nT_{em} + (n)T_{ea} + (n)T_h$	184 bytes

7. Conclusions

This paper proposes a secure communication scheme based on a multicast mechanism in software-defined MIoT. Firstly, we designed a multicast tree protocol based on DBWST. This protocol incorporates multicast mechanisms to quickly establish a multicast tree among affected online learning devices after the occurrence of emergencies. Secondly, an adaptive signature authentication scheme is devised to ensure the security of multi-party communication, enabling the system to meet security requirements such as anonymity, privacy preservation and traceability. Additionally, our scheme supports batch authentication, effectively saving resources. Furthermore, a security proof conducted under the random oracle model demonstrates that the proposed scheme satisfies the security requirements for secure communication in software-defined MIoT. The performance comparison of the scheme indicates its superior performance in both computing and communication. However, our system does not consider the actual distribution of online learning devices and does not achieve optimal efficiency. In the future, we will focus on how to group online learning devices based on the proposed scheme, which will help in managing online learning devices more efficiently in device-intensive areas.

Author Contributions: In this research paper, J.Y. conceived, designed, and wrote the cryptographic protocol; J.C. performed the experiments and analyzed the collected experimental data. All authors have read and agreed to the published version of the manuscript.

Funding: This research was funded by Foundation of Anhui Educational Committee grant number 2020jyxm0326, 2022sx020, 2022jy55; National Natural Science Foundation of China grant number 62272002.

Institutional Review Board Statement: Not applicable

Informed Consent Statement: Not applicable

Data Availability Statement: Due to restrictions on user privacy, we cannot make the data publicly available. If readers require access to the data, they can contact the authors via email to obtain it.

Conflicts of Interest: The authors declare no conflict of interest.

References

1. Gómez, J.; Huete, J.F.; Hoyos, O.; Perezc, L.; Grigorid, D. Interaction system based on Internet of Things as support for education. *Procedia Comput. Sci.* **2013**, *21*, 132–139. [CrossRef]
2. Gul, S.; Asif, M.; Ahmad, S.; Yasir, M.; Majid, M.; Malik M.S.A. A survey on role of Internet of Things in education. *Int. J. Comput. Sci. Netw. Secur.* **2017**, *17*, 159–165.
3. Konan M, Wang W. A secure mutual batch authentication scheme for patient data privacy preserving in WBAN. *Sensors* **2019**, *19*, 1608–1621. [CrossRef]
4. Vasile, R.; Olivares, S.; Paris, M.G.A.; Maniscalco, S. Continuous-variable quantum key distribution in non-Markovian channels. *Phys. Rev. A* **2011**, *83*, 042321. [CrossRef]
5. Pei, X.L.; Wang, X.; Wang, Y.F.; Li, M.K. Internet of Things based education: Definition, benefits and challenges. *Appl. Mech. Mater.* **2013**, *411*, 2947–2951. [CrossRef]
6. Li, J.L.; Choo, K.K.R.; Zhang, W.; Kumari, S.; Joel J.P.C.R.; Khan, M.K.; Hogrefe, D. EPA-CPPA: An efficient, provably-secure and anonymous conditional privacy-preserving authentication scheme for vehicular ad hoc networks. *Veh. Commun.* **2018**, *13*, 104–113. [CrossRef]
7. Liu, Y.; Wang, Y.; Chang, G. Efficient privacy-preserving dual authentication and key agreement scheme for secure V2V communications in an IoV paradigm. *IEEE Trans. Intell. Transp. Syst.* **2017**, *18*, 2740–2749. [CrossRef]
8. Phoenix, S.; Khan, F.; Teklu, B. Preferences in quantum games. *Phys. Lett. A*, **2020**, *384*, 126299. [CrossRef]
9. Shao, J.; Lin, X.; Lu, R.; Zuo, C. A threshold anonymous authentication protocol for VANETs. *IEEE Trans. Veh. Technol.* **2015**, *65*, 1711–1720. [CrossRef]
10. Trapani, J.; Teklu, B.; Olivares, S.; Paris, M.G.A. Quantum phase communication channels in the presence of static and dynamical phase diffusion. *Phys. Rev. A* **2015**, *92*, 012317. [CrossRef]
11. Wang, M.; Liu, D.; Zhu, L.; Xu, Y.; Wang, F. LESPP: Lightweight and efficient strong privacy preserving authentication scheme for secure VANET communication. *Computing* **2016**, *98*, 685–708. [CrossRef]
12. He, D.; Zeadally, S.; Xu, B.; Huang, X. An efficient identity-based conditional privacy-preserving authentication scheme for vehicular ad hoc networks. *J. Abbr.* **2015**, *10*, 2681–2691. [CrossRef]
13. Huang, J.; Qian, Y.; Hu, R.Q. Secure and Efficient Privacy-Preserving Authentication Scheme for 5G Software Defined Vehicular Networks. *IEEE Trans. Veh. Technol.* **2020**, *69*, 8542–8554. [CrossRef]
14. Cui, J.; Zhang, X.; Zhong, H.; Zhang, J.; Liu, L. Extensible conditional privacy protection authentication scheme for secure vehicular networks in a multi-cloud environment. *IEEE Trans. Inf. Forensics Secur.* **2019**, *15*, 1654–1667. [CrossRef]
15. Li, H.; Dong, M.; Ota, K. Control plane optimization in software-defined vehicular ad hoc networks. *IEEE Trans. Veh. Technol.* **2016**, *65*, 7895–7904. [CrossRef]
16. Rosati, M.; Mari, A.; Giovannetti, V. Coherent-state discrimination via nonheralded probabilistic amplification. *Phys. Rev. A* **2016**, *93*, 062315. [CrossRef]
17. Duan, P.; Peng, C.; Zhu, Q.; Shi, J.; Cai, H. Design and analysis of software defined Vehicular Cyber Physical Systems. In Proceedings of the 2014 20th IEEE International Conference on Parallel and Distributed Systems (ICPADS), Hsinchu, Taiwan, 16–19 December 2014; pp.412–417

18. Teklu, B.; Bina, M.; Paris, M.G.A. Noisy propagation of Gaussian states in optical media with finite bandwidth. *Sci. Rep.* **2022**, *12*, 11646. [CrossRef] [PubMed]
19. de Oca, E.M.; Mallouli, W. Security Aspects of SDMN. In *Software Defined Mobile Networks (SDMN) beyond LTE Network Architecture*; IEEE: Piscataway, NJ, USA, 2015; pp. 331–357.
20. Nkenyereye, L.; Nkenyereye, L.; Islam, S.M.R.; Choi, Y.H.; Bilal, M.; Jang, J.W. Software-defined network-based vehicular networks: A position paper on their modeling and implementation. *Sensors* **2019**, *19*, 3788. [CrossRef]
21. Zhu, M.; Cao, J.; Pang, D.; He, Z.; Xu, M. SDN-based routing for efficient message propagation in VANET. In *Wireless Algorithms, Systems and Applications: 10th International Conference, Qufu, China, 10–12 August 2015*; Springer International Publishing: Berlin/Heidelberg, Germany, 2015; pp. 788–797.
22. Karakus, M.; Durresi, A. Quality of service (QoS) in software defined networking (SDN): A survey. *J. Netw. Comput. Appl.* **2017**, *10*, 2681–2691. [CrossRef]
23. Lai, C.; Lu, R.; Zheng, D. Achieving secure and seamless IP Communications for group-oriented software defined vehicular networks. *Wirel. Algorithms Syst.* **2017**, *10*, 356–368.
24. Kim, H.S.; Yun, S.; Kim, H.; Shin, H.; Kim, W.T. An efficient SDN multicast architecture for dynamic industrial IoT environments. *Mob. Inf. Syst.* **2018**, *2018*, 8482467. [CrossRef]
25. Teklu, B. Continuous-variable entanglement dynamics in Lorentzian environment. *Phys. Lett. A* **2022**, *432*, 128022. [CrossRef]
26. Do, T.X.; Nguyen, V.G.; Kim, Y. SDN-based mobile packet core for multicast and broadcast services. *Wirel. Netw.* **2018**, *24*, 1715–1728. [CrossRef]
27. Zhou, S.; Wang, H.; Yi, S.; Zhu, F. Cost-efficient and scalable multicast tree in software defined networking. In Proceedings of the Algorithms and Architectures for Parallel Processing: 15th International Conference, ICA3PP 2015, Zhangjiajie, China, 18–20 November 2015; pp. 592–605.
28. Lecompte, D.; Gabin, F. Evolved multimedia broadcast/multicast service (eMBMS) in LTE-advanced: Overview and Rel-11 enhancements. *IEEE Commun. Mag.* **2012**, *50*, 68–74. [CrossRef]
29. Chen, J.; Yan, F.; Li, D.; Chen, S.; Qiu, X. Recovery and Reconstruction of Multicast Tree in Software-Defined Network: High Speed and Low Cost. *IEEE Access* **2020**, *8*, 27188–27201. [CrossRef]
30. Teklu, B.; Trapani, J.; Olivares, S.; Paris, M.G.A. Noisy quantum phase communication channels. *Phys. Scr.* **2015**, *90*, 074027. [CrossRef]
31. Garg, S.; Kaur, K.; Kaddoum, G.; Ahmed, S.H.; Jayakody, D.N.K. SDN-based secure and privacy-preserving scheme for vehicular networks: A 5G perspective. *IEEE Trans. Veh. Technol.* **2019**, *68*, 8421–8434. [CrossRef]
32. Adnane, H.; Teklu, B.; Paris, M.G.A. Quantum phase communication channels assisted by non-deterministic noiseless amplifiers. *JOSA B* **2019**, *36*, 2938–2945. [CrossRef]
33. Moulierac, J.; Guitton, A.; Molnár, M. Multicast tree aggregation in large domains. In *Networking Technologies, Services and Protocols; Performance of Computer and Communication Networks; Mobile and Wireless Communications Systems: 5th International IFIP-TC6 Networking Conference, Coimbra, Portugal, 15–19 May 2006*; Springer: Berlin/Heidelberg, Germany, 2016; pp. 691–702.
34. Li, W.; Guo, Y. A Secure Private Cloud Storage Platform for English Education Resources Based on IoT Technology. *Comput. Math. Methods Med.* **2022**, *2022*, 8453470. [CrossRef]
35. Tao, H. Online English Teaching System Based on Internet of Things Technology. *J. Sens.* **2022**, *2022*, 7748067. [CrossRef]
36. Chen, D. Application of IoT-Oriented Online Education Platform in English Teaching. *Math. Probl. Eng.* **2022**, *2022*, 9606706. [CrossRef]
37. Gao, W. Designing an interactive teaching model of English language using Internet of Things. *Soft Comput.* **2022**, *26*, 10903–10913. [CrossRef]
38. Azees, M.; Vijayakumar, P.; Deboarh, L.J. EAAP: Efficient anonymous authentication with conditional privacy-preserving scheme for vehicular ad hoc networks. *IEEE Trans. Intell. Transp.* **2017**, *18*, 2467–2476. [CrossRef]
39. Li, J.; Ji, Y.; Choo, K.K.R.; Hogrefe, D. CL-CPPA: Certificate-less conditional privacy-preserving authentication protocol for the Internet of Vehicles. *IEEE Internet Things J.* **2019**, *6*, 10332–10343. [CrossRef]
40. Xiang, D.; Li, X.; Gao, J.; Zhang, X. A secure and efficient certificateless signature scheme for Internet of Things. *Ad Hoc Netw.* **2022**, *124*, 102702. [CrossRef]
41. Hong, H.; Sun, Z. TS-ABOS-CMS: Time-bounded secure attribute-based online/offline signature with constant message size for IoT systems. *J. Syst. Archit.* **2022**, *123*, 102388. [CrossRef]
42. Khashan, O.A.; Khafajah, N.M. Efficient hybrid centralized and blockchain-based authentication architecture for heterogeneous IoT systems. *J. King Saud Univ.-Comput. Inf. Sci.* **2023**, *35*, 726–739. [CrossRef]
43. Wang, S.; Li, H.; Chen, J.; Wang, J.; Deng, Y. DAG blockchain-based lightweight authentication and authorization scheme for IoT devices. *J. Inf. Secur. Appl.* **2022**, *66*, 103134. [CrossRef]
44. Lai, C.; Zhou, H.; Cheng, N.; Shen, X.S. Secure group communications in vehicular networks: A software-defined network-enabled architecture and solution. *IEEE Veh. Technol. Mag.* **2017**, *12*, 40–49. [CrossRef]
45. Cui, J.; Zhang, X.; Zhong, H.; Ying, Z.; Liu, L. RSMA: Reputation system-based lightweight message authentication framework and protocol for 5G-enabled vehicular networks. *IEEE Internet Things J.* **2019**, *6*, 6417–6428. [CrossRef]
46. Cui, J.; Wu, D.; Zhang, J.; Xu, Y.; Zhong, H. An efficient authentication scheme based on semi-trusted authority in VANETs. *IEEE Trans. Veh. Technol.* **2019**, *68*, 2972–2986. [CrossRef]

47. Pournaghi, S.M.; Zahednejad, B.; Bayat, M.; Farjami, Y. NECPPA: A novel and efficient conditional privacy-preserving authentication scheme for VANET. *Comput. Netw.* **2018**, *134*, 78–92. [CrossRef]
48. Tzeng, S.F.; Horng, S.J.; Li, T.; Wang, X.; Huang, P.H.; Khan, M.K. Enhancing security and privacy for identity-based batch verification scheme in VANETs. *IEEE Trans. Veh. Technol.* **2015**, *66*, 3235–3248. [CrossRef]

Disclaimer/Publisher's Note: The statements, opinions and data contained in all publications are solely those of the individual author(s) and contributor(s) and not of MDPI and/or the editor(s). MDPI and/or the editor(s) disclaim responsibility for any injury to people or property resulting from any ideas, methods, instructions or products referred to in the content.

Article

Utilizing Trusted Lightweight Ciphers To Support Electronic-Commerce Transaction Cryptography

Ghanima Sabr Shyaa and Mishall Al-Zubaidie *

Department of Computer Sciences, Education College for Pure Sciences, University of Thi-Qar, Nasiriyah 64001, Iraq
* Correspondence: mishall_zubaidie@utq.edu.iq; Tel.: +964-61469869029

Abstract: Electronic-commerce (e-commerce) has become a provider of distinctive services to individuals and companies due to the speed and flexibility of transferring orders and completing commercial deals across far and different places. However, due to the increasing attacks on penetrating transaction information or tampering with e-commerce requests, the interest in protecting this information and hiding it from tamperers has become extremely important. In addition, hacking these deals can cause a huge waste of money and resources. Moreover, large numbers of connected and disconnected networks can cause significant disruption to the built-in security measures. In this paper, we propose to design a protocol to protect transaction information based on ElGamal, advanced encryption standard (AES) and Chinese remainder theorem (CRT) techniques. In addition, our protocol ensures providing scalability with high-performance security measures. We combine these algorithms with a robust methodology that supports the balance of performance and security of the proposed protocol. An analysis of our results proves that our protocol is superior to existing security protocols.

Keywords: AES; CRT; data encryption; e-commerce security; electronic trade protection; ElGamal; information hiding; Scyther

Citation: Shyaa, G.S.; Al-Zubaidie, M. Utilizing Trusted Lightweight Ciphers To Support Electronic-Commerce Transaction Cryptography. *Appl. Sci.* **2023**, *13*, 7085. https://doi.org/10.3390/app13127085

Academic Editor: Yoshiyasu Takefuji

Received: 19 May 2023
Revised: 7 June 2023
Accepted: 10 June 2023
Published: 13 June 2023

Copyright: © 2023 by the authors. Licensee MDPI, Basel, Switzerland. This article is an open access article distributed under the terms and conditions of the Creative Commons Attribution (CC BY) license (https://creativecommons.org/licenses/by/4.0/).

1. Introduction

The online shopping sector, commonly known as e-commerce, has grown dramatically in recent years as a result of technological advancements. More and more customers are choosing to utilize on-line shopping because of the quick advancement in information technology gadgets and Internet connectivity. The evolution of shopping mechanisms is influenced by a variety of social, technological, cultural, and psychological elements, which contribute to e-commerce's success. The most frequently utilized platform on the Internet is probably e-commerce websites, online auctions and mobile applications. Customers or buyers can order high-tech items, digital music files, books, services, etc., through e-commerce. Additionally, electronic apps provide a wide range of services and prospects, such as chances for developing payment invoices, buying and selling operations, and providing electronic services to customers and institutions via the Internet trade progress [1]. According to [2] in 2021, e-commerce sales increased dramatically at the level of countries; for example, the United Kingdom spent USD 169.02 million and the United States spent USD 843.15 million and USD 2779.31 million; this indicates that e-commerce has become a hugely influential economic factor around the world.

Due to the rise in credit card theft and compromised client accounts, e-commerce security has lately been a major concern. Compromising of customers' account information and credit card fraud are the two most serious security issues that are known to affect e-commerce [3]. The usage of e-commerce has significantly developed over the past several decades, and as a result, there are now exponentially greater transactions and numbers of payments made on online platforms. E-commerce has sophisticated an explosion of development, leading to security risks that threaten the personal information of users and attempt to detect private, public, and shared keys [4] in encrypting commercial and personal data/information [5]. Bitcoin, Litecoin, Freicoin, and Peercoin are among the currency-encryption approaches utilized in e-commerce applications. Some of these schemes apply cryptography algorithms to provide confidentiality and secrecy features [6]. It is common for e-commerce applications to be attacked (see Figure 1) by the types of common risks such as distributed denial of service (DDoS), phishing, wiretapping, brute force (BF), distributed guessing, financial fraud, sabotage, modification, ransomware, sniffer and zero-day. For instance, by producing a large number of malicious requests, a DDoS will crash the e-commerce applications and make them unusable for customers. Furthermore, e-commerce requests may be collected and modified through wiretapping on the transferred transaction encryption over the Internet. In addition, hackers use phishing attacks to capture the confidential information of customers through the creation of fake websites that are similar to real websites. Moreover, by using all possible combinations of characters, BF will crack passwords. Customers' private data and payment transactions have become major concerns [7]. Furthermore, financial fraud is committed through the theft of private information from credit cards when e-commerce platforms use this method to purchase services and products. Additionally, it occurs through false requests for credit returns through unauthorized transactions.

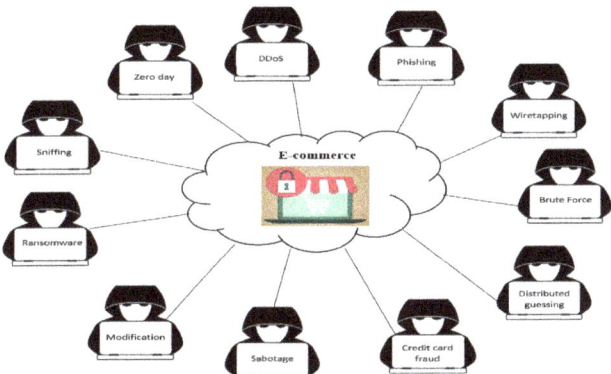

Figure 1. Various attacks against e-commerce sector.

A report published by [8] indicates that e-commerce attacks are constantly increasing; for example, from 2020 to 2021, there was an increase in credit card fraud attacks from 65% to 68%, BF from 11% to 11.5%, phishing from 56% to 71%, etc. This report also indicated that security-related incidents on Black Friday/Cyber Monday accounted for 17.5% of the total number of e-commerce requests. According to the report [9], 62% of attacks against e-commerce were automated. E-commerce transactions are exposed to various types of threats and attacks due to the rapid development of Internet websites; therefore, the system becomes unsafe. In this study, we focus on the security of commercial transactions using asymmetric and symmetric encryption protocols and algorithms. The system will provide strong security using the public key encryption algorithm (ElGamal) and the symmetric encryption algorithm (AES) to make e-commerce transactions more secure. Our main contributions to this research are:

- Designing a lightweight protocol for customer data authentication in e-commerce applications based on ElGamal for key generation and the AES algorithm for data encryption as well as relying on CRT to improve key generation performance.
- Protecting all stored security parameters associated with business application entities in a systematic and robust manner.
- Testing the e-commerce application protocol in the SYTHER tool for verification and analysis of security results, as well as performance testing of the proposed protocol and proving its superiority over existing protocols.

A quick description of how the paper is organized with the key points: Section 1 is the introduction to e-commerce and security risks. In Section 2, we describe related works of e-commerce security. The background about the used techniques with the proposed protocol is discussed in Section 3. Section 4 demonstrates the methods of the proposed e-commerce protocol. The proposed protocol results and discussion are explained in Section 5. In Section 6, we briefly provide the conclusions of this research, and future directions are presented in Section 7.

2. Related Works of E-Commerce Security

Existing research has addressed issues of using symmetric and asymmetric encryption algorithms in e-commerce applications, but the existing schemes still contain many security and performance flaws. This section will review the recent research related to the topic of our research in an extensive manner.

Hu et al. [10] submitted a proposal to develop digital signal processor (DSP) cipher modules for new embedded devices to execute a safe e-commerce app and to design a functional Rivest, Shamir, and Adleman (RSA) plug-in encryption tool that can store and encrypt confidential data originating from online transactions utilizing common web browsers. Secure online transactions are produced from the client side using the RSA algorithm. However, their scheme still has problems, such as increased cost and increased complexity, and the RSA algorithm suffers from key length and large arithmetic operations, which affect performance. Furthermore, space constraints affect the construction and utilization of Internet applications and databases, while large block sizes make execution more complex. In addition, there is a difference in the speed of encryption implementation and encryption.

Saha et al. [11] proposed a scheme to improve the security of the AES algorithm depending on cryptanalysis. Their algorithm is applied in the commercial field. They used a symmetric random function generator (SRFG) to support randomness. In addition, they used randomness in the process of generating keys in each block cipher. Nevertheless, there are some issues in their scheme, such as ignoring the execution time and the high complexity of their algorithm due to large operations, the round keys are kept separate since they are only needed for decryption and are produced at random.

Logunleko et al. [12] suggested using different methods to protect shared and sensitive data by depending on encrypting keys and implementing zero tolerance for data security in transit. Three encryption approaches—extended base64 (EB64), data encryption standard (DES) and AES algorithms—were used to increase the security and effectiveness of sensitive data. They contrasted their findings for both the encryption and decryption processes after looking at the encryption and decryption times provided at each individual testing step. The problem with their suggestion is using large and complex algebraic operations, a difference in the time of encryption and decryption, and that the amount of communication requests increased, which caused a delay in encryption and decryption.

Yousif et al. [13] introduced a proposal for secure images by integrating chaotic schemes and ElGamal public key cryptography with a scanning technique. Additionally, a permuted image was initially built using zigzag and spiral scanning. Next, the permuted image was encrypted utilizing the ElGamal encryption approach. Finally, in the confusion and diffusion phases, the pixel positions were mixed up using Lorenz and Rössler chaotic sequences. Unfortunately, some problems affect the work of their proposal negatively, which are not calculated for high randomness cost and complex operations, or for a difference in the execution time of the encryption due to the increase in the size of the images and the process of high sensitivity. Their system generated the encryption keys, which affected the sensitivity of the key to the decryption. This key sensitivity can add some complexity.

El Laz et al. [14] presented a proposal to use an effective symmetric cipher scheme in electronic systems. The ElGamal encryption system benefits from homomorphic features while maintaining semantic security, and it may be simply modified to fit a variety of cryptographic groups. This is dependent on the selected group sustaining the decisional Diffie–Hellman (DDH) assumption. Of the 26 libraries, that implement ElGamal's encryption technique, twenty were found to be semantically unsafe because they violate the DDH assumption. Four distinct message-encoding and -decoding algorithms were found and compared from the five libraries that meet the DDH assumption. However, their proposed problems include applications that generate large numbers without test randomness, and this affects security. Moreover, third-message encryption technology is generally difficult and can only be implemented for a small subset of messages where an account can be solved with a discrete logarithm by BF. In addition, the decryption tool is less important than encryption in the electronic process. Some applications do not use the safe initial setting of the ElGamal scheme, which affects security, and some libraries parse part of the information about the original message, which exposes the system to danger and makes the system unsafe.

Ali et al. [15] presented a suggestion about the design of a relational database that covered the creation of a multi-tier secure architecture for integrating the dam management framework with its tasks. They employed the AES technique and generated keys to encrypt and decode the dam data via the password-based key derivation function 2 (PBKDF2), random numbers generator (RNG) sequences generator and the slave key for salting security. However, their suggestion suffered from some problems, including low randomness, complex arithmetic operations efficiency, differences in execution time, encryption and decryption, and long keys being slow due to large dynamic operations.

Mohd and Ashawesh [16] submitted a proposal to optimize operations in encryption algorithms in order to protect digital data and to provide data security using AES cryptography. To decrease the time required for encryption and decryption while still boosting the security of digital data, they reduced the number of rounds in AES to 14. However, their proposal used large arithmetic operations that make encryption operations slow. The encryption transfer rate depends on the size of the files, as well as the speed of the encryption and decryption processes. Employing a key size of 256 makes the encryption process slower and more complex than AES-80 and AES-128. However, AES-256 is safer for applications that deal with sensitive information such as e-commerce applications.

Kumar et al. [17] adopted a recommendation regarding high-speed, low-power hardware designs for effective field programmable gate arrays (FPGA). They implemented AES cryptography to support information security. They used AES encryption and decryption in their method. Combinational logical circuits were used in their architecture to achieve SubBytes and InvSubBytes transformation. Look-up tables (LUTs) were removed from their design, eliminating any unnecessary delays, and a sub-pipelining structure was added to increase the performance of the AES algorithm. To lower the overall hardware requirements, the modified positive polarity Reed Muller (MPPRM) approach was added in this case, and comparisons with various implementations were performed utilizing AES-MPPRM. However, there were several drawbacks to their proposal. The process of generating a key led to consuming more time when expanding the key [18], and the cryptanalysis process checked the algorithm security by testing some threats such as a side channel threat, where their method was weak to some attacks such as DDoS and fraud.

Riadi et al. [19] presented a proposal to use encryption algorithms to secure text document files. They used the ElGamal algorithm. Additionally, they made use of the Fermat prime generator technique, which seeks prime random numbers, from which they derived the randomized prime numbers that made up the public and private keys. Nonetheless, there are some problems with their proposal that may hinder its implementation in real applications. Among these, the ElGamal algorithm suffers from the difficulty of computing the logarithm and large and random arithmetic operations in encryption operations. The algorithm is too complex to encrypt big text files.

Parenreng et al. [20] proposed the use of double encryption by utilizing the ElGamal encryption and the AES encryption approaches to distribute the symmetric key and to secure message data or confidential information. They claimed that their method provides sufficient security and performance when users' requests are transmitted over the network. Notwithstanding, their method did not provide appropriate performance because the method uses double encryption, the security analysis of the system was not performed in a deep or clear way, and the type of messages was not specified as to whether they were transmitted or stored, such that they were incomprehensible.

Dinata et al. [21] proposed a solution to preserve the integrity of the file and to provide the receiver assurance that the data are unaltered by outside parties. The receiver will be aware that the file is no longer validated if it has been modified, helping them to avoid utilizing the incorrect information. The message digest 5 (MD5) algorithm is used as a hash function method to construct a message digest, and the ElGamal algorithm is used as a public key cryptography to form the digital signature of the message digest in order to guarantee the data validity. However, their proposal is not secure. For example, the MD5 function has the same message digest length for each processed file, which is 32 or 128 bits of message digest. Therefore, if the attacker tries to modify the file, it takes a lot of time to find a pair of data. In the ElGamal algorithm, the public key is on a pair, only one of the private keys, and thus, the compiler cannot encrypt it utilizing any private key. It takes a private key with a pair matching the public key so that it is modified to an unknown. The performance is not balanced with security procedures.

An analysis of the relationship between privacy, security, confidence in the determination to reuse e-commerce apps, and perceived value was proposed by Anshori et al. [22]. Employing the purposive sample method, they applied this strategy to a set of customers who had at least once transacted using the Tokopedia application. The data-collection approach uses Google Forms to distribute surveys online, and the SmartPLS 3.3 program is used to analyze the data using the partial least square (PLS) approach. A total of 242 respondents participated in the survey. Nevertheless, their scheme encountered many problems including that the technique of collecting data was not more in-depth, utilizing random interview techniques with many of the participants. The application of e-commerce suffers from a set of variables such as price and method of promoting goods. This affects the security of e-commerce due to the development of technology exposing types of attacks that lead to the penetration of sensitive user information.

3. Background of E-Commerce and Used Techniques

In order to comprehensively discuss the topic of the research, this section is divided into providing information about the e-commerce methods and security techniques currently used to protect transactions in e-commerce applications.

3.1. E-Commerce Methods

In this section, we will briefly describe e-commerce methods.

- **Internet e-commerce:**
  E-commerce services provide access to a number of customers and facilitate buying and selling through the Internet. Customers, people, or businesses can use e-commerce services to access accounts, carry out business transactions, or obtain information about financial goods and services through a public or private network such as the Internet. The use of e-commerce provides convenience for the customer, less time, low cost, ease of use, rapid delivery and payment of bills via the Internet. One of the most important risks of e-commerce services is the security of transactions and the preservation of customer information [23].

- **E-commerce payment manner**
  Payment systems include e-commerce by means of credit cards or checks. The payment of e-commerce invoices is an important advantage of the use of e-commerce. Most customers utilize credit cards or checks when buying goods via e-commerce; Figure 2 shows payment manners in e-commerce applications. Mutual authentication is necessary for a secure electronic payment manner so that parties to the transaction may verify each other's identities, confidentiality, authentication of transactions, and

non-repudiation of customer and company user data. With the increasing proliferation of online shopping centers, the enhancement in payment manners has been studied, as credit cards are widely accepted on e-commerce platforms [24].

- **E-commerce merchant**

  The merchant is responsible for the time of delivery of goods, customer choices, customer questions, promoting the quality of goods, and his/her own method of persuading the customer, thus facilitating the process of selecting e-commerce products and selling goods [25].

- **E-commerce customer**

  The attraction of a customer to a vendor indicates that the customer will conduct more transactions with that provider. Providing excellent customer service is a significant approach to generate repeat transactions since clients are likely to continue business with these suppliers again. Nonetheless, any e-commerce app should use the six factors that affect service quality, which will serve as a broad guide to service quality. These factors are tangibility (facilities, equipment, display), reliability (on time), responsiveness (e-commerce provider helps customers if problems occur), assurance (the ability of e-commerce providers to convince customers), empathy (service providers are able to make customers feel personally cared) and security of requests (customer information in e-commerce requests such as selling, purchasing and invoices must be secure; this issue is the most important in making the customer adopt an e-commerce application without another application or vendor) [26].

- **Payment gateway**

  An e-commerce payment gateway authorizes payments through an intermediary system. In the middle of the payment process, a payment gateway acts as the intermediary between the merchant, customer, e-commerce app and the bank (or card issuer); see Figure 3. Due to the rising popularity of online shopping malls, improvements to credit card payment gateways on e-commerce platforms have been the subject of substantial research in recent years. Secure e-commerce activities are enabled by the public key infrastructure (PKI) authentication system, which establishes a secure connection after the server certificate is validated [27].

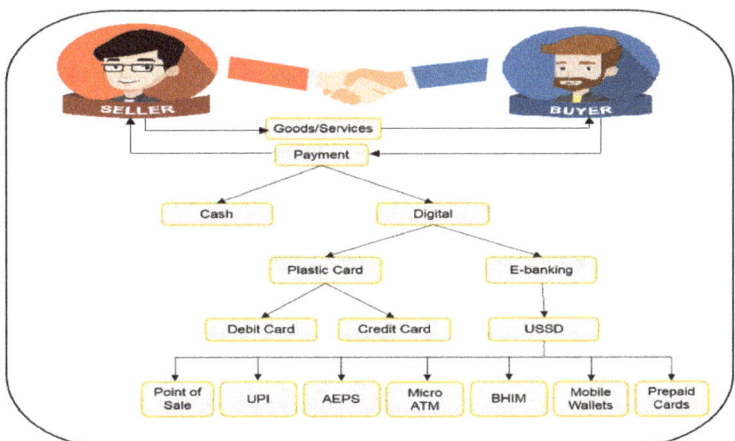

Figure 2. Payment methods in e-commerce.

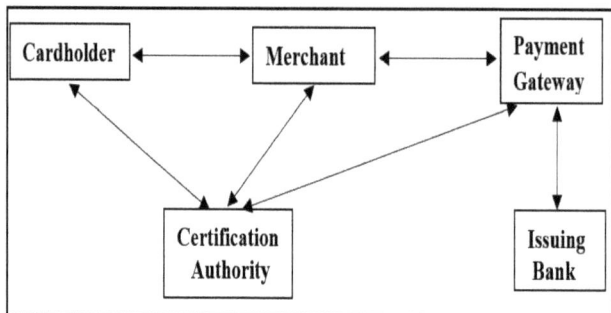

Figure 3. Payment gateway in e-commerce.

3.2. Overview of Security Techniques

This section will overview the techniques used in the proposed protocol.

- **ElGamal Algorithm**

  This is a major asymmetric encryption approach that was invented by Taher El Jamal in 1985. This algorithm depends on Diffie–Hellman key exchange. The algorithm can be an alternative manner for RSA public key encryption [28]. The primary distinction between RSA and ElGamal is that RSA relies on how difficult it is to analyze huge prime numbers, whereas ElGamal's security depends on how challenging it is to compute the discrete logarithm of large prime numbers. Table 1 shows the comparison between ElGamal and RSA in some characteristics, and ElGamal is characterized by key length, scalability, power consumption, application etc. [29]. Because it depends on the specifics in order to find all potential solutions, the discrete logarithm problem is regarded as one of mathematics's most challenging. This encryption is almost elusive or very time-consuming [13]. Figure 4 shows the use of ElGamal keys with encryption and decryption. Three procedures—key generation, encryption, and decryption—can be used with the ElGamal algorithm. The following is a brief illustration of each procedure:

ElGamal key generation procedure:

- Generating a large random prime number (Pn);
- Choosing a random number in the period [$1, Pn - 1$] as a generator number (Gn);
- Choosing an integer (Pr_k) larger than one and less than ($Pn - 2$) as the private number;
- Calculating a public key part value (Pv), where $Pv = Gn^{Pr_k} \mod Pn$;
- The private key is Pr_k, and the public key (Pu_k) is Pn, Gn and Pv.

ElGamal encryption procedure:

- Representing the transaction request (plaintext) as an integer TR, where $0 < TR < Pn - 1$, and the public key (Pn, Gn, Pv) is used to achieve encryption;
- Choosing an integer random number Rn such that $1 < Rn < Pn - 2$;
- Computing the first encryption value V_1, $V_1 = Gn^{Rn} \mod Pn$;
- Computing the second encryption value V_2, $V_2 = (Pv^{Rn} * TR) \mod Pn$;
- Encryption (E) is $E = (V_1, V_2)$.

ElGamal decryption procedure:

- Receiver receives the encryption $E = (V_1, V_2)$;
- Using the private key (Pr_k) for decryption procedure;
- Then, r is computed as follows: $r = V_1^{Pn-1-Pr_k} \mod Pn$;
- E is decrypted by $TR = (r * V_1) \mod Pn$.

The ElGamal algorithm works to increase security, and it is difficult to break [30]. Although the ElGamal cipher algorithm is a popular public-key cryptography algorithm whose security is based on a difficult discrete logarithm problem, the traditional ElGamal encryption algorithm still has some shortcomings including the long ciphertext and the time-consuming calculation, and the higher the complexity, the slower the encryption speed [31].

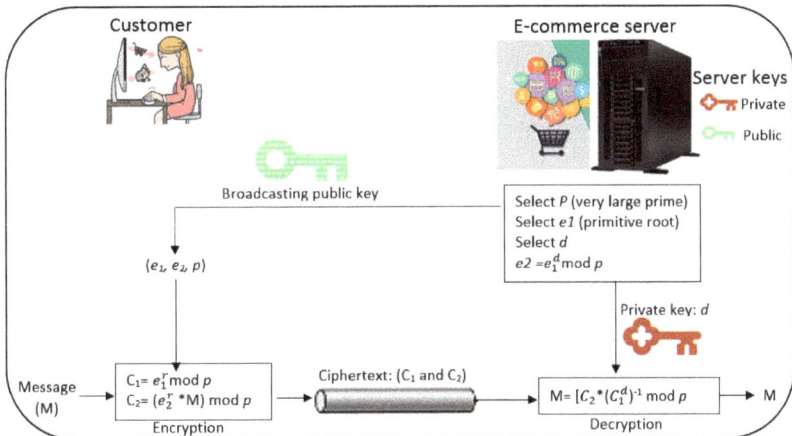

Figure 4. ElGamal keys with encryption and decryption.

Table 1. Asymmetric cryptography algorithms.

Factors	ElGamal	RSA
Developed	1985	1978
Researcher(s)	Taher ElGamal	Rivest, Shamirand, and Adleman
Key length value	$\geq$1024 bits	$\geq$1024 bits
Type of algorithm	Asymmetric	Asymmetric
Security attack	Meet in the middle attack	Timing attack
Simulation speed	Fast	Fast
Scalability	Good scalability	No scalability occurs
Key used	Different key used for encryption and decryption	Different key used for encryption and decryption
Power consumption	Low	High
Hardware and software implementation	Not very efficient	Faster and efficient
Solution problem	Multiplicative group	Integer factorization
Security strength	The difficulty of computing a discrete logarithm in a finite field	The difficulty of factoring the product of two large prime numbers
Encryption	It is more efficient for encryption	It is more efficient for encryption
Decryption	It is more efficient for decryption	It is less efficient for decryption

- **Advanced Encryption Standard**

  Block cipher technology, known as the "advanced encryption algorithm" (or "AES"), operates on 128 bit plaintext and uses the same key for both encryption and decryption. The 128 bit blocks are performed by the AES algorithm, which performs 10, 12, and 14 rounds of operations on each block. It uses an 80, 128, 192 and 256 bit cipher (see Figure 5 [32]). It is made up of a 4-byte array that identifies the state, and in each cipher round, conversions are made as SubBytes (), ShiftRows (), MixColumns and AddRoundK ().

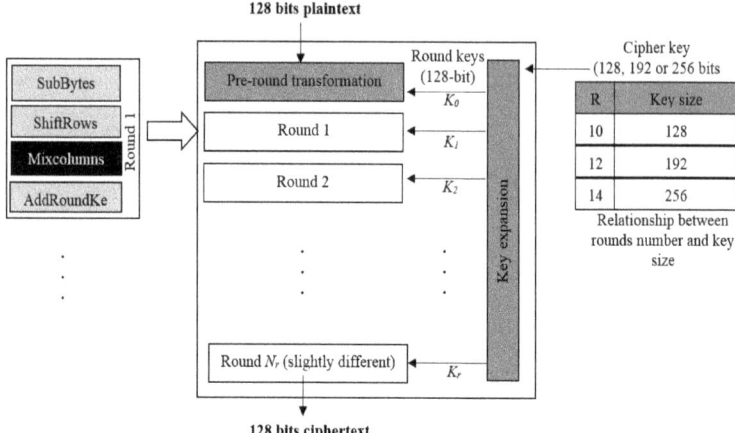

Figure 5. AES algorithm structure.

There are four primary functional blocks in AES:

1. Byte substitution: The byte of each data block is substituted to another block utilizing an S-box.
2. Rows shift: Each row receives a cyclic shift to the right relying on where it is in the state matrix.
3. Columns mix: In this matrix multiplication process, each column of the state matrix is multiplied by the fixed matrix.
4. Round key addition: The new state matrix and the round key matrix are combined using an XOR technique [33].

Distinguishing AES reduces the number of rounds of encryption, reduces data encryption, reduces power consumption and improves the level of security. Table 2 provides a comparison between existing block ciphers with the AES algorithm.

Table 2. Comparison between block cipher algorithms.

Block Cipher Algorithm	Block Size	Key Size	Number of Rounds	Algorithm Design Pattern
HIGHT	64	128	32	GFN
Pickolo	64	80/128	25/31	GFN
PRESENT	64	80/128	31	SPN
DES	64	56	16	Feistel
AES	128	128/192/256	10/12/14	SPN
Clefia	128	128/192/256	18/22/26	GFN
TEA	64	128	64	Feistel
XTEA	64	128	64	Feistel
NTSA	64	128	64	Feistel

One of the most used symmetric key encryption algorithms is AES, which encrypts and decrypts sensitive data using the same key. Due to its lower cost and simpler execution in both software and hardware, AES is considered the most secure cryptographic method. The encryption and decryption phases of the non-Feistel cipher AES use the same rounds of operations. It has been demonstrated that AES executions on hardware are both quicker and more secure than those on other cryptographic executions [17]. The use of the AES algorithm as a basis decreases the number of encryption rounds and works to increase the complexity and resistance to attacks of various paradigms, leading to more security of data and a safer algorithm [34].

- **Chinese Remainder Theorem Technique**

  A theorem in number theory involving simultaneous linear congruences is called the

Chinese remainder theorem (CRT). In general, if there are congruences of a certain form, it states:

$$S \equiv ai_1 (mod\ ppi_1), S \equiv ai_2 (mod\ ppi_2) \ldots S \equiv ai_n (mod\ ppi_n)$$

where S is a solution, $ai_1, ai_2 \ldots ai_n$ are arbitrary integers (ai) and $ppi_1, ppi_2, \ldots ppi_n$ are pairwise positive integers (ppi). If it has a solution, then the solution is unique in relation to the product $ppi_1 * ppi_2 * \ldots * ppi_n$. The equation will satisfy any other solution (OS) if S is a solution to the problem $S \equiv OS\ (mod\ ppi_1 * ppi_2 * \ldots * ppi_n)$. A system of congruences can be solved using the theorem when the moduli have no common factors except 1.

This technology was discovered in the world in the third century common era (CE) by the Chinese mathematician Yisunzi Fu Wesunzisuangjing. One of the most crucial theorems in mathematics, CRT is an algorithm for decreasing standard arithmetic by a significant amount for the same arithmetic for each coefficient aspect. In a landscape where new types of applications are open to the perfect combination of beauty and usability, the perfect combination of beauty and usability continues to emerge in new contexts [35]. The CRT algorithm is used in many areas of contemporary research and high-tech industries, including communication, coding, computer, and cryptography [36]. Most recently, the CRT technique and corresponding forms of representation of numbers and methods for reconstructing integers have been studied by residue code, which is intensively used, especially with regard to its application in high-performance calculating. The main focus is on computationally reducing calculations and complexity of the main integrative features of the residue code [37].

4. Proposed Protocol Methodology for E-Commerce

Due to the numerous and varied Internet technologies, the number and kind of sent data across e-commerce have greatly expanded in recent years, which has in turn led to the enormous expansion of e-commerce risks. Several of the data include sensitive data that could be attacked in several ways, including payment data, because security is the biggest issue currently facing all customers, and it plays a crucial role in e-commerce web services. In this study, we use a strong protocol to maintain the security of electronic commerce transactions.

The overall architecture of the proposed e-commerce network includes customers, sellers, delivery services, authenticated servers, goods and services providers (merchants), payment gateways and banking transactions. Figure 6 shows the architecture of the general e-commerce network. Costumers are users around the world who wish to buy a service or goods, sellers are users who try to sell something electronic or physical through e-commerce applications, delivery services are offices that send orders if they are physical things or send via the Internet if they are software or instructions/tips, authenticated servers are computers with large sources that perform and receive authentication requests to ensure the legitimacy of users of e-commerce applications, merchants are users who offer huge and one-class goods for sale through e-commerce applications, and payment gateways are platforms used to support payment authentication, of which there are many popular platforms such as PayPal, PayWay, BrainTree, CorvusPay, etc. A banking transaction is an entity that guarantees the transmission of payments to payment gateways and thus to sellers and merchants. In this paper, we will focus on authenticating customers, sellers and authenticated servers. Documenting the rest of the entities will be left for future research. Initially, we used an asymmetric encryption algorithm for generating keys, the ElGamal algorithm, and a symmetric encryption algorithm for encryption and decryption, the AES algorithm. The following Figure 7 illustrates the general methodology of the proposed protocol.

The diagram shows the two types of encryption algorithms we used, symmetric and asymmetric, and we used the CRT technique in the operations of encoding and decoding order information in e-commerce.

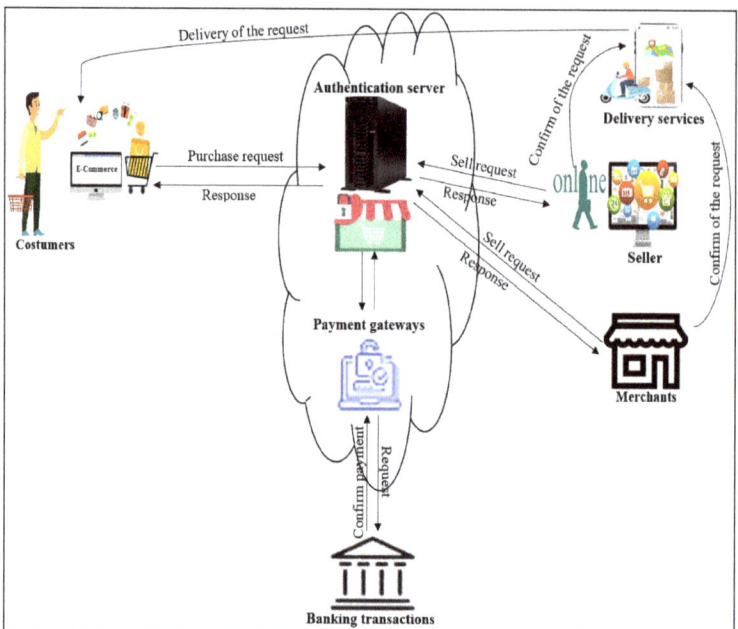

Figure 6. General network architecture of e-commerce application.

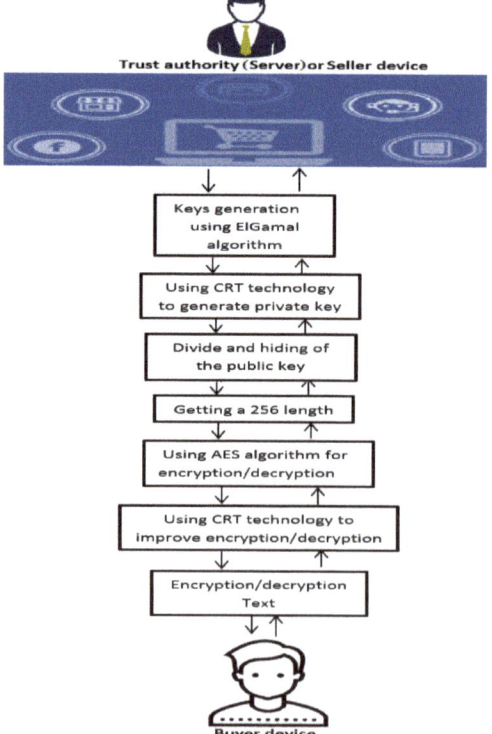

Figure 7. General diagram for our e-commerce application.

4.1. Implicated Symmetric and Asymmetric Cryptography

This section will explain the techniques used in our methodology and how these security measures are used and employed in our protocol. We explain ElGamal, AES and CRT.

4.1.1. Utilizing ElGamal

In our protocol, we need an algorithm that generates large and random keys suitable for encrypting sensitive information in e-commerce applications. There are many asymmetric encryption algorithms, the most prominent of which are ElGamal and RSA. However, we chose ElGamal because it provides faster encryption and decryption processing than RSA, and it consumes less power and provides better scalability than RSA (as shown in Table 1). Our protocol uses the ElGamal algorithm only for generating and calculating public and private keys, and not for encryption and decryption. Encryption and decryption processes are very expensive in asymmetric algorithms such as ElGamal; thus, we use ElGamal only to generate large random keys. ElGamal provides keys with lengths of 1024, 2048, 4096, etc. Our protocol generates a public key of length 1024 and a private key using CRT technology (as shown in the following algorithm).

- Generating a large random prime number (p);
- Choosing a generator number (a);
- Using CRT to generate an random integer (P_r), as the secret number and less than ($p-2$);
- Computing (d), where $d = a.P_r \bmod p$;
- The private key is P_r, and the public key is (P_u), which includes p, a, d.

Then, our protocol divides the public key into four parts, with each part of size 256, and performs the XoR processes for the four parts to obtain a secret and random key ready for use in the AES algorithm. The purpose of using ElGamal is to generate random and different keys for each user of e-commerce applications.

4.1.2. Utilizing the AES Algorithm

The AES algorithm encrypts/decrypts the buy and sell requests upon delivery from the buyer (B), seller (S) or trust authority server (TAS). However, the use of keys as small as 80 and 128 can compromise the customers' sensitive information. Therefore, our protocol relies on a key length of 256, which is enough to block attacks. In addition, our protocol addresses a scalability problem that is inherent in symmetric algorithms, whereby all users use the same secret key. Our protocol uses a different secret key for each user by using the public keys of the ElGamal algorithm. In addition to the importance of key length, fundamental reasons that AES can be vulnerable to attacks are the randomness level of keys and cryptographic randomness. Therefore, our protocol uses strong AES ciphers that provide appropriate key length (256 bit), key randomness (ElGamal), and cryptographic randomness through the use of a random salt with fewer performance expenses.

4.1.3. Utilizing the CRT Technique

The CRT technique can be used to support randomness issues for encryption algorithms. In addition, it can be used to support performance issues in encryption, decryption and keys generation. This technique is used with the ElGamal algorithm to generate random keys, especially private ones, to increase the randomness, and it is used with the ElGamal algorithm with a faster operating speed, a smaller key, and an increase in the working time capacity with the system. The keys are later used in the process of encryption and decryption for the encryption process, i.e., changing the original text into ciphertext using a public key and for the decryption procedure, which changes the ciphertext into original text/plaintext using a private key. This technique works to represent and process large operands in ciphertext polynomials and to reduce large numbers to small ones. Namely, we use CRT to reduce the private key length and to support its randomness. In our protocol, we relied on CRT to calculate Salt to support the random handling of encryption and decomposition in AES.

4.2. Buying and Selling Requests and Invoices

We implement encryption operations based on the AES algorithm for a set of encryption requests, and there are forms of requests that buy and sell requests and invoices. Figure 8 shows types of request forms. The request information is encrypted, whether it is a request to buy or sell or pay bills, based on the request procedure. Requests forms used in this research are real forms for e-commerce applications, which are forms taken from free databases [38] on the Internet and do not contain personal information or network. In order to complete the encryption process and decryption for the purchase requests to sell and invoice properly, we added some personal information and unreal request data for virtual users. We encrypt a request received from the customer or buyer based on the AES method and then sent it to the TAS. Here, information is encrypted and difficult to hack (if the encryption is strong with high key randomness) by legitimate network parties, and personal information is protected for both the client and the server.

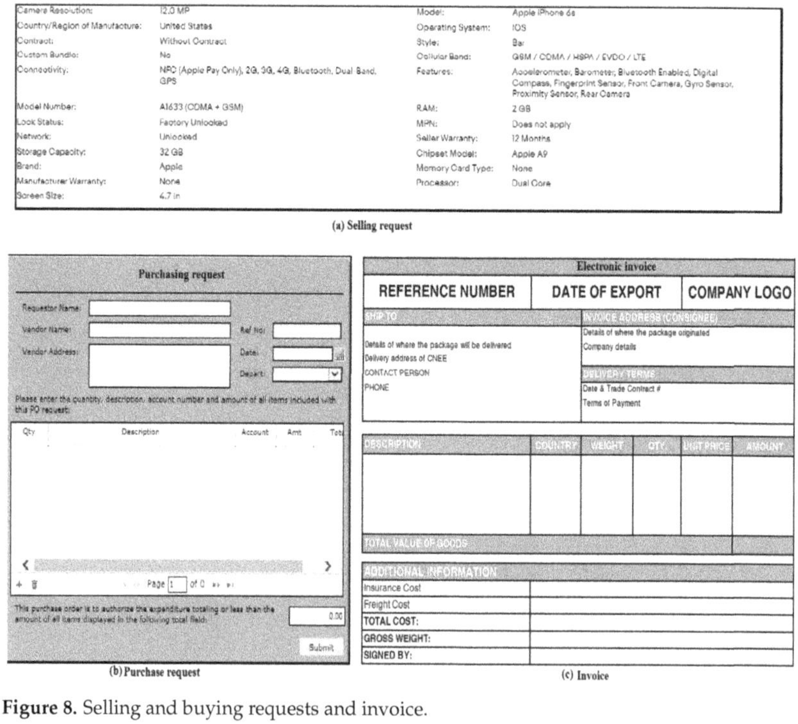

Figure 8. Selling and buying requests and invoice.

4.3. Proposed Protocol Procedures

In designing the protocol, we rely on the method of encrypting and decrypting request transactions. This is performed using symmetric and asymmetric encryption algorithms. We use the AES algorithm to encrypt the text and request information. We follow the following steps (Figure 9 shows our proposed protocol procedures):

1. We generate random keys that are the private and public keys by default using an ElGamal asymmetric encryption algorithm. Then, we divide the random key whose size is from 1024 to 256 bit to fit the AES algorithm keys.
2. We use this public key to encrypt the e-commerce requests among B, S and TAS. Our protocol performs strong encryption using high encryption randomness, which is difficult to crack when sent from B to S.

3. The request information will be decrypted using the AES and ElGamal keys. The buyer/seller receives a decrypted text that is difficult to penetrate from an attacker.
4. Public and private keys are updated when required or when the number of key mix-ups has expired.
5. Hiding information and security parameters on network devices, especially keys, is important in cases of hacking of these devices.

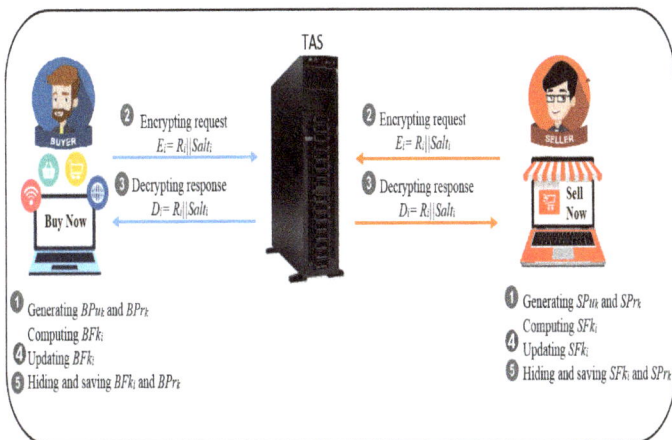

Figure 9. Proposed methodology procedures.

Keys Generation Procedure

The first procedure in our protocol is the key generation procedure. Algorithm 1 refers to the operations performed for the key generation procedure. Key generation instructions for the ElGamal algorithm are described earlier in Section 3.2. In this section, we will describe directives added to support public and private key security. Initially, the parameters P_n and G_n were used to generate the keys in ElGamal. We use ElGamal to generate Pu_k public keys with a size of 1024 bit. In addition, we make use of ElGamal-CRT to generate the private key (Pr_k). To support randomness in public keys, we split the public key (Pu_k) into subkeys (Sk_s). These Sk_s are Sk_1, Sk_2, Sk_3 and Sk_4 with a length of 256 bit, which fits the AES algorithm. Our protocol performs the operations $k_1 = Sk_1 \oplus Sk_2$ and $k_2 = Sk_3 \oplus Sk_4$. Then, our protocol obtains the final key (Fk) of length 256 bit through $Fk_i = k_1 \oplus k_2 \oplus Sk_i$ (where Sk_i can be the value of Sk_1, Sk_2, Sk_3 and Sk_4). To protect the keys Pr_k and Fk_i on network devices, they are hidden using the operations result ($Inte$) = $PW \oplus Pr_k$ (where $Inte$ represents the interim value) and final key ephemeral (Fk_e) = $Fk_i \oplus Inte \oplus PW$. At this point, $Inte$ and Fk_e are safely stored on devices using e-commerce applications. On the next connection, our protocol moves to the fourth step in Algorithm 1 without generating keys. Our protocol relies on scrambling Sks to use new public keys; for example, our protocol computes $k_1 = Sk_1 \oplus Sk_3$ and $k_2 = Sk_2 \oplus Sk_4$ and then performs the same operations in Algorithm 1 until 16 connections are completed. If the network device has made 16 connections in e-commerce applications, then in the next connection, it should start from step 1 in Algorithm 1. Bypassing key generation for 16 connections reduces computational costs, especially in TAS.

Algorithm 1 Keys generation procedure

Input: P_n, G_n values and PW
Output: Pr_k and Pu_k keys with 256 bit length
1: Use ElGamal to generate Pu_k with 1024 bit length
2: Use ElGamal-CRT to generate Pr_k
3: Divide Pu_k to four part with 256 bit length
4: Four subkeys: Sk_1, Sk_2, Sk_3 and Sk_4
5: Apply $\oplus$ with subkeys
6: Obtain Fk_i with 256 bit length
7: Protect Pr_k and Fk_i on device
8: Compute $Inte = PW \oplus Pr_k$
9: Store $Fk_e = Fk_i \oplus Inte \oplus PW$
10: Next connection, go to step 4 with changing Sk_s order
11: After 16 connections, go to step 1

Encryption Procedure

To perform the encryption process in our protocol, Pr_k, Pu_k, PW and R_i (buying, selling or invoice request) are used. However, before the encryption process can be performed, the keys Pr_k and Fk_i that are hidden on the network devices must be extracted. As described in Algorithm 2, Steps 1 and 2 represent the extractions of Pr_k and Fk_i for use in AES-256 ciphers. Next, our protocol uses a CRT technique with the key Pr_k to obtain a random $Salt_i$ with minimal computational overhead. Then, our protocol uses Fk_i and $Salt_i$ to perform the encryption operations, whereas the encryption operation Enc_{R_i} is executed through the operation $R_i||Salt_i$. Our protocol uses the operation $Pu_k \oplus Salt_i$ to obtain a hidden ephemeral salt ($Salt_e$). Finally, the $Enc_{R_i}||Salt_e$ cipher is sent to the target device. In the same way, Pr_k and Fk_i are hidden by Fk_e to prevent attackers from hacking the device and from gaining security parameters.

Algorithm 2 Encryption procedure

Input: Pr_k, Pu_k keys with 256 bit, PW and R_i
Output: Enc_{R_i} and $Salt_e$
1: Extract $Pr_k = PW \oplus Inte$
2: Extract $Fk_i = Fk_e \oplus Inte \oplus PW$
3: Use CRT to generate $Salt_i$
4: Use Fk_i 256 bit with AES encryption
5: Encrypt $Enc_{R_i}(R_i||Salt_i)$
6: Hide $Salt_e = Pu_k \oplus Salt_i$
7: Send $Enc_{R_i}||Salt_e$
8: Store $Fk_e = Fk_i \oplus Inte \oplus PW$
9: Store connection order on the sender side

Decryption Procedure

The encryption procedure is followed by a process called decryption. After the target device receives the encrypted request, it decrypts it with the public and private keys as well as security parameters such as $Salt$. For example, sellers need to decrypt buyers' requests to identify the type of request, the quantity ordered, the destination of the request, and the information that represents the invoice payment. In the same way as Algorithm 2, Algorithm 3 extracts the keys Pr_k and Fk_i stored on network devices during steps 1 and 2. Next, the receiver receives requests such as $R_i = Enc_{R_i}||Salt_e$, then subtracts $Salt_e$ from the encryption request, and then extracts $Salt_i$ from $Salt_e$ to perform the decryption process. Then, our protocol uses Fk_i and $Salt_i$ to perform the decoding of R_i by $Enc_{R_i}||Salt_i$. After the receiving device receives the explicit text of the requests, it is stored in the datasets for archiving. In the same manner as Algorithms 2 and 3, it stores keys anonymously.

Algorithm 3 Decryption procedure

Input: Pu_k keys with 256 bit, PW and Enc_{R_i}
Output: Dec_{R_i}

1: Extract $Pr_k = PW \oplus Inte$
2: Extract $Fk_i = Fk_e \oplus Inte \oplus PW$
3: Use Fk_i 256 bit with AES decryption
4: Use $R_i = Enc_{R_i} || Salt_e$
5: Remove $Salt_e$ from R_i
6: Extract $Salt_i = Pu_k \oplus Salt_e$
7: Decrypt $R_i = Dec_{R_i}(Enc_{R_i})$
8: Save R_i in dataset
9: Store $Fk_e = Fk_i \oplus Inte \oplus PW$
10: Store connection order on the receiver side

Keys Updating Procedure

For a protocol to be robustly designed for security, it should include a key update procedure (see Algorithm 4). Initially, our protocol applies steps 1 to 6 in Algorithm 1 which performs key generation operations Pr_k and Pu_k and then obtains Pr_k by ElGamal-CRT and Fk_i by mixing Sk_s. To hide Fk_e, the last salt ($LSalt_i$) is used within the process $Fk_i \oplus Fk_o \oplus LSalt_i$. The sender (buyer) sends Fk_e to the receiver (seller). Finally, public and private keys are protected on network devices in the same way as Algorithms 1–3.

Algorithm 4 Keys updating procedure

Input: P_n, G_n values and PW
Output: Pr_k and Pu_k keys with 256 bit length

1: Apply Algorithm 1, steps 1–6
2: Obtain Pr_k and Fk_i
3: Compute $Fk_e = Fk_i \oplus Fk_o \oplus LSalt_e$
4: Send Fk_e to the receiver
5: Protect Pr_k and Fk_i on device
6: Compute $Inte = PW \oplus Pr_k$
7: Store $Fk_e = Fk_i \oplus Inte \oplus PW$

5. Security and Performance of Proposed E-Commerce Applications

This section will discuss security analysis by testing the ability of our protocol to block e-commerce attacks; after that, the Scyther tool is used to test the security of our protocol in practice.

5.1. Attacks Analysis on Our Protocol

The security analysis of a range of e-commerce attacks is summarized as follows (Table 3 provides a comparison of cryptographic protocols in terms of blocking attacks within the scope of this research):

- **DDoS**
  An attacker tries to stop all the services provided by the servers and makes them unavailable to the customers/buyers/sellers, and the goal is to prevent user requests from being fulfilled by servers in e-commerce applications, whether buying or selling or e-commerce payment operations. DDoS attacks are more perilous than DoS attacks, and the reason is that DDoS uses several different systems to attack from multiple locations, which makes the impact of stopping the network bigger and faster. In addition, it is difficult to track. Moreover, e-commerce applications deal with sensitive information, and any delay or blocking of user requests can cause economic disasters. Preventing these attacks completely is very difficult. However, limiting its impact and mitigating its severity are crucial. Our protocol uses a small token inside $Salt_e$ that

proves the legitimacy of the connected device. This process is inexpensive to perform $(Salt_i \oplus Pu_k)$. Thus, our protocol is able to mitigate the risk of DDoS attacks.

- **Phishing**

  An attacker tries to penetrate the personal information (usernames, passwords and credit card) of the buyers or sellers or to penetrate the information of requests or the information of a company or institution that is sensitive and important in e-commerce applications. Phishing attacks rely on mined links or malicious malware to steal confidential information. Our protocol does not allow e-commerce applications to transmit or send links between users (buyers and sellers). Even if a user downloads malware without knowing it or accidentally clicks on a link in other programs, the malware or the attacker will not receive clear and useful information about that user. In addition, PW is not stored on users' machines. Therefore, our protocol repels phishing attacks.

- **Wiretapping**

  An unauthorized intruder or attacker tries to access the company's or user's data by eavesdropping on purchase and sale requests between the buyer/seller and the servers by revealing and analyzing the transmitted request. This attack is resisted using a request information encryption ($Enc_{R_i}(R_i||Salt_i)$ process) based on the AES 256 algorithm. These requests can be decrypted with only their private and public key. Process breaking the encryption is impossible because the buying/selling request data are hidden.

- **Brute force**

  In this attack, the attacker tries to access confidential information such as PW, Pr_k and Pu_k in e-commerce applications. This attack relies on trial and error to gain access to the PW or login credentials. Our protocol does not transmit any confidential information in the encryption and decryption procedures. For example, $Enc_{R_i}||Salt_e$ does not contain any explicit secret parameters (see Algorithms 2 and 3). No matter how hard the attacker tries to hack/crack PW, Pr_k and Pu_k, it is not possible because it is not transmitted through the unsecured channel. Additionally, PW is not stored on network devices. Moreover, PW is selected according to strict security criteria (such as uppercase and lowercase letters, symbols, etc.). As a result, our protocol is able to completely prevent brute force attacks.

- **Distributed guessing for electronic payment**

  The guesser's probability of succeeding on a randomly chosen key depends on the probability of guessing PW. The guesser attempts to capture the packet passing from the sender to the receiver in order to decrypt it using a single guess or distributed multiple guesses. An attacker can use distributed guesses to reveal secret parameters if they are sent explicitly, use PW as an encryption key, or use weak security measures. In addition, the guesser uses a large number of guesses to make this attack more effective. The attacker cannot decrypt the electronic payment details (see Figure 8c) because we rely on a sufficiently long, random 256 bit key to fend off this type of attack. Our protocol does not send secrets over the insecure channel. In addition, when the guesser captures the packet, it cannot parse it to derive the keys Pr_k and Pu_k. Therefore, our protocol deservedly resists this attack.

- **Credit card fraud**

  A fraudster tries to access a customer's account and compromises a credit card account in order to obtain secret parameters (such as the credit card number, the card security code, or knowing the expiration of the attack value) for the user/company. An attacker uses document falsification and fraudulent information using credit card fraud attacks. Even if the fraudster receives some credit card details or uses some fake details, he/she does not have secret parameters such as PW and Pr_k without which he/she cannot complete the e-commerce transactions. Thus, our protocol is able to prevent this type of attack.

- **Sabotage**

    A saboteur intends to destroy, subvert or obstruct by penetrating certain websites, stopping the system of a company/institution, stopping the sale/purchase requests or online payment operations, or sending sensitive information from the client or server to another party. Infecting an e-commerce app with a malicious program is an example of online buying and selling environment sabotage. A more extreme instance is causing e-commerce in a nation to go down. To counter this attack, our protocols use Pu_ks that change each time the buyer and seller's devices connect to the e-commerce network.

- **Data modification**

    An attacker attempts to penetrate the exchanged e-commerce information then modifies or deletes the information of the e-commerce requests (purchasing, selling and invoices), and changes some of its contents or prevents access to the information receiver. In order to prevent this attack, we maintain the confidentiality of the information by implementing an encryption algorithm (AES-256). In our protocol, any change in e-commerce requests will be detected by the receiver app because our protocol uses specific forms for e-commerce requests. If the attacker makes a change to the encrypted requests, upon decryption, the change will be exposed and not match the forms used.

- **Ransomware**

    An attacker compromises a website or application by injecting or analyzing to try to obtain secrets such as a credit card number, encryption keys and PW, and they use this information to demand a ransom from the targeted victims. Then, attackers can demand the ransom online payment or even set up a ransom program. If the victim does not pay or execute the ransom, the attacker either destroys the data, publishes the data, or encrypts the data in a way that the victim cannot access. In our protocol, if an attacker can access Pr_k, Pu_k and $Salt_i$ (which is impossible) on the current connection, the attacker will not benefit from these parameters because they will not be used on the next connection. That is, the attacker cannot demand ransom for the secret parameters even if he/she receives them. We use a protocol that combines encryption algorithms such as ElGamal-1024 and AES-256, which are difficult to penetrate due to their high security.

- **Sniffing**

    An unauthorized sniffer monitors, intercepts and captures all sensitive request data for the targeted network that passes through the sending and receiving processes of a certain request. The goal of this attack is to expose login credentials and financial information or to hijack a target's device by sending a packet or group of packets to the victim's device to gain access to sensitive information. In our protocol, any packet that does not use legitimate parameters such as Pu_k for the receiver device will be rejected outright. Thus, our protocol does not handle requests that use hijacking packets. Our protocol applies encryption and decryption procedures to all network devices (buying, selling and server), namely, our protocol resists these attacks.

- **Zero day**

    The attacker tries to exploit security vulnerabilities in e-commerce software or applications to use them to carry out malicious attacks on network devices and applications. In commerce institutions, an attacker tries to obtain sensitive transaction information or execute fraudulent threats. After the attacker carries out this attack, he/she tries to exploit the documents, files and information to apply his/her attack on the entire network. When detection of this attack is delayed, this can give the attacker time to apply their attack on a larger scale. If we assume that the attacker penetrates one of the network devices (buyer, seller or server device) and obtains requests for buying, selling or invoices, then he will not benefit from these files because they are all encrypted on the network devices. In addition, all security parameters are hidden (such as Pr_k) on network devices. Therefore, our protocol supports robust protection of e-commerce applications and controls zero day attacks.

Table 3. Comparison of threat resistance between cryptography protocols.

Attack	[39]	[30]	[40]	[13]	[16]	[41]	[22]	[42]	Proposed Protocol
DDoS	✓		✓		✓	✓			✓
Phishing			✓		✓	✓	✓		✓
Wiretapping	✓	✓		✓					✓
Brute force		✓			✓				✓
Distributed guessing		✓		✓		✓			✓
Credit card fraud						✓	✓		✓
Sabotage			✓						✓
Data modification	✓	✓	✓	✓	✓		✓		✓
Ransomware			✓		✓		✓		✓
Sniffing	✓				✓				✓
Zero day					✓				✓

5.2. Security Analysis Using Scyther

One automated tool for verifying security protocol is called Scyther. It has a number of intriguing characteristics, including the ability to characterize protocols and produce a finite representation of all conceivable protocol behaviors. It can also verify protocols with an infinite number of sessions and nonces. This tool is the result of research by Cremers Cas in 2006. During that time, Cremers Cas published his research related to a methodology for formal analysis and verification of encryption. It is a tool designed to analyze formal security protocols and their security requirements and was designed assuming full or unbreakable encryption. Furthermore, Scyther is used to verify security claims and to find potential attacks against authentication protocols, for instance, sales, purchases or payment operations in e-commerce. This tool analyzes the secrecy (confidentiality) and authentication property in the cryptographic protocol. Using the Scyther tool can ensure that objectivity of the formal verification of the protocol is performed by means of security analysis and proof.

Scyther description with the proposed e-commerce protocol: This tool uses security protocol description language (SPDL) and a set of roles depending on the protocol designed. Each role represents an e-commerce network entity. We wrote a set of commands to configure our network entities, which are buyer (B), seller (S) and trust authority server (TAS). These commands simulate the procedures of our methodology. Furthermore, in order to communicate between network entities, Scyther provides us with send() and recv() directives. To verify our protocol, this tool enables us to implement a set of claims and to test events to achieve security and authentication properties and to protect data and e-commerce requests. The scyther tool can be utilized to search problems that emerge from the manner the protocol is constructed. The following claims (Alive, Niagree, Nisynch, Secret and Weakagree) are checked for the elements in the exchanged requests. The process of achieving the intended communication with some events is described as "Alive". "Niagree" stands for non-injective agreement and ensures that a protocol assures a sender B non-injective agreement with a receiver TAS or S on a set of request elements. "Nisynch" stands for non-injective synchronization, which ensures that the intended sender sends all requests received by the receiver in a synchronized manner. "Secret" is used to protect secrecy parameters. "Weakagree" stands for weak agreement and ensures that a protocol guarantees to a sender B weak agreement with another entity TAS or S. If B completes a run of the protocol, apparently with receiver S, then S has previously been running the protocol, apparently with B.

Scyther test results: Here, we describe a test of the proposed e-commerce protocol by the Scyther tool. Figure 10 shows the results of testing our protocol based on the "Alive", "Niagree", "Nisynch", "Secret" and "Weakagree" claim events. The tests show that the public ($BPuK$, $TASPuK$ and $SPuK$) and private keys ($BPrK$, $TASPrK$ and $SPrK$) and buyer/seller requests (BR/SR) are secret. The figure shows that requests are securely exchanged between network entities (B, S and TAS) without any threats or attacks that compromise network entities, security parameters or e-commerce request data transmitted over the network. This analysis proves that the proposed e-commerce protocol resists the scope of attacks in this research.

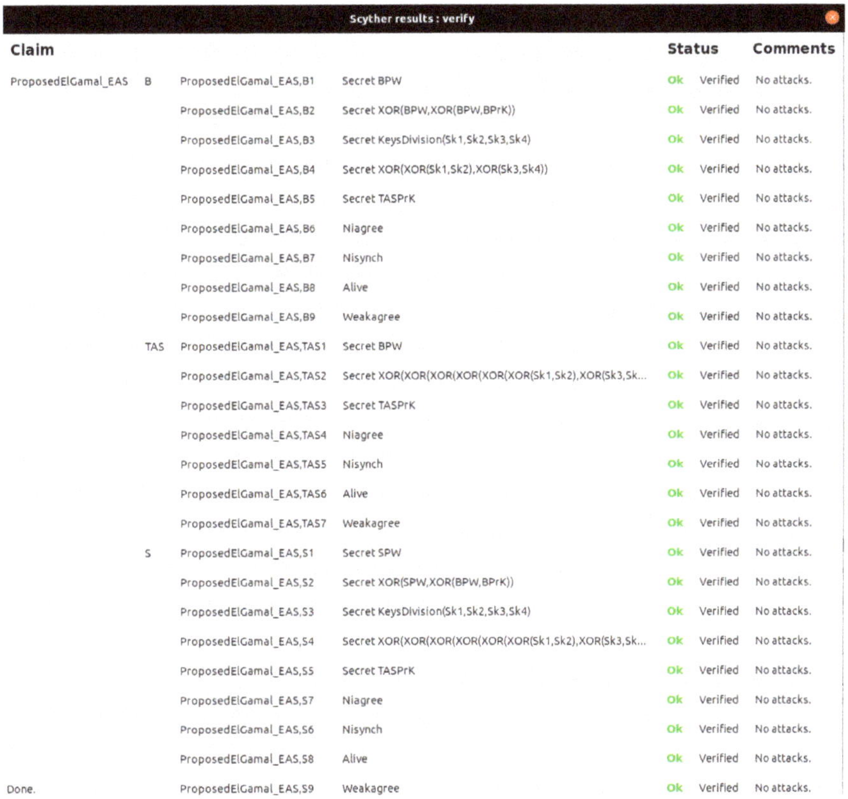

Scyther results : verify

Claim				Status		Comments
ProposedElGamal_EAS	B	ProposedElGamal_EAS,B1	Secret BPW	Ok	Verified	No attacks.
		ProposedElGamal_EAS,B2	Secret XOR(BPW,XOR(BPW,BPrK))	Ok	Verified	No attacks.
		ProposedElGamal_EAS,B3	Secret KeysDivision(Sk1,Sk2,Sk3,Sk4)	Ok	Verified	No attacks.
		ProposedElGamal_EAS,B4	Secret XOR(XOR(Sk1,Sk2),XOR(Sk3,Sk4))	Ok	Verified	No attacks.
		ProposedElGamal_EAS,B5	Secret TASPrK	Ok	Verified	No attacks.
		ProposedElGamal_EAS,B6	Niagree	Ok	Verified	No attacks.
		ProposedElGamal_EAS,B7	Nisynch	Ok	Verified	No attacks.
		ProposedElGamal_EAS,B8	Alive	Ok	Verified	No attacks.
		ProposedElGamal_EAS,B9	Weakagree	Ok	Verified	No attacks.
	TAS	ProposedElGamal_EAS,TAS1	Secret BPW	Ok	Verified	No attacks.
		ProposedElGamal_EAS,TAS2	Secret XOR(XOR(XOR(XOR(XOR(XOR(Sk1,Sk2),XOR(Sk3,Sk...	Ok	Verified	No attacks.
		ProposedElGamal_EAS,TAS3	Secret TASPrK	Ok	Verified	No attacks.
		ProposedElGamal_EAS,TAS4	Niagree	Ok	Verified	No attacks.
		ProposedElGamal_EAS,TAS5	Nisynch	Ok	Verified	No attacks.
		ProposedElGamal_EAS,TAS6	Alive	Ok	Verified	No attacks.
		ProposedElGamal_EAS,TAS7	Weakagree	Ok	Verified	No attacks.
	S	ProposedElGamal_EAS,S1	Secret SPW	Ok	Verified	No attacks.
		ProposedElGamal_EAS,S2	Secret XOR(SPW,XOR(BPW,BPrK))	Ok	Verified	No attacks.
		ProposedElGamal_EAS,S3	Secret KeysDivision(Sk1,Sk2,Sk3,Sk4)	Ok	Verified	No attacks.
		ProposedElGamal_EAS,S4	Secret XOR(XOR(XOR(XOR(XOR(XOR(Sk1,Sk2),XOR(Sk3,Sk...	Ok	Verified	No attacks.
		ProposedElGamal_EAS,S5	Secret TASPrK	Ok	Verified	No attacks.
		ProposedElGamal_EAS,S7	Niagree	Ok	Verified	No attacks.
		ProposedElGamal_EAS,S6	Nisynch	Ok	Verified	No attacks.
		ProposedElGamal_EAS,S8	Alive	Ok	Verified	No attacks.
Done.		ProposedElGamal_EAS,S9	Weakagree	Ok	Verified	No attacks.

Figure 10. Scyther security tool test of proposed e-commerce protocol.

5.3. Performance of Proposed E-Commerce Applications

To test the eligibility of the proposed protocol, this section illustrates the performance results of the algorithms and techniques used in our protocol. Our codes were implemented on a laptop with Intel ® Core ™ i5-2540M CPU @ 2.60 GHz, RAM 4 GB, operating system Ubuntu 18.04.6 LTS and OS type 64 bit. In addition, we used Java language to deal with the ElGamal, AES and CRT algorithms. Our protocol relied on ElGamal public and private keys of 1024 bit length, the AES algorithm of 256 bit keys to encrypt e-commerce requests and the CRT approach to generate fast 256 bit private keys.

At first, we implemented the encryption and decryption procedures without e-commerce requests to find the execution/running time one hundred times, as shown in Figure 11. The previous figure shows that the encryption operations in the AES-256 algorithm require more execution time than the decryption operations. Our proposed protocol uses real e-commerce files (see Figure 8) with various sizes such as an invoice file with 1.6 KB, purchasing file with 3.9 KB and selling file with 2.9 KB. Next, we performed AES-256 encryption operations on e-commerce requests (invoice, purchasing and selling) to find the execution time, as shown in Figure 12. From the aforementioned figure, purchasing request encryption requires the most execution time, and the reason for this is that the size of the purchasing files is larger (3.9 KB) than the invoice and selling files. In addition, Figure 13 shows the implementation of AES-256 decryption operations for invoice, purchasing and selling requests, where we note that invoice files require less execution time than the rest of the files because the invoice file size is 1.6 KB, which is the smallest among the rest of the files. Figures 12 and 13 show that the encryption procedures require more execution time than the decryption procedures. Furthermore, Figure 14 shows the execution time of the public and private keys of the ElGamal-1024 algorithm as well as the use of a CRT to generate the private keys. As we can see from the previous figure, the private keys need less execution time than the public keys of the ElGamal algorithm, and the CRT approach generates the private keys faster than the private keys of the ElGamal algorithm. In addition, Table 4 provides an execution time comparison of the private keys for both traditional ElGamal and ElGamal-CRT. We can see from the previous figure that ElGamal-CRT achieves less execution time than traditional ElGamal. Table 5 shows a comparison of memory consumption between public key algorithms such as traditional ElGamal, RSA and ElGamal-CRT. The table shows that the ElGamal-CRT algorithm uses less memory than RSA and traditional ElGamal. Finally, the total running time for encryption with XOR operation and keys division is 0.369143 ms, and the total running time for decryption is 0.274815 ms.

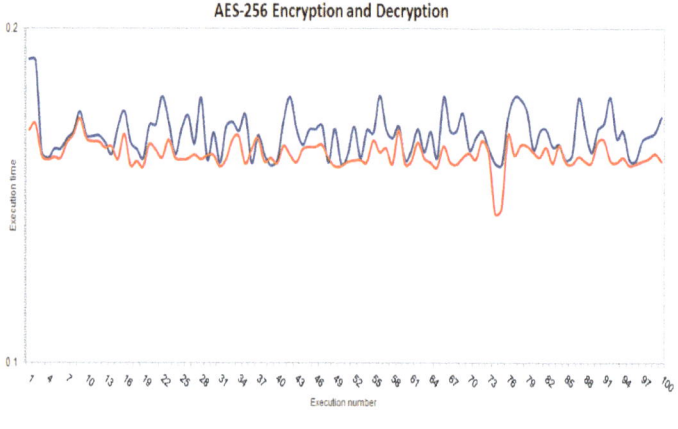

Figure 11. Running time for AES-256 encryption and decryption.

Figure 12. Running time for AES-256 file encryption (invoice, purchasing and selling).

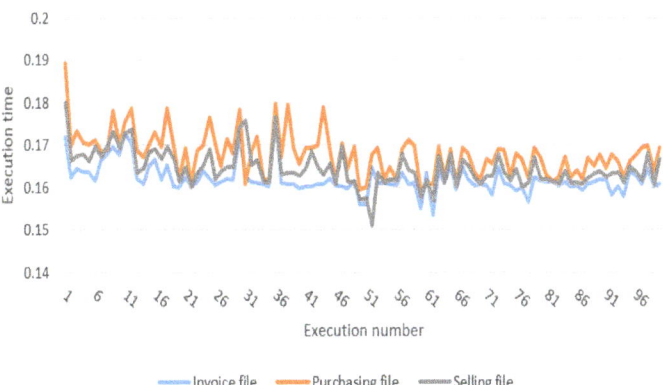

Figure 13. Running time for AES-256 file decryption (invoice, purchasing and selling).

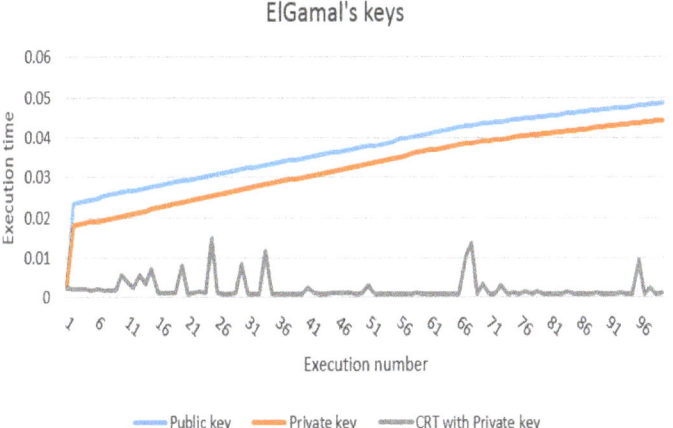

Figure 14. Running time for ElGamal keys (public, private and CRT with private key).

Table 4. Key generation comparison of traditional ElGamal and ElGamal-CRT.

Key Length	ElGamal Private Key in ms	ElGamal-CRT-Private in ms
1024	0.0181114	0.0021469
2048	0.0362228	0.0042938
3072	0.0543342	0.0064407
4096	0.0724456	0.0085876
7680	0.1358355	0.01610175
15,360	0.271671	0.0322035

Table 5. Comparison of public key algorithms in terms of memory used.

Traditional ElGamal (bits)	RSA (bits)	Proposed ElGamal-CRT (bits)
1024	1024	256
2048	2048	512
3072	3072	768
4096	4096	1024
7680	7680	1920
15,360	15,360	3840

5.3.1. Theoretical Discussion

E-commerce networks are considered huge networks due to the dependence of buyers and sellers from all over the world on the use of online transactions, which causes major problems in the consumption of hardware/software and network resources such as memory and execution time. Our protocol uses several lightweight methods that make it suitable for e-commerce applications. It relies on relatively small and random keys compared to public key algorithms (see Table 5), which lead to reduced memory usage and consumption, especially in networks that use large organizations and companies. In addition, the AES-256 encryption algorithm is fast when compared to public encryption algorithms such as elliptic curve cryptography (ECC) and RSA. In addition, our protocol relies on the CRT approach to generate small and fast keys, which greatly affects the speed of key generation, encryption and decryption. It changes the public keys every sixteen times depending on the four partitions of size 256. This means that the customer does not need to change the public key every sixteen times, which contributes to performance improvement. It eliminates the expense of generating public keys. Based on the above, the solid methodology used in designing our protocol makes it eligible for application in the e-commerce environment.

For more detail, our protocol is lightweight because, first, it uses hybrid encryption based on ElGamal-AES. It uses AES-256 bit for encryption and decryption. It is common knowledge that symmetric algorithms have high performance compared to asymmetric encryption algorithms because the latter use complex operations and generate very large keys. That is, our protocol encrypts with the AES algorithm and not with asymmetric encryption algorithms, as in some existing research that uses ECC, RSA and ElGamal. Second, symmetric encryption algorithms suffer from a major problem, which is the use of one shared key for all users. Our protocol generates keys using the ElGamal-1024 bit algorithm, taking advantage of CRT technology to speed up the process of generating private keys, and then converting these public keys into a suitable length for the AES algorithm, which is 256 bit using an XOR gate that does not require complex calculations. This means that our protocol uses an asymmetric key exchange in the algorithm and does not use a single key for all users. If one user's keys are exposed, it will not affect the rest of the users (providing solid security); at the same time, ElGamal's algorithm generates keys only every 16 times (see Algorithm 1, step 10) based on a permutation of SK_s and random addition (providing high performance). This confirms that our protocol balances performance and security.

5.3.2. Results, Comparison and Analysis

In practice, our protocol performs lighter security measures for e-commerce applications than existing protocols. Although the environments, parameters and algorithms used in our protocol are not very identical to existing protocols, we investigated finding some comparable aspects between our protocol and existing protocols. Table 6 provides a comparison of performance parameters (key lengths, encryption algorithm, key generation algorithm, key generation support techniques, and encryption type) between our protocol and existing protocols.

Hu et al. [10] relied on RSA to encrypt e-commerce requests. However, we indicated in Table 1 that ElGamal is more efficient than RSA. In addition, our protocol uses ElGamal only for generating public and private keys and not for encryption and decryption procedures. Saha et al. [11] used AES to encrypt the data with the shared key of all users. However, their scheme does not have the flexibility offered in our protocol to generate separate keys for each user. Imran et al. [30] used ElGamal for encryption and decryption in their scheme. This means that encryption of any data request will require a lot of execution time, especially in large networks such as e-commerce. In comparison with our protocol, it only uses ElGamal to generate public and private keys, and the encryption and decryption process is only performed by the AES-256 algorithm, which is fast and efficient. Yousif et al. [13] also used the ElGamal algorithm with a scanning technique to encrypt the data. In terms of performance, their proposal does not concern memory overheads and key sizes since traditional ElGamal uses 1024, 2048 keys, etc. When the number of data encryption requests is large, it will affect the memory size. Fortunately, our protocol generates ElGamal random keys and converts them into small sizes of length 256, which are suitable for encryption in AES and e-commerce environments. Ali et al. [15] utilized several built-in methods such as PBKDF2, RNG and slave key to generate shared keys. However, their protocol is complex and increases implementation running time costs. In addition, the key remains shared between the source and the target, while our protocol uses a CRT-only approach to improve private key generation performance. Although Mohd and Ashawesh [16] indicated that they improved the performance of AES by reducing the number of rounds, the execution time for encryption and decryption is 15 s, which is very large compared to our protocol, as the execution time for encryption is 0.369143 ms, and for decryption, it is 0.274815 ms (taking into account the different environments, such as the different processor speeds).

Table 6. Comparison of performance parameters between our protocol and existing protocols.

Protocol	Keys Length	Encryption Algorithm	Key Generation Algorithm	Key Support Technique	Encryption Type
Hu et al. [10]	512/1024/2048	RSA	RSA	-	Asymmetric
Saha et al. [11]	256	EAS	AES	SRFG	Symmetric
Imran et al. [30]	1024	ElGamal	ElGamal	-	Asymmetric
Yousif et al. [13]	1024	ElGamal	ElGamal	Scanning	Asymmetric
Ali et al. [15]	256	EAS	RNG	PBKDF2	Symmetric
Mohd and Ashawesh [16]	256	EAS	AES	-	Symmetric
Our protocol	256	EAS	ElGamal	CRT	Symmetric and Asymmetric

6. Conclusions

Providing security requirements for electronic commerce transactions, such as buying and selling transactions or payment operations, as well as the customer and server information are sensitive and personal, and this information requires high security. In this study, we designed a protocol that enhances security and that is difficult to penetrate from various attacks as well as that supports high performance. The proposed e-commerce applications have been designed to use asymmetric encryption algorithms such as ElGamal generation random incremental keys and symmetric algorithms such as AES 256 in encryption and decryption operations. After security (attack analysis and Scyther results) and performance (Tables 4–6) analyses, we conclude that our protocol provides secure and strong procedures with high performance.

7. Future Works

For future directions, we will improve on server encryption because the server encryption and decryption processes are many times greater than on the buyer's device. In addition, we plan to use an attack detection method that will help to improve network performance significantly. Furthermore, one of the future contributions that we would like to improve in our protocol is to focus on the merchant's requests from suppliers and companies, because when the merchant buys a large commodity, it costs him/her a lot of money, as any breach of the merchant's information in e-commerce will cause a great loss compared to the regular customer, which can even affect the country's economy. Moreover, we plan to study post-quantum cryptography (PQC) to support the security of our protocol. Finally, to broaden the scope of analysis, we aspire to analyze more attacks such as fault and side-channel attacks on our protocol in addition to the attacks analyzed in this research.

Author Contributions: All authors provided contributions to the work. Conceptualization, G.S.S. and M.A.-Z.; methodology, G.S.S. and M.A.-Z.; software, G.S.S. and M.A.-Z.; validation, G.S.S. and M.A.-Z.; formal analysis, M.A.-Z.; investigation, G.S.S. and M.A.-Z.; writing—original draft preparation, G.S.S. and M.A.-Z.; writing—review and editing, M.A.-Z.; supervision, M.A.-Z.; project administration, M.A.-Z. All authors have read and agreed to the published version of the manuscript.

Funding: This research received no external funding.

Conflicts of Interest: The authors declare no conflict of interest.

Abbreviations

In this research, the following acronyms are utilized:

AES	Advanced encryption standard
B	Buyer
CRT	Chinese remainder theorem
E-commerce	Electronic commerce
Pr_k	Private key
Pu_k	Public key
RSA	Rivest, Shamir, and Adleman
S	Seller
Sk_s	Subkeys
TAS	Trust authority server

References

1. Florea, N.; Ionescu, C.; Duică, M.; ăpusneanu, S.; Paschia, L.; Stanescu, S.D.; Coman, M. Trends and perspectives of Romanian e-commerce sector based on mathematical simulation. *Electronics* **2022**, *11*, 2295. [CrossRef]
2. Liu, X.; Ahmad, S.; Anser, M.; Ke, J.; Irshad, M.; Ul-Haq, J.; Abbas, S. Cyber security threats: A never-ending challenge for e-commerce. *Front. Psychol.* **2022**, *13*, 4863.
3. Cebeci, S.; Nari, K.; Ozdemir, E. Secure e-commerce scheme. *IEEE Access* **2022**, *10*, 10359–10370.
4. Muhajjar, R.; Flayh, N.; Al-Zubaidie, M. A perfect security key management method for hierarchical wireless sensor networks in medical environments. *Electronics* **2023**, *12*, 1011. [CrossRef]
5. Al-Zubaidie, M.; Zhang, Z.; Zhang, J. Efficient and secure ECDSA algorithm and its applications: A survey. *Int. J. Commun. Netw. Inf. Secur. (IJCNIS)* **2019**, *11*, 7–35. [CrossRef]
6. Al-Zubaidie, M.; Zhang, Z.; Zhang, J. RAMHU: A new robust lightweight scheme for mutual users authentication in healthcare applications. *Secur. Commun. Netw.* **2019**, *2019*, 3263902. [CrossRef]
7. Jahnavi, P.; Kumar, B. Survey paper on the various security algorithms used for e-commerce security. *EPRA Int. J. Res. Dev. (IJRD)* **2021**, *6*, 39–46.
8. WEBSCALE. The Global Ecommerce Securityreport 2022. 2022. Available online: https://www.webscale.com/global-ecommerce-security-report-2022/ (accessed on 18 March 2023).
9. Imperva. The State of Security within Ecommerce in 2022. 2022. Available online: https://www.imperva.com/resources/reports/The-State-of-Security-Within-eCommerce-in-2022_report.pdf (accessed on 19 March 2023).
10. Hu, J.; Hoang, X.; Khalil, I. An embedded DSP hardware encryption module for secure e-commerce transactions. *Secur. Commun. Netw.* **2011**, *4*, 902–909. [CrossRef]
11. Saha, R.; Geetha, G.; Kumar, G.; Kim, T. RK-AES: An improved version of AES using a new key generation process with random keys. *Secur. Commun. Netw.* **2018**, *2018*, 9802475. [CrossRef]
12. Logunleko, K.; Adeniji, O.; Logunleko, A. A comparative study of symmetric cryptography mechanism on DES AES and EB64 for information security. *Int. J. Sci. Res. Comput. Sci. Eng.* **2020**, *8*, 45–51.
13. Yousif, S.; Abboud, A.; Radhi, H. Robust image encryption with scanning technology, the El-Gamal algorithm and chaos theory. *IEEE Access* **2020**, *8*, 155184–155209. [CrossRef]
14. Laz, M.; Grégoire, B.; Rezk, T. Security analysis of ElGamal implementations. In Proceedings of the SECRYPT 2020-17th International Conference on Security and Cryptography, Lieusant, Paris, 8–10 July 2020; pp. 310–321.
15. Ali, H.; Jawad, T.; Zuhair, H. Data security using random dynamic salting and AES based on master-slave keys for Iraqi dam management system. *Indones. J. Electr. Eng. Comput. Sci.* **2021**, *23*, 1018–1029. [CrossRef]
16. Mohd, N.; Ashawesh, A. Enhanced AES algorithm based on 14 rounds in securing data and minimizing processing time. *J. Phys. Conf. Ser.* **2021**, *1793*, 012066. [CrossRef]
17. Kumar, T.; Reddy, K.; Rinaldi, S.; Parameshachari, B.; Arunachalam, K. A low area high speed FPGA implementation of AES architecture for cryptography application. *Electronics* **2021**, *10*, 2023. [CrossRef]
18. Al-Zubaidie, M. Implication of lightweight and robust hash function to support key exchange in health sensor networks. *Symmetry* **2023**, *15*, 152. [CrossRef]
19. Riadi, A.; Furqan, M.; Kurniawan, R. Document based text data security using the prime generator algorithm fermat's and the ElGamal algorithm. *INFOKUM* **2021**, *10*, 810–817.
20. Parenreng, J.; Maulida, S.; Wahid, A. The E-mail security system using El-Gamal hybrid algorithm and AES (advanced encryption standard) algorithm. *Internet Things Artif. Intell. J.* **2022**, *2*, 1–9. [CrossRef]
21. Dinata, D.; Mayasari, N.; Hardinata, R. Keeping file authenticity with digital signature technique using a combination of MD5 and ElGamal algorithm. *INFOKUM* **2022**, *10*, 350–356.

22. Anshori, M.; Karya, D.; Gita, M. A study on the reuseIntention of e-commerce platform applications: Security, privacy, perceived value, and trust. *J. Manaj. Teor. Dan Ter. J. Theory Appl. Manag.* **2022**, *15*, 13–24.
23. Chaimaa, B.; Najib, E.; Rachid, H. E-banking overview: Concepts, challenges and solutions. *Wirel. Pers. Commun.* **2021**, *117*, 1059–1078. [CrossRef]
24. Kim, S.-I.; Kim, S.-H. E-commerce payment model using blockchain. *J. Ambient. Intell. Humaniz. Comput.* **2020**, *13*, 1673–1685. [CrossRef]
25. Deng, J.; Lin, J.; Hu, J.; Qian, J. A multi-party secure e-commerce voting scheme based on SDGHV algorithm. *J. Phys. Conf. Ser.* **2021**, *1827*, 012195. [CrossRef]
26. Suharto, S.; Junaedi, I.; Muhdar, H.; Firmansyah, A.; Sarana, S. Consumer loyalty of indonesia e-commerce smes: The role of social media marketing and customer satisfaction. *Int. J. Data Netw. Sci.* **2022**, *6*, 383–390. [CrossRef]
27. Al-Zubaidie, M.; Zhang, Z.; Zhang, J. PAX: Using pseudonymization and anonymization to protect patients' identities and data in the healthcare system. *Int. J. Environ. Res. Public Health* **2019**, *16*, 1490. [CrossRef]
28. Al-Zubaidie, M.; Zhang, Z.; Zhang, J. REISCH: Incorporating lightweight and reliable algorithms into healthcare applications of WSNs. *Appl. Sci.* **2020**, *10*, 2007. [CrossRef]
29. Guruprakash, J.; Koppu, S. EC-ElGamal and genetic algorithm-based enhancement for lightweight scalable blockchain in IoT domain. *IEEE Access* **2020**, *8*, 141269–141281. [CrossRef]
30. Imran, O.; Yousif, S.; Hameed, I.; Abed, W.; Hammid, A. Implementation of El-Gamal algorithm for speech signals encryption and decryption. *Procedia Comput. Sci.* **2020**, *167*, 1028–1037. [CrossRef]
31. Wan, P.; Liao, T.; Yan, J.; Tsai, H. Discrete sliding mode control for chaos synchronization and its application to an improved El-Gamal cryptosystem. *Symmetry* **2019**, *11*, 843. [CrossRef]
32. Zodpe, H.; Sapkal, A. An efficient AES implementation using FPGA with enhanced security features. *J. King Saud-Univ.-Eng. Sci.* **2020**, *32*, 115–122. [CrossRef]
33. Arab, A.; Rostami, M.; Ghavami, B. An image encryption method based on chaos system and AES algorithm. *J. Supercomput.* **2019**, *75*, 6663–6682. [CrossRef]
34. Yang, C.; Chien, Y. FPGA implementation and design of a hybrid chaos-AES color image encryption algorithm. *Symmetry* **2020**, *12*, 189. [CrossRef]
35. Hidayat, A.; Arifudin, R.; Akhlis, I. Implementation of RSA and RSA-CRT algorithms for comparison of encryption and decryption time in android-based instant message applications. *J. Adv. Inf. Syst. Technol.* **2020**, *2*, 1–10. [CrossRef]
36. Selianinau, M. Efficient implementation of Chinese remainder theorem in minimally redundant residue number system. *Comput. Sci.* **2020**, *21*. [CrossRef]
37. Selianinau, M.; Povstenko, Y. An efficient CRT-base power-of-two scaling in minimally redundant residue number system. *Entropy* **2022**, *24*, 1824. [CrossRef] [PubMed]
38. 123FormBuilder. E-Commerce Forms. 2023. Available online: https://www.123formbuilder.com/free-form-templates/gallery-ecommerce/ (accessed on 14 April 2023).
39. Fang, W.; Xu, M.; Zhu, C.; Han, W.; Zhang, W.; Rodrigues, J. FETMS: Fast and efficient trust management scheme for information-centric networking in internet of things. *IEEE Access* **2019**, *7*, 13476–13485. [CrossRef]
40. Noor, U.; Anwar, Z.; Altmann, J.; Rashid, Z. Customer-oriented ranking of cyber threat intelligence service providers. *Electron. Commer. Res. Appl.* **2020**, *41*, 100976. [CrossRef]
41. Kumar, V.; Sinha, D. A robust intelligent zero-day cyber-attack detection technique. *Complex Intell. Syst.* **2021**, *7*, 2211–2234. [CrossRef] [PubMed]
42. Mitra, D.; Kulkarni, P.; Pathak, P.; Natrai, N. Importance of coping with cyber security challenges in e commerce business. In Proceedings of the 2022 International Interdisciplinary Humanitarian Conference for Sustainability (IIHC), Bengaluru, India, 18–19 November 2022; pp. 1596–1601.

Disclaimer/Publisher's Note: The statements, opinions and data contained in all publications are solely those of the individual author(s) and contributor(s) and not of MDPI and/or the editor(s). MDPI and/or the editor(s) disclaim responsibility for any injury to people or property resulting from any ideas, methods, instructions or products referred to in the content.

Systematic Review

A Systematic Literature Review of Information Security in Chatbots

Jing Yang [1], Yen-Lin Chen [2,*], Lip Yee Por [1,*] and Chin Soon Ku [3,*]

1. Department of Computer System and Technology, Faculty of Computer Science and Information Technology, Universiti Malaya, Kuala Lumpur 50603, Malaysia
2. Department of Computer Science and Information Engineering, National Taipei University of Technology, Taipei 106344, Taiwan
3. Department of Computer Science, Universiti Tunku Abdul Rahman, Kampar 31900, Malaysia
* Correspondence: ylchen@mail.ntut.edu.tw (Y.-L.C.); porlip@um.edu.my (L.Y.P.); kucs@utar.edu.my (C.S.K.)

Abstract: Chatbots have become increasingly popular in recent years, but they also present security risks and vulnerabilities that need to be addressed. This systematic literature review examines the existing research relating to information security in chatbots, identifying the potential threats, proposed solutions, and future directions for research. The review finds that chatbots face various security threats, including malicious input, user profiling, contextual attacks, and data breaches, and that solutions such as blockchain technology, end-to-end encryption, and organizational controls can be used to mitigate these concerns. The review also highlights the importance of maintaining user trust and addressing privacy concerns for the successful adoption and continued use of chatbots. A taxonomy developed in this review provides a useful framework for categorizing the articles and their findings. The review concludes by identifying future research directions that include developing more sophisticated authentication and authorization mechanisms, exploring the use of privacy-enhancing technologies, and improving the detection and prevention of security threats, among others. This review contributes to the growing body of literature on information security in chatbots and can guide future research and practice in this field.

Keywords: chatbot; information security; systematic literature review (SLR); ChatGPT; security

Citation: Yang, J.; Chen, Y.-L.; Por, L.Y.; Ku, C.S. A Systematic Literature Review of Information Security in Chatbots. *Appl. Sci.* **2023**, *13*, 6355. https://doi.org/10.3390/app13116355

Academic Editor: Luis Javier García Villalba

Received: 6 March 2023
Revised: 17 April 2023
Accepted: 20 April 2023
Published: 23 May 2023

Copyright: © 2023 by the authors. Licensee MDPI, Basel, Switzerland. This article is an open access article distributed under the terms and conditions of the Creative Commons Attribution (CC BY) license (https://creativecommons.org/licenses/by/4.0/).

1. Introduction

Chatbots are also known as conversational agents [1]. They are computer programs designed to simulate human conversation through artificial intelligence, natural language processing, and machine learning technologies [2]. The rise of chatbots has brought new levels of convenience and efficiency to a wide range of industries and applications, from e-commerce and healthcare to finance and education. However, as these systems become more ubiquitous, they also become more vulnerable to a range of security threats and attacks, raising concerns about the safety and privacy of users' sensitive data [3].

Recently, information security has actually received increasing attention [4,5]. One of the major challenges of information security in chatbots is the protection of users' sensitive data [6–11]. As chatbots become more widely used across various industries and applications, the amount of personal information being shared through them is increasing, including financial data, health information, and personally identifiable information. This makes them an attractive target for cybercriminals, who may try to exploit vulnerabilities in chatbots to gain unauthorized access to user data.

For example, if a healthcare chatbot is compromised, an attacker may gain access to sensitive patient data such as medical histories, prescriptions, and other personal information. Similarly, if a finance chatbot is breached [12,13], an attacker may gain access to users' financial data, such as credit card numbers, bank account details, and transaction histories.Another important aspect of information security in chatbots is the need to maintain user trust and confidence in these systems [6–9,14–18]. Users must feel confident that their personal information is secure and protected when using chatbots. A security breach or data leak can erode user trust, which can have significant consequences for businesses and organizations that use chatbots to provide services and support.

For example, the companies set hidden rules in the website's terms and conditions and disclaimers to get user consent to use their data. In this case, the companies can store personal data legally. However, the user might not be aware that their data is disclosed to third parties [19,20].

In addition, an aspect to take into special consideration for user trust is that older adults seem to differ from younger adults when choosing a chatbot for customer service versus connecting to a live agent [21,22]. Older adults may still value the human touch more, which would mean that relying on chatbot communication solely or predominantly can alienate older consumers, whereas they constitute such a large share of the population [23].

In terms of research challenges, one of the major challenges is the evolving nature of security threats and vulnerabilities [6–10,16]. As chatbots become more intelligent and capable, new types of attacks may emerge that exploit previously unknown vulnerabilities. This requires ongoing research and development to identify and mitigate emerging threats. For example, GPT-4 (which surpasses ChatGPT) was trained on Microsoft Azure AI supercomputers. It uses a deep learning approach that leverages more data and more computation to create increasingly sophisticated and capable language models [24]. It needs to be trained on large datasets of respective domain information (such as patient information and user conversation information) to predict outcomes [25]. However, a chatbot cannot train on encrypted data. Therefore, there is a risk of the disclosure of data to third parties when decrypting data for training purposes.

Additionally, the development of secure chatbots requires a multidisciplinary approach that encompasses not only technical security measures but also user trust, privacy, and ethical considerations [6–9,14–17]. Developers must consider the potential impact of chatbots on society and ensure that chatbots are designed and deployed in an ethical and responsible manner [26]. This can be a challenging task that requires collaboration between security experts, developers, policymakers, and users.

Furthermore, the diversity of chatbot contexts and scenarios presents unique security challenges that require tailored solutions. For example, a chatbot used in healthcare may require different security measures than one used in finance or e-commerce [27–29]. This requires a nuanced approach to security that takes into account the specific needs and requirements of each use case.Overall, the importance of information security for chatbots cannot be overstated. The protection of user data and the maintenance of user trust are critical factors in the success and widespread adoption of chatbots. To address these challenges, we conducted a systematic literature review to identify and analyze studies focused on the security of chatbots. The goal of this review was to provide a comprehensive analysis of the major security threats and vulnerabilities faced by chatbots and to highlight the strategies and technologies that can be used to mitigate these risks.

2. Method

Figure 1 shows the literature review methodology used in this study. To ensure a comprehensive and transparent review of the literature, we followed the Preferred Reporting Items for Systematic Reviews and Meta-Analyses (PRISMA) guidance in conducting this systematic literature review on chatbots and security.

The PRISMA methodology is a widely recognized and accepted approach for conducting systematic literature reviews (SLRs) [30]. It provides a transparent and reproducible framework for conducting literature searches, screening and selecting relevant articles, and synthesizing the findings.

In the context of a SLR focused on security threats and vulnerabilities in chatbots, the PRISMA methodology was considered an appropriate approach as it helps to ensure a comprehensive and systematic search of the literature and a rigorous process for screening and selecting relevant articles. Additionally, the PRISMA methodology includes a detailed reporting checklist, which can help ensure that the review is reported in a clear and transparent manner.

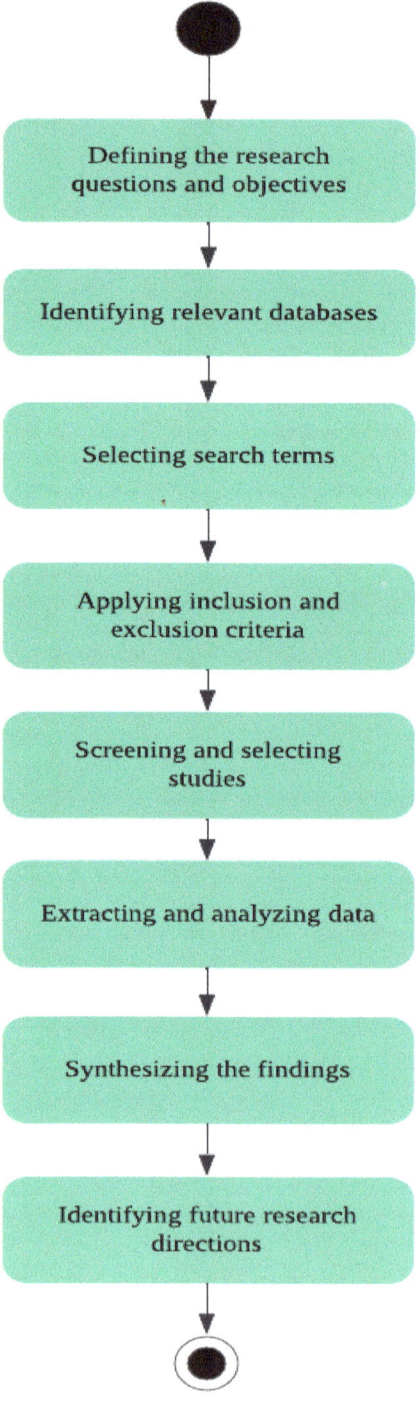

Figure 1. Literature review methodology.

Other approaches to conducting SLRs, such as the Cochrane methodology [31], may also be appropriate for certain research questions or topics. However, in the case of this specific SLR, we may have found that the PRISMA methodology was the most suitable based on its emphasis on transparency and reproducibility.

There are 8 sequential steps involved the literature review methodology, and they are as follows:

Step 1. Defining the research questions and objectives: The research questions and objectives were defined to guide the search and analysis of the literature. The research questions and objectives are as follows:

Research Questions:

1. What are the major security threats and vulnerabilities faced by chatbots?
2. What strategies and technologies can be used to mitigate these risks?

Objectives:

1. To provide a comprehensive analysis of the major security threats and vulnerabilities faced by chatbots.
2. To highlight the strategies and technologies that can be used to mitigate these risks.

We believe that the findings of this literature review can guide future research and practice in the field of information security in chatbots.

Step 2: Identifying relevant databases: Several databases, including the ACM Digital Library, IEEE Xplore, ScienceDirect, and Web of Science, were selected to ensure a comprehensive search of the literature.

Step 3. Selecting search terms: The search terms were selected based on the research questions and objectives. The chosen search terms were "chatbot" OR "ChatGPT" AND "security" OR "information security".

Step 4. Applying inclusion and exclusion criteria:

Inclusion Criteria:

We included peer-reviewed research articles that focused specifically on the security of chatbots and were published between 2016 and 2023. Additionally, we only considered studies that were available in full-text format and published in English.

Exclusion Criteria:

We excluded studies not relating to the security of chatbots, such as those that focused on the development, technology, and applications of chatbots, natural language processing, or user experience. Only peer-reviewed research articles were considered for inclusion in this review.

Step 5. Screening and selecting studies: The selected studies were screened based on their relevance to the research questions and objectives. Full-text articles were then reviewed, and studies that did not meet the inclusion criteria or were not relevant to the research questions were excluded.

Step 6. Extracting and analyzing data: Relevant data, such as the research methods used, the types of chatbots examined, and the specific security issues addressed, were extracted from the selected studies. The extracted data were then analyzed to identify common themes, patterns, and gaps in the literature.

Step 7. Synthesizing the findings: The synthesized findings were presented in a narrative format, with tables and figures used to provide visual representations of the data.

Step 8. Identifying future research directions: Based on the analysis of the literature, future research directions were identified and presented in the conclusion section of the paper.

3. Result

Figure 2 shows the PRISMA flow diagram [30] for a systematic review of the security aspects of chatbots. There are three phases involved (identification, screening, and eligibility phases). During the initial identification phase, we retrieved 1193 articles from the electronic database search. After removing duplicates, 179 articles remained. The screening phase involved reviewing the titles and abstracts of the articles, resulting in the exclusion of 62 articles. During the eligibility phase, full-text screening was conducted on the remaining 19 articles, and 10 articles were excluded for not meeting the inclusion criteria.

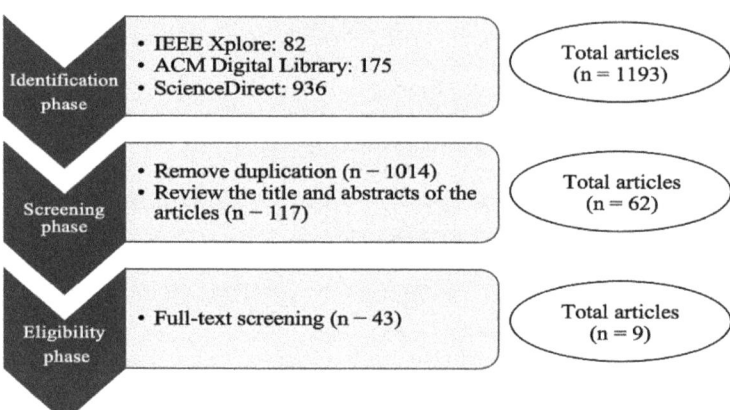

Figure 2. PRISMA flow diagram [30] for systematic review of security aspects of chatbots.

The nine articles that met the inclusion criteria were analyzed and synthesized to provide an overview of the major security threats and vulnerabilities associated with chatbots and the approaches that have been proposed to address them. The following presents the results of our systematic literature review.

Figure 3 shows the articles and their corresponding fields relating to information security. From the systematic literature review, we have identified several articles related to security threats and vulnerabilities in chatbots. Specifically, five articles [6–8,10,16] were found to be related to security threats and vulnerabilities in chatbots. These articles discussed potential attacks that could compromise the security of chatbots, such as malicious input, user profiling, contextual attacks, and data breaches. The articles emphasized the importance of developers being aware of these potential vulnerabilities and taking measures to secure their systems against attacks.

The review also identified seven articles [6–10,14,16] relating to approaches proposed to address chatbot security threats and vulnerabilities. These articles proposed various solutions to mitigate security concerns relating to chatbots, such as the use of blockchain technology, the implementation of end-to-end encryption, and the provision of organizational, managerial, and technical controls in the service level agreement.

The review identified one article [17] relating to determinants of continuance intention in the domain of AI assistants with a focus on information security. This article emphasized the importance of maintaining user trust and addressing privacy concerns in order to ensure the successful adoption and continued use of AI assistants.

Additionally, one article [14] discussed the importance of raising cyber threat awareness and improving the cyber security of companies. It proposed an AI-based conversational bot that acts as a personal assistant to enhance cyber threat awareness and deliver the latest information and training to the employees of a company.

Article [15] discussed security risks and ethical problems relating to information security in chatbot implementation. It emphasized that human behavior provides neural networks with examples of both appropriate and inappropriate behavior and proposed a mechanism for detecting socio-cultural and information security threats by monitoring the interests and motivations of users, specialists, and programmers.

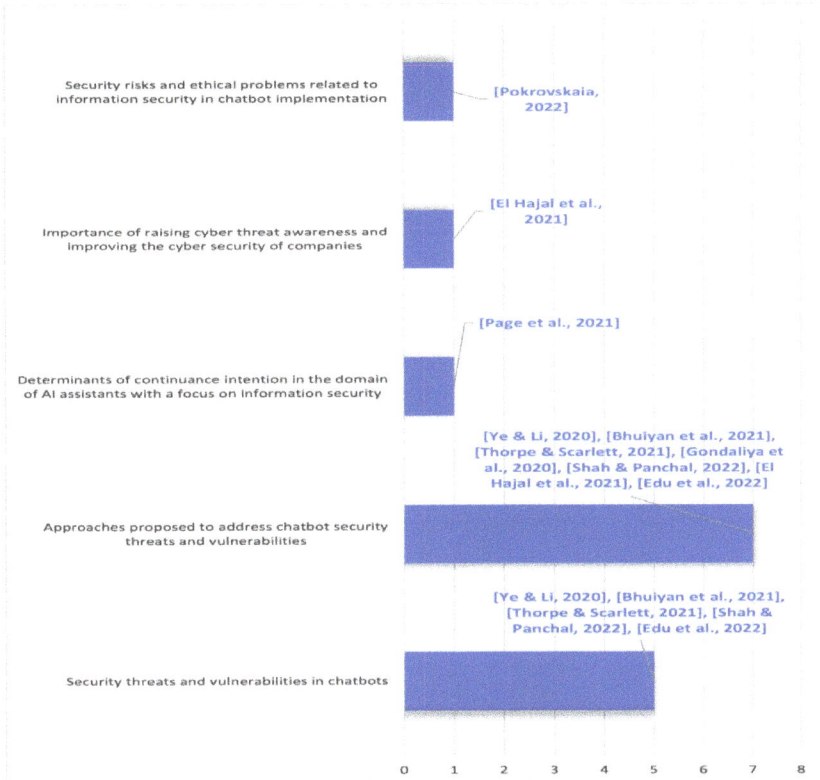

Figure 3. Articles and their corresponding fields relating to information security [6–10,14–16,30].

Table 1 shows the finding and their related articles. Article [6] focuses on the security and privacy vulnerabilities in the chatbot. The article highlights the potential vulnerabilities that could compromise the security of the system and the privacy of the user. These include malicious input, user profiling, contextual attacks, and data breaches. Attackers could insert malicious input into the chatbot, such as SQL injection or cross-site scripting, to exploit vulnerabilities in the system. Chatbots could collect sensitive information about the user, such as personal data or behavioral patterns, which could be exploited by attackers for identity theft or targeted attacks. Attackers could exploit the context of the conversation to manipulate the user or the chatbot, for example, by impersonating the chatbot or deceiving the user into revealing sensitive information. Chatbots could be vulnerable to data breaches, where the user data or chatbot data are exposed to unauthorized parties. The article suggests that developers should be aware of these potential vulnerabilities and take measures to secure their systems against attacks. Despite the great potential of chatbots for many applications, it is important to address these vulnerabilities to ensure the security and privacy of users.

Article [7] discusses some of the vulnerabilities identified in chatbots, which include insecure authentication, data integrity issues, system availability, transparency, and privacy concerns. These vulnerabilities can potentially be exploited by attackers to compromise the security of a chatbot, gain unauthorized access to sensitive information, or disrupt the chatbot's operations. The paper proposes the use of blockchain technology to mitigate some of these security concerns in financial chatbots. However, chatbot vulnerabilities may vary depending on the specific implementation and context, and other studies may identify additional or different types of vulnerabilities.

Table 1. Finding and their related articles.

Findings	Related Articles
Chatbot vulnerabilities exist in various modules	[6,7]
Chatbots can collect sensitive information	[6]
Attackers can exploit the context of the conversation	[6]
Chatbots could be vulnerable to data breaches	[6]
The use of end-to-end encryption in chatbots enhances security	[10]
Trust and concerns about the surroundings are major determinants of continuance intention in using AI assistants	[17]
A comprehensive security analysis of chatbots is important	[6–9,16]
Raising cyber threat awareness among employees is important	[14]
Machine learning procedures can ensure etiquette and data protection	[15]
Static and dynamic analysis can assess security and privacy issues in messaging platform chatbots	[16]

The vulnerabilities in chatbots are not explicitly discussed in article [8]. The paper proposes a design and framework for a cyber-aware chatbot service that detects and helps prevent malware behavior from spreading on the user's machine. The malicious behavior modeled in the paper is based on the vulnerabilities observed within the Open Web Application Security Project (OWASP) top ten, which outlines the security vulnerabilities of the Web. However, the paper does not discuss vulnerabilities specific to chatbots.

Article [9] highlights the potential risks associated with chatbots, including risks relating to the confidentiality and integrity of user data, the reliability of chatbot responses, and risks relating to the service level agreement (SLA) provided by chatbot providers. The proposed checklist provides security managers with a tool to assess these risks prior to chatbot implementation. The paper also proposes a set of controls that can be provisioned in the SLA to manage these risks, such as organizational, managerial, and technical controls, and provides examples of how these controls can address specific risk factors, such as DDoS attacks on third-party infrastructure. The proposed analysis allows customers to be informed about the risks associated with the service before signing an SLA with a chatbot provider.

Article [10] highlights the security issues in chatbots, which could provide opportunities for information flowing through the chatbot interface to be accessed by cybercriminals or hackers. As a result, the authors propose a solution to make chatbots secure by utilizing authentication (session) timeouts in combination with encryption mechanisms, such as the Double Ratchet algorithm modified with Paillier Cryptosystems. The use of end-to-end encryption in the proposed chatbot ensures that only the intended recipients can decrypt messages, thus protecting an organization's valuable data. The primary goal of a secure educational chatbot is to protect students' data from cyber-criminals, hackers, or attackers, so the conversation is entirely secure using end-to-end encryption (E2EE), thus maintaining data privacy, confidentiality, integrity, and authentication.

Article [14] discusses the importance of raising cyber threat awareness and improving the cyber security of companies by focusing on the weakest link—the human factor layer. The paper proposes an AI-based conversational bot that acts as a personal assistant to enhance cyber threat awareness and deliver the latest information and training to the employees of a company. The bot is designed to communicate with the user through WhatsApp and is capable of maintaining records of each employee, evaluating their progress, and proposing training to reduce weaknesses. The implementation of this bot has shown great impact on the employees, and the bot is able to update its database of any security breach and suggest ways to behave in case of an attack. However, the paper also highlights that cyber security is a constantly evolving field, and there is a need to add new features to the bot to keep up with the latest threats. The paper suggests adding a feature to verify the application of procedures and to inform the IT team immediately in case of a fatal attack. The addition of a voice generation alternative is also proposed to keep the employee focused, and the linkage of the bot to the most up-to-date security webpage and databases is suggested to inform employees and the IT department about new threats.

Article [15] discusses the security risks and ethical problems relating to information security in chatbot implementation. It emphasizes that human behavior provides neural networks with examples of both appropriate and inappropriate behavior, and it proposes a mechanism for detecting socio-cultural and information security threats by monitoring interests and motivations of users, specialists, and programmers. The article identifies key approaches to ensuring etiquette and data protection and proposes procedures for machine learning in relation to chatbots in corporate ecosystems. The article suggests that the society members should conceive a system of cultural transmission, transfer of knowledge, and civic education to foster the clear identity of a national society, and a regional or professional community.

Article [16] discusses the security and privacy issues that arise from the use of chatbots in messaging platforms. It highlights the potential risk that chatbots pose to users, as they could steal information from channels without the victim's awareness. The paper proposes a methodology that incorporates static and dynamic analysis for automatically assessing security and privacy issues in messaging platform chatbots. The research focused on the popular Discord platform and found that 55% of chatbots from a leading Discord repository request the "administrator" permission, which could be a security risk. Additionally, only 4.35% of chatbots with permissions actually provide a privacy policy. These findings suggest that there are significant security and privacy concerns associated with the use of chatbots in messaging platforms that need to be addressed to protect users.

Article [17] investigated the determinants of continuance intention in the domain of AI assistants, with a focus on information security. The results revealed that trust and privacy concerns regarding the surroundings are major antecedents of continuance intention. This suggests that users consider the security of their personal information when using AI assistants and that maintaining trust and privacy are essential factors for the successful adoption and continued use of these technologies.

As a summary, the articles reviewed address various types of chatbots and security threats, including malicious chatbots, unsecured communication channels, authentication and authorization, data privacy, and social engineering. The studies also proposed various approaches to address these threats, such as utilizing end-to-end encryption, incorporating static and dynamic analysis, and implementing organizational, managerial, and technical controls. The determinants of continuance intention in the domain of AI assistants were also explored, with a focus on information security.

Table 2 summarizes the research methods used, types of chatbots examined, specific security issues addressed, and related articles for nine studies relating to chatbot security. The studies employed various research methods, including case studies, surveys, and experimental studies, and examined different types of chatbots, such as financial chatbots, educational chatbots, and messaging platform chatbots. The specific security issues addressed in the studies include malicious chatbots, unsecured communication channels, authentication and authorization, data privacy, social engineering, and user trust and privacy concerns. The related articles provide further insights into the importance of maintaining user trust, addressing privacy concerns, and improving cyber threat awareness and security. Overall, the table provides a comprehensive overview of the major security threats and vulnerabilities associated with chatbots and the approaches proposed to address them.

Table 2. Overview of research methods, chatbot types, and security issues addressed in the chatbot security literature review.

Study	Research Methods	Chatbot Types	Specific Security Issues Addressed
[6]	Comprehensive analysis	N/A	Malicious input, user profiling, contextual attacks, and data breaches
[7]	Analysis and proposal	Financial chatbots	Insecure authentication, data integrity, system availability, transparency, and privacy concerns
[8]	Proposal and modeling	Malware-detecting chatbots	Open Web Application Security Project (OWASP) top ten vulnerabilities
[9]	Proposal and case studies	N/A	Confidentiality and integrity of user data, reliability of chatbot responses, and risks relating to SLA
[10]	Proposal and testing	Educational chatbots	Information exposure, data privacy, confidentiality, integrity, and authentication
[14]	Proposal and implementation	Conversational bot	Cyber threat awareness, employee training, and security breach verification
[15]	Proposal and case studies	Corporate chatbots	Socio-cultural and information security threats, and machine learning procedures
[16]	Proposal and testing	Messaging platform chatbots	User information theft, administrator permission requests, and privacy policy provision
[17]	Survey and analysis	AI assistants	Trust and privacy concerns

Note: N/A means the study did not focus on a specific type of chatbot.

4. Taxonomy

Table 3 summarizes the common themes and patterns identified across the literature on chatbot security. The literature highlights the importance of identifying security threats and vulnerabilities in chatbots and implementing approaches to address them. There is also an emphasis on the importance of maintaining user trust and addressing privacy concerns, as well as the need for improved user education and awareness. The role of AI and machine learning in chatbot security is also highlighted, along with the importance of secure communication channels and encryption. Standardized security measures and regulations are seen as necessary, but there are challenges in evaluating and testing chatbot security. The literature also points to the lack of focus on insider threats and social engineering attacks.

Table 3. Common themes and patterns of the literature.

Common Themes and Patterns	Related Articles
Identification of security threats and vulnerabilities	[6–8,10,16]
Approaches proposed to address chatbot security threats and vulnerabilities	[6–10,14,16]
Importance of maintaining user trust and addressing privacy concerns	[14,15,17]
Need for improved user education and awareness	[7,8,10,14,16]
Role of AI and machine learning in chatbot security	[7,9,15]
Importance of secure communication channels and encryption	[6,8,10,15]
Need for standardized security measures and regulations	[7–9,15]
Challenges in evaluating and testing chatbot security	[8,10,16]
Lack of focus on insider threats and social engineering attacks	[8,16]

Figure 4 depicts the taxonomy of information security in chatbots that we developed based on the information in Table 3. The taxonomy is used to provide a framework for understanding the different aspects of information security in chatbots and to help identify gaps and areas for further research. In general, the common themes and patterns identified across the literature on chatbot security can be classified into four themes: Themes 1: Security threats and vulnerabilities; 2: Solutions to mitigate security concerns; 3: User trust and privacy concerns; and 4: Ethical and socio-cultural issues. Theme 1 covers four aspects, and they are malicious input, user profiling, contextual attacks, and data breaches. Theme 2 covers three aspects: the use of blockchain technology, the implementation of end-to-end encryption, and the provision of organizational, managerial, and technical controls. Theme 3 covers two aspects: maintaining user trust and addressing privacy concerns. Theme 4 also covers two aspects: the impact of human behavior on neural networks and the need for a system of cultural transmission and civic education.

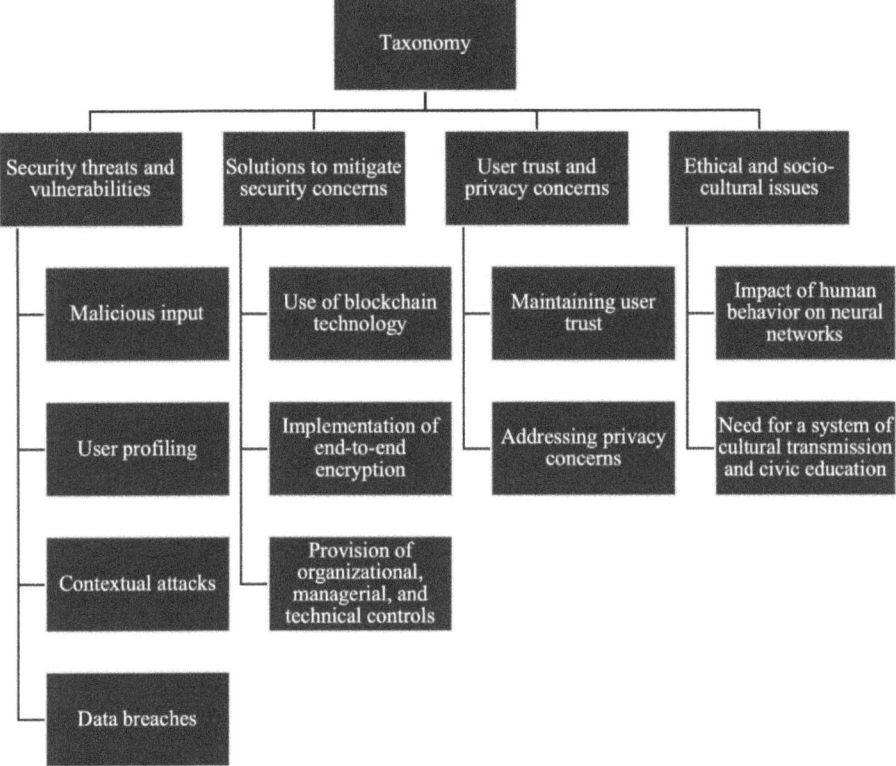

Figure 4. Taxonomy of information security in chatbot.

Theme 1: Security threats and vulnerabilities.

One of the major challenges in addressing security threats and vulnerabilities in chatbots is the constantly evolving nature of cyber threats. New attack vectors and vulnerabilities are being discovered all the time, and developers need to stay up to date with the latest security measures to ensure ongoing protection of their chatbots. For example, the recent rise in phishing attacks using chatbots highlights the importance of implementing measures to prevent malicious input and contextual attacks.

Another challenge is the need to balance security with usability. Chatbots need to provide a user-friendly experience while also ensuring the confidentiality, integrity, and availability of user data. Developers must carefully consider the trade-offs between security measures and user experience and find a balance that meets both requirements. For instance, chatbots in the healthcare industry must comply with strict regulations regarding data privacy and security while also providing timely and accurate medical advice.

Theme 2: Solutions to mitigate security concerns

The lack of standardized security measures for chatbots poses a significant challenge in addressing security concerns. Developers need to determine which security measures to implement, how to implement them, and how to ensure their effectiveness. For example, while end-to-end encryption is a promising solution to protect user data, its implementation may be difficult for small- or medium-sized chatbot providers due to cost constraints.

Another challenge is the need for effective organizational, managerial, and technical controls. Chatbots are often developed and deployed by teams with varying levels of expertise and experience in information security. Developers must ensure that all team members are properly trained in information security and follow best practices to prevent security breaches. Additionally, developers must ensure that their chatbots have appropriate technical controls, such as access control mechanisms and monitoring tools, to detect and respond to security threats in a timely manner.

Theme 3: User trust and privacy concerns

One of the challenges in addressing user trust and privacy concerns is the lack of transparency in chatbot operations. Users may be uncomfortable sharing sensitive information with chatbots if they do not know how their data are being used or who has access to it. Developers must ensure that their chatbots are transparent about how user data are collected, stored, and used. For example, chatbots that collect user data for personalized marketing must provide clear and concise information about how the data are used and allow users to opt out if they choose.

Another challenge is the need to address cultural and regional differences in privacy expectations. Different cultures and regions may have different expectations and norms around data privacy and security. Developers must take these differences into account when designing and implementing chatbots to ensure that they are culturally appropriate and respectful of user privacy.

Theme 4: Ethical and socio-cultural issues

One challenge in addressing ethical and socio-cultural issues in chatbots is the potential for unintended consequences. Chatbots are designed to interact with humans and learn from those interactions, but their ability to do so can also lead to unintended biases and discrimination. For example, chatbots that are trained on biased datasets may unintentionally perpetuate stereotypes or discriminate against certain groups of users.

Another challenge is the need for effective cultural transmission and civic education. Chatbots may interact with users from a variety of cultural and linguistic backgrounds, and developers must ensure that their chatbots are sensitive to these differences. This may involve incorporating cultural sensitivity training into the development process or partnering with local organizations to better understand cultural norms and expectations.

The following are some potential solutions to achieve the security goals outlined in each of the themes:

Security threats and vulnerabilities: To address the potential security threats and vulnerabilities in chatbots, developers can conduct regular security audits and vulnerability assessments, implement appropriate security measures to address any weaknesses, and stay up to date with the latest security threats and vulnerabilities by attending security conferences and training sessions, participating in online forums, and following industry experts on social media.

Regular security audits and vulnerability assessments entail reviewing the chatbot system's security controls and identifying any weaknesses or vulnerabilities that attackers could exploit. To identify and address potential security issues, developers can use a variety of tools and techniques, such as penetration testing and vulnerability scanning. Once vulnerabilities have been identified, proper security measures can be put in place to address them. This could include updating software and firmware to address known security flaws, implementing access controls to limit who has access to sensitive data, and encrypting data in transit and at rest.

Staying up to date with the latest security threats and vulnerabilities is also crucial. Developers can attend security conferences and training sessions to learn about emerging threats and best practices for addressing them. They can also participate in online forums and follow industry experts on social media to stay informed about the latest developments in chatbot security.

Solutions to mitigate security concerns: To mitigate security concerns in chatbots, developers can implement end-to-end encryption to protect user data from unauthorized access, use blockchain technology to enhance data security, and provide organizational, managerial, and technical controls to ensure the confidentiality, integrity, and availability of user data.

End-to-end encryption is an essential security measure that can be implemented in chatbots to protect user data. This encryption method ensures that the data transmitted between the chatbot and the user is secure and cannot be intercepted or accessed by unauthorized third parties. End-to-end encryption provides users with privacy and security, and it can also help to build trust in the chatbot system.

For example, a chatbot used by a financial institution may use end-to-end encryption to protect users' financial information, such as bank account details and transaction history. With end-to-end encryption, the data transmitted between the user and the chatbot is encrypted and can only be decrypted by the user or the chatbot, ensuring that it remains confidential and secure.

Another security measure that can be implemented is the use of blockchain technology. Blockchain is a distributed ledger that can be used to store and share data securely. By leveraging blockchain technology, chatbots can store sensitive data in a decentralized and tamper-proof way, ensuring that it remains secure and cannot be tampered with or altered by unauthorized parties.

For example, a healthcare chatbot may use blockchain to store and share sensitive patient data, such as medical histories and prescriptions, securely. By using blockchain technology, the data can be stored in a decentralized manner, making it more resistant to cyberattacks and ensuring that patient data remain secure and private.

In addition to these technical solutions, developers can also implement organizational, managerial, and technical controls to ensure the confidentiality, integrity, and availability of user data. This includes implementing access controls, conducting regular security assessments, and providing security awareness training for employees and users.

For example, a chatbot used by a government agency may implement access controls to ensure that only authorized personnel can access sensitive data. Regular security assessments can also be conducted to identify vulnerabilities and ensure that the chatbot system remains secure. Finally, security awareness training can be provided to users to help them understand the importance of data security and how to protect their personal information.

User trust and privacy concerns: To address user trust and privacy concerns, developers can maintain transparency and open communication with users regarding the data that are collected and how they are used, obtain explicit consent from users before collecting or processing their data, and implement appropriate security measures to protect user data from unauthorized access or disclosure.

Maintaining user trust and addressing privacy concerns are critical for the successful adoption of chatbots. To achieve this, developers can implement a number of strategies. Firstly, they can ensure that users are fully informed about the data that are collected and how they are used. This can be performed by providing clear and concise privacy policies and terms of service that are easily accessible to users. These policies should explain what data are collected, how they are used, and with whom they are shared.

Secondly, developers can obtain explicit consent from users before collecting or processing their data. This can be achieved through a variety of methods, such as pop-up consent forms, checkboxes, or other interactive mechanisms that clearly explain what data are being collected and why. It is also important for developers to ensure that users have the option to opt out of data collection or processing if they do not wish to share their information.

Thirdly, developers can implement appropriate security measures to protect user data from unauthorized access or disclosure. This can include implementing encryption, access controls, and other technical safeguards to prevent data breaches or leaks. Additionally, developers can ensure that their chatbots comply with relevant data protection laws and regulations, such as the General Data Protection Regulation or the Health Insurance Portability and Accountability Act, and obtain appropriate certifications or third-party audits to demonstrate compliance.

Ethical and socio-cultural issues: To address ethical and socio-cultural issues in chatbots, developers can consider the potential impact of chatbots on society and ensure that chatbots are designed and deployed in an ethical and responsible manner. This could involve developing a system of cultural transmission and civic education to ensure that users understand the potential risks and benefits of chatbots and implementing appropriate safeguards to prevent the use of chatbots for malicious or unethical purposes.

For instance, chatbots may perpetuate biases or stereotypes if they are not programmed to be inclusive and respectful of diversity. Developers need to ensure that chatbots are designed and trained to be culturally sensitive, taking into account the diversity of the users they will interact with. Moreover, chatbots may impact the social dynamics of communication, especially in sensitive areas such as mental health, where chatbots are increasingly being used to provide support and guidance to users. In such cases, developers need to ensure that the chatbots are not replacing human interaction but rather supplementing it, and users are given the option to seek human help if needed.

Developers also need to consider the potential for malicious use of chatbots, such as the spread of disinformation or the manipulation of public opinion. In such cases, appropriate safeguards need to be implemented, such as robust authentication mechanisms and controls to prevent unauthorized access to chatbots.

Overall, it is important for developers to take a holistic approach to chatbot security, considering not only technical security measures but also user trust, privacy, and ethical considerations. By following best practices and staying up to date with the latest security threats and vulnerabilities, developers can ensure that their chatbots provide a secure and user-friendly experience.

5. Discussion

Although the reviewed literature provides a comprehensive overview of the security threats and vulnerabilities associated with chatbots and the approaches proposed to address them, there are still areas where additional research is needed to address specific security issues.

One such area is the need for more research on authentication and authorization mechanisms for chatbots. Article [7] highlights the vulnerability of chatbots to insecure authentication and data integrity issues, which can be exploited by attackers to gain unauthorized access to sensitive information. While some studies, such as article [10], propose solutions for secure authentication and encryption mechanisms, more research is needed to identify effective and scalable solutions that can be implemented in different chatbot contexts and scenarios.

Another area where additional research is needed is the detection and prevention of malicious chatbots. Article [3] discusses the potential of malicious chatbots to harm users and highlights the need for more research on identifying and detecting malicious chatbots. Additionally, more research is needed to develop effective and efficient methods for monitoring chatbots and detecting suspicious behavior, such as that described in article [8], which proposes a design and framework for a cyber-aware chatbot service that detects and helps prevent malware behavior from spreading on the user's machine.

Furthermore, more research is needed on the security risks and ethical issues relating to information security in chatbot implementation, as highlighted in article [15]. Specifically, more research is needed to develop frameworks and guidelines for ensuring the confidentiality, integrity, and availability of user data, as well as address ethical concerns relating to user privacy and data ownership.

Lastly, there is a need for more research on the impact of chatbots on social engineering attacks. Article [2] suggests that chatbots could be exploited by attackers to conduct social engineering attacks, but more research is needed to understand the extent to which chatbots are vulnerable to these types of attacks and to identify effective countermeasures.

Besides additional research, we might also consider some best practices for developing secure chatbots. The following are some best practices for developing secure chatbots:

Conduct comprehensive security assessments: One of the best practices for developing secure chatbots is to conduct comprehensive security assessments throughout the entire chatbot development process. Developers should conduct security testing at different stages of development to identify and mitigate vulnerabilities before the chatbot is deployed. These assessments should cover all modules in the chatbot architecture, including the client module, communication module, response generation module, and database module. For example, a developer could use tools such as static analysis to identify code-level vulnerabilities such as buffer overflows or SQL injections and dynamic analysis tools to test for vulnerabilities during runtime.

Implement user authentication and authorization: Another best practice for developing secure chatbots is to implement user authentication and authorization. Developers should ensure that the chatbot requires users to authenticate themselves before accessing sensitive data or services. Authentication could involve traditional username and password combinations, two-factor authentication, biometric authentication, or autonomous inquiry-based authentication [32]. Additionally, authorization should be implemented to ensure that users only have access to data or services that they are authorized to access. For example, a chatbot used for banking should only allow users access to their own accounts.

Use encryption for data protection: To protect sensitive data in chatbots, developers should implement encryption. Encryption can protect data from being intercepted and viewed by unauthorized parties during transmission. Developers can use techniques such as end-to-end encryption or transport layer security to secure data in transit using authenticated key agreement schemes [33–35] in different environments and symmetric or asymmetric encryption to protect data stored on the chatbot's database.

Regularly update and patch chatbots: Chatbots should be regularly updated and patched to fix vulnerabilities and improve security [36]. Developers should monitor for security alerts and advisories and ensure that their chatbots are up to date with the latest security patches. Additionally, chatbots should be monitored for unusual activity, and logs should be analyzed regularly to detect potential security breaches.

Educate users on security best practices: Developers should educate users on security best practices to ensure that they are aware of the risks associated with chatbots and how to protect themselves [37]. For example, developers can provide guidance on creating strong passwords, avoiding clicking on suspicious links, and reporting suspicious activity. Additionally, chatbots should provide clear privacy policies and obtain user consent before collecting any personal data.

Based on the information presented above, the future directions for information security in chatbots indicate several areas that will necessitate ongoing research and development. These include concerns about privacy and security, regulations and ethics, and security threats and countermeasures.

5.1. Privacy and Security

In terms of privacy and security, chatbots present a unique set of challenges that require ongoing research and development to address. One potential area of future research is the development of more sophisticated authentication and authorization mechanisms to protect against unauthorized access to chatbot data. For instance, multi-factor authentication methods, which use blockchain, image recognition, a secure one-time PIN, and biometric authentication [38–40], may be used to improve the security of chatbots. Additionally, secure encryption [41] and end-to-end encryption can be used to ensure that messages and data are protected from interception or tampering [42]. Another area of research may focus on developing more comprehensive and user-friendly security and privacy policies for chatbots to ensure that users understand how their data is collected, used, and protected. Furthermore, chatbots may be vulnerable to data breaches where user data or chatbot data is exposed to unauthorized parties. As such, research in this area may focus on developing advanced threat detection systems that use artificial intelligence and machine learning algorithms to improve the detection and prevention of security threats. Overall, research and development in this area will be important for maintaining user trust and making sure that chatbot systems are safe and private.

5.2. Regulation and Ethical Concerns

In terms of regulation and ethical concerns, there is a growing need to ensure that chatbots are developed and deployed in a responsible and ethical manner, in accordance with relevant regulations and industry best practices [43,44]. Future research in this area may focus on developing more comprehensive frameworks for chatbot development and deployment that incorporate ethical considerations such as transparency, accountability, and non-discrimination. Additionally, research may explore the use of privacy-enhancing technologies, such as differential privacy or homomorphic encryption, to ensure that chatbots can process sensitive data while preserving user privacy. Another area of research may focus on developing more comprehensive and user-friendly privacy policies for chatbots to ensure that users understand how their data are collected, used, and protected. Moreover, regulatory bodies may need to monitor the development and use of chatbots to ensure that they comply with relevant laws and regulations and to hold developers and operators accountable for any violations. As chatbots become more prevalent in various industries, it will be increasingly important to ensure that they are used in a responsible and ethical manner and to maintain user trust and confidence in these systems. Overall, it will be important to keep researching and developing in this area to make sure that chatbots are made and used in a way that respects user privacy, rights, and freedoms and follows laws and ethical guidelines.

5.3. Security Threats and Countermeasures

In terms of security threats and countermeasures, chatbots face a range of potential vulnerabilities and attacks that can compromise the security and privacy of users [37,45]. Future research in this area may focus on developing more comprehensive threat models for chatbot systems that take into account the various types of attacks that may be used against them, such as social engineering attacks, phishing attacks, and malware attacks. For example, as chatbots become more intelligent and capable of carrying out more complex tasks, they may also become more vulnerable to social engineering attacks. Social engineering is a type of attack where an attacker uses psychological manipulation to trick a user into revealing sensitive information or taking an action that may compromise the security of a system [46]. Future research in this area may focus on developing algorithms and techniques for detecting and preventing social engineering attacks on chatbots. This could include the use of natural language processing and machine learning to identify patterns of suspicious behavior and language that may indicate a social engineering attack. Additionally, research may explore the use of user education and training to improve awareness of social engineering tactics and help users avoid falling victim to such attacks. Overall, continued research and development in this area will be important to make sure that chatbot systems are safe and that people keep trusting and using them.

These are some of the future directions for chatbot research in information security. Addressing these areas will be important for the continued growth and success of the technology in the information security research and beyond.

6. Conclusions

It is important to provide context on how chatbot security differs from security in other areas. While security threats and vulnerabilities exist across various technologies and systems, the unique nature of chatbots and their use of natural language processing present specific security challenges. For example, chatbots rely heavily on user input, which can be manipulated or altered by malicious actors to exploit vulnerabilities. Additionally, chatbots may inadvertently reveal sensitive information based on the context of a conversation, which requires careful attention paid to privacy and confidentiality.

Furthermore, the use of chatbots for customer service and support presents additional security considerations, such as the authentication and authorization of users, protection of personal information, and maintaining the integrity of the chatbot's responses.

By understanding the specific security concerns and challenges relating to chatbots, researchers and practitioners can develop targeted solutions and best practices to mitigate these risks and ensure the secure use of chatbots.

This systematic literature review (SLR) provides a comprehensive summary of the research relating to information security in chatbots. This SLR highlights the significant security threats and vulnerabilities that chatbots face. The review reveals that malicious input, user profiling, contextual attacks, and data breaches are among the most common security concerns for chatbots. The findings also demonstrate that there is a need for effective and scalable solutions for chatbot security that can be implemented in different contexts and scenarios.

To address these challenges, the studies reviewed suggest various solutions, such as the use of blockchain technology, end-to-end encryption, and organizational, managerial, and technical controls. Furthermore, the review emphasizes that maintaining user trust and addressing privacy concerns are critical factors for the successful adoption and continued use of chatbots and AI assistants.

The taxonomy developed in this review provides a useful framework for categorizing the articles and their findings, which could inform future research and practice in this field. Based on the review, it is clear that there is still much research to be conducted in the field of chatbot security. Future research should focus on developing more sophisticated authentication and authorization mechanisms, comprehensive and user-friendly security and privacy policies, advanced threat detection systems, and frameworks for chatbot development and deployment that incorporate ethical considerations.

Overall, the findings of this review suggest that information security is a critical factor that must be addressed for the successful adoption and continued use of chatbots and AI assistants. The failure to address these security concerns could undermine user trust and lead to negative consequences for organizations and individuals alike. The insights provided in this review can serve as a roadmap for researchers and practitioners to develop and implement effective security solutions for chatbots and AI assistants.

7. Limitations

Several limitations should be considered when interpreting the results of this review. First, this review only includes articles published up to 31 December 2022, which means that more recent research may not be included. Additionally, the review focuses solely on information security relating to chatbots and does not cover other potential issues, such as usability concerns. Furthermore, the studies included in this review used different methods and approaches to assess chatbot security, which could limit the comparability of findings across studies. Finally, the review is limited by the quality and scope of the articles included, as some articles may be more comprehensive or relevant than others. Despite these limitations, this review provides a valuable overview of the current state of research in this area, and it highlights areas for future research to address the limitations identified.

Author Contributions: Conceptualization, J.Y. and L.Y.P.; methodology, J.Y.; validation, L.Y.P., Y.-L.C. and C.S.K.; formal analysis, J.Y.; investigation, J.Y.; resources, J.Y.; data curation, L.Y.P.; writing—original draft preparation, L.Y.P.; writing—review and editing, L.Y.P., Y.-L.C. and C.S.K.; visualization, J.Y.; supervision, L.Y.P.; project administration, L.Y.P.; funding acquisition, Y.-L.C. and C.S.K. All authors have read and agreed to the published version of the manuscript.

Funding: This research was funded by the National Science and Technology Council in Taiwan, grant number NSTC-109-2628-E-027-004–MY3, NSTC-111-2218-E-027-003, and NSTC-111-2622-8-027-009 and the Ministry of Education of Taiwan, official document number 1112303249.

Institutional Review Board Statement: Not applicable.

Informed Consent Statement: Not applicable.

Conflicts of Interest: The authors declare no conflict of interest.

References

1. Dhinagaran, D.A.; Martinengo, L.; Ho, M.-H.R.; Joty, S.; Kowatsch, T.; Atun, R.; Car, L.T. Designing, Developing, Evaluating, and Implementing a Smartphone-Delivered, Rule-Based Conversational Agent (DISCOVER): Development of a Conceptual Framework. *JMIR Mhealth Uhealth* **2022**, *10*, e38740. [CrossRef] [PubMed]
2. Adamopoulou, E.; Moussiades, L. An Overview of Chatbot Technology. In Proceedings of the Artificial Intelligence Applications and Innovations 2020, Neos Marmaras, Greece, 5–7 June 2020.
3. Adamopoulou, E.; Moussiades, L. Chatbots: History, technology, and applications. *Mach. Learn. Appl.* **2020**, *2*, 100006. [CrossRef]
4. Chen, C.-M.; Liu, S.; Li, X.; Islam, S.H.; Das, A.K. A provably-secure authenticated key agreement protocol for remote patient monitoring IoMT. *J. Syst. Arch.* **2023**, *136*, 102831. [CrossRef]
5. Chen, C.-M.; Li, Z.; Kumari, S.; Srivastava, G.; Lakshmanna, K.; Gadekallu, T.R. A provably secure key transfer protocol for the fog-enabled Social Internet of Vehicles based on a confidential computing environment. *Veh. Commun.* **2023**, *39*, 100567. [CrossRef]
6. Ye, W.; Li, Q. Chatbot Security and Privacy in the Age of Personal Assistants. In Proceedings of the 2020 IEEE/ACM Symposium on Edge Computing, San Jose, CA, USA, 12–14 November 2020.
7. Bhuiyan, M.S.I.; Razzak, A.; Ferdous, M.S.; Chowdhury, M.J.M.; Hoque, M.A.; Tarkoma, S. BONIK: A Blockchain Empowered Chatbot for Financial Transactions. In Proceedings of the 2020 IEEE 19th International Conference on Trust, Security and Privacy in Computing and Communications, Guangzhou, China, 29 December 2020–1 January 2021.
8. Thorpe, S.; Scarlett, H. Towards a Cyber Aware Chatbot Service. In Proceedings of the 2021 IEEE International Conference on Big Data, Orlando, FL, USA, 15–18 December 2021.
9. Gondaliya, K.; Butakov, S.; Zavarsky, P. SLA as a mechanism to manage risks related to chatbot services. In Proceedings of the 2020 IEEE 6th Intl Conference on Big Data Security on Cloud, IEEE Intl Conference on High Performance and Smart Computing, and IEEE Intl Conference on Intelligent Data and Security, Baltimore, MD, USA, 25–27 May 2020.
10. Shah, M.; Panchal, M. Privacy Protected Modified Double Ratchet Algorithm for Secure Chatbot Application. In Proceedings of the 2022 3rd International Conference on Smart Electronics and Communication, Trichy, India, 20–22 October 2022.
11. Belen-Saglam, R.; Nurse, J.R.C.; Hodges, D. An Investigation Into the Sensitivity of Personal Information and Implications for Disclosure: A UK Perspective. *Front. Comput. Sci.* **2022**, *4*, 1–22. [CrossRef]
12. Patil, K.; Kulkarni, M.S. Artificial intelligence in financial services: Customer chatbot advisor adoption. *Int. J. Innov. Technol. Explor. Eng.* **2019**, *9*, 4296–4303. [CrossRef]
13. Ali, H.; Aysan, A.F. What will ChatGPT Revolutionize in Financial Industry? *Soc. Sci. Res. Netw.* **2023**, 4403372. [CrossRef]
14. El Hajal, G.; Daou, R.A.Z.; Ducq, Y. Human Firewall: Cyber Awareness using WhatApp AI Chatbot. In Proceedings of the 2021 IEEE 3rd International Multidisciplinary Conference on Engineering Technology, Beirut, Lebanon, 8–10 December 2021.
15. Pokrovskaia, N.N. Sociocultural and Information Security Issues in the Implementation of Neural Network Technologies in Chat-bots Design. In Proceedings of the 2022 XXV International Conference on Soft Computing and Measurements, Saint Petersburg, Russia, 25–27 May 2022.
16. Edu, J.; Mulligan, C.; Pierazzi, F.; Polakis, J.; Suarez-Tangil, G.; Such, J. Exploring the security and privacy risks of chatbots in messaging services. In Proceedings of the 22nd ACM Internet Measurement Conference, Nice, France, 25–27 October 2022.
17. Jo, H. Impact of Information Security on Continuance Intention of Artificial Intelligence Assistant. *Procedia Comput. Sci.* **2022**, *204*, 768–774. [CrossRef]
18. Nadarzynski, T.; Miles, O.; Cowie, A.; Ridge, D. Acceptability of artificial intelligence (AI)-led chatbot services in healthcare: A mixed-methods study. *Digit. Health* **2019**, *5*, 1–12. [CrossRef]
19. Waheed, N.; Ikram, M.; Hashmi, S.S.; He, X.; Nanda, P. An Empirical Assessment of Security and Privacy Risks of Web-Based Chatbots. In Proceedings of the International Conference on Web Information Systems Engineering, Biarritz, France, 1–3 November 2022.
20. Hasal, M.; Nowaková, J.; Saghair, K.A.; Abdulla, H.; Snášel, V.; Ogiela, L. Chatbots: Security, privacy, data protection, and social aspects. *Concurr. Comput. Pract. Exp.* **2021**, *33*, 1–13. [CrossRef]
21. Følstad, A.; Nordheim, C.B.; Bjørkli, C.A. What makes users trust a chatbot for customer service? An exploratory interview study. In Proceedings of the International Conference on Internet Science, St. Petersburg, Russia, 24–26 October 2018.
22. van der Goot, M.J.; Pilgrim, T. Exploring Age Differences in Motivations for and Acceptance of Chatbot Communication in a Customer Service Context. In Proceedings of the International Workshop on Chatbot Research and Design, Amsterdam, The Netherlands, 19–20 November 2019.
23. United Nations, Department of Economic and Social Affairs, Population Division. Available online: http://esa.un.org/wpp/ (accessed on 12 May 2023).
24. GPT-4 Is OpenAI's Most Advanced System, Producing Safer and More Useful Responses. Available online: https://openai.com/product/gpt-4 (accessed on 12 May 2023).

25. Corsello, A.; Santangelo, A. May Artificial Intelligence Influence Future Pediatric Research?—The Case of ChatGPT. *Children* **2023**, *10*, 757. [CrossRef] [PubMed]
26. Kooli, C. Chatbots in education and research: A critical examination of ethical implications and solutions. *Sustainability* **2023**, *15*, 5614. [CrossRef]
27. Giansanti, D. The Chatbots Are Invading Us: A Map Point on the Evolution, Applications, Opportunities, and Emerging Problems in the Health Domain. *Life* **2023**, *13*, 1130. [CrossRef]
28. Aggarwal, A.; Tam, C.C.; Wu, D.; Li, X.; Qiao, S. Artificial Intelligence–Based Chatbots for Promoting Health Behavioral Changes: Systematic Review. *J. Med. Internet Res.* **2023**, *25*, e40789. [CrossRef]
29. Sallam, M. ChatGPT utility in healthcare education, research, and practice: Systematic review on the promising perspectives and valid concerns. *Healthcare* **2023**, *11*, 887. [CrossRef]
30. Page, M.J.; McKenzie, J.E.; Bossuyt, P.M.; Boutron, I.; Hoffmann, T.C.; Mulrow, C.D.; Shamseer, L.; Tetzlaff, J.M.; Akl, E.A.; Brennan, S.E.; et al. The PRISMA 2020 statement: An updated guideline for reporting systematic reviews. *Syst. Rev.* **2021**, *10*, 89. [CrossRef]
31. Tarsilla, M. Cochrane Handbook for Systematic Reviews of Interventions. *J. Multidiscip. Eval.* **2010**, *6*, 143–148. [CrossRef]
32. Voege, P.; Abu Sulayman, I.I.M.; Ouda, A. Smart Chatbot for User Authentication. *Electronics* **2022**, *11*, 4016. [CrossRef]
33. Wu, T.-Y.; Meng, Q.; Chen, Y.-C.; Kumari, S.; Chen, C.-M. Toward a secure smart-home IoT access control scheme based on home registration approach. *Mathematics* **2023**, *119*, 2123. [CrossRef]
34. Wu, T.-Y.; Kong, F.; Meng, Q.; Kumari, S.; Chen, C.-M. Rotating Behind Security: An enhanced authentication protocol for IoT-enabled devices in distributed cloud computing architecture. *EURASIP J. Wirel. Commun. Netw.* **2023**, *2023*, 36. [CrossRef]
35. Wu, T.-Y.; Meng, Q.; Yang, L.; Kumari, S.; Pirouz, M. Amassing the Security: An Enhanced Authentication and Key Agreement Protocol for Remote Surgery in Healthcare Environment. *Comput. Model. Eng. Sci.* **2023**, *134*, 317–341. [CrossRef]
36. Chow, J.C.; Sanders, L.; Li, K. Design of an educational chatbot using artificial intelligence in radiotherapy. *AI* **2023**, *4*, 319–332. [CrossRef]
37. Addington, S. ChatGPT: Cyber Security Threats and Countermeasures. *Soc. Sci. Res. Netw.* **2023**, 4425678. [CrossRef]
38. Carrillo-Torres, D.; Pérez-Díaz, J.A.; Cantoral-Ceballos, J.A.; Vargas-Rosales, C. A Novel Multi-Factor Authentication Algorithm Based on Image Recognition and User Established Relations. *Appl. Sci.* **2023**, *13*, 1374. [CrossRef]
39. Ahmad, M.O.; Tripathi, G.; Siddiqui, F.; Alam, M.A.; Ahad, M.A.; Akhtar, M.M.; Casalino, G. BAuth-ZKP—A Blockchain-Based Multi-Factor Authentication Mechanism for Securing Smart Cities. *Sensors* **2023**, *23*, 2757. [CrossRef] [PubMed]
40. Binbeshr, F.; Por, L.Y.; Kiah, M.M.; Zaidan, A.A.; Imam, M. Secure PIN-Entry Method Using One-Time PIN (OTP). *IEEE Access* **2023**, *11*, 18121–18133. [CrossRef]
41. Alexan, W.; Chen, Y.L.; Por, L.Y.; Gabr, M. Hyperchaotic Maps and the Single Neuron Model: A Novel Framework for Chaos-Based Image Encryption. *Symmetry* **2023**, *15*, 1081. [CrossRef]
42. Bartusek, J.; Garg, S.; Jain, A.; Policharla, G.V. End-to-end secure messaging with traceability only for illegal content. In Proceedings of the Advances in Cryptology–EUROCRYPT 2023: 42nd Annual International Conference on the Theory and Applications of Cryptographic Techniques, Lyon, France, 23–27 April 2023; pp. 35–66.
43. Rivas, P.; Zhao, L. Marketing with ChatGPT: Navigating the Ethical Terrain of GPT-Based Chatbot Tech-nology. *AI* **2023**, *4*, 375–384. [CrossRef]
44. Torres-Castaño, A.; Abt-Sacks, A.; Toledo-Chávarri, A.; Suarez-Herrera, J.C.; Delgado-Rodríguez, J.; León-Salas, B.; Serrano-Aguilar, P. Ethical, Legal, Organisational and Social Issues of Teleneurology: A Scoping Re-view. *Int. J. Environ. Res. Public Health* **2023**, *20*, 3694. [CrossRef]
45. Uma, S. Conversational AI Chatbots in Digital Engagement: Privacy and Security Concerns. In *Trends, Ap-plications, and Challenges of Chatbot Technolog*; IGI Global: Hershey, PA, USA, 2023; pp. 274–317.
46. Salahdine, F.; Kaabouch, N. Social Engineering Attacks: A Survey. *Future Internet* **2019**, *11*, 89. [CrossRef]

Disclaimer/Publisher's Note: The statements, opinions and data contained in all publications are solely those of the individual author(s) and contributor(s) and not of MDPI and/or the editor(s). MDPI and/or the editor(s) disclaim responsibility for any injury to people or property resulting from any ideas, methods, instructions or products referred to in the content.

MDPI
St. Alban-Anlage 66
4052 Basel
Switzerland
www.mdpi.com

Applied Sciences Editorial Office
E-mail: applsci@mdpi.com
www.mdpi.com/journal/applsci

Disclaimer/Publisher's Note: The statements, opinions and data contained in all publications are solely those of the individual author(s) and contributor(s) and not of MDPI and/or the editor(s). MDPI and/or the editor(s) disclaim responsibility for any injury to people or property resulting from any ideas, methods, instructions or products referred to in the content.

www.ingramcontent.com/pod-product-compliance
Lightning Source LLC
LaVergne TN
LVHW070438100526
838202LV00014B/1619